The History of St. Catherine of Siena and Her Companions

Drane, Augusta Theodosia

BIBLIOLIFE

ST. CATHERINE OF SIENA.

From the Engraving by Francesco Vanni.

THE HISTORY

OF

St. Catherine of Siena

AND HER COMPANIONS

With a Translation of her Treatise on Consummate Perfection

BY

AUGUSTA THEODOSIA DRANE

AUTHOR OF "CHRISTIAN SCHOOLS AND SCHOLARS," ETC.

IN TWO VOLUMES

VOL. I.

Second Edition

LONDON: BURNS AND OATES, Limited

New York: Catholic Publication Society Co.

PREFACE TO THE SECOND EDITION.

THERE already exist in various languages more than sixty Lives of St. Catherine of Siena. In presence of such a fact, an apology seems called for on the part of any one who should propose to add to their number. It will, however, be borne in mind that most of these Lives are little more than translations or abridgments of the original Legend written by Raymund of Capua, the Saint's Confessor: they furnish us with no new facts, and do not even attempt to restore that chronological order of events which was entirely neglected by St. Catherine's first biographer. There are two notable exceptions indeed to which this remark does not apply: the *Storia di Santa Caterina da Siena, e del Papato del suo tempo*, by Mgr. Alfonso Capecelatro ; and the *Histoire de Ste. Catherine de Sienne*, by M. Emile Chavan de Malan.[1] Of the first-named work it is impossible to speak too highly. The author has brought the public life of St. Catherine and her relations with the Papacy within the compass of a single volume, full of historical research, and has made excellent use of some of the Saint's letters. But, as may be gathered from the title of the book, he deals almost exclusively with her public career, and cannot therefore be said to have given us her complete biography. M. Chavan de Malan has attempted a restoration of the chronology of St. Catherine's life, and has consulted many valuable authorities. He has also

---

[1] To these we must now add the Life published in 1880 by Madame la Comtesse de Flavigny, carefully compiled from original sources.

included in his volumes illustrations from Italian history which
throw more or less light on the state of society in the fourteenth
century. His interesting work, however, is open to one objec-
tion; he has not been able to refrain from filling up the historic
outline of his narrative with materials purely imaginary; so that
fact and fiction are often mingled in his pages, which thus, in
some parts, assume the colouring of a romance. Neither of these
works has found an English translator, and we, as yet, possess but
two (Catholic) Lives of St Catherine in the English language.
The first is a translation of the Legend, published at Philadelphia
in the year 1860. It has the disadvantage of being the translation of a translation, being made, not from the Latin original,
nor even from the Italian version of that original, but from M
Cartier's French translation of that version. Hence it is not
surprising that the result has been unsatisfactory, and that in
many places even the sense of the author has not been conveyed
The second work above alluded to is a reprint from the old
English translation of F. Ambrogio Caterino Politi's abridgment
of the Legend This translation was made in 1609 by Father
John Fen, Confessor to the English nuns at Louvain. It was
re-edited in 1867 by the Very Rev Father James Dominic
Aylward, English Provincial of the Order of Preachers, and is
now out of print. The translator has contrived to give to his
version all the charm of an original work. Nothing can surpass
the pathos and animation of some of the narratives, as related in
the fine old English of the *bel secolo* of our language. Several
such passages, the unction of which could never be equalled by
a modern pen, have been freely embodied in the following pages.
Nevertheless, the superior merit of this little book is entirely one
of style. Father Politi's chronology is quite as confused as that
of the Legend which he abridges; and neither from one nor the
other can we gather any clear notion of the consecutive order of
the events narrated.[1]

[1] To be strictly accurate, we must add to the above the *Lyf of St. Katherin
of Senis*, printed by Caxton, a copy of which bibliographical rarity is in the
Chatsworth Library, having been purchased by the Duke of Devonshire for

In the present volume the writer has aimed at giving the facts of St. Catherine's life as recoided by other biographers, restoring their chronological order, and at the same time supplementing them with additional matter drawn from original sources hitherto either partially or entirely neglected. Very ample use has been made of St. Catherine's own letters, those wonderful compositions of which we as yet possess no English translation, but a knowledge of which is essential to our forming any real acquaintance with the saintly writer. Yet the letters themselves cannot be understood without some explanation of the history and circumstances of those to whom they were addressed ; and this naturally introduces the reader to the members of that spiritual "family" of which she was the Mother and Head.

The position occupied by St. Catherine was altogether an exceptional one. She was never the member of a religious community, yet neither was she a secular, nor a recluse. She appears before us surrounded by a group of disciples bound to her by no other ties than those of personal affection, and numbering among them men and women of every variety of age, station and character. Blessed Raymund himself, and her other confessors ; her three secretaries Neri, Stephen, and Barduccio ; Master Matthew, whom she cured of the plague, and the English hermit, William Flete ; her sister-in-law Lisa, and Alexia her chosen friend, with all these we make acquaintance in a passing way in the pages of the Legend, and the wish must have occurred to many readers that we could know them better, and interrogate them concerning their intercourse with her to whose daily life it was their privilege to be thus associated. To respond in some measure to this wish the writer has endeavoured to include in the history of St. Catherine such notices of her companions as can be gathered from authentic letters and records still preserved ; and at the same

the sum of £231. Another copy is preserved in the Grenville Library in the British Museum. Caxton's Life of the Saint was reprinted by Wynkyn de Worde. A summary of her doctrine, containing extracts from her Dialogue, was also printed in 1519 by Wynkyn de Worde, entitled, "Booke of Dyvyne Doctrine," by Richard Sutton, London.

time to gather up in their own words the testimony which they
have borne to the sanctity of which they were so long the eyewitnesses.

It remains to enumerate the chief authorities from which the
following narrative has been compiled, giving at the end of each
notice the abridged word by which reference is made to the works
in question.

1. *Vita della Serafica Sposa di Gesu Christo, Sta Caterina da
Siena.* This is the Italian version of the original life, commonly
called the *Legend.* It was written in Latin by Raymund of Capua,
the Saint's confessor, and was first translated into Italian by her
secretary, Neri di Landoccio dei Paglieresi, and another anonymous writer. When in 1707 Girolamo Gigli, Professor of *Belles
Lettres* in the University of Siena, undertook the publication of
St. Catherine's Life and complete Works, he caused a new translation of the Legend to be made by the Canonico Bernardino
Pecci, and this now forms the first volume of the *Opere di Santa
Caterina,* the second and third volumes containing her Letters,
and the fourth her Dialogue. It was Gigli's intention to have
published besides these a considerable number of other precious
manuscripts preserved at Siena; but the troubles in which he
became involved with the Academy *della Crusca* and the Tuscan
Government, which ended in his banishment, prevented the completion of his design. In the learned Prologues, however, which
he has prefixed to his published volumes, he has done much to
facilitate the study of what we may call the literature of St.
Catherine, and has left stamped on his writings the marks of
that tender devotion to the Saint which moved him, whilst engaged
in these labours, daily to visit her relics, and there to implore
with tears that she would obtain for him, by her intercession, the
salvation of his soul. (*Leg*)

2. *La Leggenda Minore.* This is an abridgment of Raymund's
work, written in Latin by F. Tommaso d' Antonio Nacci Caffarini,
and translated into Italian by Stephen Maconi. It contains several
additions that are not to be found in the original Legend. Caffarini
was well acquainted with St. Catherine many years before she

became known to Raymund, and the events of her earlier life which Raymund gathered from the lips of others, had fallen under his own personal observation. The *Leggenda Minore* finds a place in the very rare *Santuario* of Mombrizio (Milan, 1479), whence the Bollandists extracted the additional matter, and printed it as an Appendix to the Latin Legend, under the title of *Analecta de S. Catherina, ex vita Fr. Thomæ collecta.* In the year 1868 Stephen Maconi's Italian translation of the work was edited by Signor F. Grottanelli, the learned librarian of Siena, who enriched it with a number of valuable notes. It forms one of the volumes of that "Collection of Rare and inedited Works," which has been published by the Royal *Commissione pe' Testi di Lingua* (*Leg. Min*)

3 *Supplimento alla Leggenda di Santa Caterina.* The Supplement to Raymund's Legend was written in Latin by Caffarini, and contains much additional and interesting information. In 1754 an Italian translation of the work was published at Lucca by F. Ambrogio Ansano Tantucci. This translation has now become extremely rare, and M Cartier, who has made a French translation from it, calls it *presque introuvable.* Valuable as it is, Tantucci's translation is far from being a perfect or exact version of Caffarini's work. He has entirely omitted some treatises, and abridged others. Considerable use has been made of the work in the following narrative, but in some places references will be found given to the *Latin* Supplement, when the passages referred to have been omitted or altered in the Italian translation. Caffarini's original work is preserved in the Communal Library of Siena, whence authentic copies of some of the missing portions have been obtained for the present work. (*Sup or Lat. Sup.*)

4. *Lettere di Santa Caterina.* Several editions of the Saint's Letters have at various times been published : the first being the Aldine Edition, printed at Venice in 1500, which was followed by another in 1548 by Toresano, and another in 1579 by Farri; both likewise published at Venice. In the present work the edition of Girolamo Gigli has generally been quoted, enriched as it is by the explanatory notes of F. Federigo Burlamacchi, S. J.,

whose researches into contemporary history may be said to have exhausted the subject. They form in fact the chief and best authority for reconstructing the History of St. Catherine. A later edition of the Letters was published at Florence in 1860, by F. Tommaseo, which contains nothing of additional value. A good French translation has been made by M. Cartier, who has prefixed to his volumes an admirable sketch of the Saint's public career. He has also attempted a restoration of the chronology, for the satisfactory completion of which, however, he lacked the necessary materials. In all references to the letters the numbers given are those of Gigli's edition.[1]

* 5. *Note originali d'illustrazione alla Leggenda compendiata dal Caffarini.* These notes to the *Leggenda Minore* are from the pen of Burlamacchi, and are of great value. They have never been printed and exist in MS. only in the Library of Siena. They do not even seem to have been prepared for publication, for the authority for each separate statement is not precisely given; though the materials are all gathered from the Supplimento and the Process of Venice. (*Notes to Leg. Min.*)

6. *Processus contestationum super sanctitate et doctrina B. Catherinæ de Senis.* (*Martene et Durand. Ampliss. Coll. Vet. Script. Tom.* vi.) This is the famous *Process of Venice*, containing the depositions of certain persons who were cited to appear before Francis Bembo, Bishop of Venice, in 1411, to answer the charges brought against them of rendering public honours to Catherine of Siena before she had yet been canonised by the Church. The result of the investigation was a declaration that in all that they had done to honour Catherine's memory, the Friars of her Order had incurred no blame; and the depositions of the witnesses were afterwards used in the Process of her Canonisation. The document, as it appears in the pages of Martene and Durand, is exceedingly imperfect, containing the

---

[1] The authorities marked (*) are all inedited MSS. preserved in the Communal Library of Siena, whence authentic copies have been procured for the use of the writer, through the generous kindness of Signor Bernardo Fabbricotti, of Leghorn.

depositions of seven witnesses only, whereas the original Process, of which a copy is preserved at Siena, contains twenty-four. The seven depositions above-named are, however, some of the most important, and they have been largely drawn from in the compilation of the following narrative. Three of the missing depositions have been printed by Baluze, in the fourth volume of his Miscellanea. (*Process.*)

7. *Deposition of Don Francesco Malevolti.* This very important memoir, which forms part of the original Process, has never been printed, and strange to say, it has rarely even been quoted. References to it will often be found in Gigli's Prologues; but these give a most imperfect idea of the contents or value of the original. A perfect copy of it is preserved in the *Biblioteca Casanatense* at Rome; from which, through the kindness of the late Most Rev. Père A. V. Jandel, Master General of the Order of Preachers, an authentic copy was made for the Library of St. Dominic's Convent, Stone. This document will be found frequently quoted, and at a considerable length; nor will the reader fail to appreciate Malevolti's merit both as a witness and a writer.

* 8. *Sommario del Processo di Santa Caterina, fatto dal Padre Angiolo Maria Carapelli.*

* 9. *Sommario di cose appartenente a Santa Caterina.*

* 10. *Sommario di Notizie della Vita di S. Caterina.* These three manuscripts contain the sum of the Depositions, including those which remain unpublished, and have proved of very great value. They are all of them copies of manuscripts preserved at Siena.

* 11. *Corso Cronotastico della Vita di Santa Caterina da Siena. Dal R. P. Fra Angiolo Maria Carapelli, O. P.* This invaluable work, together with many others from the pen of the same learned writer, who devoted himself with such ardour to the study and illustration of St. Catherine's life, exists only in manuscript, in the library of Siena. In compiling his chronology the writer has consulted every authority within his reach, and has thrown great light on many difficult points, though his conclusions sometimes appear

open to question. When, however, we have found ourselves obliged to differ from an authority so deserving of respect, the reasons for such difference have been carefully assigned in a foot note. (*Corso Cron.*)

* 12. *Sermo in reverentiam Beatæ Katherinæ de Senis,* 1382.

13. *Epistola ad Māgm Raimundum da Capua.* These two curious documents are of great interest to the English reader, as being from the pen of F. William Flete, the English Augustinian hermit, who was one of St. Catherine's confessors and chosen friends. They have never hitherto been quoted at any length, though many references to F. William will be found in Gigli's Prefaces, and in Burlamacchi's Notes to the letters. Independent of the interest which attaches to the author from his connection with St. Catherine, he was in his own time a notable English worthy, whose words had no little weight with his countrymen, and whose authority was respectfully appealed to by the Parliament of the realm.

* 14. *Notale relative ad alcune Visioni avute da Santa Caterina nella terra di Voragine.*

* 15. *Relazione del passagio di S. Cath. in Voragine.* These two MSS. restore to us a lost page in St. Catherine's history, the narrative, namely, of that visit to Voragine which finds no record in the Legend, though it is alluded to in the Process.

16. *Sommario della disputa a difesa della sacre Stimate di Santa Caterina da Siena: dal R. P. Fra Gregorio Lombardelli, O. P.* This is a summary of the great work of Lombardelli on the Stigmas of St. Catherine, which is preserved in MS. in the Vatican Library. The *Sommario* alone was printed at Siena in 1601, but has now become so rare as to be, practically speaking, unattainable. Through the courteous kindness, however, of the Rev. P. F. Thomas Bonnet, Librarian of the *Biblioteca Casanetense,* at Rome, a transcription has been made from the copy preserved in that library for the present work.

17. *Breve Relazione del modo come fu portata da Roma a Siena la sacra testa di Santa Caterina.* (*Siena,* 1683) The history of the removal of St. Catherine's head from Rome to Siena is accu-

rately given in this narrative, published anonymously, but written, as we learn from F. Angiolo Carapelli, by F. Tommaso Angiolini, O. P.

18. *Alcuni Miracoli di Santa Caterina da Siena, secondo che sono narrati da un anonimo, suo contemporaneo.* This little memoir was well known both to Gigli and F. Burlamacchi, who frequently quote from it. It was among the manuscripts which Gigli promised to publish, but it remained inedited until the year 1862, when it was printed from the MS. at Siena by Signor Grottanelli, only 250 copies, however, being struck off. The narrative is of great interest, though the statements of the writer betray just that kind of inaccuracy which is incident to those who attempt to write of contemporaneous events.

19. *Memorie di Ser Christofano di Galgano Guidini, da Siena.* This very curious autobiography of one of the most devoted of St. Catherine's disciples has been frequently quoted, both by Gigli, and other writers It remained unpublished, however, until 1842, when it was printed in the 4th volume of the *Archivio Storico Italiano*, to which valuable collection we are likewise indebted for the *Chronica Antiqua Conventus S. Catherinæ in Pisis*, which appears in the 6th volume.

20. *Lettere dei discepoli di Santa Caterina da Siena.* This collection of letters long preserved in manuscript in the library of Siena, was printed for the first time by Signor Grottanelli in 1868, at the end of the *Leggenda Minore*. The letters furnish us with most valuable and interesting information, and admit us into the private circle of the Saint's spiritual family.

21. *Lettere di Santi e Beati Fiorentini.* (*Florence*, 1736.) In this collection are to be found two letters from Don John of the Cells referring to St Catherine, and one from the Blessed John Dominic.

22. *De Vita et Moribus Beati Stephani Maconi Senensis, Auctore D. Bartholomeo Senensi. Siena*, 1626. (*Vit. Steph. Mac*)

23. *Divæ Catherinæ Senensis Vita, per Joannem Pinum, Gallum Tolosanum* John Pino's "Life of St. Catherine" was

published at Bologna in 1505. It contains some additional details concerning the Saint's visit to Avignon; and Gigli, who notices the book in the Prologue to the Legend, thinks it possible that the author derived his information from authentic sources, collected on the spot. Baronius speaks of him as "an exact writer." (*Pino.*)

24. *Vita da S. Caterina da Siena, da P. Paolo Frigerio.* (*Roma,* 1656.) This life by P. Frigerio, of the Oratory, is noteworthy as one of the very few in which any attempt has been made to add to the materials collected by Raymund. It includes extracts from the life of Stephen Maconi, and from some manuscripts furnished to the writer by Pope Alexander VII., by whose command the work was undertaken.

25. *Capitolo in terza rima in laude di Santa Caterina da Siena, per Anastagio da Monte Altino, vivendo ancora lei nella presente vita.*

26. *Uno Capitolo in rima fatto per Jacobo di Monte Pulciano in reverentia di Santa Caterina.*

27. *Uno Capitolo in rima fatto per Ranicro de' Paglieresi, da Siena.* These poetical compositions, made by three of St. Catherine's attached disciples, are of great interest and value. Anastagio writes of her as one still living, and depicts her as she appeared at the moment before his bodily eyes. They are printed (complete) at the end of the Venice Editions of her letters.

28. *Storia di Santa Caterina da Siena, e del Papato del suo tempo, per Alfonso Capecelatro.* (Florence, 1863.) This excellent work has been already named, and to the researches of the author all subsequent biographers of St. Catherine must express their obligation. The value of the book is much increased by the full and accurate *Elenca,* or catalogue of all works, whether printed or in MS., relating to the Saint, which is given as an appendix in the third and fourth editions. It is from the pen of Signor Grottanelli, and an attentive study of it places at our command all the treasures of the Roman and Sienese Libraries which contribute any additional materials to our stock of know-

ledge in what concerns the history of St. Catherine. (*Capece-latro*)

29. *Annales Ecclesiastici; continuatio Oderici Raynaldi.* These volumes contain the continuation of the Church Annals of Cardinal Baronius by Oderico Rinaldi, and have been the chief authority consulted for the historical notice of the Great Schism. (*Rinaldi.*)

30. *Vitæ Paparum Avenonensium: Steph. Baluzii.* (Paris, 1693)

31. *Muratori. Italicarum Rerum Scriptores.* The 15th volume of this collection contains the Sienese chronicles of Andrea Dei, continued by Angelo Tura; and those by Neri Donato.

32. *The Chronicles of St. Antoninus of Florence.* In his third volume St. Antoninus gives a life of St. Catherine abridged from the Legend, but interspersed with some valuable remarks of his own.

33. *Diario Sanese (Diar. San.)*

34. *Vocabolario Caterimano (Vocab. Cat.)* These two works are by Girolamo Gigli. In the first he has collected every information regarding the churches, monuments, festivals, and customs of Siena which can be of interest to the historian or the antiquary. In the second he gives a vocabulary of such words in St. Catherine's works as differ from the Tuscan approved by the Academies of Florence, and belong rather to the Sienese dialect. His preference of the latter, and his witty sarcasms on the Florentines, gave offence at the court of the Grand Duke of Tuscany, and were the cause of his disgrace and exile. By a decree of the Grand Duke, every copy of his book was ordered to be given up and publicly burnt. A sufficient number were actually destroyed to render the work a choice rarity; but many persons who possessed the prohibited volume relished its contents so much that they concealed their copies, and only gave up sham imitations to the flames ; while the book was eagerly sought for by collectors, especially those of the English nation.

35. *Il Dialogo della Serafica Santa Caterina da Siena. (Dial.)* This forms the fourth volume of Gigli's edition of St. Catherine s

works, which contains likewise her Treatise on Consummate Perfection and her Prayers, together with a few other fragments and documents.   The Dialogue has more than once been translated into French, the latest edition being that of M. Cartier; but no English version as yet exists.   May we live to see the day when the English reader shall possess a complete edition of St. Catherine's works, from which alone can be obtained any just conception of her illuminated wisdom !

In the above list are not included the more generally known Italian historians—references to whose works will be found in the foot-notes, and who have been quoted only so far as was strictly necessary to elucidate the course of the narrative.   For the object aimed at in these pages has been less to present the reader with a complete history of the age of St. Catherine than to make him better acquainted with the Saint herself.   It is her character as a woman that most requires to be made known, for it has hitherto been partially concealed by the very splendour of her historical reputation.   Stupendous as is the story of her life, it has, nevertheless, a side which brings her within the reach of ordinary sympathies.   Catherine, the Seraphic Bride of Christ, espoused to Him at Siena; stigmatised at Pisa; supported on the Bread of Life ; the Pacificator of Florence ; the Ambassadress of Gregory ; the Councillor of Urban; the Martyr for the unity of the Holy See ;—this is indeed a character that overwhelms us with its very greatness.   But Catherine, the Lover of God and man, who gave away her will with her heart to her divine Spouse ; the tender mother of a spiritual family; the friend of the poor ; the healer of feuds, the lover of her country ;—Catherine, with all her natural gifts of prudence and womanly tact ; with her warm affections, and her love of the beautiful; with her rare genius refined, spiritualised, and perfected by Divine illumination ; surrounded by men and women like ourselves, with whose infirmities she bore, and whom she loved as heartily as they loved her in return ; Catherine, with her wise and graceful words, her " gracious smile," and her sweet attractive presence,—this is a being to be loved and imitated; we open our very hearts to receive her within them, and to enshrine her there, not as a Saint only, but as a mother and a friend.

In conclusion, it need only be remarked that in the attempt so to represent our glorious Saint, the rule has been strictly adhered to of excluding all imaginary details, and introducing nothing for which there do not exist unimpeachable authorities   Where such authorities have failed to fill up the gaps in our Biography, they have been left unfilled.

The Frontispiece to the present volume is a *fac simile* of that prefixed to the pictured Life of St Catherine engraved in 1597 by Francesco Vanni, and reprinted at Antwerp by Cornelius Galle, in 1603.

Appended to the present Edition will be found a translation of the Treatise on Consummate Perfection, which it is hoped will find a welcome from every lover of St. Catherine.

A. T. D.

St Dominic's Convent, Stone,
May 30, 1887.

CONTENTS OF VOL. I.

—◦—

Part I.

ST. CATHERINE AT SIENA.

CONTENTS.

Part II.

ST. CATHERINE'S EMBASSIES.

ILLUSTRATIONS IN VOL. I.

Part I.

ST. CATHERINE AT SIENA.

SIENA.

1. *Duomo*
2. *La Scala*
3. *Palazzo Pubblico*
4. *La Misericordia*
5. *Palazzo Saraceni*
6. { *Piazza Tolomei &* *Ch. di S. Christoforo* }
7. *S. Francesco*
8. *Piazza del Mercato*
9. *S. Domenico*
10. *Sta Caterina*
11. *Valle Piatto*
12. *Collegio Tolomei*
13. *Servites*

Porta Camolia

Porta Ovile

Fortress

Porta San Viene

Campo

Porta Laterina

Porta Romana

Porta S. Marco

Porta Tufi

CHURCH OF S. DOMENICO, SIENA.

CHAPTER I.

CATHERINE'S FAMILY AND CHILDHOOD, 1347-1359.

THE plains which occupy the centre of Tuscany, lying between the sources of the Arno, the Tiber, and the Ombrone, present few of those distinctive features of beauty which we are wont to associate with an Italian landscape. The wide and desolate levels are broken only by insignificant sandhills which scarcely interrupt our view of the vast horizon. As we approach the southern boundary of this district, however, the country becomes more hilly and diversified; villages and cultivated farms everywhere appear; and these, together with the frequent recurrence of the familiar foliage of the oak, may possibly carry back the thoughts of an English traveller to scenes nearer home. It needs but a second glance, however, to remind him that he is treading the soil of Italy, as his eye catches the glitter of the silvery olive on the hillsides, or, in lieu of the tapering spire of an English village church, rests on the tall and graceful campanile. Above all, he will recognise in the heavens which shine over these Tuscan plains a beauty such as our northern latitudes can never boast; for the sky is as full of light as that of Attica, and its brilliancy is reflected in the gay and lively character of the people over whom it smiles.

It is then in this part of Tuscany, as it approaches nearer to the mountains, on an eminence 1300 feet above the level of the sea, that stands Siena, "the city of the Virgin," lifting her quaint towers into that luminous atmosphere, and seeming by her very position to command the surrounding plains. So her poets have loved to describe her, "towering from the hills, basking in the light of those serene and glowing heavens; full of all that is gay and graceful in manners; all her sons brave and courteous, and all her daughters beautiful." [1]

There is probably no city in Italy which retains so exclusively medieval an aspect. When the storm of the classical Renaissance swept over the land, it spared the red brick towers of Siena, and left her churches and palaces standing almost as they stood in the fourteenth century. Her walls are still unlevelled, and her gates retain not only their ancient names, but the very pictures of the Blessed Virgin placed there centuries ago by the magistrates of the republic in thanksgiving for her signal protection of the city. The view from those walls has its resemblances and its contrasts with that which would have met the eye five hundred years ago. Within their enclosure lies the ancient city, covering the space of three hills, each of which is crowned by some dome or tapering campanile, while from the very centre of the group rises the lofty tower of the Palazzo Pubblico. At the time to which our story belongs there would have been seen a fair display

---

[1] " Siena, dal colle ove torregia e siede."—*Alfieri.*

" Di leggiadria, di bei costumi è piena,
Di vaghe donne e d'uomini cortesi,
L'aere è dolce, lucida e serena."—*Fazio degli Uberti.*

of other towers, which gave to Siena an appearance of splendour which is now considerably diminished   Permission was granted to the great families to attach such appendages to their palaces, in reward of any distinguished service, and no more ignominious sentence could be decreed against an offender, were he of noble blood, than the destruction of his tower.   But in the sixteenth century, when Siena had long lost her freedom, they were most of them ruthlessly levelled by Diego di Mendoza, the Spanish lieutenant of the Emperor Charles V., and the materials used in the construction of a fortress.

If the interior aspect of the city is thus shorn somewhat of its ancient dignity, the suburbs and surrounding country have proportionably gained.   We look now over plains covered with cultivation, where the white walls of convents and villas gleam through olive woods and vineyards, or the darker foliage of the cypress or the stone pine.   And hidden away in their recesses lies many a pleasant garden, for the Sienese are now, as ever, great lovers of flowers.   In the fourteenth century the country presented a far more desolate appearance, continually ravaged as it was by hostile armies or bands of freebooters.   But the main features are nevertheless the same : there is the torrent of the Tressa still flowing fast below the walls; to the north there is that immense horizon which has its transparent vastness for its solitary beauty, to the south we behold rising in the distance the rugged heights of Radicofani, and Monte Amiata.

Of the three hills on which Siena is built, one is surmounted by the Duomo, or cathedral, an unfinished fragment consisting of what, were the work completed, would form only the transept of the edifice.   Yet even thus it claims to be the masterpiece of Italian Gothic, and on it, century after century, the artists and sculptors of Siena have lavished the best efforts of their genius. There may be seen the curious pavement inlaid with stories from the Old Testament, which is thought by some to have suggested to Dante a famous passage in the Purgatorio ;[1] there in the frieze on either side of the nave are the long rows of tiara'd heads, the

[1] Purgatorio, Canto xii 9-33, 56-67.

portraits of the Popes from St. Peter to Alexander III., so
wonderful in their expression of majesty; there, fixed against the
pilasters which support the dome, are the poles of the Florentine
Carroccio, or Car of the Standard, captured by the Sienese in
1260, at their great victory of Monte Aperto; and there is the
pulpit, the most magnificent work of Nicolo da Pisa, from which
the great patriarch St. Dominic preached when first he visited this
city, when, according to the ancient legend, the Blessed Virgin
was seen standing by his side and inspiring his discourse.

On the hill to the north of that occupied by the Duomo, standing apart from other buildings on a kind of cliff with gardens and
underwood creeping up its sides, there rises another church which,
if possessing less architectural beauty, nevertheless fails not to
rivet the eye by its commanding position. It is the Church of
San Domenico, occupying the site called the Campo Reggio, from
the circumstance that Henry, king of the Romans, encamped
his army here when he came to besiege Siena in 1186. It was
then outside the city walls, and was the property of the Malevolti,
a family devoted to the Imperial cause, one of whom, Malevolti
the Strong Arm, as he was called, bestowed it in 1220 on the
founder of the Friars Preachers. It is, alas! no longer in the
possession of the Order to which it is linked by a thousand associations, having passed in 1784 into the hands of the Benedictines
of Monte Cassino. But for the moment we will only remind
ourselves that it was the third foundation of our Holy Father St.
Dominic, that within its walls he gave the habit to Tancred Tancredi, that beneath its altars repose the ashes of Blessed Ambrose
Sansedoni, and that for thirty years its pavement was almost daily
trodden by the footsteps of St. Catherine of Siena.

Its dimensions have been added to since her time, the transepts
not having been opened until 1465. But the lower church or
crypt where the friars used to assemble for the office of the dead,
and where was the burial place of her family, is now abandoned,
and in Gigli's days was used to contain the straw and other stores
of the neighbouring fortress. Formerly it boasted of a tower of
extraordinary beauty, built by the Tancredi family, who were

great benefactors to the Order. Next to the tower of the Palazzo Pubblico it was reckoned the most beautiful in Tuscany. Above the topmost cornice rose a lofty pinnacle, with other smaller pinnacles at the corners ; but these were so frequently struck and injured by lightning that at length the friars pulled them down, to the intense indignation of the citizens, who denounced them as unworthy of possessing so exquisite an edifice if they cared not to keep it in repair.

The depression between the two hills of which we have spoken is known as the Valle Piatta, at the bottom of which appears the famous fountain of Fontebranda, first erected in 1081 by the family of Branda, and enlarged in 1198, which supplies all this part of the city with water, and has found a notice in the pages of Dante.[1] Turning to the right hand you enter the Strada dell' Oca leading up a steep ascent, on the left-hand side of which stands a house commonly known as the "Fullonica." Over the door of this house you may read in golden letters the words, "*Sponsæ Christi Katherinæ Domus.*" Five hundred years ago it was the residence of Giacomo Benincasa, the dyer, and the father of St. Catherine ; it is now one of the holy places of Siena, and the devotion of the citizens has preserved with scrupulous care every apartment once consecrated by the presence of their glorious countrywoman. Enter, and you will see her father's workshop, the stairs she so often ascended on her knees, the kitchen where she discharged her humble household duties, the chamber she was permitted to use as a chapel, and the little cell which for so many years was the scene of her prayers, her penances, and the marvels of her daily intercourse with God. This is "the house of Catherine, the spouse of Christ," the least footprints of whose life have been thus jealously preserved and religiously venerated.

It was a life cast in the midst of days most sorrowful for her country and for Christendom. The latter half of the fourteenth century was rife with those signs of decay which mark the interval between the extinction of an old form of civilisation and the establishment of its successor. The age of chivalry, properly so

[1] *Inferno,* xxx

called, was over, and together with the glories of the holy wars
we miss those grand Pontificates, under which the brute force of
semi-barbarous nations was subdued to the dominion of the faith.
The triumph achieved by Philip le Bel over Boniface VIII. had
resulted in the removal of the Popes to Avignon, an event equally
disastrous to the interests of the Holy See and the welfare of
Italy. Rome, abandoned by her legitimate rulers, was left the
prey of contending factions; her population dwindled into insig-
nificance; her palaces and sacred temples were crumbling to
ruins. The very year which witnessed the birth of St. Catherine
was rendered memorable by the seven months' tribuneship of
Nicolas Rienzi; but his brief assumption of power was succeeded
by fresh revolts, which extended to every part of the Papal
dominions, and considerably weakened the authority of the
Roman Pontiffs.

Nor was the condition of the Italian republics at this time
much more prosperous. It was in great measure through the
protection afforded them by the Holy See that so many of the
cities of Northern Italy had, at an earlier period, obtained their
municipal freedom. Even those which continued to acknowledge
the authority of the German Emperors, succeeded in securing for
themselves privileges so considerable as to place them in a position of virtual independence, though, by the time of which we
are speaking, many of these Ghibeline States had resigned their
liberties into the hands of certain families such as the Visconti, who,
as lords of Milan, ruled over the greater part of Lombardy. The
Guelph cities, on the other hand, retained their republican institutions, though often at a bloody cost. The freedom of Florence
and Siena was purchased at the price of revolutions, so numerous
and so fruitful in social misery that Dante compares his native
city to a sick man tossing on his couch and vainly seeking for
ease by a change of posture. The triumph of one faction was
followed by the proscription of its rival, and hence arose those
deadly family feuds which gave a yet more acrimonious character
to party strife.

It was not merely the old contest between Guelph and

Ghibeline, kept alive and embittered as the exiles from one city took refuge in a neighbouring state, and were ever ready to avenge their wrongs by turning their swords against their fellow-citizens. A new source of civil contention arose in the thirteenth century, when the people, growing jealous of the power of the nobles, began to league together to exclude them from all share in the government, until at length this jealousy of their rulers, whether noble or plebeian, became so preposterous that in most of the Tuscan republics no man was allowed to exercise the higher offices of state for more than two months at a time. This was the case in Siena, where at the period of St. Catherine's birth the government was in the hands of the *popolani*, or middle-class tradesmen.

Their supremacy had not been established without a fierce struggle. In the twelfth century Siena adopted the consular form of government, and the head of the republic enjoyed the title and authority of Podesta. This office was generally held by one of noble birth, but in 1267 the rivalries of Guelph and Ghibeline brought about a revolution, which resulted in the establishment of a new constitution, and the exclusion of the nobles (who mostly belonged to the Ghibeline faction) from all offices of state. The popular party, who represented the Guelphs, now prevailed; nine magistrates were annually chosen from the plebeian class to form the Signoria, but the number of electors was extremely limited, and the government of the Nine, as it was called, came soon to be regarded as an odious oligarchy. In 1355 the arrival in Siena of the Emperor Charles IV. brought about a counter-revolution. The nobles made common cause with the discontented citizens, and encouraged by the Emperor, succeeded in overthrowing the Nine, some of whom were put to death in the heat of popular commotion. In their place were chosen twelve magistrates, two of whom governed conjointly for the space of two months, when they were succeeded by other two. Charles, dissatisfied with this arrangement, made a strenuous effort to obtain the appointment of his natural brother, the Patriarch of Aqueleia, as virtual Chief of the Republic; but the appointment though made, lasted only a few weeks; the jealousy of the citizens saw in it a design upon their independence, and in May 1355 the Patriarch was forced to offer his resignation, and the government of the Twelve was re-established. This state of things lasted until 1368, when, as we shall see, Siena became the scene of a fresh revolution. These various changes increased the bitterness of existing feuds; the nobles struggled hard to regain some share of political power, and were often in arms against the people; and if to these sources of social disorder we add the frequent plagues which then ravaged Italy, and the lawless bands of the Free Companies, who roamed from state to state, levying contributions on the unwarlike inhabitants, or making them victims to their ferocious violence, we may gather some notion of the wounds of that society to which St. Catherine was sent as an angel of peace.

The family of Benincasa, of which she was a member, belonged to the class of *popolani*, just alluded to, as at that time holding the chief rule in Siena.[1]   Giacomo Benincasa himself at one time filled the office of chief magistrate, and the name of his brother Ambrogio, a goldsmith by trade, occurs as one of the " Defenders " of the republic in the months of September and October 1371. It is affirmed by some writers that the families of Benincasa and Borghese had a common origin; but though the fact seems sufficiently authentic, it is certain that the Benincasa made no claim to nobility.   They were in the position of substantial tradesmen, enjoying a fair share of worldly prosperity, and owning a little country estate near Santa Maria a Pili, which came into the possession of Lisa, St. Catherine's sister-in-law, after the death of her husband, Bartolo Benincasa.   Giacomo was married to Lapa di Puccio di Piagenti, whose father, Mucio·Piagenti, is said to have been a poet of some little reputation.   Giacomo had a sister, Agnes, married to Chele di Duccio   After she became a widow, she entered among the Sisters of Penance of St. Dominic, and

---

[1] Raymund of Capua, in the Legend, only says that they held a respectable position among their fellow-citizens ; but Caffarini, in the *Leggenda Minore*, particularly notices that " they belonged to the class which then ruled and governed the city of Siena "

her portrait is painted in the dormitory of the Convent of San
Domenico, inscribed with the words, *Beata Agnese Benincasa.*
Lapa also had a family connection with the order of Preachers,
for a document is preserved signed and sealed by F. Erveo,
Master General of the Order, granting to Mucio Piagenti and his
wife, Cecca, a participation in all the prayers and good works of
the brethren in return for their great devotion to the Order.

The pious, simple, and charitable character of Giacomo made
him beloved and respected by all his neighbours. He was so
mild and guarded in his words that, no matter how much he was
provoked, he never gave way to anger : and if he saw any member
of his family vexed or disturbed, he would try and calm them,
saying, "Now do not be angry, that God may bless you." Once
when a fellow-citizen had greatly wronged and calumniated him,
Lapa was giving free vent to her indignation, but her husband
would not hear his enemy ill-spoken of. "Let him alone, wife,
and God will bless us," he said; "it is God who will show him
his error, and be our defence." Another virtue in which he
excelled was a singular modesty of speech, so that no freedom of
language was ever tolerated in his family. His daughter, Bonaventura, having married Niccolo Tegliacci, a citizen of Siena, was
often required to entertain her husband's young friends, whose
conversation was far from being blameless. Her health broke
down, and Niccolo observing that she was pining away from some
secret grief, inquired the cause. "In my father's house," she
replied, "I was never used to hear such words as those I now
daily listen to; be sure that if this goes on you will soon see me
dead." Struck with wonder and respect, Niccolo lost no time in
making his companions understand that nothing must be said in
his wife's presence that could wound her sense of modesty, and
ere long the good customs of Giacomo's household were established also in that of his son-in-law.

Lapa Benincasa was an honest and industrious woman, though
possessed of very ordinary mind. She bore her husband twenty-
five children, the names of thirteen appearing on the family tree.
Catherine and her twin sister, Jane, were born on the 25th of

March, 1347. Four of her brothers lived to man's estate, Benincasa, Bartolo, Stephen, and Sandro. Of the last named we know no more than that at the close of the fifteenth century his grandson was still living in Siena. The names of the other three often occur in St. Catherine's life and letters. Benincasa was old enough in 1346 to take a shop and business of his own,[1] he married, and had several children and grandchildren. Bartolo, the second son, was married to Lisa di Golio di Piccio, first cousin to St. John Colombini : Stephen appears to have remained single, and died in Catherine's lifetime. Of the daughters, Nicoluccia was married to Palmiero della Fonte, to which family belonged Father Thomas della Fonte, the Saint's first confessor, who was brought up in her father's house. Magdalen married Bartolo di Vannini; of Bonaventura we have already spoken, and direct descendants from the two last-named sisters were living at Siena in Gigli's time ; a fourth sister, Lisa, remained unmarried, and died of the plague in 1374.

The sons, after their marriage, continued, according to the custom of the age, to live with their parents ; and up to the time of Giacomo's death in 1368, the large family remained undivided, occupying the house of which we have already spoken as "the Fullonica." Catherine, as the youngest,[2] was the special object of her mother's tenderness. Nor was she the favourite of her own parents alone. As soon as she could walk, her winning ways attracted the notice of the neighbours, who were so charmed with her childish talk that they were always trying to entice her to their houses, so that Lapa found it no easy matter to keep her at home. They gave her the pet name of *Euphrosyne*, which in Greek signifies joy ; for, says F. Raymund, "as soon as any one conversed with her, sadness was dispelled from his heart." As she grew in years she grew also in grace and intelligence, and

---

[1] See the documents printed by Grottanelli. Note 49 to *Leggenda Minore*.

[2] She is so called by F. Raymund, but on the family tree appears the name of "Nanna, *ultima nata*," who died April 18, 1363 The probability, however, is, that this date is incorrect, and that Nanna was identical with Catherine's twin sister Giovanna, who died immediately after their birth.

when no more than five years old, having learned the Hail Mary, she would recite it on each step of the stairs as she went up and down, kneeling on her knees with great reverence. "Whilst yet a mere baby," says a contemporary writer,[1] "the child delighted in going to churches and places of devotion." One day, when she was about six years old, her mother sent her, in company with her brother Stephen who was a little older, to the house of their married sister Bonaventura. Having discharged their errand they returned homewards, and crossing the Valle Piatta were about to turn into the street now known as the *Cortone* which leads down to Fontebranda, when raising her head and looking towards the Church of San Domenico on the opposite hill, Catherine saw in the heavens a majestic throne set, as it were, upon the gable-end of the church, on which throne appeared our Lord and Saviour Jesus Christ crowned with a tiara and wearing pontifical robes, while beside Him stood St. Peter, St. Paul, and St. John the Evangelist, and several men in white garments. As she gazed in wonder at the heavenly vision she beheld how our Lord stretched out His right hand towards her, and made over her the sign of the cross, as when a bishop gives his blessing, at the same time bestowing on her a look full of majesty and tenderness. Rapt into a kind of ecstasy, she continued to stand and gaze, wholly absorbed, and as it were united spiritually with that most glorious Lord whom she there beheld, so that she forgot not only whither she was going, but her own self also, and remained there motionless, giving no heed either to men or beasts that passed that way; and so she would have remained even longer had no one called her away. But at length her brother, Stephen, who had gone on his way and imagined her to be following, turned back, and seeing her thus standing still in the midst of the road and gazing into the air, he called her aloud by her name, but she gave him no answer, and seemed not so much as to hear him. Then he drew nearer, still calling to her; until at last, coming up to the spot where she stood, he took her by the hand, saying, "What are you doing, why are you staying here?"

[1] *Miracoli,* p. 7.

At which words, roused as it were out of a deep sleep as she felt him pulling her by the hand, she cast down her eyes, and looking at him for a moment, "Oh, did you but see the sight I saw," she said, "never would you have disturbed me." Then she once more raised her eyes, thinking again to have seen the lovely vision; but all had vanished; and full of grief she began to weep bitterly, supposing that she had through her own fault, by turning away her looks, deserved to lose that precious favour. "Having reached home," says the author of the *Miracoli*, "she said nothing to father or mother of what she had seen; but from that day there grew up in her a certain carefulness of soul, a fear and remorse of conscience, and dread of committing sin as far as was possible to one at her age. And ever as she grew in years there increased in her this anxiety, and she bethought her what means she might take to offend God less, and was always seeking to be alone, and to steal away somewhere out of her parents' sight that she might be able to say her prayers in secret."[1] This was the event which, young as she was, for ever drew her heart to the Supreme Beauty; to Him, whom once beheld, she never forgot, and in comparison of whom all earthly things from that hour became as nothingness. From that day she seemed no longer a child, for "the heavenly fire of God's love had wrought such an attraction in her heart, such a light in her understanding, such a fervour in her will, such a pliantness in all her powers both of body and soul to follow the instinct of His Holy Spirit, that to those who saw her behaviour, and took good heed to her words and deeds, it seemed that she was made wholly conformed to Jesus Christ her sweet Spouse and Saviour."[2]

In speaking of this time afterwards to her confessor, F. Raymund, she acknowledged that it was not by reading, or by any human teaching, that the desire arose in her of following a

---

[1] *Miracoli*, 8, 9 The exact spot where this vision took place was marked by Gigli by a painting and an inscription in the street called the *Cortone*, which leads down to Fontebranda A few years since the painting having faded, it was restored at the public expense. It is now no longer to be seen, but the inscription remains

[2] Fen, p. 6

manner of life similar to that of which we read in the lives of the Fathers of the desert, and other Saints. It was God Himself who inspired it, until she could think of nothing but how she might best bring it to pass. She began, therefore, to plan for herself a new way of life, giving up all childish sports, diminishing her food, and practising other kinds of penance. She also sought out for herself a retired part of the house, where she would scourge herself with a little discipline which she had fashioned out of some cords. Nor did she rest content until she had persuaded some of the neighbours' children to follow her example, so that gathering themselves together with her, they would do the same, saying, meanwhile, a certain number of Paters and Aves, so many as she prescribed; and persevering in these exercises of piety, the more she shunned the company of men the more did she grow in favour with God, so that often when she set herself to go up and down the stairs in her father's house, after the manner that has been already described, she was seen by many persons to be carried in the air without so much as touching any of the steps with her feet, and that with so great rapidity that her mother, who more than once beheld her so borne to the top, trembled lest she should fall.

But the great desire which at this time took possession of her heart was to seek out some solitary place in the wilderness where she might serve God after the manner of the ancient hermits; and following this dream of a childish imagination she determined to leave her father's house, and to set forth in search of the desert. One morning, therefore, prudently providing herself with a loaf of bread, she directed her steps towards the residence of her married sister, which was near the Gate of St. Ansano.[1] Passing through this gate, she found herself for the first time in her life outside the city walls, and going on she came at last to

---

[1] Frigerio, and after him the Bollandists and P. Capecelatro, identify this as the present Gate of St. Mark. But Signor Grottanelli has corrected this error. The Gate of St. Ansano (which was so called from being close to the spot where, according to tradition, the martyr St. Ansano was thrown into a vessel of boiling pitch) no longer exists; and its site is now occupied by the Church of St. Sebastian, near the *Fosso di St Ansano.*

where she saw the houses standing one here and another there, and not together as she was wont to see them in the city, for which reason she was glad, hoping that now she must be near to the wilderness. However, she held on her way a little further, and came at last to a place where she found a sort of cave under a shelving rock, which she entered with great joy, believing that she had found at last her much-desired solitude. Without more delay, then, she fell on her knees and began to pray, and gave thanks to God, who was pleased to give her a sensible token that He accepted her good intention, although it was not His purpose to call her to that manner of life. For as she prayed with great fervour she was lifted up above the ground as far as the height of the cave would suffer her to rise; and so she continued until the hour of None. But at that same hour when our Lord was taken down from the Cross, she began by little and little to descend, and understanding at the same time by a secret inspiration that it was not the wish of her Divine Master that she should serve Him after this manner, she thought within herself how she should return home. But coming out of the cave, and finding herself all alone, and a long way from the city gate, she began to fear lest she should not be able to get so far, and considered also the trouble which her father and mother would feel, believing her to be lost. She therefore again had recourse to prayer, and as she herself afterwards acknowledged to her sister-in-law, Lisa, God failed not to supply her weakness, for He sent a little cloud which lifted her from the ground and carrying her in the air set her down very shortly at the gate of the city, whence she made her way home with all speed and found that her parents were in no anxiety about her, supposing her to have been spending the day with her sister Bonaventura.

The failure of this attempt in no way abated Catherine's ardour, and understanding that she was not called to follow the life of the ancient hermits, she resolved at least to imitate those holy virgins of whom she had heard that they dedicated themselves to God by a vow of virginity in their earliest years. Knowing nothing of the world and its pleasures, she yet longed to renounce them for the love of Him, the vision of Whom " had utterly extinguished in her," says F. Raymund, "the love of this life." One day, therefore, when she was about seven years old, after praying much that our Blessed Lady, the Queen of virgins, would inter- cede for her with her Divine Son, that she might be shown the way in which she might best please Him, she retired to a secret place where she felt sure of being neither seen nor heard, and kneeling down she spoke aloud to the Blessed Virgin in the fol- lowing words · " O most Blessed Lady, and Sacred Mother of God ! who before all other women didst by vow consecrate thy virginity to God, I beseech thee to obtain for me such grace and favour with thy Son that, from this day forward, I may take Him to be the Spouse of my soul. And I here give my faith and pro- mise to Him and to thee, that I will never take other spouse but Him, and so far as in me lies will keep myself pure and unspotted for Him alone to the end of my days."

This done, she set herself to consider what steps she might best take to secure her own fidelity to that which she had promised. She regarded herself as henceforth bound to a life of perfection. "She often assured her confessors," says Caffarini,[1] "that from the time she thus consecrated herself to God (which she did when little more than six years old), if she entertained so much as an idle thought, or fell into any fault which, however trifling, seemed enormous in her eyes, she lost no time in humbling herself and doing penance." Moreover, by a secret instinct of grace, she understood that she had now entered on a warfare with nature which demanded the mortification of every sense. She resolved, therefore, to add fasting and watching to her other penances, and in particular to abstain entirely from meat; so that when any was placed before her, she either gave it to her brother Stephen who sat beside her, or threw it under the table to the cats, in such a manner as to avoid notice. She began also to feel a great zeal, not only for her own sanctification, but also for that of other souls whom she longed to gain to God. On this account she cherished a singular devotion towards those saints who had

[1] Sup., Part I, Trat. 2, § I.

laboured most for the salvation of souls. And learning that the great patriarch, St. Dominic, had founded his Order expressly for this end, she conceived a special love for him, and was accustomed to hold the brethren of that Order in such reverence that when she saw any of them passing her father's house, she would go after them and humbly kiss the very steps where they had set their feet. In her childish imagination she even longed to embrace their rule, and disguising herself as a man to be received among them in some distant cloister where she, too, in the livery of St. Dominic, might spend her days in winning souls to God; a thought which had perhaps been first suggested by the history of St. Euphrosyne, by whose name, as has been said, she was commonly called, and with whose legend on that account she was probably familiar.

Yet with the lively imagination of a child there mingled, even at this early age, in the character of Catherine, a sense and maturity far beyond her years. Her parents and their neighbours often had occasion to admire the gravity and discretion of her words, which inspired them with a feeling of respect. One instance of this was often related by Lapa, and has been preserved by all her biographers. She was not yet ten years old when one day her mother called her, and bade her go to their parish church [1] and ask the priest to say a mass in honour of St. Antony, at the same time giving her some money and candles which were to be offered at the altar. Catherine gladly obeyed, and having discharged her commission, she stayed for her own devotion till the end of the mass. But her mother thought that she would have returned home after making her oblation to the priest; and on her reappearance addressed her in angry words, "Cursed be the tongues!" she exclaimed, "that said my daughter should come no more; [2] she has come at length, though she has tarried long on the way." The child hearing these words

---

[1] Of St. Antonio in Fontebranda, Diario San., 2. 71.

[2] Raymund explains this as a sort of idiom in use among the vulgar when expostulating with any one who delays : "Cosi suol dirsi da alcuni del volgo a coloro che troppo indugiano." Leg , Part I, cap. 3.

held herself still for a while and returned no answer. But after a little space, when she had, as it were, taken counsel with herself, she drew her mother aside, and said with great gravity and respect, "My honoured mother,[1] when you see me transgress any of your commands, beat me with a rod if you think well, that I may be more wary another time, for it is only right that you should do so. But one thing I pray, that for my faults you curse no man or woman in this world, for it is unseemly for you to do so, and a great grief for me to hear." Her mother wondered as she listened to the wise words of the child; but not wishing to show what she felt, she asked her why she had stayed so long away. "I only stayed," she replied, "to hear the mass which you bid me ask for, and that done, I came straight home again, and went nowhere else." Lapa was greatly edified at this reply, and as soon as her husband came home she told him all that had passed, and both gave thanks to God for the singular tokens of grace and prudence which became daily more apparent in their little daughter.

[1] Leg, Part I, cap. 3. *Madonna Madre;* an expression of unusual respect, which Catherine used because she was about to say what implied a reproof of her mother; and she desired therefore to express it in the most humble and deferential language.

CHAPTER II.

HER DOMESTIC PERSECUTION, 1359-1363.

WHEN Catherine was about twelve years old, her father and mother began to think how they might bestow her in marriage, and according to the custom of the country with young maidens of that age, she was kept more strictly at home, while at the same time her mother began to urge her to give more time and attention to her dress and the adornment of her hair and person. These exhortations were very unwelcome to Catherine, who was far indeed from desiring to make herself more attractive to the eyes of men. On the contrary, she avoided them with a kind of horror, and as her confessor informs us, if she chanced, at this time, to meet any of her father's apprentices who lived in the house, she fled from them as if they had been serpents. Neither would she even approach the door or window to gaze at passers-by, her whole anxiety being to keep herself hidden from all notice It may well be supposed, therefore, that she showed small willingness to comply with her mother's wishes; so that after many fruitless contentions, Lapa was forced to call in the aid of her married daughter Bonaventura, whom she begged to use her influence with her sister and persuade her to adopt the dress and ornaments suitable to her age. She well knew the special affection which Catherine bore towards her elder sister, and trusted that Bonaventura might succeed where she had failed. Nor were her hopes disappointed The example and persuasive words of Bonaventura won so far upon her sister, that she was induced to give more time to her toilette, and particularly to the care of her hair, which was of great beauty. John Pino, in his

Life of the Saint, describes it as being of a golden brown,[1] an expression confirmed by F. Bartholomew Dominici in his deposition. Hair of this particular hue has always been held in singular esteem by the natives of Italy, and Lapa might therefore have been well content with the personal advantages which nature had bestowed on her daughter. But there existed at that time the ridiculous fashion of using certain unguents for the purpose of altering the natural colour of the hair, and Lapa could not be satisfied until Catherine's beautiful tresses had been subjected to this ill-advised treatment [2]

Her triumph, however, was of short duration. If, in compliance with her sister's persuasion, Catherine had yielded somewhat to the besetting folly of her sex, she no sooner had time for reflection than she conceived an intense remorse for her weakness, believing herself to have been thereby guilty of a grievous offence against God And in this light she ever continued to regard it , weeping over her fault, and again and again seeking to wash away the stain which she thought she had contracted by humble self-accusation. She used often to make a general confession of her whole life, and whenever she came to this point, says F. Raymund, "she could make no end of weeping and lamenting." As she appeared to consider this fault as one deserving of eternal punishment, he once took occasion to question her whether at that time she had any purpose of acting contrary to her vow. To which she replied that such a thought had never once entered her heart. Then he inquired if she had desired to be liked or admired by men , and she answered by saying that there was nothing that grieved her more than when by any necessity she was seen by them. "Why, then," said he, "do you take your offence to be

---

[1] Flavum illum capillum et aureum, jubet abicere. Pino, *Vita*, p. 8. Capillos flavos quos habebat, abscidit. Process, 1314

[2] We gather this from the expression used by Caffarini in the *Leggenda Minore*, "Era sollecita, che Caterina *facci e' capegli biondi.*" Signor Grottanelli has drawn attention to this circumstance, hitherto overlooked, but which throws considerable light on the whole story, and he quotes a recipe for the preparation of this singular cosmetic, which is preserved in the Siena Library.

so grievous in the sight of God?"   "Because," said she, sobbing
and sighing from the bottom of her heart, "I think that at that
time I preferred the love of my sister before the love of God;
and while I was afraid of offending a silly creature, I offended
the Divine Majesty of the everlasting Creator and the sweet
Spouse of my soul, Jesus Christ." Then her confessor, desiring
to comfort her, said to her, "Although there was some excess,
yet considering that it was but little and done for no evil intent,
but only for a vain pleasure at that time, I take it, it was not
against the commandment of God." When she heard her confessor say so, she lifted up her eyes to heaven, and cried with a
loud voice. "O my Lord God, what a ghostly father is this, that
excuses my sins?" Then turning to her confessor again, she
said: "Father, think you that a vile creature who has received
so many graces and gifts of her Creator, of His mere goodness,
without any merit on her part, could without sin withdraw any
time from the service of such a loving and bountiful Lord, and
bestow it upon this miserable carcass?"[1]   When he heard these
words and saw that they proceeded from a heart inflamed with
the love of God, he said no more.   Nevertheless, examining into
the whole state of her conscience, he takes occasion from this
passage of her life to notice how great must have been the purity
of that soul which could charge itself with no more heinous
offence than the one in question

Light, however, as her fault might appear in the judgment of
the world, it brought with it a certain relaxation of fervour, so
that Catherine perceived in herself that she was slacker and
colder in her prayers than she had been before.   But her Beloved,
who would not suffer that his chosen Spouse should, in ever so
small a degree, become estranged from His Heart, was pleased to
remove out of the way that too natural affection which seemed
the only obstacle that could endanger the closeness of her union
with Himself.   Bonaventura died in the flower of her age, in the
August of 1362,[2] and Catherine, more than ever impressed by

[1] Fen, p 20.
[2] The date of this event, which fixes the chronology of this part of St.

her sister's death, with the vanity of all earthly ties, devoted herself with renewed fervour to the service of God. Prostrating in the presence of God and uniting herself in spirit with the great penitent St Mary Magdalene, she wept anew over her infidelity with bitter regret, until at length she deserved to hear those comfortable words spoken by our Lord in her heart, " Thy sins are forgiven thee " And from that day forward she began to bear a special love towards St. Mary Magdalene, and to take her as an example of penance.

The death of Bonaventura was made by her parents the occasion for busying themselves yet more seriously how to bestow Catherine in marriage. But as she opposed a resolute resistance to all such plans, they addressed themselves to Father Thomas della Fonte, a Friar Preacher, and a connection of the family, and besought him to procure her consent. Father Thomas was well known to Catherine. He had, as we have said, been brought up in her father's house, and to him she had confided the history of her first vision. When he found how firm was her will and purpose to devote herself to God, he was far from seeking to oppose her resolution, and instead of arguing with her, offered his advice as to the most prudent manner of acting. " My daughter," he said, " since you are fully resolved to serve God in the holy state of virginity, being called thereto by God Himself, I have no more to say : you have chosen the better part, and may our Lord give you grace to follow it. And now if you think well to follow my counsel, I would advise you to cut off your hair, which will prove to your parents that they must give up all hopes of your marriage, and will also save you the time that must needs be spent upon its care and adornment." Catherine was not slow in following this advice, and that the more willingly as she regarded her beautiful hair with a certain displeasure as having been the occasion to her of the fault she so profoundly

Catherine's life, is thus stated in the Necrology of St. Dominic's Convent : 1362, *Domina Bonaventura filia Jacobi tintoris de Fontebranda, uxor Nicolai Tegghacci, sepulta est die decima Augusti.*" This would make Catherine fifteen years of age at the time of her sister's death.

regretted. Taking a pair of scissors, therefore, she cut it all away, and to conceal what she had done, she covered her head with a coif, contrary to the custom of young maidens of her tender age. When Lapa perceived this, she inquired the reason of her going thus with her head covered; but Catherine, who dared neither to utter a falsehood nor to avow the truth, gave but a faltering and indistinct answer. Then Lapa hastily seized the coif, and as she removed it, beheld her daughter's head bare, and shorn of its golden tresses. On this she raised a cry of anger, which quickly summoned to the spot the rest of the family. They were all much offended with her, and gave her plainly to understand that in spite of her opposition their plans regarding her would not in any wise be abandoned. Catherine appealed to her brothers,[1] assuring them that she cared not how they might deal with her · she desired to be no sort of charge to the family, and would be content to live on bread and water, so that they would consent to leave her in peace; but their pride would not suffer them to yield the point in dispute. It was agreed that her spirit must be conquered, and to effect this, they insisted on a thorough change in her manner of life. Henceforward, it was agreed that she should no longer have any private chamber of her own to which she might resort, but that she should be continually occupied about the household service, so as to have no time left for prayer and meditation. To show how little account they made of her, the kitchen-maid was dismissed, and Catherine was appointed in her place to do all the menial drudgery. Nor was she even left at peace whilst so occupied, but as she went about her work, they constantly reproached her in severe and cutting language, seeking thus to weary out her constancy and force her to yield to their wishes. They even selected a suitable person whom they designed for her husband, and left no means untried to win Catherine's compliance. " But," says her biographer, " her heart was so thoroughly possessed with the love of Christ, her chosen Spouse, that she would not hear of any other And whereas they had debarred her of a secret place to which

[1] *Miracoli*, p. 11

she might withdraw herself for prayer and meditation, our merciful Lord taught her, by the inward instinct of His Holy Spirit, how she should build a secret chamber or oratory in her own heart, where she might dwell delightfully with her sweet Spouse so long as she desired, and never be plucked out, whatever befell. And whereas, before, she was forced sometimes to go out of her chamber, and so to be distracted with outward affairs, now, contrariwise, she shut up herself so closely in this cell, and took such passing delight in the presence of her love and joy, Jesus Christ, whose delight it is to dwell in pure hearts, that howsoever they cried and called about her, reproaching her in words or deeds, she passed with all such things so quietly, as if they had never been spoken or done to her.

" And as for their abasing her to the vile services of the house, that turned but little to the advantage of the enemy. For when she saw that her father and mother had appointed her to do all the works of drudgery in the kitchen and other places of the house, she never repined at it, but turned it all to her greater merit by this holy imagination. She had this conceit with herself that her father represented in the house our Saviour Christ ; her mother, our Blessed Lady , her brethren, sisters, and others of the family, the apostles and disciples of Christ. The kitchen she imagined to be the innermost tabernacle of the temple, called *sancta sanctorum*, where the principal sacrifices were offered up to God. And with this holy imagination she went up and down the house like a diligent Martha, and in her father, mother, and brethren, served Christ with His blessed Mother and Saints so cheerfully, and with such a glad heart, that the whole house had great wonder of it." [1]

However, as she could not be without some chamber in which to rest, and she was denied any to her own use, she chose to be in her brother Stephen's room, where, when he was away, she might sometimes retire by day, and where also she might pray in the night-time when he was asleep. The sweetness and constancy with which she bore herself under these hard trials began mean-

[1] Fen., 30–32.

while to open the eyes of her parents, and they humbly confessed it to one another, saying, " She has conquered us." Her father in particular, having more spiritual discernment than his wife, began to see that his daughter's conduct had been inspired by something higher than mere stubbornness. This impression was confirmed by an accidental circumstance that happened about this time. One day when Catherine was in her brother's chamber at prayer, leaving the door open (for her father and mother had given her charge that she should be nowhere with the door shut upon her), her father entering into the chamber by chance and seeking something there of his son's that he had need of at that time, found her in a corner kneeling devoutly on her knees ; and, casting up his eyes, saw a little white dove sitting over her head, which dove, so soon as he was entered, to his seeming, flew out at the chamber window, at which being somewhat amazed, he asked her what dove that was. "Sir," said she, " I never saw dove nor other bird in the chamber that I know of." When he heard this, he was very much astonished, but kept the matter secretly to himself. Nevertheless, reflecting on what he had seen, and comparing it with the constancy and patience exhibited by his daughter, he was led to conclude that she was truly following the inspiration of the Holy Spirit.

At the same time Catherine was permitted more clearly to understand the state of life to which God was pleased to call her. From her very childhood, as we have seen, she had entertained a special love towards the great patriarch, St. Dominic, and a desire to be enrolled among his children. One night as she slept, it seemed to her that she beheld all the founders of the different religious rules, and among them St. Dominic, whom she recognised by his habit and by the lily which he carried in his hand. They appeared to invite her to choose one of their rules in which to serve God for the remainder of her life. Casting her eyes on St Dominic, that loving father drew near to her, holding in his hand the habit of his Third Order of Penance,[1] and addressed

---

[1] The Third Order founded by St. Dominic, and called by him the " Militia of Jesus Christ," became known after his death as the " Order of Penance of

her with these consoling words : "Daughter, be of good cheer, fear no obstacle, you shall one day wear this habit."

The comfort she received from this assurance was so great, that the next day she assembled her parents and brothers, and addressed them with no less grace than courage in the following terms :—" It is now a long time since you began to treat with me that I should marry with some mortal man, which talk, however much I abhorred, I never declared plainly but concealed it in part, for the reverence that I bear you. But now I may no longer hold my peace ; and, therefore, I must open my heart and purpose to you in plain words. I have made a full resolution and promise to my Lord and Saviour, and to His most glorious Mother, the Blessed Virgin Mary, that I will serve them all the days of my life in the pure and holy state of virginity, and I give you to understand that this is no new thing, or lately come upon me, but a thing that I have desired even from my infancy, being moved thereto not by any childish lightness, but after careful thought and not without evident tokens of the will of God ; therefore I have vowed that I will never incline my heart to accept any other husband, but only Him. Now, then, being come, by His gracious goodness, to the years of discretion, I thought it my duty to tell you in express terms, that thus much I have, by the will of God, faithfully promised, and thus much I will, by the grace of God, truly observe. This purpose is so deeply imprinted in my soul, that it will be more easy to make a hard flint soft than to take this resolution out of my heart. Wherefore, I humbly beseech you, lose no more time in treating with me about marriage, for in this matter I may not condescend to your request, because I

St. Dominic." It included members of both sexes, and B. Andrea Gallerani, the founder of the Casa della Misericordia, is called by some the first Dominican Tertiary. The Sisters were not cloistered nuns bound by the three vows of religion, though in process of time regular communities were formed among them. As originally founded they lived in their own houses, one of their own members who bore the title of Prioress governing them according to their rule, under the direction of the Friars. The Dominican Sisters of Penance were at this time very numerous in Siena ; and in 1352, a hundred of them voluntarily bound themselves to wear the habit even until death.

have plighted my faith and truth to Jesus Christ alone, whose love I must prefer before all earthly creatures. If it shall please you to keep me in your house, with this condition, as your common servant, I will serve you willingly and obediently to the uttermost of my power. If you think, by putting me out of your house, to force me to yield to your command for lack of necessary provision, assure yourselves no such fear can alter my mind in this matter. For I have chosen Him for my Spouse who giveth food to all living creatures, and who will not suffer them that repose themselves with confidence in His goodness to be destitute of necessary things."

These words were said with such grace and modesty that those who heard her were struck to the heart, and so overcome with tears, that for a good space they were unable to give her one word for answer. At last Giacomo, who was a good man and full of the fear of God, and who moreover called to mind the dove which only a day or two before he had seen over her head, and the other tokens of heavenly favour which he had observed in her behaviour, mastered his emotion so far as to be able to reply. "Dearest daughter," he said, "God forbid that we should desire anything contrary to the will of God, from whom this determination of yours proceeds. Your patience and constancy sufficiently declare to us that this your choice comes from no caprice, but from a fervent love of God. In His name, therefore, follow freely what you have vowed; from this day forth none in this house shall hinder you. Only pray for us to your heavenly Spouse that we may be found worthy of the eternal life which He has promised" Then turning to his wife and his other children, he continued, "From this day forward let none be so bold as to molest my daughter's freedom ; for in truth the alliance she has chosen is more honourable for us than that which we sought to accomplish. We have no cause to complain of what she has done, she has made a fair exchange. She has refused to be matched with a mortal man, and has chosen to be espoused to the immortal God and man, Christ Jesus." When he had finished speaking, Lapa still wept, for she loved her daughter sensibly ;

and it seemed to her that it was hard to renounce the worldly hopes regarding her on which she had set her heart; but Catherine rejoiced with unspeakable gladness, and from that hour had no other care in her heart than how she might best make profit of the liberty that had been granted to her.

CHAPTER III.

CATHERINE ENTERS THE ORDER OF PENANCE, 1363, 1364.

AFTER having obtained from her parents the freedom of serving God according to her desire, Catherine set herself to order her life after an entirely new manner; and first she begged to have some room to herself, no matter how mean or inconvenient it might be. The chamber assigned her, and of which she joyfully took possession, was a little cell under her father's house, no more than five metres long and three in width. It was lighted by one small window to which a few brick steps led up, the remains of which may still be seen, and on which it is said she often rested her head when sleeping. Here she retired as into the solitude of a desert, giving herself up to rigorous penance and uninterrupted prayer. Up to this time, as Lapa would often testify, Catherine was possessed of unusual physical strength, so that she had no difficulty in taking a horse load on her shoulders and running with it up two flights of stairs to the attics But this robust temperament soon gave way under the austerities to which she now subjected herself. From this time she entirely abstained from flesh-meat, as well as from all kinds of sweet or savoury things, so that in process of time it became impossible for her to swallow them without extreme suffering. Wine also she renounced, drinking nothing but pure water. And she went on daily retrenching some new article of food till she came at last to take only a little bread and some raw herbs, and even these she swallowed with difficulty. A few planks composed her bed, with a log of wood for her pillow. She wore a rough haircloth which, from a motive of cleanliness, she afterwards exchanged for an iron chain;[1] she also gradually prolonged her night-watches till she so entirely overcame the disposition to sleep, as to allow herself no more than half an hour of repose, and that only every other day; but as she afterwards acknowledged to F. Raymund, no victory over nature had cost her so dearly as this.

When her mother became aware of these practices, she was greatly concerned; and set herself to do what she could to soften the rigour of Catherine's austerities. In particular she entreated her for a time to give up her hard bed and to come and sleep with her. Catherine would not vex her mother by a refusal, and accompanied her therefore to her chamber, but with no intention of giving herself any extra indulgence. When her mother was laid in one side of the bed, she went and laid herself down in the other side, where she continued watching in prayer and meditation, until at length perceiving her mother to be fast asleep, she rose up softly, without making any noise, and applied herself to her wonted exercises. But Lapa, whose mother's heart was ever wakeful, soon discovered her daughter's stratagems and took them in very ill part. Whereupon Catherine, who had always a great care to do nothing that might grieve her mother, hit on a new device, by which she thought she might both satisfy her mother's mind and exercise in some degree her accustomed discipline. She took two pieces of wood and put them secretly into the bed, under the sheet, on the side where she should lie, and laid herself down upon the same. But it was not so privately done but that the mother, who had a great jealousy of all her doings, within a short time found it out. So when she saw that, however diligent and careful she was to qualify the rigour of her daughter's life, she would, on the other side, be as inventive to find means of continuing the same; as one overcome, she gave it up, and said to her: "Daughter, I see well it boots not to strive with you any

[1] Portions of her hair-shirt are preserved in the chapel of the Fullonica, and elsewhere. The iron chain is kept in the Sacristy of San Domenico. It originally possessed twenty-four links, but several have been given away to various Dominican convents. Three were sent in 1714 to the Church of St Catherine at Leghorn. The discipline, also made of iron chains armed with points, is kept in the Sacristy of San Domenico.

longer, I do but lose my labour. Wherefore, in God's name, go
your way and take your rest in your own chamber at what time
and in what manner you may think best." [1]   And she resolved to
make no further attempt to control her. But from this resolution
she was soon moved by a fresh discovery. Catherine had a great
desire to imitate her holy father, St. Dominic, in his triple disciplines, and following his example she was wont to chastise her
body three times every day with a discipline made of iron chains
garnished with sharp points, offering this penance the first time
for her own sins ; the second time for the souls of others, and
the third for the dead. These disciplines lasted for an hour and
a half at a time, and were so severe, that the blood flowed abundantly. One day when Lapa chanced to be near the chamber
she heard the sound of blows, and entering suddenly, beheld the
piteous sight ; on which, losing all command over herself, she
raised such a cry that the neighbours came running in to see what
ailed her, and so were witnesses with her of the rigorous penances
of her daughter.

All this time Catherine had not forgotten the promise given
her in her dream, that she should one day receive the habit of
Penance of the Blessed Dominic. Day and night she prayed
that the happy day might soon appear which should bring the
accomplishment of her wishes. And fearing that until she had
taken this step she should never be quite safe from molestation
on the part of her family, she herself begged her mother to inter-
cede for her with the *Mantellate* (as the Sisters of the Third
Order were then commonly called), that they would admit her
to their number. This petition was very unwelcome to Lapa,
and to divert her thoughts into another channel, she proposed
that Catherine should accompany her to some hot baths in the
neighbourhood of Siena, hoping that by forcing her thus to take
some recreation she might win her over to give up her present
severe manner of life, as well as her plans for the future. Catherine
made no difficulty in agreeing to her mother's request, and they
set out for the baths, which are supposed to have been those of

[1] Fen., p. 44

Vignone, on the right bank of the Orcia.[1] But she had no thought of giving herself any bodily indulgence. On the contrary, she took occasion of this visit to the baths to practise a new kind of penance. She begged her mother that they might enter the bath alone, and Lapa willingly consenting, having no suspicion of her daughter's intention, she went and placed herself under the spout where the sulphureous water came scalding hot into the bath, and there suffered patiently greater pains from the heat of the water, than she was wont to do at home when she beat herself with the iron chain. When her mother perceived this, and saw that whatever she devised for the comfort of her daughter was, by her contrivance, turned to a contrary end, she determined to return home, but failed not on the road to make Catherine understand how much she was displeased with these excessive penances. Catherine never argued the point with her mother; she listened to all she had to say with modesty and in silence, but it did not still the voice of God which sounded in her heart, and drew her by a powerful attraction to a life of heroic sacrifice, of which Lapa little understood the secret. Caffarini tells us that as they returned from the baths, it was observed that she walked with her eyes shut, her mind abstracted from the bodily senses and wholly absorbed in God. "As I, who write," he continues, "have many times seen her walk, and if I had not seen it, I never could have believed it."[2]

The suffering which Catherine had endured at the baths proved the immediate occasion of her long-cherished desire being granted. On her return home she pressed her mother to undertake her suit with the Sisters of Penance, and overcome with her importunity, poor Lapa at last complied; and going to the Sisters, presented her daughter's request. It met at first with no success. They answered that it was not their custom to receive young

---

[1] There was a chapel here in St. Catherine's time, dedicated to St. Catherine the Martyr, as we learn from a survey of Siena made in 1334 by Simon da Fondi This chapel was rebuilt in 1660, and dedicated to St. Catherine of Siena.

[2] Caff, Leg. Min , cap. 7.

maidens among them, but only widows of mature years, who might be expected to behave with becoming gravity; because not living in community or keeping enclosure, it was necessary to exercise great prudence in the admission of members. Lapa returned with this answer to her daughter, who was not discouraged, but entreated her mother to try again, which she did, but with no better result than before. Meanwhile Catherine fell sick, her malady being partly caused, as it would seem, by her adventure at the baths. Lapa, who tenderly loved her child, was overcome with sorrow, and watched by her sick-bed with unremitting care. Catherine profited of the occasion to win from her mother the promise that she would make a third appeal to the Sisters of Penance. "If you wish me to recover health," she said, "obtain for me this favour; otherwise, be well assured that God and St. Dominic will take me from you altogether."

At such a moment Lapa could refuse her nothing, and once more returning to the Sisters she pressed her request with such importunity, that they were in a manner forced to yield consent. "If your daughter," said they, "be not over fair we are content to receive her. If she be, the malice of the world is such that you would hazard the good name, both of your daughter and all of us, and, therefore, we could in no wise receive her." On which the mother answered, saying, "Come, yourselves, and judge whether she be fair or no." They sent therefore two discreet matrons, chosen from among themselves, to examine both her personal appearance and her dispositions of mind. On coming to the house they found Catherine lying on her bed, and so altered by sickness that they were satisfied her beauty was at any rate not excessive. By her words, however, they judged that she had a most fervent desire to serve God, and were greatly astonished at the wisdom which appeared in one of such tender years. And so, taking their leave, they went home to the rest of their company, and declared to them what they had heard and seen. Upon this report, the Sisters communicated the matter to the Brethren of the Order, and that done, resolved with full consent to receive her to the habit, sending word to Lapa, that so soon as her daughter was recovered, she should bring her to them without longer delay.[1] At these tidings Catherine wept for very joy, and gave thanks to God and St. Dominic; praying that her recovery might be hastened, so that she might speedily be fit to receive the holy habit. In fact, the joy of her heart seemed to give back health to her body, so that the malady from which she had been suffering rapidly disappeared. But the enemy was allowed to assail her constancy by one more trial, which is thus related by Caffarini in his Supplement —"One day towards the close of evening, not long before the holy virgin obtained the habit of St. Dominic, as she was shut up in the chamber which her father had given her, praying after her custom before the crucifix, the evil spirit appeared to her in a form rather pleasing than terrifying, bringing with him a quantity of rich dresses and stuff of the finest silk which he displayed before her, whilst he tried with flattering words to induce her to accept them. Catherine repulsed him with scorn and drove him away; but as he disappeared she felt herself for the first time assaulted by a strange temptation. There arose within her a violent desire to go forth and show herself abroad, dressed not only in the gay attire commonly worn by girls at her age, but in the more luxurious costume which at that time was adopted by newly-married women. Tormented by the presence of so odious a temptation, she turned to the crucifix, saying, "My sweetest Lord, you know I have never desired a mortal spouse; help me in this trial, I ask not to be delivered from it, but to have strength to overcome." As she prayed, there appeared to her our Blessed Lady, who showed her a garment of dazzling richness, which she had drawn out of that casket of all treasures, the wounded side of her Divine Son. And as she clothed Catherine with this inestimable robe, she said to her, "My daughter, know this, that the garments drawn from the side of my Son surpass in beauty all that can be fashioned by the hand of man."[2]

Her reception of the holy habit of St. Dominic took place on a Sunday, in the chapel assigned to the use of the Sisters in the

[1] Fen., p 54   [2] Sun., Part I, Trat. I, § 4.

Church of St. Dominic, commonly called *Delle Volte.* The date of this event is not given by Raymund, and we have no means by which to fix it precisely, but it was probably about the year 1364 [1] He merely tells us that the ceremony took place according to the accustomed form, in the presence of the Brethren and the Sisters. Catherine's name is twice inscribed in their register, once as " Katerina Jacobi Benincasa," and a second time as " Catherina di Lapa." From that day, according to the custom of the Sisters, she constantly wore the white veil and habit and the black mantle of the Order, from which they received the vulgar name of the " Mantellate." This " black mantle of humility" was specially dear to Catherine. Her secretary, Neri di Landoccio, writing to Caffarini, told him that she always regarded the mantle in which she was first dedicated to her Spouse as a most precious thing, and was accustomed to say : " It shall never be taken from me." If it was ever torn, she would patch and mend it with her own hands, for she would say, " I wish it to last after I am gone." Yet dearly as she loved her mantle, she once parted with it at the call of charity. " One day," says Stephen Maconi in his letter to Caffarini, which is inserted in the Process, " as she was setting out with her companions she met a poor person who begged an alms with much importunity. She said to him : ' I assure you, my dear brother, that I have no money.' ' But,' said he, ' you could give me that mantle.' ' That is true,' said Catherine, giving it to him. Those who accompanied her had much difficulty in redeeming the mantle, because the poor man made them pay very dear for it ; and when they asked her how she could resolve to walk out without the mantle of her Order, she replied in these noble words : ' *I would rather be without my mantle than without charity.*' "

[1] P. Capecelatro, who is followed by M Cartier, supposes her to have received the habit of Penance so early as 1362. But this is manifestly impossible, as Bonaventura's death did not take place until the August of that year, so that under this supposition all the subsequent events narrated above would have occupied no more than four months.

On her deathbed the saint left this mantle as a legacy to her first confessor, F. Thomas Della Fonte, from whose hands she had probably received it. He left it when dying to his niece, Catherine Cothi, also one of the Mantellate, and she gave it as a sacred relic to F. Thomas Caffarini. By him it was carried to Venice in 1398, where many persons out of devotion chose to be invested with it when received into the Third Order. It was long kept by the Sisters of Penance of that city in a chest of gilt wood, and was the means of working many cures both corporal and spiritual.

(38)

CHAPTER IV.

CATHERINE IN SOLITUDE, 1364-1366.

" ON the same day that Catherine received the holy habit of
Penance," says Caffarini,[1] " she entered her little chamber
and began to meditate on the strange and sorrowful problem how
men could love and follow after the perishable things of this world,
whilst the voice of God was ever inviting them to taste of His
consolations.   As she so pondered, there appeared before the eyes
of her soul a magnificent tree loaded with the richest fruit, but
hedged about with prickly thorns that made it difficult to approach.
Not far from the tree was a fair hill covered with ears of golden
corn, but the ears though beautiful to look upon, were black and
foul within, and withered at the touch.   Some persons came and
gazed at the tree, admiring its beauty, but when they saw the hedge
of sharp thorns they feared to approach, and turned aside to satisfy
themselves with the empty ears of corn that poisoned those who
ate them.   Others more courageous pierced the hedge and reached
the foot of the tree, but perceiving how high its branches were
from the ground, they too lost courage, and made choice of the
withered ears.   Only a few were found who feared neither the
sharp thorns nor the fatigue of climbing, and these, mounting the
lofty branches, ate the delicious fruit, which after once tasting
they lost all relish for earthly food."

Catherine understood the vision well, and long ago she had
made her choice.   The blasted ears of worldly pleasure with all

[1] Sup., Part I, Trat I, § 5.

their gilded show had no charms for her, neither did the sharp thorns of penance or the labour of perseverance present any terrors to her heroic soul. For one brief moment in her early childhood Heaven had been open to her gaze, and her election had been irrevocably made. Now, therefore, that she found herself clothed with the holy garb of religion, her only thought was, how most completely to die to the world and give herself to God. Though it was not the custom for Tertiaries to bind themselves by the three vows of religion, yet she fully purposed in her heart to live thenceforward according to their spirit. Her vow of perpetual chastity had long since been pronounced , and so precise was her observance of the obedience due to her superiors, that when she came to die she was able to say that she had never knowingly transgressed it ; as to poverty, she neither possessed nor desired to possess anything superfluous The prosperity enjoyed by her father and brothers, whose affairs were at this time in a flourishing condition, was far from pleasing to her. " Thou knowest, Lord," she would say, "that these are not the goods I desire for my family " She even besought Almighty God that if it were for their greater spiritual profit, this abundance of earthly things might be taken from them ; and it seemed that her prayer was granted, for in the end, through no fault of theirs, they were reduced to great penury. Although not bound then by the obligation of religious vows, Catherine practised with the greatest exactitude the virtues which they prescribe ; whilst the rule of life which she now embraced probably surpassed in strictness that of the most austere cloister. She began by imposing on herself a rigorous law of silence. F. Thomas Della Fonte left it written in his notes of her life, that for three years after her entrance into the Third Order she never spoke save in confession, and never left the house except to go to the church. Probably this rule admitted of certain relaxations, for it was during this period of retirement that she made the acquaintance of F. Thomas Caffarini and F. Bartholomew of St Dominic, who visited her from time to time in the company of her Confessor, "without whose leave, however," says F. Bartholomew, "she never spoke to any man except her

father and her brothers."[1]   And thus, in the words of her old
biographer, "she contrived to find out a wilderness in the midst
of the city, and to make for herself a solitary place where there
was great resort of people." Her prayer was all but continual,
and she loved to unite it in spirit with the choral offices of the
Order to which she belonged.. The Church of St. Dominic was
close to the Fullonica, and Catherine from her chamber could
catch the sound of its bell calling the brethren to choir at the
appointed hours   She so arranged her time as to watch while
the friars were sleeping, and when she heard the second toll
for midnight matins she would address her Divine Spouse, saying,
"Lord, until now my brethren have slept and I have watched
for them in Thy presence, praying Thee to guard them from the
wiles of the enemy ; now that they are rising to offer Thee their
praises, suffer me to take a little repose." And then she would
lie down to her scanty rest.

Her Divine Spouse was not willing to leave her without
necessary direction in the arduous course she had embraced ;
but He chose neither man nor angel for the purpose : He
deigned Himself to be her teacher ; so that from this time began
that wonderful intercourse between Catherine and her Beloved,
the closeness of which, says F. Raymund, can be compared to
nothing but the familiar intimacy of two friends.   She herself so
described it : "Father," she said, "take this for a certain truth,
that I was never taught the rule of spiritual life by any man or
woman, but only by my Lord and Master Jesus Christ, who
made it known to me either by secret inspiration or else appearing openly to me and speaking to me as I now speak to you."
She declared also, that in the beginning, her visions were for the
most part only wrought in the imagination, but they were afterwards sensible, so that she saw with her eyes the Form that
appeared to her, and heard with her ears the sound of the Voice
that spoke.   At first she feared, doubting the illusions of the

---

[1] Process, fol. 139, 140. The seeming contradiction is clearly enough
explained by Raymund when he says that our Lord "*gradually* introduced
Catherine to the active life." Leg., Part 2, cap 1.

enemy, but our Lord, whilst commending her prudence, gave her certain notes and tokens by which she might always discern between the true visions of God and the deceits of Satan. "Daughter," He said, "it were an easy matter for Me to inform thy soul inwardly with the secret instinct of My Spirit, so that thou shouldest at all times discern perfectly and without error between true visions and 'counterfeit illusions; but because My will is to profit others as well as thee, therefore I will teach thee a general rule and lesson, which is this: My vision beginneth evermore with fear and dread, but in process of time setteth a soul in great joy, quietness, and security. It beginneth with some kind of bitterness, but in continuance it waxeth more delightful and sweet. The visions of the enemy are contrary, for in the beginning they show a kind of security and gladness, but in process they turn to fear and bitterness, which increase afterwards and wax greater and greater. And it standeth with good reason, because My ways and the ways of the enemy have this special difference: My ways are the keeping of the commandments in perfection of a virtuous and godly life. These seem at the beginning to be full of difficulty; but in time they become easy and pleasant. But the ways of the enemy are the transgressing of My commandments in the liberty of the flesh and licentiousness of life, which seem at the beginning to be delightful and pleasant; but in continuance of time they prove, in very deed, dangerous and painful. Take this also for a most certain and infallible rule to discern between true and false visions; because I am Truth, it cannot be otherwise than that the soul of man must needs, by My visions, receive a greater knowledge of truth; by which he cometh to understand both his own baseness and the worthiness of God, and so consequently to do due honour and reverence to God, and to make little account of himself, which is the proper condition of humility. The contrary happeneth in the visions of the enemy; for he, being the father of lies and king over all the children of pride, can give none other thing but only what he hath; and therefore in his visions there must needs ensue in a soul ignorance and error, whereby it conceiveth a false esteem of itself, which is the proper condition of pride. Therefore by this thou mayest know if thy visions be from Me or from the enemy ; of Truth or of falsehood · if they come of Truth they will make thy soul humble, if they come of falsehood they will make thee proud " [1]

Dating then from this period, Catherine's union with her Divine Spouse became uninterrupted , never was she separated from His presence ; but whether she prayed or read, whether she watched or slept, He was ever with her. There was not a part of the church which she frequented which was not marked by some gracious manifestation of His watchful tenderness ; her little chamber and the garden [2] attached to her father's house were all filled with memories of this unspeakable intercourse. Truly it might be said of her that " she walked with God. ' " On her lips and in her heart," says Caffarini, " she had nothing but Jesus · in the streets she walked with Jesus ; her eyes were set to look on Jesus only ; never were they open out of curiosity to behold any other objects unless they were such as might lead her to Jesus, and thus it was that she was so often rapt in wonderful ecstacies and abstractions of mind " [3]

Nor was this union weakened or obscured in after years by her converse with the world ; but when outwardly speaking with men, her heart was always inwardly engaged with God, and in this lay the secret of that marvellous power which she exercised over all who approached her. Flesh and blood, however, could not long sustain such closeness with Divine things without a suspension of the faculties and a wasting of bodily strength, and these supernatural graces were the origin of that state of bodily suffering and incapacity for food which made the remainder of her life a daily martyrdom.

Among the precious lessons which she received at this time there was one which must be regarded as the foundation-stone

[1] Fen , Part I, cap. 17.

[2] This garden now forms the site of the Church of the Confraternity of Sta. Catherina in Fontebranda

[3] Sup , Part I, Trat. 2, § 11.

of her whole spiritual edifice, and which is thus narrated and
expanded by her biographer. One day as she was praying, our
Lord appeared to her and said : "Daughter, knowest thou what
thou art, and what I am? If thou perfectly know this truth thou
art blessed. Give heed then to My words, that thou mayest be
able to understand it Thou art she that is not, and I am He
who am. Art thou not she that was made out of nothing? for-
asmuch as every creature is made out of nothing, and has no
being save in My Almighty power, and evermore of itself tends
to nothing Now if a man were thoroughly persuaded of this,
that in truth he were nothing, how could he be proud, or how
could he glory in himself or in any of his works, if he knew that he
had nothing of his own but defects and sin? But because if he
considered this truth alone he would fall away into despair, therefore is it needful also that he know that I am He that am. God
only is, of Himself. He alone is unchangeable and incorruptible
The creature, therefore, that sees this, and knows that he can
have no being in himself, or find any good or blessedness in himself or any other creature, turns himself to God and beholds Him,
the Creator and Preserver of all things, Who maintains all things
in their being and blessedness, the everlasting spring and fountain
of all goodness, Who alone is able to slake the thirst of his natural
desires and longings. And so beholding Him, the creature
begins to sigh towards Him and to be inflamed with the love of
Him. And he conceives a certain holy fear, which is the guardian
of the soul, so that he will not suffer the least motion in his heart
which could offend so sweet and bountiful a Master. And he
rests so firmly on the provident goodness of God that no adversity
disturbs him, because he knows that Almighty God permits it
for his salvation ; and he understands that there is no labour
or sorrow in this world, however grievous, that can be compared
to the glorious reward which he looks for from the hands of God."

This steadfast trust in the providence of God was also taught
her by another of these Divine words "Think of Me," He said,
"and I will think of thee!" which words she understood as
though He had said · "Have no thought or care of thyself either

for soul or body, because I who know better what is good for thee will think and provide for all thy necessities. Be careful only to think on Me, for in that is thy perfection and beatitude." It cannot be expressed with what joy and confidence Catherine henceforth dwelt on those words, " I will think of thee." She never wearied of speaking of them, and they formed the text and chief subject-matter of the treatise which she afterwards composed on Divine Providence. If at any time she saw any of her companions troubled or pre-occupied by some vexation, "Leave all to God," she would say, "what have you to do of yourselves? For you to bestow care about these things is to take from God His care and providence, as though He could not or would not provide."

She would often speak with her Confessor on the state of a soul that is united to God in perfect charity. "A soul that loves God perfectly," she would say, "ends by forgetting herself and all other creatures. Such a soul, seeing that of herself she is nothing, and that all her being depends on God, in Whom alone, and in no creature, she finds by experience that her happiness must rest, forsakes both herself and all things to plunge herself as it were into the love of Him, directing to Him all her works, and thoughts, and powers. Without Him she cares not to be, because in Him she finds all that can delight the heart, all beauty, all sweetness, all quietness, and all peace. And so, the bond of love between her and God drawing closer, she comes as it were to be wholly transformed in Him. And at length it comes to pass that she can love, delight, think, and remember no other thing than Him only. All other creatures she loves and considers in Him, even as a man who dives and swims under the water sees and feels nothing which is not either the water or what is contained in the water; and even if he sees anything that is out of the water, he sees it not properly as it is in itself, but as the likeness of it appears in the water. A soul thus plunged in the love of God hates herself as much as she loves Him. She sees that her own sensuality is the root and origin of all sin, and the cause of her separation from God, her Supreme End. Therefore on that account she conceives a certain holy hatred of her own inclinations and a desire to kill the root of them, which is self-love. And because the root of this self-love lies so deep that it cannot utterly be removed, but something will still remain which from time to time will molest her, therefore there daily grows in her this holy hatred and contempt of self, which increases her desire to advance nearer to God ; and for His love she is ready to endure the sharpest discipline that may subdue that proneness to sin which keeps her back from her desired joy." All her disciples notice how frequently she dwelt on this lesson of "holy hatred," and how often she would quote the saying of St. Bernard, " Destroy self-love, and there will be no more hell." It was a lesson that lay at the root of her whole interior life, and will be found embodied in that abridgment of her Spiritual Doctrine which was taken down from her lips at a later period by her English Confessor, F. William Flete.[1]

As in her words, so also in her writings, the same truth returns again and again. She saw in the disorder of self-love the great antagonist of the love of God, "the root of all vices, which has poisoned the entire world and stricken the mystical Body of Christ as with a pestilence."[2] And she understood that it was the business of a loving soul to make war on this great rebel and deliver it to death by the relentless practice of mortification. She would not tolerate the idea that there is any state of the soul, however exalted, in which the warfare with our own passions can ever be relaxed, and regarded it as a deadly delusion to suppose that this is only a practice for beginners. Hence in her Dialogue, after describing various sublime stages of the spiritual life, she concludes with the emphatic warning, that "there is no condition of the soul in which it ceases to be necessary for a man to put his own self-love to death."[3]

Following the course of our history we shall presently have to relate some of those wonderful favours granted to Catherine in her solitary cell, which have been recorded by Raymund and her

[1] For a translation of this precious document see Appendix A.
[2] Dialogo, cap. 7. .   ..   [3] Ibid., cap 56.

other confessors   But lest any should gather from such narratives
the notion that St. Catherine's ecstatic life rested on a different
basis, and was subject to wholly different conditions from the
spiritual life, as we understand the term, it will be profitable, in
addition to what has been said above, to gather from the writings
of those who knew her longest and best a few most significant
facts as to her ordinary manner of prayer. First, then, we learn
from the evidence of F. Thomas Caffarini, whose acquaintance
with her began as early as the year 1366, that it was her habitual
practice to meditate on the life of our Lord.   "I witnessed," he
says, "how she prolonged her vigils till matins, meditating, according to her custom, principally on the life of Christ and the
truths of the Gospel."[1]   And in his Supplement he relates, how
"going one day into the church of the Friars Preachers *to meditate there at her leisure on the mysteries of our Lord's Incarnation,*
she was suddenly illuminated by a Divine revelation."[2]   And
again, "she was sweetly and powerfully drawn to an affectionate
love and compassion for the sufferings of Christ, *meditating on
which* she found comfort and refreshment for her soul whenever
it was afflicted.   This was the real secret of her victories over the
enemy, and she was never weary of recommending to others the
practice of continual prayer.   In truth, her own prayer may be
said to have been continual, for there never was a moment that
she was not thinking of God." These meditations were fed by
spiritual reading; her most constant study, after she learnt to
read, being the Holy Gospels, on which she composed a devout
treatise, now unhappily lost.[3]

Next, it may be observed, that much as she valued meditation,
she did not despise vocal prayer. Besides her recital of the
Divine office, of which we shall speak hereafter, she was accustomed to the frequent use of ejaculations, one of those most
familiar to her being the words, *"Peccavi, Domine, miserere mei."*
These words, says Caffarini, "she always used at the end of her

---

[1] Process, fol. 18.   [2] Sup., Part I, Trat I, § 9.
[3] Quoted by Gigli from the deposition ... F. Thomas Caffarini. I have
been unable, however, to verify the passage in the Process.

prayers, folding her hands and bowing her head," and the habit of a lifetime showed itself upon her deathbed, when we are told she used this same ejaculation "more than sixty times" "She did not care," says F. Bartholomew of St. Dominic, "to pray much at a time, but in praying or reading she would, as it were, ruminate each word, dwelling upon it, and finding in it something to feed her soul with spiritual savour; and in this manner she came at last to be unable to say one Our Father without being rapt in ecstacy." [1]

Moreover, her prayer, if sublime, was also simple and practical. "Catherine never ceased to pray for the virtues," says Caffarini,[2] "and specially for true and perfect charity." At one time, before a season of temptation, we find her inspired by God to pray for fortitude, and at another for purity of heart. During her whole life she constantly made use of the prayer of petition, asking particular graces for herself, or for others, and persevering in her requests a long time together. She would address our Lord with sighs and tears, saying with filial confidence, "Lord, I will not stir from your feet till your goodness has granted me what I desire." But she often said that she dared not so pray, unless she knew by manifest tokens that what she asked was in conformity with the will of God." [3]

The third point to be noticed, as full of encouragement, is that St. Catherine's growth in prayer and in the spiritual life was *gradual and progressive.* Prevented by grace, as she manifestly was, even from her infancy, she was yet, not all at once and without labour, raised to the heights of contemplation. "In her heart she disposed to ascend by steps;" and she passed "from virtue to virtue." [4] This is apparent from many expressions of Raymund, as well as from the spiritual instruction she dictated to F. William Flete. But it may suffice to quote here a passage from the Supplement of Caffarini, as being less generally known:

"On a certain feast of the Holy Cross, as she was meditating on the immense love of Jesus Christ displayed in His Passion,

---

[1] Process, 140.   [2] Sup., Part I, Trat. I, § 12.
[3] Sup., Part 2, Trat. 3, § 14.   [4] Ps. lxxxiii. 6, 7.

she felt herself washed from head to foot in that Precious Blood shed by Him for our redemption. Then our Lord appeared to her carrying a cross of gold, and said to her, ' Daughter, take this Cross and follow Me ' She obeyed promptly, but when she had taken a few steps she met another cross, higher and larger, on which our Lord mounted, saying 'Approach thy lips to the wound of My side ' And when she had done so with ineffable consolation, He took her by the hand and drew her higher, till her face rested upon the Face of her Beloved. Then He gave her to understand that by these three steps were signified three states of the soul, concluding with these words : ' When thou shalt have reached the third, or last degree, thou shalt enjoy My Divine embrace with quiet and tranquillity, for so I render My chosen ones blessed even before I call them to My kingdom.' And Catherine having been guided, while yet a young girl, through the first and second degrees, found herself at last at the third, or supreme degree of union with God which is described in Holy Writ under the figure of an embrace, or ' the Kiss of His Mouth.' Thence she obtained the grace, even whilst living in this world, of an unalterable peace and tranquillity ; never feeling her heart disturbed, though struck down by many sicknesses, attacked by cruel calumnies, and worn out with fatigues and responsibilities far beyond her age and sex. She desired nothing save to be released from the bondage of the flesh that she might be united to her spouse. But He, designing to employ her in affairs of importance for the service of Holy Church, deferred for a time the fulfilment of her desires. She mitigated the sadness which from time to time made itself felt, by resignation to the Divine decrees, knowing that one day, at any rate, she should die and pass to His presence : and therefore it was that she so willingly employed herself in burying the dead, showing great signs of joy whenever she learnt the happy departure out of this world of some soul who had lived a holy life." [1]

But when all has been said that can be said to exhibit this great Saint as using the same methods of prayer and exercises of

[1] Sup., Part 2, Trat. 2, § 3.

perfection as are common to the faithful, and as raised to her exalted sanctity only by progressive steps, there yet remains the fact, declared in the Bull of her Canonisation, that her doctrine was "not acquired but infused." Caffarini says she had attained that highest degree of contemplation, of which St. Thomas affirms that its fruits are "light in the intellect and love in the heart." When she came out of her ecstacies, he says, she spoke with so wonderful an intelligence of Divine things that she seemed to know more than the wisest doctors; but all her illumination was from God.

Of this sublime light she has written admirably in her Dialogue, describing it as a ray proceeding from the fire of charity. " Proud ignorance remains blind to this light because its eye is clouded by self-love. Such souls can never penetrate beyond the letter of the Scriptures : they may read much and turn over many books, but the pith and marrow they never taste. They wonder to see the simple and illiterate possessed of a clearer knowledge than they of spiritual things, but there is nothing to wonder at in it, because these humble souls are illuminated by grace, which is the true source of knowledge "[1] "What Catherine taught," says Raymund, "she had learnt by experience, like the disciple of whom St. Denys, the Areopagite, speaks." He is referring to a passage in the works of St. Denys, which runs as follows :— " Hierotheus learned these things, instructed by some special inspiration, having not only *learned, but also experienced, Divine things, and being fashioned by such teaching of the heart* (if I may so express it) to that faith and mystic union which can never be acquired by any human lessons."[2]

Let us now take a glance at that little cell where Catherine, alone with her Divine Spouse, was "being fashioned by this teaching of the heart;" and to do so we shall but gather up the words of those who shared her confidence, and who themselves were witnesses of the marvels they described. It was a life of

---

[1] Dialogo, cap. 85.
[2] De Div. Nom., cap. 2. The exact sense of the original is, that "Divine things came upon him without his action."

mingled penance and ecstacy. " Every evening, for many years, when it began to grow dusk," says Caffarini, "she felt herself drawn by an irresistible force to God, passing into a rapture which generally lasted six hours, during which time she conversed with the Eternal Wisdom, her bodily senses remaining suspended."[1] Another time, we read, how standing one night at the window and gazing up into heaven, she thought of the Divine Beauty which she saw reflected in the heavenly orbs ; when suddenly from the blue vault above her there came a sound of exquisite melody, such as mortal ear had never heard, which rapt her in ecstacy, filling her with the joys of Paradise[2] Once as she prayed for the virtue of charity, and understood that her prayer was granted, she was so overwhelmed with the sweetness of the Divine Presence that for ten days she could neither eat nor drink, nor engage in her ordinary occupations.[3] Another time. when in like manner she had continued praying a long time for purity of heart, an angel appeared bearing a garland of spotless lilies which he placed as a crown upon her head. The beauty and fragrance of these lilies was so unearthly that she declared the mere thought of that precious garland sufficed to cause her a kind of rapture. Occasionally we catch sight of that same love of the Office of the Church which was so remarkable in St. Gertrude. On the first Vespers of a certain feast of St. Lucy she seemed to see all Paradise preparing to celebrate the festival, and full of joy, she ran to the church, desiring to have the bells rung that the Church on earth might take part with the Church in Heaven Our Lord was pleased that her wish should be accomplished without causing the people any astonishment, for suddenly the sky clouded over and announced the approach of a tempest, and, according to the custom of the times, the church bells were rung to exorcise the powers of the air. When they ceased Catherine seemed to hear solemn vespers sung in heaven by a choir of virgins, led by one of surpassing beauty, to whom all paid homage The privilege of listening to the chants of Paradise was often granted to her.[4]

---

[1] Sup , Part 2, Trat 3, § 8.   [2] Ibid , Part 1, Trat 2, § 6.
[3] Ibid., Part 1, Trat. 2, § 12.   [4] Ibid. Part 1, Trat 2, § 20

On the 11th of January one year she was permitted to hear the heavenly canticles of the Saints and Angels, and speaking of this to her Confessor, she told him that these blessed spirits did not all sing in unison, but those sang in the highest key and the most sonorous voices who on earth had most ardently loved the Supreme Goodness. She specially distinguished the voices of St. John the Evangelist and St. Mary Magdalen, though she confessed herself unable to understand the meaning of what she heard. As she was still speaking, she stopped to listen; "Father," she said, "do you not hear with what a high sweet voice the blessed Magdalen sings in the choir of the Saints?" And she remained listening intently as if she heard the heavenly music even with her bodily ears.[1]

The memory of this favour was probably in her mind when she wrote the following passage in her Dialogue: "All the affections and powers unite in perfect souls to produce one harmonious sound, like the chords of a musical instrument The powers of the soul are the great chords, the senses and sentiments of the body the smaller ones. And when all these are used to the praise of God and in the service of our neighbour, they produce one sound like that of a harmonious organ. All the Saints have touched this organ and drawn forth musical tones. The first who sounded it was the sweet and loving Word, whose Humanity united to His Divinity made sweet music on the wood of the cross. And all His servants have learnt of Him as of their Master to give forth the same music, some in one way and some in another, Divine Providence giving all the instruments on which to play."[2]

Very often she received from God whilst in her ecstacies the understanding of different passages in Holy Scripture, as for example the 99th Psalm (*Jubilate Domino*), which she explained, showing the connection between serving God with joy and coming before Him with confidence; or, again, the history of the young man in the Gospels whom our Lord desired to sell all and follow Him Her Divine Master gave her to understand that this did

---

[1] Sup, Part I, Trat. 2, § 19.   [2] Dialogo, cap 147.

not refer merely to temporal goods, but implied a yet larger sacrifice, even that of the thoughts and affections of the heart, which if they are given to God, so that a man no longer belongs to himself, he will receive the hundredfold in the abundance of grace which will be poured out upon him.[1]

Not once, but as it would seem many times, Catherine received the favour of being mystically washed in the Precious Blood of our redemption. The first time was soon after she had taken the habit of Penance, and often from that time when she beheld the colour of red, it reminded her so powerfully of the Blood of our Lord that she could not refrain from tears.[2] In fact, Catherine's devotion of predilection was undoubtedly that which she bore to the inestimable Price of our Redemption. Hence many of the favours she received had reference to this great gift. In her supernatural sicknesses, which were caused by nothing else than the excess of divine love, she was sometimes bathed in a sweat of blood. Often when in ecstasy she was seen to change colour, appearing now white as snow, now red as fire. Those who beheld her thus were filled with wonder and devotion, and her Confessor on one occasion questioned her as to the cause of these changes in her aspect. She endeavoured to answer him, but the power failing her, she could only weep, and he perceived that the very tears she shed were not of the ordinary kind, but *tinged with blood*.[3]

[1] Sup., Part 2, Trat. 5, § 13.   [2] Ibid., Part 2, Trat. 2, § 4.
[3] Ibid., Part 2, Trat. 3, § 16.

CHAPTER V.

HER TEMPTATION, DELIVERY, AND ESPOUSALS, 1366, 1367.

"WHEN thou comest to the service of God," says the wise man, "prepare thy soul for temptation. Take all that shall be brought upon thee, and in thy sorrow endure, and in thy humiliation keep patience. For gold and silver are tried in the fire, but acceptable men in the furnace of humiliation."[1] These inspired words are for all times and for all souls ; and the more exalted the height to which any soul attains, so much the more profoundly must it make experience of their truth. Catherine was not to be exempted from this universal law, but He who designed to perfect her under trial, was pleased to prepare her for it, by inspiring her to pray in a special manner for the gift of fortitude. She persevered in this prayer for many days, at the end of which time our Lord, to recompense her prayer, gave her the following instruction : "Daughter, if thou wilt have the virtue of fortitude, thou must follow Me. True it is that I was able to overcome the power of the enemy in many ways. But, for your example, I chose rather to vanquish him by dying upon the Cross, that you that are only men might learn, if you have a mind to encounter with the enemy, to take the Cross as I did, and so, by the virtue of the same, to overcome all his wiles and strength. And be well assured that this Cross shall be a refreshment to you in your temptations, if you think of the pains that I suffered on it for your sake. If you suffer with Me for My love, you shall also be rewarded with Me. And the more like you are to Me in this life by persecutions and pains, the more like shall you be to Me in

[1] Ecclesias. ii. 1.

the life to come in joy and rest   Therefore, my dear daughter, embrace the Cross ; regard for My sake all sweet things as bitter and all bitter things as sweet, and so be certain that you will always be strong.   Accept all adversities with a willing and cheerful heart, and dread no power, neither of man nor of the devil.   For in whatever manner they shall assault you, by this means you will easily withstand and drive them back."[1]

When our Lord had thus armed and prepared her for the combat, He permitted the evil spirits to assail her with their most cruel temptations.   Waking or sleeping she was beset by frightful and humiliating phantoms which sought to defile her eyes and ears, and to torment her in a thousand ways.   These attacks Catherine met courageously, chastising her flesh with her iron chain, and prolonging her vigils so as almost to deprive herself of sleep.   But her enemies would not retire ; they whispered in her ear words of pity and counsel ; " Alas, poor little one," they said, " why thus torture thyself in vain ?   Thinkest thou to be able to endure thus to the end ?   What gain shall it be to thee to kill thyself by excessive penance ?   Thou wilt suffer all thy life in this world only to suffer afterwards in hell.   Far better to pause ere life be utterly spent, whilst youth is left and the pleasures of the world may yet be tasted and enjoyed."   But while these words resounded in the ears of her soul, Catherine admitted them not into her heart, nor did she enter into any argument with the tempter, save only that in reply to his suggestions of despair, she answered humbly, " I trust in my Lord Jesus Christ, and not in myself."   Then Satan laying aside his arguments returned to his former method of attack, so that she was pursued everywhere, in her cell, and even in the church, with horrible spectres ; and to complete her affliction, her Divine Spouse, who had been wont to visit and console her with His presence, seemed now to forsake her, and thus her soul was plunged in a profound sadness.   But not on that account did she interrupt her prayers or her penances.   " O miserable creature ! " she exclaimed, turning her indignation against herself, and exciting within her heart

[1] Fen., Part I, cap 20.   Legend, Part I, cap. 10.

a sentiment of holy self-hatred, "who art thou to look for comfort from God's hands? Thinkest thou that it is *comfort* that thy sins have deserved? It is much for thee that thou art not now in hell, and if thou escape those endless pains, cannot thy Spouse and Creator give thee joy and consolation in an endless eternity? Arise, then, and be of good heart, now is the time to fight manfully: for thee be labours and sufferings, and to His holy Name alone be honour and glory."

One day on her return from the church these terrific assaults were renewed with such violence, that casting herself on her face upon the ground, she remained there for a long space in prayer beseeching God of His mercy to come to her assistance. Then there came to her mind a remembrance of the lesson which she had learned but a short time before, when she had been praying for fortitude; and understanding that all which she now endured proceeded only from the malice of the enemy, she took courage, and resolved from that day to endure all temptations gladly for the love of her Divine Spouse. It was not long before the foul fiends again presented themselves, and sought to drive her to despair, saying, "Miserable wretch, think not to resist us; never will we give thee an hour's peace till thou yield to our will, but during thy whole life we will pain and vex thee continually." But Catherine, full of confidence in God, gave them this heroic answer: "I have chosen pain to be my comfort, and therefore it will not be difficult, but rather pleasant and delightful, for me to endure these and all other afflictions for the love of my Lord and Saviour Jesus Christ, and as long as it shall please His Majesty."

Immediately all the company of unclean spirits fled away in confusion, and a marvellous and beautiful light shone from heaven, illuminating her room with its brightness, in the midst of which appeared our Saviour Christ in the same form as He bore when He hung upon the Cross, and there shed His most precious blood for the redemption of the world; Who called her unto Him, and said these words: "Mine own daughter, Catherine, seest thou not what I have suffered for thy sake? Think it not much, therefore, to suffer for Me." After that He approached nearer to her in another form, to comfort her, speaking to her many sweet and loving words Then she said, using the words of St. Anthony, "O Lord, where wert Thou when my heart was so vexed with foul and horrible temptations?" "Daughter," said He, "I was in thine heart." Then said she again: "O Lord, saving always Thy truth and my dutiful reverence to Thy Divine Majesty, how is it possible that Thou shouldst dwell in a heart filled with so many shameful thoughts?" "Tell Me, daughter," He replied, "did those thoughts cause in thy heart grief or delight?" "Surely," said she, "they caused very great grief and sorrow." "Who, then," said our Lord, "was He that caused that grief and horror in thine heart? Who was it but only I, who abode secretly in the centre of thy soul? Assure thyself of this: if I had not been there present, those foul thoughts that stood round thine heart vainly seeking means to enter had without all doubt prevailed, and made their entry into thy soul with full consent of thy will ; but it was My presence that caused in thee that horror, and moved thy heart to resist those temptations as much as it was able ; and because it could not do so much as it would, it conceived a great displeasure both against them and also against itself. It was My gracious presence that wrought all these effects in thine heart, wherein I took great delight to see My love, My holy fear, and the zeal of My faith planted in thy soul, My dear daughter and spouse. And so when I saw My time (which was when thou hadst, through My grace and assistance, thoroughly vanquished the pride and insolence of thine enemy), I sent out certain external beams of My light that put these dark fiends to flight. For, by course of nature, darkness may not abide where light is. Last of all, by My light I gave thee to understand that those pains were thy great merit and increase of the virtue of fortitude. And because thou offeredst thyself willingly to suffer for My love, taking such pains with a cheerful heart, and esteeming them as welcome, according as I had taught thee ; therefore, My will and pleasure was that they should endure no longer. And so I showed myself, whereupon they vanished quite away. My daughter, I delight not in the pains of My servants, but in their good-will and readiness to suffer patiently and gladly for My sake. And because such patience and willingness is shown in pains and adversity, therefore do I suffer them to endure the same. In this time of battle I was in thy heart, fortifying thee with My grace against the enemy, but secretly, to exercise thy patience and increase thy merit. Now, that by My help thou hast manfully fought out thy battle, know that I am, and will be ever, in thy heart more openly, and that I will visit thee yet oftener and more lovingly than before." The vision disappeared, and Catherine was left full of overabundance of joy and sweetness, such as no words may express. And specially she took comfort in dwelling on those words by which our Lord had addressed her, saying, "*Mine own daughter, Catherine.*" And she entreated her confessor to use the same words when he spoke to her, and to call her "My daughter, Catherine," that by hearing them repeated, the sweetness of that happy moment might often be renewed." [1]

From that time our Lord was pleased to bestow on her a greater abundance of favours than she had ever before enjoyed; He visited her, says her biographer, "even as one friend is wont to visit another," sometimes alone and sometimes in company with his Blessed Mother and other Saints. More often, however, He came alone and conversed with her "as a friend with a friend."

It was at this time that Catherine, by the Divine help, acquired the art of reading. She had never learned to read in childhood; but she very early felt a great desire to recite the Office of the Church. She therefore begged one of her sisters to get her an alphabet and teach her the letters, which being done, she spent many weeks in the fruitless endeavour to learn; but at length, finding her efforts of no avail, she resolved to give up the attempt, and rather to seek what she desired from God. One day, therefore, she prostrated upon the ground in prayer, and thus made her petition :—" Lord, if it be agreeable to Thee that I may know how to read, in order that I may recite the Divine Office and sing Thy praises, vouchsafe to teach me what I cannot learn of myself. If not, I am well content to remain in ignorance, or spend my

[1] Fen., Part I, chap. xxi.

time in such simple meditation as it shall please Thee to grant."
God heard her prayer, and gave her the faculty she asked for, and
that so perfectly that she was able to read any kind of writing as
quickly and easily as the most experienced person. She at once
procured the necessary books, and began to say her office daily
with great devotion. She specially delighted in the versicle with
which the hours begin: "*Deus in adjutorium meum intende!*"
which she translated and used as an habitual ejaculation. Another
of her favourite verses was the following: "*Illumina oculos meos
ne unquam obdormiam in morte,*" and these words she wrote on
a little tablet and hung at the head of her bed.

St. Catherine's recitation of the Divine Office is inseparably connected with the memory of one favour which she received at this
time. Very often when her heavenly Spouse deigned to visit her
with His sensible presence, He would walk with her in her room
and recite the Psalms with her "as though they had been two
religious saying their office together." And coming to the *Gloria*
at the conclusion of a Psalm, it was her wont to change the words,
and instead of "*Gloria Patri et Filio et Spiritui Sancto,*" to say,
"*Gloria Patri et Tibi et Spiritui Sancto,*" thus addressing Him
Who condescended to bear her company.[1]

As soon as St. Catherine had learnt to read, she began to give
considerable time to this occupation. It is evident that she did
not merely recite the words of the office, but pondered their sense
in her heart. Caffarini remarks in his Supplement, that whenever
her first confessor, F. Thomas della Fonte, went to see her, he
always found her praying or reading, sometimes bathed in tears,
sometimes recreating herself with singing, but never idle. She
soon acquired a wonderful knowledge of the Holy Scriptures,
especially of the New Testament; and took such a passing delight
in speaking and meditating on the life of Jesus Christ as set forth
in the Holy Gospels, that if she could find any one to converse
with her on that subject she would forget the necessity of food or

---

[1] The memory of this favour is preserved by an inscription in the chapel
Della Volte, where it had been often granted to her. It also forms the subject
of a painting by Gamberelli, which adorns the same chapel.

sleep. But if in her hours of solitude she knew how to nourish her soul with study and meditation, no less was she sensible of the charms of other pursuits which bear witness to her possession of a graceful and artistic taste. She had a singular love of flowers. "Often, before her appearance in public," says Caffarini, "divine love would cause her to fall into a holy languor, at which time she solaced herself by singing hymns, surrounded by earthly flowers, which reminded her of those of her heavenly Spouse. She twined them into garlands, or arranged them with admirable skill into the form of crosses; and these she afterwards distributed in order to excite other souls to the love of God." The same is testified by other witnesses, who speak of her great love for roses, lilies, and violets, and tell us how after she had finished her accustomed penances, she would arrange them into exquisite bouquets, singing over her work.[1]

But the time was fast approaching, when this life of silence and retirement was to be exchanged for one of active labour; not indeed, all at once, but gradually and, as it would seem, in obedience to *two distinct notifications* of *the divine will*, each preceded by a special increase of heavenly grace, and accompanied by mysterious, sensible signs, as their outward pledge and assurance. It was a change, which, on the part of Catherine, entailed a costly sacrifice. God, Who would prepare her for it, and Who designed to make her the pliant instrument of His all holy purposes, inspired her at this time to seek, by means of earnest and continual prayer, no less a gift than the *perfection of faith*, so that henceforth nothing might separate her from Him. In answer to this prayer, in which she persevered for a long time, He caused her to hear in her heart these words, " I will espouse thee to Me in faith." And still as she renewed her request with ever-increasing earnestness, the same answer was repeated, and in the same words. At length

[1] F. Raymund says in the Legend (Part 2, chap. xi.), that "God was pleased to work many miracles by His spouse on inanimate things, and specially on flowers, in which the holy virgin greatly delighted." Of these miracles, however, he gives no examples. In consequence of Catherine's singular love of flowers the custom arose of celebrating her feast (even before her canonisation) by extraordinary floral decorations.

as Lent drew near, on the last day of the Carnival, when, according to custom, the city was given up to the riotous festivities usual at that season, Catherine shut herself up in her cell, and sought by prayer and fasting to make reparation for the offences committed by the thoughtless crowds who passed her door. And she besought our Lord that He would vouchsafe at this time to perform His promise, and bestow on her that perfection of faith she had so long desired. Then He appeared to her, and answered her in these words: "Because thou hast forsaken all the vanities of the world, and set thy love upon Me, and because thou hast, for My sake, rather chosen to afflict thy body with fasting than to eat flesh with others, especially at this time, when all others that dwell round about thee, yea, and those also that dwell in the same house with thee, are banqueting and making good cheer, therefore I am determined, this day, to keep a solemn feast with thee, and with great joy and pomp to espouse thy soul to Me in faith." As He was yet speaking, there appeared in the same place the most glorious Virgin Mary, Mother of God, the beloved disciple St. John the Evangelist, St. Paul the Apostle, and the great patriarch and founder of her order, St Dominic; and after these came the kingly prophet and poet David, with a musical psalter in his hand, on which he played a heavenly song of inestimable sweetness. Then our Blessed Lady came to her and took her by the hand, which she held towards her Divine Son, and besought Him that He would vouchsafe to espouse her to Him in faith. To which He consented with a very sweet and lovely countenance, and taking out a ring that was set about with four precious pearls and had in the other part a marvellous rich diamond, He put the same on the finger of her right hand, saying thus: "Behold, I here espouse thee to Me, thy Maker and Saviour, in faith, which shall continue in thee from this time forward, evermore unchanged, until the time shall come of a blissful consummation in the joys of heaven. Now then, act courageously: thou art armed with faith, and shalt triumph over all thine enemies."[1] The vision disappeared, but the ring,

[1] Fen., Part 1, ch. xxiii. Caffarini in the *Leggenda Minore* specifies the

invisible indeed to other eyes than Catherine's, remained upon her finger; mysterious token of a favour no less mysterious, yet one the signification of which is not obscure to the student of Holy Scripture. If every faithful soul is knit to its Creator by the tie of a spiritual espousal,[1] what must not have been the closeness of that union which Catherine contracted when she received as her dowry "the perfection of faith?" That precious ring was to her the token of her Divine Vocation ; the pledge of an indissoluble union with her Beloved. "She was destined," says Raymund, "to save innumerable souls from the stormy ocean of this world, without dreading for herself shipwreck or tempest." God therefore prepared her as a fit instrument for the Divine work He was about to entrust to her, and when the instrument was perfected, the word was spoken which called her to a new manner of life.

last day of the Carnival as that on which this favour was granted. This, in Siena, was the *Tuesday* before Quinquagesima. Following the more general custom, however, the movable feast, formerly kept as the Espousals of St. Catherine (now merged in that of her Translation), is kept on the Thursday before Quinquagesima Sunday. In 1705 the High Consistory of Siena published a decree to be observed for ever in the Contrada di Fontebranda, forbidding masks, dances, and other Carnival festivities to be held "on the last day of the Carnival, dedicated to the sacred Espousals of their seraphic fellow-citizen, Catherine Benincasa." It is somewhat remarkable that Catherine appears from this time to have worn a real material ring. One such is preserved at Città di Castello, said to have been hers.

[1] "I have espoused you as a chaste virgin to Jesus Christ."—2 Cor. xi. 2.

CHAPTER VI

CATHERINE IN HER FAMILY, 1367.

THE cell in which Catherine had now spent three years hidden from the world had become to her the gate of heaven, and had she followed her own attraction she would never more have quitted it. But God had other designs over her, and after the celebration of her mystic Espousals, He began little by little to call on her to return once more to her place in the family, and to hold converse with men. Not that He withdrew from her any of His former favours, or ceased those heavenly visitations which she had hitherto enjoyed; but from time to time He would make known to her His will, saying, "Behold the hour of dinner is at hand, go up [1] therefore and take thy place at table with thy family, and then return to Me." When first this intimation of the Divine will was given to her, Catherine was overwhelmed with sorrow, and entreated with many tears that she might not be required to forego her solitude, or to return to such intercourse with the world as would separate her from the blessed presence of her Spouse "O my good Lord!" she said, "wherefore wilt Thou have me to go and eat with them? Doth man live by bread only, and not by every word that cometh from Thy mouth? Hast Thou not caused me to forsake the conversation of men that I might the better converse with Thee; and now that I have found Thee must I again lose so precious a treasure, and return to the world which shall dim the purity and clearness of my

[1] In the Legend it stands, "Go quickly," in the English version, "Go down;" Caffarini in the *Leggenda Minore* has it, more correctly, "Go *up*," *i. e.*, from her cell *under* her father's house.

faith?" But in reply our Lord opened to her gaze the sublime path in treading which she was "to fulfil all justice." Souls that would do this must be profitable not only to themselves but also to others. Nor need they on that account be separated from God, but rather united to Him more firmly. For the perfection which He requires of them is the love of God and of their neighbour, in which twofold love stand all the law and the prophets. That zeal which made itself felt in the heart of Catherine whilst yet a child, and which had first moved her to enrol herself as a daughter of St. Dominic, was now to find its proper scope, and wearing the habit of an apostolic Order she was to be called to the apostolic life. In vain did she in her humility and simplicity represent her unworthiness for such a function, whether by the weakness of her sex or other infirmities. "How can I, a poor and miserable woman, be able to do any good in Thy Church?" she would say; "how shall I instruct wise and learned men, or how will it be even seemly for me to live and converse with them?" But He made her to understand that in the counsels of His wisdom He had chosen her, a weak woman, to confound the pride of the strong. Her mission was to exhibit to a world "lying in wickedness" the power of the Divine Word, made known to them by the feeblest of human instruments. "Daughter," He said, "I will impart to thee My secret in this matter. Know thou that nowadays pride so abounds in the world, and specially among those who hold themselves for wise and learned, that My justice may no longer bear it. Now the proper punishment as well as the sovereign medicine for pride is to be confounded and put to shame. Therefore I have determined that those men who are wise in their own conceits should be made ashamed by seeing weak and frail women, whom they account as things vile and abject, to understand the mysteries of God, not by human study, but only by infused grace; confirming such doctrine by many marvellous signs above the course of nature. I will do now as I did when I was conversing in this world, and sent simple and unlearned men, and poor fishermen replenished with the strength of My Spirit, to confound the wisdom of the world. So will I now, in like manner, send thee and other ignorant persons, both men and women, to humble the pride of those who are wise in their own eyes. If they will embrace My doctrine spread throughout the world by such weak vessels, I will regard them with mercy, but if they refuse to do so they shall be brought to shame. Wherefore, daughter, set thyself in readiness to go forth into the world ; for I will be with thee at all times, and in all places, and will direct thee in all things that I shall send thee to do."

When once the will of her Divine Spouse had thus been manifested, Catherine had no thought save to bow her head and to obey. Yet she owned to her confessor that each time our Lord ordered her to quit her cell and mix with the world outside, it cost her so lively a sorrow, that it seemed to her as if her heart must break. From that time her love and desire for Holy Communion greatly increased, because by the more frequent reception of the Body of her Divine Spouse, she trusted to persevere, and as it were to rivet the closeness of those bonds which she feared a renewed intercourse with the world might sever. It is quite certain that Catherine did not interpret the command she had received as requiring her at once to undertake extraordinary work for souls of her own choosing. On the contrary, she waited until it should be made manifest what our Lord demanded of her, and the rule she had made for herself was still enforced, according to which she spoke to no man beyond the limits of her family without the permission of her confessor. As regarded the injunction to mix with the household, however, she set herself to accomplish it with all possible fervour, and made her return to the family circle the occasion for taking on herself fresh practices of penance and humility. She chose to perform every menial office in the house, such as sweeping, washing the dishes, and serving in the kitchen. Not content with this she would rise at night when the others were asleep, and wash all the dirty clothes which she found ; and when the servant fell sick, she not only supplied her place, but nursed and attended to her wants during her sickness. Yet none of these exterior actions disturbed the interior recollection of her soul, or withdrew her in the least degree from the Divine presence, and her ecstasies became even more frequent.

Such was her manner of life when, in 1366, Father Thomas Antonio Caffarini first made her acquaintance. He belonged to the convent of St. Dominic, and was still very young when he was admitted into the family on terms of intimate friendship. His recollections of Catherine in those early days are touching from their very simplicity. He often sat with her at her father's table, and saw that she ate next to nothing, but during the meal she would talk to them of God, and was always to be seen with a gay and smiling countenance.[1] Wonderfully circumspect in her words, never idle or in any way reprehensible, never disturbed save when God was offended, she was always affable, kind, and full of joy, specially in time of sickness or affliction. The robust frame which she possessed as a young girl was fast wasting under the fire of Divine love, joined to her continual austerities. Eating was a daily torture to her, for her digestion had become so weak that she was incapable of retaining any solid food. Nevertheless, to please and satisfy her parents, she would force herself to swallow something, and would call the summons to the family meal ' going to execution," so terrible was the suffering it cost her. "Nevertheless," he continues, "I always saw her cheerful. I remember once, when she was covered with wounds, she called them her flowers, saying, ' These are my flowers and roses.' Only in time of worldly prosperity was she ever sad, for she would say, ' I desire not such gifts for my family, but rather the eternal joys of heaven.' " She often bestowed on him some of the nosegays she was in the habit of making and distributing to her friends ; and her confessor, F. Thomas della Fonte, more than once gave him some bread which she had made with her own hands. "Nor did I think it a little thing to have eaten it," he observes. "And whatever she did, whether she made the bread or busied herself in any other household work, she was always on fire with the love

---

[1] The same was observed by all those who were familiar with her. It is one of the features which Anastagio di Monte Altino introduces in his poetical portraiture of her : " *Ella è sempremai lieta e ridente.*"

of God." The same Father Thomas della Fonte showed him one of her disciplines, composed of cords with iron points, "which looked as if it had been steeped for a long time in a vessel of blood, and then dried." He was an eye-witness of her vigils and her ecstasies ; and on one occasion, when she was rapt in God, he listened to the burning words which fell from her lips, and was conscious of an exquisite perfume which seemed to escape from her, and which caused him for many days afterwards a sense of unspeakable consolation. The same fact was testified by other witnesses, who affirmed that this heavenly fragrance was perceptible on merely approaching her cell, and had been the means of inspiring many with sentiments of profound compunction.

The home-circle, in which Catherine now resumed her place, deserves a few words of notice. Giacomo was still living, a prosperous tradesman, beholding with honest pride the numerous children and grandchildren who gathered round his hearth and assisted him in his business. From the street that rises above the Fullonica we can still look down on the meadows where he and his workmen were accustomed to wash their wool and lay it out for bleaching. Within the house all things were well regulated by Lapa, the most industrious of housewives, unchanged in all respects from the old Lapa with whom we have already made acquaintance, and who was ever oscillating between an indulgent tenderness towards her favourite daughter and the despair excited by her practices of charity or penance. Of the brothers we know but little ; besides those whose names have been already given, there was one, a wild and heedless youth, who, growing weary of trade, resolved to try his fortune as a soldier, and, to the sorrow of his parents, set out for the wars. In the first encounter he was severely wounded, and left for dead on the field of battle. At the moment when he fell Catherine was supernaturally warned of what had happened, and shed bitter tears, fearing lest her brother's soul might be in no less grievous danger than his body. With characteristic prudence, however, she said nothing of the matter to her mother, but had recourse to prayer. The wounded youth found means of returning home, where the tender care of his mother and sister restored him to health, and becoming a wiser man by his experience, he made no further trial of the military career. Perhaps it was this same brother of whom we read that, having cause to be uneasy regarding the state of his soul, Catherine, being one day in the church, set herself to pray for his conversion, and addressing our Lord with her accustomed confidence, she said, "O Lord, I will not rise from my knees until Thou grant me this favour." Then, feeling in her heart a certain assurance that her prayer had been heard, she returned home, and found her brother in his room, weeping over his sins. She sweetly consoled him, and found no difficulty in inducing him at once to go to confession. But there was one member of the family who was bound to Catherine by even closer ties than those of blood. It was her sister-in-law Lisa, the confidante of her childhood, the friend and companion of her maturer years. Her numerous children were the objects of Catherine's tenderest affection : she had a singular love for children, and had she followed her inclination, would have had them always with her. "Were it becoming,' she would say, "I should never weary of caressing them." [1] The greater number of these little ones were taken away in early youth, for Lisa was destined to be drawn closer to God by the stroke of domestic affliction. Two of her daughters, however, lived to take the religious habit in the convent of St. Agnes of Montepulciano, and a letter is preserved addressed by St. Catherine to one of them, named Eugenia. The strong mutual affection existing between Catherine and Lisa is apparent from many passages both in the Legend and in the letters of the Saint. In one of the last she addresses her friend as "*Mia cognata secondo la carne, mia sorella secondo Cristo*" In fact, after the death of her husband, Lisa put

---

[1] Sup., Part 1, Trat. 2, § 12. Lisa was often in danger of death when giving birth to her children, and on two occasions both mother and child owed their safety to the prayers of the Saint. This seems to have been the origin of the very special love she bore to these little ones—the children of her prayers.

on the habit of Penance, and became Catherine's inseparable
companion even until her death.   Their close intimacy gave her
opportunities of becoming acquainted with many circumstances
of Catherine's life, which were unknown to others, and from her
F. Raymund collected some of the most interesting facts which
he has introduced into the Legend.   She had personal experience
within their own family of that wonderful knowledge of hearts
which God had communicated to the holy virgin—a supernatural
gift which often brought anguish to its possessor.   It was not
easy to escape the glance of her gentle but penetrating eye.
One day, having opened her breviary to say Vespers, Catherine
was rapt in ecstasy, and remained in that state for four hours.
Coming to herself, she was conscious of an insupportable odour
which often indicated to her the presence of a soul stained by
mortal sin.   At the same moment it was made known to her that
one of her brothers had grievously offended God.   Pierced with
sorrow, she interceded for the unfortunate youth ; then, hearing
his footstep at the door, she rose to meet him.   As he listened
to her words of sad reproof, he stood abashed and conscience-
stricken, and found, to his surprise, that before those grave and
weeping eyes the secrets of his heart lay open.[1]   Another of these
domestic incidents was of a less sorrowful character.   Lisa had
determined on making a general confession, but, wishing to keep
the matter private, she said nothing to any of the family, and
chose the remote corner of an unfrequented church, where, having
made her confession to one who was not her ordinary confessor,
she returned home, as she imagined, unperceived.   But Catherine
met her, and embracing her with tenderness, exclaimed a little
archly, " Oh ! now you are really my good little sister ! "   Lisa
inquired the meaning of her unusual salutation, and was somewhat disconcerted on finding that her whole proceedings were
perfectly known.   Seeing her confusion, Catherine sweetly consoled her, saying, " I shall always love you the better, my Lisa,
for this morning's work." [2]

Mention has been made of F. Thomas Caffarini as at this time

[1] Sup, Part 2, Trat. 5, § 7   [2] Sup., Part 2, Trat. 5, § 8

a frequent visitor at the Fullonica; and a little later another
of the Friars was introduced to Catherine by his old friend and
fellow novice, F. Thomas della Fonte. This was F. Bartholomew
Dominic, who seems first to have made her acquaintance early
in 1368, and who for the remaining twelve years of her life continued to enjoy her most intimate friendship. When first he was
admitted into the little chamber to which she retired when her
presence with the rest of the family was no longer required, it
bore the same aspect of austerity and recollection which has been
already described. The door and window[1] were always kept
closed, and a lamp burnt day and night before the crucifix and
the image of the Blessed Virgin and other Saints. There was the
bed of boards, which in the day-time she used as a bench on
which to sit; there were the brick steps, which may still be seen,
and which often served as her only pillow; and, above all, there
was the wasted form of one whose very beauty was so unlike the
beauty of earth that it told its own tale of a nature purified and
sublimated by penance. "When first I began to visit her," he
says, "she was young, and her countenance was always serene
and joyful. I was also young, yet, far from experiencing in her
presence the embarrassment which I might have felt in the company of other women of her age, the longer I conversed with her,
the more utterly were all earthly passions extinguished in my
breast. I have known many—both laymen and religious—who
experienced the same thing; there was a something in her whole
appearance so redolent of purity as to be far more angelic than
human."[2]

Besides these friends and the members of her own immediate
family, Catherine admitted into her privacy some of the other
Mantellate, and with them Bartholomew often found her, after
the labours of the day were over, singing hymns and making
garlands. Then she would converse with them on the things of
God, but would break off, saying with a sigh, "It were better to

[1] Out of this window, according to local tradition, Catherine was wont to
distribute alms to the poor.
[2] Process, 1314.

be silent than to speak of such things in such a way. It is like
dipping pearls in mud to attempt to relate them with a tongue
of flesh." "As to my repetition of her words," he adds, "it is as
insipid as a dish of meat without salt." Gradually others of the
Friars came to visit her, and listened with wonder to her words.
"How often," says Caffarini, "have I heard her exhort them to
be true sons of their Holy Father, to abide in the cell of self-
knowledge, to feed on souls, and to weep over sinners ! Sometimes she would exclaim, 'Let us live in our cell !' or again, 'Let
us weep, let us weep over all these dead souls !' And I know by
experience that by her prayers and exhortations, and her own holy
example, devotion and penance revived in our convent at Siena ;
the use of fasts, disciplines, and haircloths increased among us,
and primitive observance began to be restored."

The unbroken union with God which Catherine enjoyed, and
which was never interrupted by her active employments, often
caused her to be rapt in ecstasy even when engaged in the home-
liest household duties. It could not be otherwise, says Raymund,
"for her heart ever tended heavenward, and drew the body with
it. At such times her limbs became stiff, her eyes closed, and her
body, raised in the air, often diffused a perfume of exquisite sweetness." He declares in the Legend that she had been thus seen
by him and his brethren a thousand times, and her other disciples
all speak to the same effect. In consequence, she was exposed to
exactly the same kind of annoyance, on the part whether of the
curious or the devout, which in all times falls to the lot of an
Ecstatica. People were always trying to see her, asking her confessor to admit them to her chamber when the Saint was in ecstasy,
or plotting with her companions to bring her to some place on a
mission of charity, where they might have a chance of beholding
the prodigy. And the embarrassment was the greater from the
impossibility she was under of restraining that suspension of her
bodily faculties which the very thought of God would suffice to
occasion. If this took place in the presence of others it caused
her the utmost confusion. "You see, father," she would say,
addressing her confessor, "I am not fit to converse with others ;

I entreat you, let me go elsewhere."[1] But if he refused her the permission to do so, she never disobeyed, but, bowing her head, submitted meekly to the hard command.[2] One instance of these unwelcome visits of pious intruders may suffice as a sample. Fra Niccolo of Cascina had come to Siena from Pisa, as he said, upon business; but says Caffarini, more probably out of nothing else than his desire to behold the Ecstatica, of whom he had heard through his brethren, for he too was a Friar Preacher. Persuading F. Thomas to take him to her father's house, they entered her chamber, and found her in abstraction, unable to hear or speak with them. "She appeared like a statue which retains nothing but the human form."[3] Suddenly they beheld her raised gently into the air, and sustained there as by some invisible hand, after which there began to fall from her lips the following broken exclamations: "O inestimable Charity! O eternal Truth! when shall I have the happiness of suffering something for Thy glory? Yet if in this desire Thou seest aught of vanity or self-love, I conjure Thee annihilate it, destroy it, tear it out of my heart!" Fra Niccolo listened with awe and tender devotion, and with humble reverence extending his hand, he touched her lightly with one of his fingers. And that slight touch communicated to his hand so wondrous a fragrance, that for the entire day it seemed to infuse a strength and consolation as well to his corporal as to his spiritual senses.[4]

It very often happened that persons, out of mere curiosity, would obtain permission from F. Thomas to secrete themselves somewhere in order to behold Catherine in this state of abstraction. But again and again it happened that when such persons beheld her absorbed in prayer, the mere spectacle so moved them to compunction as to effect an entire change of heart. Then, after they were gone away, the Saint, returning to herself, would say to her confessor, "Who were those persons you brought here just now?" "And how do you know I had any person with

---

[1] Sup., Part I, Trat. 2, § 14.   [2] *Ibid.*, Part 2, Trat. 3, § 4.
[3] "*Quasi statua che ritenesse la sola figura di donna.*"
[4] Sup., Part 2, Trat 3, § 3.

me?" he would reply. Then, with an air of gravity, she would say, "Father, such and such persons were here, and they came in your company, being curious to see me thus;" and he soon found that it was impossible to deceive her.

These prodigies were not equally well understood by all who witnessed them, and it sometimes happened that Lapa, who had no great experience in the phenomena of ecstasies,[1] would find her daughter in this condition, and try to bend her rigid limbs, not always in the gentlest manner. On one of these occasions she used so much force as nearly to break her daughter's neck, and Catherine, on returning to herself, suffered great pain in consequence. Another day, being engaged in the kitchen according to her custom, she sat down by the fire and began to turn the spit; as she did so she was rapt in ecstasy, and became wholly insensible to exterior things. Her sister-in-law, Lisa, observing this, and being better acquainted than Lapa with the nature of these heavenly raptures, quietly took her place at the spit, leaving her to enjoy undisturbed the Divine communications. When the meat was roasted, supper was served to the family, Lisa still discharging all those services which were generally rendered by her sister; and when supper was ended, having attended to the wants of her husband and put her children to bed, she returned to Catherine, intending to watch by her till she should recover consciousness. On re-entering the kitchen, however, she was terrified to find that Catherine had fallen forwards, and was lying with her body on the burning coals. The fire was large and fierce, for an unusual quantity of wood was always kept burning in the house for the sake of preparing the dyes. "Alas!" cried Lisa, "Catherine is all burnt," and so saying, she ran and drew her out of the smoking embers, but found, to her wonder, that she had received no injury either in her person or even her clothes, on which the "smell of fire had not passed." "And yet," says her old English biographer, "it was a great fire, and she a long time in it. But the fire of God's love that burnt within her heart was of such force and virtue that it would not suffer that

---

[1] "*Non consapevole di quest' estasi*," says Raymund.

outward fire to prevail over her." This was not the only occasion when fire seemed to have no power of injuring her. One day, when praying in the Church of San Domenico, and leaning, according to her custom, against the pilaster that supports the roof of the chapel *Delle Volte*, it chanced that, some candles having been set up before the image of some saint that stood in that place, one of them fell upon her head, she being at the time in ecstasy, and continued burning there, without, however, doing her any kind of harm, or so much as singeing her veil.

Other anecdotes which seem to belong to this time are of a less homely character. Her companions tried sometimes to induce her to accompany them on little expeditions, whether of charity or otherwise, beyond the city gates. One of the places which they visited was the Monastery of St. Abondio, the favourite resort of St. John Columbini, who was buried there, and whose only daughter was a nun within its walls. Possibly this circumstance may explain their visit, as Lisa, who, no doubt, accompanied her sister-in-law, was the saint's near relative. Catherine, when they set out, was suffering from an affection of the chest, which made any exertion painful to her; nevertheless, with her usual sweet charity, she complied with the wishes of her Sisters, and set out in their company. She had not gone far when, overwhelmed, as it seemed, by some glorious vision, she exchanged her feeble steps for a pace so rapid that none of her companions could keep up with her. They followed as best they might, and beheld her carried forward with wonderful impetuosity, her eyes being all the while closed. Reaching the convent, she at once entered the church, and prostrated before the altar. When the others came in they found her in ecstasy, and in that state she began to utter such sweet and wonderful things that they were stupefied with astonishment; and the rumour of what was passing spreading through the house, the community gathered in the upper choir and other parts overlooking the church, whence they could behold and listen to her.

Another time they took her to a neighbouring village, and, as usual, she became so absorbed in meditation, that, though indeed she walked with the others, her senses were quite abstracted, nor could they rouse her by pushing or shaking her.   At last, however, they were surprised to hear her begin to sing, and were very soon sensible of a new kind of marvel; for, as they listened to her sweet voice, they were themselves made sharers in the holy jubilee which filled her breast, and felt as though transformed into different persons.   They returned to the city singing the Divine praises, and heedless of the rain which fell in torrents; and such was the supernatural grace infused into them, that for three entire days they remained recreated by it, nor so much as thought of taking their ordinary food.

CHAPTER VII.

CATHERINE'S CHARITY TO HER NEIGHBOUR, 1367, 1368

CATHERINE had not been drawn from the privacy of her little chamber merely to take part in household duties, or even to diffuse among her family and those who from time to time visited her in her home the good odour of her virtues. In abandoning her solitude she had feared at first to lose that continual presence of her Beloved which was dearer to her than life itself. But He is pleased to abide in other sanctuaries than the solitary cell, and Catherine learnt to seek Him and find Him in His two chosen dwelling-places—the Sacrament of His love and the person of His poor. And indeed it would have been impossible for a love like hers to have rested content with devout affections without seeking for relief in action. It is her own maxim that "the love we conceive towards God we must bring forth in acts of charity towards our neighbour. God Himself is beyond our reach, therefore the services we cannot render directly to Him, He wills we should render to our neighbour."[1] In conformity with this principle, she very soon began to exercise herself in charitable labours for the sick and needy; but having nothing of her own to bestow, and considering herself bound by her religious character to the practice of poverty, she besought her father to allow her to deduct the share of the poor from the abundance of temporal things which were enjoyed by the family. Giacomo willingly consented: his reverence for his daughter had increased with years, and he made known to the whole house-

[1] Dialogo, ch. vii.

hold the permission he had granted her. "Let no one hinder
my dear daughter from giving alms," he said; "if she give all
there is in the house, I am well content." Catherine carried out
his permission almost to the letter; but her liberality, however
large, was always discreet. She sought out certain poor families
whom she knew to be in great distress, yet ashamed to beg, and
gave them relief as secret as it was timely. For, rising very
early in the morning, she would load herself with corn, wine, oil,
and other necessaries, and stealing to their houses, she would
gently place her store of provisions within the door, and return
home without being perceived. One day, when she was lying sick
in bed, suffering great pain in every part of her body, she learnt
that a poor widow of the neighbourhood was in a state of great
distress, not having even a loaf of bread to give to her children.
Catherine spent the night praying to our Lord that He would
give her strength enough to go and help the poor woman, and
rising before it was day, she procured a large sack, and went about
the house gathering together meal, wine, oil, and any other food
that she could find. Whe she had carried all these things to her
cell, she began to fear lest it would be impossible for her to carry
such a burthen. Nevertheless, lifting up her heart to God, she
made the attempt; and as soon as the morning bell had rung
(before which no person was suffered to leave their house), she
went forth into the street, feeling her load "no more than if it
had been a wisp of straw." By the providence of God she found
the widow's door half open, and thrusting in her sack of provisions,
she would have hurried away, when her strength forsook her, and
she was nearly sinking to the ground. But, turning to her Spouse,
between game and earnest, she began to say, "O Lord, why hast
Thou deceived me? Is it Thy pleasure that all the neighbours
should see my folly and laugh me to scorn? Behold, the day is
coming on, and I shall be discovered by all men. Give me so
much strength that I may be able to return home to my chamber,
and then lay on me as much weakness as Thou pleasest." Then
our Lord heard her, and, pitying her case, gave her strength enough
to make her way home again, where, as soon as she had arrived,

the grievous sickness from which she had been suffering returned upon her as before.

Two other incidents must be related in the beautiful language of the old Legend :—

"While Catherine was one day in St. Dominic's church, there came to her a poor man, who besought her, for God's love, that she would give him somewhat ; to whom, because she had nothing there to give (for it was not her manner to carry either gold or silver about her), she spake very gently, and prayed him that he would have so much patience as to wait there till she might go home and come again. The poor man made answer that he could not tarry so long, but if she had anything there to give, she should give it, for otherwise he must needs go his way. She was loth that he should go away from her without something, and there-fore bethought herself carefully what thing she might have about her to serve that poor man's need ; and it came to her mind that she had a little cross of silver that hung by her beads, which she broke off with all speed, and gave gladly to the poor man, who likewise, when he had received this alms at her hand, went his way, and was seen no more to beg that day, as though his coming had been for that cross only. The night following, as she was occupied in prayer, after her accustomed manner, our Saviour Christ appeared unto her, having that same cross in His hand, set with divers and sundry precious stones, and said unto her, ' Daughter, knowest thou this cross ? ' ' Yes, Lord,' said she, ' I know it right well ; but it was not so richly decked when I had it.' Then said our Lord to her again, ' Yesterday thou gavest Me this cross with a cheerful heart and great charity, which love and charity are signified by these precious stones. And, therefore, I promise thee that at the day of judgment I will show the same, in the pre-sence of men and angels, to the increase of thine everlasting joy and glory ; for I will not suffer to be hidden such deeds of charity as are done by thee.' With that, this apparition ceased, and left her replenished with unspeakable joy and gladness. And from that time forward her desire of relieving the poor greatly increased."

One day, when the office was finished in the church of the Friars, she remained behind alone with one of her sisters to pray; and as she was coming down from the chapel belonging to the Sisters of Penance, our Lord appeared to her in the likeness of a poor pilgrim, of the age, as it seemed, of three and thirty years, half naked, and besought her that she would give him clothes for the love of God. " Tarry here a little while," said she, "until I go to yonder chapel and come again , and then, God willing, I will help thee with clothes." With that she went up again to the chapel, and undid her kirtle, under which she wore a sleeve-less petticoat, which she took off, and came down again and gave it to the poor man very sweetly. When the poor man had received the coat, he besought her furthermore that, seeing she had given him a woollen garment to wear outwardly, she would also be so good as to give him some shirt of linen to wear next his body. "Willingly," said she; "come home with me, and I will seek out one for thee." And so she went on before, and the poor man came after. When she was come home she went to the chests and presses where the linen clothes of her father and brothers were laid up, and took out a shirt and certain other linen clothes, and gave the same gladly to the poor man. When the poor pilgrim had received all these things at her hand, he did not depart, but prayed her yet more that she would give him sleeves to his coat to cover his arms. " With a goodwill," said she; "for otherwise, I grant, this coat were to no great purpose." And with that she went and sought all about for sleeves, and at last found a new coat of a maid-servant that was in the house, which had never been worn, and took off the sleeves from the same and gave them cheerfully to the poor pilgrim, who received those sleeves also thankfully at her hand, as he had done all the rest, and said unto her, " Mistress, ye have now clothed me thoroughly : He for whose love ye have done it thanks you for it : but yet one demand more I have to make unto you. I have a companion lying in an hospital here by, who standeth in great need of clothes; if it shall please you to send him any, I will carry them unto him in your behalf with a very good will." This new request troubled her somewhat, and caused her to have a

certain conflict within herself. On the one side, she was much
moved with compassion for that poor man, and had a great desire
to supply his necessity. On the other side, she considered the
murmuring and grudging of as many as were in the house, who
waxed so weary of her dealing out their things, that, to keep
them from her hands, they began, every one, to keep their apparel
and other goods under lock and key. Again, she thought she had
done enough to take away the sleeves of the servant's new coat
that was never worn, and that she could not with discretion take
any more from her, being herself also needy and poor. Then
she began to reason with herself whether she might conveniently
part from her own garment or no. She was much inclined to do
it, because she knew it was a great work of charity, and saw also
that she was better able to bear that lack of clothes than the poor
man was. But, on the other hand, she considered that if she
should spoil herself of her clothes, she should in so doing transgress
the rules of prudence, which might cause great offence in the minds
of men. All which things thus considered and discreetly weighed,
she resolved in herself that in this case it was far better to abstain
from giving her alms than, by giving the same, to cause offence
to her neighbour. She spake, therefore, to the poor man after
a very gentle and sweet manner, and said, "Truly, good man,
if I might do it with modesty, I would spoil myself even of this
coat that I wear, with all my heart, and bestow it upon thy companion; but because I have no more garments to put on but
only this, I must needs pray thee to hold me excused, for in
truth there lacketh no goodwill in me, but only ability." With
that the poor man smiled upon her, and said, "Mistress, I see
right well that if ye had ought to give, you would gladly give it.
I thank you for your goodwill: God reward and keep you!"
And so he took his leave of her, and went his way in such sort
that she gathered, by certain signs, that this poor pilgrim was
indeed He that was wont to appear unto her. But such was
her lowliness and base esteem of herself, that she thought herself
unworthy to receive such honour at God's hand, and therefore,
with an humble mind, she returned to her wonted services in the

house, where, notwithstanding, she kept her heart evermore fixed upon her dear Spouse, Jesus Christ, who the next night following appeared unto her again (as she was praying) in the likeness of the poor man, holding in His hand [1] that coat which she had given Him, all set and decked with goodly pearls and precious stones that shone all over the chamber, and said unto her, " Dear daughter, knowest thou this coat?" "Yes, Lord," said she, " I know it very well; but it was not so richly decked when it was with me." Then said our Lord to her again, "Yesterday thou gavest Me this coat very freely and charitably to cover the nakedness of My body, and to keep it from cold and shame. This day, for recompense of thy great charity towards Me, I give thee a coat that shall be invisible to other men, but to thee alone visible and also sensible, by virtue whereof thou shalt be defended both in body and soul from all hurtful cold; and with this garment thou shalt be clad until the time come that in the presence of angels and saints I shall put on upon thee the blissful and glorious garment of immortality." When He had said these words, He drew out of the wound of His side a robe of sanguine colour, shining all about and yielding a marvellous, beautiful light; and putting the same upon her with His own hands, said, "This garment I give thee for all the time that thou shalt live here upon the earth, in token and pledge of that immortal garment that thou shalt receive at My hands in heaven." And with these words that vision ceased, and left her endowed with such a strange grace and quality, not only in soul, but also in body, that from that very instant she never felt alteration in her body, but continued evermore in one temperature, whether it were winter or summer, hot or cold, wind or rain; and whatsoever weather came, she never wore more clothes under her habit than one single garment." [2]

[1] In the *Leggenda Minore* we read that our Lord appeared *wearing* her garment, and the following marginal note is written on the original MS. preserved at Siena : " *Questo atto è dipinto a Roma assai adornatamente.*" Thus showing that St. Catherine was venerated as a Saint almost immediately after her death.

[2] Fen , Part 2, chaps. vi., vii

Sometimes these acts of charity were accompanied by other miraculous tokens, as when, hastening to the relief of a poor man who was dying of hunger, she took a bag of eggs under her mantle. But on her way, stepping into a church, the door of which was open, and intending only to make a passing visit, she was seized with an ecstasy, and fell down on the eggs so heavily as to crush a metal thimble which happened to be in the bag, the eggs themselves suffering no injury. One more story was attested by more than twenty persons, witnesses of the fact. At the time when she had her father's leave to give out to the poor whatever she chose, it happened that the vessel of wine which was being used by the family had run low, and what remained in it seemed to her not good enough to give to the poor; for it was her custom in giving alms always to give the best, for God's sake. She went therefore to the next vessel which had not been touched, and drew out of it largely, without its coming to the knowledge of any of the household. When the first butt had been quite exhausted, the person who had charge of the wine-cellar came to this vessel and began to draw out of it for the use of the family, whilst Catherine likewise continued to draw from it as before. According to the size of the butt, it would have sufficed the household for fifteen or twenty days, but instead of this a whole month passed, and the wine decreased neither in quantity nor quality. Everybody wondered that the vessel should hold out so long, and declared that in their lifetime they had never tasted better wine; but Catherine felt no wonder about it, understanding that it was the work of God, whose wont it is to bless and multiply the substance of those who are ready to help the poor, for His love. One month had expired and another was begun, and still the wine continued as fresh and abundant as ever. At last, when the time came when the grapes were ripe and ready for the press, all the wine-butts being required to receive the new wine, he who had the charge of the vintage desired that this vessel should be emptied of its contents, that it might be filled afresh. They imagined little or nothing could be left in it, but to their surprise found that the tap ran as copiously as ever. At last they resolved

to gauge the vessel and see what was in it, when lo ! they found
it perfectly dry, as if it had stood without liquor for many months,
which caused them no less wonder than they had felt before at
the abundance and excellence of the wine.

F. Bartholomew in his deposition relates either the same story
with different circumstances, or, which is very possible, an entirely
different incident. He says that Giacomo had forbidden a
certain vessel of wine to be used for the family, on account of
its being of superior quality. Catherine, hearing this, considered
that the better the quality, the fitter it was to be dispensed to the
poor, and drew from it till it was empty. One day, he continues,
her father desired the maid to go and draw wine out of that cask ;
but she returned, saying there was nothing in it. Every one was
dismayed, and some began to reproach the servant, as though
it were she who had secretly taken it, whilst Giacomo angrily
insisted on knowing who had disobeyed his orders. Catherine
was in her own chamber, but hearing the tumult, and guessing
the cause, she went to the assembled family, and said sweetly,
"Dear father, why are you troubled ? Be not disturbed ; I will
go and draw the wine." Going therefore to the spot, she knelt
down by the wine cask, and full of confidence prayed, saying, "O
Lord, Thou knowest that the wine has been consumed for Thy
glory and the necessities of the poor, therefore permit not that it
should be a cause of scandal to my father and the family." Then
rising, she made the sign of the Cross over the cask, and the wine
began to flow abundantly. And giving thanks, she carried it to
them, but said nothing of the miracle [1] Bartholomew was not
himself a witness of what he relates, which happened, he says,
"before he knew her." The event, in fact, is placed by Carapelli,
in his *Corso Cronotastico*, as far back as the year previous to her
reception of the Dominican habit, but the expressions used by F.
Raymund in the Legend oblige us to assign it to this period of
her life, when she had her father's permission to dispense the
goods of his household. He adds that "the thing was known
throughout all Siena, and caused great wonder," and the citizens

[1] Process, 1317

still speak of "the cask of St. Catherine," when they wish to describe something which never comes to an end.

But Catherine's charity was not confined to the easy exercise of almsgiving. How often, as she passed through the streets of Siena, seeking out fresh objects who needed relief, must she not have meditated over the words in the Gospel, "I was sick, and ye visited Me." They sounded in her heart as the Voice of her Beloved, and she may have responded in those other words, " I will rise and will go about the city: in the streets and the broad ways, I will seek Him whom my soul loveth." If some things that are related of her service of the sick seem to pass the limit of what is possible to flesh and blood, let it never be forgotten that Catherine, possessed of that magnificent gift, "the perfection of faith," beheld in each poor sufferer to whom she ministered nothing less than the person of her Lord. She sought Him then in the streets and broad ways of her native city, and she found Him in the hospitals of the lepers, and wherever sickness had assumed its most terrible and repulsive forms.

There was at that time in Siena a poor woman named Cecca, who, falling sick and being entirely destitute, was received into one of the city hospitals, which, being very poor, was barely able to supply her with necessaries. At last, her malady increasing, she became covered with leprosy; and no one in the hospital choosing to have the care of such a case, it was agreed to send her to the leper-house, which in Siena was outside the Porta Romana, on the spot now called St. Lazzaro, about a mile out of the city. But before she was removed thither, Catherine, hearing of the matter, went to the hospital, and first visiting the poor sufferer and reverently kissing her, she offered to serve her daily with her own hands, and to supply her with all she might need, if they would allow her to remain where she was. Her offer was accepted, and from that day she came to visit the poor woman morning and evening, dressing her wounds and doing all that was requisite for her "with as much care and reverence as if she had been her own mother."

At first Cecca took her charitable services in very good part,

but as time went on, and she grew accustomed to see the holy
virgin bestowing on her a care and attention such as no hired
servant would have rendered, there arose in her a sentiment of
pride, so that, far from rendering any thanks to her benefactress,
she took all that she did as a matter of duty, and as no more
than she had a right to expect If anything was done otherwise
than pleased her, she would reproach and revile her with such
unseemly words as might be addressed to a bond slave. If
Catherine came to the hospital a little later than usual, having
been detained by her devotions in church, Cecca would greet her
in mocking and bitter terms: "Good morning, my lady-queen
of Fontebranda," she would say; "where has my lady been so
long? At the Church of the Friars, I'll be bound; it seems that
my lady-queen can never have enough of those Friars!" Then
Catherine, without replying, would go about her work; and when
she saw her time, would speak to her in her accustomed lowly
and gentle manner, saying, "Good mother, have patience; I am
a little late, it is true, but all your wants shall be seen to presently."
Then lighting the fire and putting on water, she would prepare
the food, and serve it with such sweet words that Cecca herself
could only wonder at her forbearance. This went on for some
time, to the admiration of all who knew it, with one notable
exception. Lapa was much aggrieved both at the service her
daughter had undertaken, and the ungrateful return she met
with, and she remonstrated in no gentle terms, saying, "Daughter,
if this goes on, you will in your turn become a leper, a thing I
will never put up with, wherefore, I charge you, give over this
business." "Have no fear about that, dear mother," she replied,
"what I do for this poor woman I do for God, and He will not
let me suffer for it." At length, however, as though to test her
to the uttermost, He permitted that the leprosy should indeed
attack the hands with which she daily dressed the infected sores
of her patient; and those who before had praised her charity,
now blamed her imprudence. More than this, they avoided her
company as one contaminated, and spoke of her with disgust
and contempt. All this in no way moved or disturbed her: she

counted her body as dust, and cared not what became of it, so long as she might employ it in God's service. "Cecca's sickness continued many days," says the old legend, "but Catherine thought them very few, by reason of the great love she had to our Lord, whom she thought she served in that sick woman." At last Cecca died, assisted by Catherine's prayers and exhortations up to her last moment. And as soon as she was dead Catherine washed the body and prepared it for burial; she caused the dirge and other prayers to be said for the departed soul, and then carried the body herself to the grave, and covered it with earth with her own hands. When that last act of charity had been accomplished, it pleased God that the leprosy which until then had disfigured her hands, should suddenly and completely disappear; they even remained whiter and fairer than the rest of her person, as was attested by the evidence of many eyewitnesses.

About the same time there was among the Sisters of Penance in Siena one named Palmerina, who had given herself and all her wealth, which was considerable, to the service of God; but her many good works were poisoned by a secret pride: and the praise which she heard bestowed upon Catherine excited in her such an envy that at length she could not bear to see her, or to hear her name spoken. Unable to repress her malice, she even broke forth in public, cursing and calumniating the servant of God, if ever she was named in her presence. Catherine, when she understood this, did what she could to win her over by sweet and humble words, but finding it of no avail, she contented herself with recommending the poor Sister to God. Not long after, Palmerina was seized with a grievous sickness, which when Catherine heard she hastened to her, and left nothing undone to touch her heart, fearing that if she departed this life in such a state of malice her soul would be lost eternally. But the hatred which Palmerina had conceived in her heart was so deep and bitter, that she rejected all her courtesy, returning it with reproaches and execrations, and bidding her depart out of her chamber. And so, growing worse, without showing any change of disposition, or having been able to receive the last sacraments, she approached her end. Penetrated to the heart with pity for her sister's unhappy state, Catherine returned home, and casting herself prostrate on the ground, she poured out her soul before God in prayer. "O Lord," she said, "suffer it not to be that I, who ought to be to my sister an instrument of salvation, should become the cause of her everlasting woe ! Are these the promises Thou didst make me when Thou didst say that I should win many souls to Thee ! Doubtless my sin is the cause of this, and yet I am well assured that Thy mercies are not diminished, nor Thy hand shortened to save." But no comforting answer came to her prayer. On the contrary, she did but understand more clearly the danger of that soul which was, as it were, hanging on the very brink of destruction. The thought that she should in any way cause the loss of a soul pierced her with anguish, and she continued her prayers with many tears and groans, beseeching God, if need be, to lay on her the sins of the dying woman, and to chastise her, if only Palmerina might be spared; and raising her heart to God with the boldness of a loving confidence, she exclaimed, "Never, O Lord, will I rise from this place till Thou show mercy to my sister !" Such a prayer, as the event proved, had power to pierce the clouds. For three days and nights the sick woman lay, as it seemed, at the point of death, and yet unable to depart, all which time was spent by Catherine in unwearied and earnest intercession for her. At last, as it were, she wrested the sword of God's justice out of His hand, and obtained for the dying woman grace to see the enormity of her sin, and truly to repent of it. When next Catherine visited her chamber, she was received with love and reverence ; and, as well as she could, Palmerina signified her deep contrition for her uncharitable conduct, and besought the Saint to pardon her ; after which, receiving the sacraments of Holy Church, she gave up her soul to her Maker.

After her departure out of this life it pleased God to make known to Catherine that the soul of her sister had indeed, through her means, been saved. He showed her also how beautiful that soul had become in its state of grace, decked with a loveliness that no tongue of man is able to express   Then He said to her,

" How sayest thou, daughter, is not this a fair and beautiful soul which through thy care has been recovered from the hands of the enemy? What man or woman would refuse to suffer somewhat for the winning of so noble a creature? If I, the Sovereign Beauty, was nevertheless so overcome by the love and beauty of man's soul that I refused not to come down from heaven and to suffer labour and reproaches for many years, and in the end to shed My blood for his redemption, how much more ought you to labour one for another, and do what in you lieth for the recovery of a soul? And for this cause have I shown it to you that hereafter you might be more earnest about the winning of souls, and induce others also to do the same." Catherine thanked our Lord with all humility, and besought Him to vouchsafe her the grace of seeing the state of such souls as she might hereafter converse with, in order that she might be the more moved to seek their salvation ; a grace which she received, and that in so abundant a measure that, as her biographer says, "she saw more distinctly the souls than the bodies of those who appoached her." Many years later F. Raymund, being then her confessor, took occasion to rebuke her for not preventing those who came to see her from kneeling in her presence, a custom which gave great offence to some who observed it. "God knows," she replied, "I do not often notice the outward gestures of those who come to see me ; I am so engaged beholding their souls, that I pay little attention to their bodies" "How, mother," he said, "do you see their souls?" "Yes," she replied, "our Lord deigned to grant me that grace, when in answer to my prayer He withdrew from eternal flames a soul that was perishing. He clearly made me see the beauty of that soul, and since that time I seldom see any one without becoming conscious of their interior state. O father," she continued, "could you but know the beauty of one immortal soul, you would think it little to give your life a hundred times over for its salvation."

Meanwhile a great and sorrowful change was preparing for the household of the Fullonica. Giacomo, the tender father and the brave and honest citizen, was drawing to his end. Between him and his saintly daughter there had existed a mutual sympathy

which added a deeper character to the tie of blood by which they
were united. Catherine daily prayed for her father's salvation,
whilst he beheld her sanctity with a love mingled with reverence,
and trusted by her intercession to find favour with God when his
last hour should come. And now at length it seemed close at
hand; he was attacked by his last illness, and night and day
Catherine knelt by his bedside assisting him with her loving words
and pious exhortations. At first she prayed earnestly for his
recovery, but understanding from our Lord that his time was
come, and that it was not expedient for him to live longer, she
bowed to the will of God, and went forthwith to her father to visit
him and announce to him his approaching departure. Giacomo
was resigned and ready to leave the world; and Catherine gave
thanks to God when she saw his holy dispositions. Yet her deep
filial love could not rest satisfied, without seeking an assurance
from God, not only that her father's soul should depart in good
hope of a blessed eternity, but also that it might be granted to
him to pass at once out of this sorrowful life to the joys of heaven,
without tasting the pains of purgatory. This, however, she understood from our Lord could not be granted; because though her
father had led a virtuous life and done many good works, among
which one was his maintenance of her in the holy state she had
chosen, yet his soul had contracted some rust of earthly conversation which in justice must be purified in the fires of purgatory.
"O most loving Lord!" rejoined Catherine, "how may I abide
the thought that the soul of my dear father who nourished and
brought me up, and from whom I have received so many proofs
of loving goodness, should now go forth to suffer in the flames
of purgatory? I entreat Thee permit not that he depart hence
until, by some means or other, his soul shall have been so perfectly cleansed of its stains as to need no other purgation." Our
Lord in His amazing pity condescended to grant her request.
Though Giacomo's strength seemed utterly spent, yet whilst
Catherine continued as it were to wrestle with Almighty God in
prayer, it was plainly seen that his soul could not depart, but
was in some way held within his body. At last when she saw

that the justice of God must needs be satisfied, she spoke as follows:—"O most merciful Lord! if Thy justice must indeed have its course, I beseech Thee turn it on me, and whatever pains are appointed for my father, lay the same on me and I will willingly bear them." "Daughter," He replied, "I am content that it should be so, therefore the pains due to thy father I lay on thee, to bear in thy body even to thy life's end." Catherine joyfully gave thanks to God for this grant of her request, and hastening to her father's dying bed, she filled his heart with comfort and hope, and did not quit him till he had drawn his last sigh And at the very instant that his soul had departed out of the body she was attacked by a grievous pain in the side, which from that day never left her. She made little of the suffering, however, rejoicing in her inmost heart to think of the blessedness of the departed soul; and when others in the house were weeping and lamenting the loss of so good a father, she who loved him better than them all was seen to smile sweetly as she arranged the body on the bier with her own hands, saying to herself with a joyful countenance, "Dear father, would God I were as you are now! Our Lord be blessed!"[1]

Giacomo's death took place on the 22d of August, 1368.[2] On the evening of the same day Catherine went to the neighbouring church to pay her devotions, while Lapa retired to an inner chamber, and there gave free vent to her sorrow. It happened that a poor man knocked at the door of the house to ask an alms, but no one heard him, for the servants were all gone out, and Lapa was too much absorbed in her grief to attend to anything else. Catherine, however, had a full knowledge of what was passing, and returning home she made her mother promise never again to permit that any person should leave their door without relief Lapa, astonished at her daughter's knowledge of the circumstance, gave the promise and kept it.[3] Caffarini in his deposi-

---

[1] Leg., Part 2, ch vi , Sup., Part 1, Trat. 2, § 7.

[2] It is so registered in the Necrology of St. Dominic's Church, and the date fixes the chronology of this part of St. Catherine's life.

[3] Sup., Part 2, Trat 5, § 1.

tion speaks of the pain which from that day caused Catherine continued suffering Yet she bore it not only patiently but gladly, and if any one asked what ailed her, would answer gaily, "*Sentio un pici dolce fianco.*" For to her, indeed, it brought a sweet confidence that the father she had loved so tenderly was now beyond the reach of suffering.

As Catherine had procured that her father's soul should not pass through the fires of purgatory, so she also delivered her mother from a yet more grievous danger. Lapa, though a good woman in her way, was inordinately attached to the things of this life and had a great horror of death. After the loss of her husband she fell ill, and Catherine praying for her recovery, understood from our Lord that it would be for her happiness if she were to die then, inasmuch as she would thereby escape many grievous trials. Catherine, therefore, endeavoured to bring her mother to accept the holy will of God, but entirely without success. Lapa would not hear the name of death so much as mentioned in her presence, and implored her daughter to obtain her recovery. The answer she received to her prayer was to this effect, "Tell thy mother who is unwilling to die *now*, that the day will come when she will sigh for death and not obtain it." Some days later Lapa died without having received the sacraments, or, as it seemed, resigned herself to God's will. Catherine was in great anguish, and those who were present, among whom were Lisa and two of the Sisters of Penance, heard her sobbing and repeating aloud, "Ah, Lord God! are these the promises that Thou gavest me that none of mine should perish? I will not leave Thy presence till Thou hast restored my mother to me alive." Her prayer was granted : Lapa did indeed arise from the bed of death, and lived to a great age ; but she had so much to endure in the course of her long life, from the loss of worldly prosperity and the death of her children and grandchildren and all whom she held most dear, that, as our Lord had foretold, she often complained that "He had riveted her soul in her body, so that it could not escape." This event is assigned by Raymund to the month of October, 1370.

CHAPTER VIII.

THE FALL OF THE TWELVE, 1368.

PALAZZO PUBBLICO, SIENA.

IN the very heart of Siena is a spot to which every street converges as to a common centre, and which in the days of the Republic was known as the *Piazza del Campo.* It bears another name now, but we shall retain the title which was familiar to St. Catherine's ears, and which has found a place in the poetry of Dante.[1] The shape of this famous Piazza is semi-circular, like that of an amphitheatre, and its whole appearance seems to suggest the idea of a republican forum. It

[1] " Quando vivea piu glorioso, disse
Liberamente nel Campo di Siena
Ogni vergogna deposta, s'afflisse."—Purg. xi.

This name has been exchanged in our day for that of the *Piazza Vittorio Emanuele.*

is surrounded by public offices, the most remarkable of which is
the Palazzo Pubblico, a noble building, finished about fifty years
before the time of which we write, and assigned to the use of the
Executive Government. It may be taken as a fair monument
of the ideas which prevailed at the time of its erection. The
frescoes which decorate the great hall called the *Sala della Pace*
represent, in a series of allegories, the republic of Siena maintaining peace, yet ready for war; the beloved city being personified
by a majestic figure, seated and clad in baronial robes. All
around her appear the symbols of those virtues which alone can
form the sure foundations of a state, Concord, Wisdom, and
Magnanimity; while the three theological and four cardinal
virtues remind us that it is a Christian and not a pagan republic
which is here represented. On another wall appears a painting
of the city itself, girt about with moat and battlement, but, as it
would seem in the mind of the painter, only strong in her military
defences that she may more surely preserve to her people the
blessings of peace; for peasants stream through the open gates
bringing into the town the produce of their farms. The streets
are full of busy citizens; we see the craftsmen at their trade,
merchants leading mules laden with bales of goods, a hawking
party setting out for their sport, and the plain outside the walls
scattered over with huntsmen, while in the open squares within,
there are young girls dancing, and little children at play. Nay,
we even have a school of the fourteenth century presented to our
eyes, and the schoolmaster is there watching his scholars, while
the sculptured figures of Geometry, Astronomy, and Philosophy
remind us that in a free and well governed state, science and the
arts will be sure to flourish. And as though to complete the
moral of his pictured epic, the artist gives in his last fresco a
hideous representation of the reverse of the medal. He shows
us Tyranny, with all its attendant monsters of cruelty, injustice,
and fraud. The same city again appears, but no longer the
scene of peace and plenty; the streets are now filled with crime
and bloodshed, and are as revolting to look upon as before they
were beautiful and attractive. Ambrogio Lorenzetti, himself one

of the magistrates of the republic, was the painter of these grand
political allegories, which read many a wholesome lesson to those
before whose eyes they were daily displayed. Nor was he content with conveying his instructions by means of his pencil only,
for under each painting he added a versified explanation, in
which, as in the frescoes themselves, are conveyed the doctrines
of Aristotle, whose teaching was at that time held in such great
esteem.

The palace has its chapel, too, erected as a votive offering after
the great plague of 1348, in which mass was said very early for
the convenience of the market people. And attached to the
chapel is the beautiful bell-tower, the *Torre del Mangia,* as it is
called, a thing of such grace that Leonardo da Vinci is said to
have travelled to Siena for the sole purpose of beholding it. The
great bell that hangs there bears inscribed on it the Ave Maria;
and in olden times the figure of a man stood by the bell, which
was made by mechanism to strike the hours with a hammer. The
citizens bestowed on this figure the appellation of *Il Mangia,*
which was possibly that of the bell-founder, and hence the tower
derives its name.

No one who has once stood in the Campo of Siena will easily
forget the scene; that forum which we re-people with the stalwart
citizens who struggled here five centuries ago to preserve their
republican institutions; that quaint old palace, so rich in its historic memories, lifting to the clouds its graceful campanile, whence,
still as ever, thrice a day comes the call to prayer. We like to
think that Catherine's eyes must often have rested on it, and that
her ear must have caught those sounds falling shrill and clear
through the morning air, announcing that the hour was come for
the citizens of Siena to go forth to work. At the summons she,
too, went forth to her work and to her labour until the evening;
sometimes even she anticipated the signal when the work was
pressing, as when the hours of some poor criminal, to whose
scaffold she was hastening, were already numbered.[1] And many
times she must have passed the Fonte Gaja in the midst of the

---

[1] "Poi la mattina, *innanzi la Campana,* audai a lui."—Letter 97.

Piazza, destined one day to bestow its name on the sculptor who was to decorate it with his bas-reliefs ; and whose chisel was also to reproduce the very act of charity in which Catherine had on one such morning been engaged.[1] Truly, these are but fancies, yet localities are solemn things. We perish, and they endure : they stand now as they stood centuries ago, with a thousand memories hanging about their walls, memories of things that perish not when all that is mortal of us has fallen into dust : the fire of genius, the self-devotion of the patriot, the heroism of the saint.

To the Piazza del Campo, then, I must now conduct my readers, interrupting the narrative of Catherine's personal history for a brief moment, in order to notice some important changes which in the year 1368 were taking place in the government of her native city. Within a month after the death of Giacomo Benincasa a fresh revolution broke out in Siena. The "Twelve," who had held the chief rule since 1355, had by this time lost favour with the fickle populace. Assisted by the nobles and particularly by the powerful, though rival, families of the Tolomei and the Salimbeni, the malcontents rose against the magistrates, and assembling in the Campo, soon made themselves masters of the Palazzo Pubblico. They met with but a feeble resistance, and almost without a struggle the power of the Twelve was abolished But the two parties who had united to bring about this revolution found themselves at variance one with another, when it became a question what form of government was to replace that which had been overthrown The nobles being for the moment masters of the situation proclaimed the restoration of the old Sienese consulate, and ten consuls were appointed, two from each of the great families of the Malevolti, the Salimbeni, the Tolomei, the Saraceni, and the Piccolomini, with every one of which, Catherine, as we shall see, had close relations. But the popular leaders resolved not to be excluded from power; and unable to

---

[1] Jacopo della Quercia, called "Della Fonte" in memory of his works at this fountain, is also the author of a beautiful bas-relief representing Catherine bestowing her garment on Jesus Christ in the person of a poor pilgrim.

come to terms, the two parties once more appealed to the
Emperor Charles IV., and invited him to act as moderator between them. The first step taken by Charles was to send Malatesta Unghero to Siena as his Imperial Vicar with a body of 800
German soldiers, with whose aid he trusted to secure possession
of the city, but the haughty Sienese nobles resented the humiliation, and sounded the call to arms. A bloody street fight ensued,
in which, after disputing every inch of ground with fruitless
valour, the nobles were driven out of the city and forced once
more to retire to their mountain fastnesses. A new government
was now installed, which was a coalition of various parties. It
consisted of fifteen persons, eight chosen from the most plebeian
ranks, out of a class of citizens who had not hitherto been admitted to any power in the state; four from the party of the
"Twelve," and the remaining three from that of the "Nine."
This government was known by the name of the "Reformers"
(Riformatori), and the fifteen magistrates received the title of
"Defenders of the Republic."

They did not keep the ascendancy they had gained without a
struggle. Though a few of the adherents of the "Twelve" were
admitted among the Riformatori, their party as a whole had been
crushed; and to regain their old footing in the state they leagued
with some of the defeated nobles, and agreed once more to call
in the aid of the emperor. In the January, then, of 1369, Charles
entered Siena at the head of his troops. He could reckon on the
firm support of the Salimbeni, who were suspected at aiming at
the sovereign power.

Charles was just then sorely in want of money, and it was
commonly whispered that his plan was to make himself master of
the city and then sell it to the Pope. His first act excited the
suspicion of the citizens. It was a proposal that they should
deliver up into his keeping four strong fortresses, together with
the stronghold of Talamon on the sea-coast, which was the key
of the republic. These haughty demands being rejected, Charles
thought to carry the day by a *coup-de-main*, and together with his
adherents in the city, concerted plans for a joint attack on the

Palazzo Pubblico. But the spirit of the old Roman tribunes seemed to awaken in the hearts both of the people and their rulers. In defence of their liberties they showed themselves fearless alike of emperor or nobles, and their brave captain, Menzano, undauntedly attacked the well-armed Imperial troops, and put them to flight. The emperor found himself in a position of the greatest peril : for seven hours he watched the struggle from the windows of the Tolomei Palace, and saw the streets piled up with dead and dying as the struggle was ten times renewed. He listened to the sound of the combat as it swept on towards the city gates, telling him of the ignominious rout of his followers. Then fearing for his personal safety, he escaped to the stronger palace of the Salimbeni, and there awaited in anguish the end of that terrible day. It resulted in the complete triumph of the popular cause. "The emperor," says the republican chronicler, Neri di Donato, "was alone in the Salimbeni Palace, a prey to abject fear. He wept, he prayed, he embraced everybody, apologising for his *mistake*, and at the same time offering his forgiveness. Every one, he said, had betrayed him, the Twelve, the Salimbeni, and his own vicar Malatesta. Nothing that had been done was his doing, he was only anxious at once to depart from the city." This was not so easy, for he had neither horses nor money. Menzano, however, at that moment could afford to be generous, and restored to him some of the property which had been seized by the mob. Charles provided himself with the means of departure, but before taking his leave had the meanness to demand a compensation in money for the affronts he had endured, and the favours (!) he had granted. He was asked to name his price ; twenty thousand gold florins, he modestly replied, payable in four years. It was an answer fitter for a shopkeeper than an emperor ; but the citizens threw him the first year's contribution with well-merited contempt, acquiring as their sole condition that he would at once rid them of his presence.

After the signal triumph of the popular party, the nobles, once more expelled from the city, continued to carry on a desultory warfare for the purpose of recovering their civil rights ; nor was it until the June of 1369 that peace was re-established through the friendly intervention of the Florentines. The nobles were re-called, and allowed to hold some offices in the Government, though still excluded from the chief power, and thus a certain amount of harmony was restored. But the seeds of bitter dissension had been sown among the rival parties; and far from seeking to heal these, it was rather the secret object of the republican leaders to foment them. They dreaded nothing so much as a solid and lasting alliance between the various noble families whom they regarded as their common enemy. The Salimbeni, in particular, had shown themselves during the late events the firm adherents of the emperor, and were naturally therefore the object of special distrust, a fact not to be lost sight of as explaining the jealousy afterwards excited by Catherine's close friendship with this family. No efforts were therefore spared to keep up the hereditary feuds between the Tolomei and the Salimbeni, who, as respective heads of the Guelph and Ghibeline factions, were the Capulets and Montagues of Siena; so that the internal harmony enjoyed by the republic was of a doubtful sort; and Larenzetti's frescoed ideal of a state made strong by concord presented a sorrowful contrast to the reality.

In all these sad scenes the Benincasa family had borne their part; they belonged to the party of the Twelve, and shared its ruin. Giacomo indeed did not live to see the outbreak of the revolution, but Catherine's brothers were exposed to imminent danger, and on one occasion owed their lives to the respect with which the populace regarded their saintly sister. The story is thus told by the author of the Miracoli :—" It happened at that time that there was a revolt in Siena, and the brothers of Catherine being opposed to the victorious party, and their enemies seeking either to kill them or do them some hurt, as they had done to others, there came to the house in great haste one of their intimate friends, saying, 'The whole band of your enemies is coming here to seize you; come along with me at once, and I will place you safe in the Church of St. Anthony (which was near the house), where some of your friends have already taken refuge.'

At these words, Catherine, who was present, rose from her seat, and said to her friend, 'They shall certainly not go to St. Anthony's, and I am heartily sorry for those who are already there,' and then she bid him depart in God's name. As soon as he was gone, she took her mantle and putting it on, said to her brothers, 'Now, come with me and fear nothing;' and so she went between them and led them straight through the Contrada, which was occupied by their enemies. Meeting and passing through the midst of them, they inclined to her with reverence, and so all passed through safe and sound. Then she conducted her brothers to the Hospital of St. Mary,[1] and recommended them to the care of the master of the hospital, and said to them, 'Remain concealed here for three days; at the end of that time you can come home in safety.' And so they did. When the three days were passed, the city was quiet again, but all who had taken refuge at St. Anthony's were either killed or cast into prison. Soon afterwards, Catherine's brothers were fined one hundred gold florins, which they paid, and so were left in peace." Nevertheless the family never recovered its former prosperity. Bartolo, indeed, appears to have held office in the republic under the Riformatori, and his name appears as one of the "Defenders" for the May and June of 1370. But in that same year he and his two brothers, Benincasa and Stephen, removed to Florence, where they were inscribed as Florentine citizens. Even there their bad fortune followed them, and we find from one of Catherine's letters to F. Bartholomew Dominic, that her great friend, Nicolas Soderini, had come to their help and lent them money. Their children meanwhile remained at Siena under the care of Lapa, and the business at the Fullonica seems to have been carried on by some other member of the family, for it continued to be Catherine's home for many years later. All these troubles, and the loss of worldly prosperity which they entailed, brought sad distress to the poor mother, and what was worse, she did not always meet from her sons the return which her

---

[1] The Hospital of St. Mary, that is, of Santa Maria della Scala, of which we shall speak in a subsequent chapter.

maternal devotion to their interests justly deserved. Among
Catherine's letters three are preserved addressed to Benincasa,
her eldest brother, besides one which is a joint letter to them all.
To Benincasa she writes, consoling him in his misfortunes, but
at the same time gravely reproving him for his ingratitude to
their mother. "Try and bear your trials with patience, my dear
brother," she writes, "and do not forget what you owe to our
mother, for you are bound to show her gratitude by the commandments of God. We will admit the fact that you had it not
in your power to assist her; but even if you had possessed the
power, I do not feel sure you would have used it, for you have
not given her so much as one good word. You will pardon me
in saying this; you know I could not have said it if I did not
love you."[1] In the other letter, addressed to all three, she urges
them to mutual charity. "You, Benincasa," she says, "as the
eldest, must make yourself the last of all; and you, Bartolo, must
be less than the least; and you, Stephen, I beg of you to be
subject to your brothers, that so you may all live together in the
sweetness of charity."[2]

Lisa accompanied her husband to Florence, and her separation from Catherine was keenly felt by both. From childhood
her sister-in-law's sympathy and affection had been Catherine's
best earthly solace. No souls are so capable of solid and lasting
friendship as those whose hearts are truly detached, for they,
and they alone, can love *in God*, and to them belongs the happy
privilege of giving free course to a tenderness, which, binding
them only the closer to His sacred Heart, is exempt from all
peril of selfishness. Such a soul was that of Catherine of Siena,
whose heart was keenly alive to all that is most holy in human
affection, and among whose characteristics this one is to be noted,
that she loved and was beloved beyond what is ordinarily granted
to mortals. And it is precisely at this period of her life that we
begin to hear of some whose names will ever be associated with
her own, and who are dear and venerable to us, for this one
reason that they were the chosen friends of Catherine. As the

[1] Letter 250.   [2] Letter 252.

world began to make larger demands on her, she was careful, with her accustomed prudence, to have one or other of her religious sisters constantly in her company. One of these, who is very early named in the Legend as her habitual companion, was Catherine Ghetti, or Enghecti,[1] whom we learn from the "Processus" to have been one of her nieces. But among all the Mantellate none was admitted to such close familiarity with her as a young widow named Alexia, of the noble family of the Saraceni. After her husband's death, she devoted all her wealth to pious objects, and took the habit of Penance. She seems to have been well deserving of Catherine's affection, and was, says F. Raymund, "the first of her disciples, not in order of time but in that of perfection." After her first acquaintance with the Saint, she became so attached to her that she could not separate from her, and by her advice distributed all she possessed to the poor, and embraced a life of great devotion and penance. "Towards the end of her life," he continues, "Catherine made her the depository of all her secrets," and as we shall see, they were very seldom parted, Alexia sometimes entertaining her friend as a guest in her own house for days and weeks together.

It is evident from what has been already said, that at the time of the revolution of 1368, Catherine was gradually becoming known to her fellow-citizens. During the time of her strictest retirement she had been almost forgotten. A few years before, indeed, there had been a momentary stir and gossip when it was rumoured about that the Mantellate had received into their society the dyer Benincasa's youngest daughter. But the life of shop and market went on as before in the busy streets, political feuds and bloody revolutions broke in many a disastrous storm, and still the citizens for the most part remained unconscious of the presence among them of her whose fame should one day

---

[1] In a copy of the register of the Sisters of Penance, which is in the possession of the writer, carefully annotated in the margin by the hand of Signor Grottanelli, Catherine Ghetti's name has this little note scribbled against it: "*nipote di S. Cat. Proc. MS. fol.* 28, *recto.*" We do not know which of St Catherine's numerous brothers or sisters was her parent, but, like most of the Mantellate, she was probably a widow.

be their proudest boast. Little by little, however, it became whispered about that the young maiden, who day after day was to be seen going to and fro on her errands of charity, was a great servant of God. One had beheld her in ecstasy in the Friars' church ; another had sat with her at her father's table, and seen how, amid the abundance of good cheer around her, she contented herself with a mouthful of bread and a raw lettuce. The story of the wonderful butt of wine had been in every one's mouth, and readily appealed to the wonder of the multitude ; and hence they began to think of her as a saint, and to regard her with no little reverence. We have seen her presence respected by the mob at the very moment they were thirsting for the blood of their enemies. Those ferocious men in pursuit of their prey had stopped short at the sight of one in whose form they recognised her who had stood by the sick-beds of their wives and daughters, who had found her way into their hovels when they were dying of hunger, and fed them, as it were, by stealth ; of one, moreover, whose life, they knew, was not supported by meat and drink, like the lives of those around them, and of whom it might almost literally be said, that "she had a meat to eat that the world knew not of."

Nevertheless, as is often the case, the very enthusiasm of her admirers excited in the minds of some who did *not* know her a totally contrary sentiment ; and there were not wanting those who found matter of blame precisely in those very things which were quoted as proofs of her sanctity Bartholomew Dominic says that at first he used to be publicly derided for his folly in going to see such a person, and that the examples of her charity were so far beyond the comprehension of worldly minds, that what they could not understand they did not fear to judge as presumptuous. Among those who were loudest in their condemnation was a certain Franciscan professor of philosophy, named Father Lazzarino of Pisa, who had been sent to the convent of his Order in Siena, where he was at that time lecturing with great success. He was a man of no ordinary learning, and although a Franciscan, closely followed the theology of St Thomas. "It was at the period," say F. Bartholomew Dominic, "when Catherine was still abiding in her secret cell, before she appeared much in public. She never at that time spoke to or saw any man, except her own family, without leave of her confessor, and yet the odour of her sanctity had filled the whole city. Those who were simple and right of heart praised her; but the proud and envious blamed and detracted, and among these was Lazzarino. One day, on the Vigil of St. Catherine the Martyr, he came to my room at about vesper time and proposed that we should go together and see Catherine. I consented, believing him touched with compunction, though in reality he only wished to find matter for speech against her, I therefore obtained the permission of her confessor, F. Thomas della Fonte, and we set out together. We entered her chamber, where Lazzarino seated himself on a chest that was in the room; Catherine sat on the floor, as was her custom, whilst I remained standing. There was silence for a few minutes, which was at length broken by Lazzarino: 'I have heard many persons speak of your sanctity,' he said, 'and of the great understanding which God has given you of the Holy Scriptures; I wished, therefore, to come and see you, hoping to hear something that would be of edification to my soul.' Catherine replied with her usual humility, 'And I, too, rejoice to see you, for I think our Lord must have intended to give me an opportunity of profiting by that learning with which you daily instruct your disciples. I hoped that you might be led out of charity to help my poor soul, and I beg you to do so for the love of God.' The conversation continued in this strain for some time, till as the evening drew on, Lazzarino rose to depart, saying that it was late, and he could not stay, but hoped to come again another day at a more suitable hour. Catherine knelt, and asked his blessing, which Lazzarino gave. Then she begged him to pray for her, and more out of politeness than sincerity he asked her to do the same for him, which she readily promised. He went away, thinking that Catherine was a good woman no doubt, but far from deserving any extraordinary reputation.

"The night following when he rose and set himself to prepare the lecture which he was next day to deliver to his pupils, Lazzarino began, he knew not why, to weep abundantly. He dashed aside his tears, and tried to set to his work, but in spite of himself they continued to flow, and he could not divine their cause He asked himself in perplexity: 'What is the reason of all this? Did I drink anything before I went to rest, or have I slept with my head uncovered?' In the morning they came to summon him to the lecture-room, but it was impossible for him to speak to his class. At the first attempt he broke down, and continued weeping like a child. He went back to his cell ashamed of his own weakness. 'What ails me, I wonder,' he said to himself, 'can my mother have died suddenly, or has my brother fallen in battle?' So the whole day passed, till when evening came he fell asleep, weary and exhausted, but soon awoke, and then his tears began to flow afresh, and he could not restrain them. Then he set himself to reflect if perchance he might not have committed some grave fault, and begged of God, if so, to make it known to his conscience; and as he was thus examining himself, a little voice seemed to whisper in his heart, 'Have you so quickly forgotten how yesterday you judged My servant Catherine in a spirit of pride, and asked her to pray for you out of formal politeness?'

"As soon as Lazzarino saw the truth, and owned his fault, his tears ceased, and now his heart became full of the most eager desire to return to Catherine and once more to converse with her. At the first break of day he came and knocked at the door of her chamber. Catherine was no stranger to what had passed, and opening her door, Lazzarino at once prostrated at her feet. Catherine also prostrated out of humility: then they sat down side by side, and Lazzarino, whose pride had all melted away, conjured her to direct him in the way of salvation. Catherine at last moved by his entreaties answered in these words: 'The way of salvation *for you* is to despise the vanities and applause of the world, and to become poor, humble, and despised after the pattern of Jesus Christ and your holy father, St. Francis.' At these words the professor saw that Catherine had read his inmost soul; that she was conscious of the pride and ambition which nestled there like a serpent ; and with renewed tears he promised at once to do whatsoever she might command him.   And he was as good as his word, for at her bidding he distributed his money and the useless furniture of his cell, and even his very books.   He only kept a few notes to help him in preaching, and embracing the poverty of his rule led thenceforth a holy life.   He continued one of Catherine's most faithful disciples, and his devotion to her was so great that his worldly friends used to call him '*be-Catherined*' (*Caterinato*), an epithet very commonly bestowed on those who were known to frequent her company." [1]

[1] This story does not occur in the Legend ; it is related by F. Bartholomew Dominic in his deposition, and, as we see by his express words, belongs to the early period of the Saint's life, though no precise date is given.   Probably, however, it happened in the year 1369.   See Process., 1374.

CHAPTER IX.

HEAVENLY FAVOURS, 1370.

THE departure from Siena of Catherine's brothers, which took place some time in the year 1370, caused many changes in the household of the Fullonica. It was no longer the bustling scene of trade that it had formerly been, and Catherine's domestic life was naturally more free from restraint. Lapa and the rest of the family had long ceased to offer any opposition to the manner of life which she had embraced; her example seems even to have drawn her elder sister Lisa[1] to imitate it, for we find her numbered among the "Sisters of the Hospital," a title bestowed on those who served the hospital of Campo Reggio, which was formerly attached to the convent of San Domenico, but was afterwards made over to the Tertiary Sisters.

The year 1370 was a memorable one to Catherine; and at no period of her history are the records of her supernatural graces more abundant, or more precisely recorded. It is no easy matter to speak of such things; she herself shrank from doing so, and would often say that to put into human words the secret intercourse of a soul with its Creator was like offering clay instead of gold, or dipping a rare jewel in the mire. Entering on this chapter in her life, therefore, we are prompted to exclaim with

---

[1] Not her sister-in-law Lisa, who accompanied her husband to Florence, but her own sister of the same name, who died in the plague of 1374.

Another of these Hospital Tertiaries was Catherine "della Spedaluccio," to whom two of the Saint's letters are addressed, one of her most intimate disciples. Catherine herself is sometimes spoken of as one of the Sisters of the Hospital, which she doubtless served.

the prophet, "Woe is me, for I am a man of unclean lips!"[1] and to desire that the Seraph might touch our mouth also with the coal from off the altar, as reverently drawing aside the veil, we dare to contemplate the communications between the Beloved and His chosen spouse.

From the moment when Catherine had received from our Divine Redeemer the mysterious favour of her spiritual Espousals, the prodigies of her supernatural life were constantly increasing. "Grace became so abundant in her soul," says Raymund, "that she might be said to live in ecstasy. . . . God began from that time to manifest Himself to her not only when she was alone as formerly, but even when she was in public." But whatever might have been the mysterious sweetness which Catherine was thus privileged to enjoy, she was ever seeking for something better than the purest and most Divine consolations. As she had formerly desired *the perfection of Faith*, so now she longed after *the perfection of Charity*, and the light of the Holy Spirit which illuminated her intellect gave her fully and thoroughly to comprehend in what that consisted. She understood perfection in no other sense than the substitution of the holy will of God in the place of our own perverse and disordered will. Hence she desired to have no other will, no other heart, than His; and a connected series of wonderful and beautiful revelations are related by Raymund from the MS. notes left by her confessor, F. Thomas della Fonte, which show in what manner her prayer was granted. On the eve of the feast of St. Alexis, 1370, desiring greatly to receive Holy Communion, yet dreading lest she might not be worthy, a rain of blood mingled with fire seemed to descend on her soul, "not merely washing away the stains of sin, but banishing the very first principles of evil."[2] The next day, though so ill she could scarcely rise from her bed, she went to the church, but remembering that she had been forbidden by her superiors to receive Communion, except from the hand of her confessor, she felt a great wish that he might come to say mass

---

[1] Isaias vi. 5, 6.

[2] *Corruzione fomitale*; see Leg. Min, 74, and note 44.

in the chapel where she was praying. F. Thomas has left
recorded the circumstances that followed. He had not intended
that morning to celebrate, and knew not that Catherine was in
the church. But suddenly he felt his heart touched by an
unusual fervour and desire for the holy mysteries, so that preparing himself at once he went to the very altar before which
Catherine was kneeling, though it was never his habit to say
mass there.

When he came and found her there awaiting his coming and
desiring to communicate, he understood that it was our Lord who
had moved him to say mass that day, and to choose that altar,
contrary to his usual custom. He offered the Holy Sacrifice,
therefore, and gave her Communion, and beheld how, as she was
receiving, her face appeared all red and shining, and bedewed
with an abundance of tears. After that she remained lost in
God, and so unspeakable was the sweetness with which she was
drawn to Him, that even after she came to herself she was unable
for the rest of that day to utter one word to any creature. On
the morrow her confessor asked her what had been the cause of
such unusual devotion, and why at the moment when she received
the Blessed Sacrament her face had been of that shining red.
"Father," she replied, "of what colour my face may have been
at that time I know not; but this I know very well. when I,
unworthy wretch that I am, received the Blessed Sacrament at
your hand, It drew me into Itself after such a sort, that all other
things save It alone waxed loathsome to me, not only temporal
things and delights of the world, but also all other comforts and
pleasures, were they never so spiritual. I made my humble
prayer then to our Lord, *that He would take all such comforts and
delights from me, that I might take pleasure in none other thing but
only in Him. I besought Him also that He would vouchsafe to
take away my will, and to give me His will;* which petition He
granted me, saying: 'Behold, dear daughter, now I GIVE THEE
MY WILL, by the virtue whereof thou shalt be so strong, that
whatever shall happen to thee from this time forward, thou shalt
never be altered or moved, but shalt continue evermore in one

state.'" And this promise God fulfilled; for all who knew her were able to testify that from that moment Catherine appeared content in all events and circumstances, so that no contradiction, however vexatious, seemed to possess the least power to disturb her. Then she continued, speaking to her confessor: "Father, do you know what our Lord did to-day in my soul? He acted as a tender mother does towards a beloved infant. She extends her arms from a little distance so as to excite his desire, and when the child has wept for a few moments she smiles and catches him, clasping him closely to her heart, and there she satisfies his craving thirst. Our blessed Lord did the same with me: He showed me in the distance the Wound in His Side; the desire I felt to press my lips to it excited me to burning tears. He seemed at first to smile at my grief, and then after a few moments He came to me and took my soul in His arms, and placed my lips upon His Sacred Wound, and my soul was able to satisfy its desires, to hide itself in His Sacred Breast, and there find heavenly consolations. Oh! did you but know, you would be amazed that my heart is not utterly consumed with love, and that I still live after experiencing such a burning fire of charity!"

The same day [1] Catherine was meditating on those words of the Psalmist, "Create in me a clean heart, O Lord, and renew a right spirit within me;" and again the thought and desire with which her soul was at that time filled found utterance in the earnest petition that our Lord would condescend utterly to take from her *her own heart and will.* Her heavenly Spouse was pleased not merely to grant her request, but moreover to make

---

[1] That is, July 18th. In the Legend (Part 2, ch. v.), the Communion on St Alexis' Day is spoken of *after* the exchange of hearts and the appearance of St. Mary Magdalen. But it is expressly said that all these events, and others that followed, took place in the same year, 1370. If so, by observing the date of the several feasts, it is easy to restore them to their proper chronological order; namely, July 17th, July 20th, and July 22d. Some days elapsed between the loss and restoration of Catherine's heart, and as the date of the latter event is fixed to the 20th of July, it is evident that this first appearance of our Lord could only have been on the 18th, *i.e.*, the day after St. Alexis.

the same known to her by a sensible sign. For it seemed to her that He appeared in His own person, and opening her side, took out her heart, and carried it away.

Two days later, being in the chapel *Delle Volte* in the Dominican Church, together with the other Sisters to whose use that chapel was assigned, she remained, when her companions had gone away, and continued her prayers ; until at last, as she arose and prepared to return home, a great light surrounded her, and in the midst of the light our Lord again appeared, bearing in His hand a Heart of vermilion hue, and casting forth bright rays as of fire. Then He approached her, and once more opening her side He placed there this Heart, and said, " Daughter, the other day I took thy heart; to-day I give thee Mine, which shall henceforward serve thee in its place." And from that day it was her custom when she prayed, no longer to say as she had done before, " My God, I give Thee *my* heart," but instead, " My God, I give Thee *Thy* heart," because she knew and understood that in very deed there had been given to her in the place of her own human will and affections the will and affections of her eternal Spouse.

F. Thomas della Fonte, in speaking of this favour granted to the Saint, says that it seemed to her as if her heart had entered into the side of our Lord to be united and blended with His. Dissolved in the flames of His love, she exclaimed repeatedly, " My God, Thou hast wounded my heart ! My God, Thou hast wounded my heart ! " And he says that the event took place on the feast of St. Margaret (July 20th), 1370.

St. Catherine, then, was one of the first of those to whom our Lord thought fit to reveal " THE SECRET OF HIS SACRED HEART " They are her own words repeated again and again in her Dialogue and her letters. Contemplating the Body of Christ crucified on the Cross as the mystical bridge whereby the soul is to be united to its Creator, she says, " His nailed Feet are a step whereby thou mayest reach the Side which shall reveal to thee *the secret of His Heart.*" [1] . . . . " In His wounded Side you will discover the

[1] Dialogo, ch. xxvi.

love of His Heart, for all that Christ did for us, He did out of
the love of His Heart. . . . Let us go to the great refuge of His
charity which we shall find in the Wound of His Side, where He
will unveil to us the secret of His Heart, showing us that the
sufferings of His Passion, having a limit, were insufficient to
manifest His infinite love, as He desired to manifest it, and to
give us all that He desired to give." And in one of her letters,
glancing back to the memory of these supernatural favours, she
exclaims, "Place your lips to the wounded Side of the Son of
God : from that opening comes forth the fire of charity, and the
Blood which washes away all our sins. The soul that hides itself
there and gazes on that Heart opened by love, becomes like to
Him, because seeing itself so loved, it cannot refrain from loving "

Nor was this first vision the only one in which the Sacred
Heart of Jesus was revealed to Catherine as the sanctuary of
His love. Another day, when she was praying in the same
church, she suddenly saw Jesus Christ by her side, with so
wonderful a light streaming forth from His Breast that the whole
of that vast building was illuminated by it.[1] This seems to have
been about the same time as, or very shortly after, the events
already narrated.

That there should appear from this time a change, and an
extraordinary increase of Divine grace in the soul of Catherine,
can be no cause for wonder. If there were those who, measuring
her by their appreciation of her exterior actions, already regarded
her as a saint, it is not rash to suppose that between Catherine
as she was before, and after, her change of heart, there was as
much difference as between a saint and an ordinary Christian.
She herself testified to the fact. "Father," she said to her confessor in broken sentences, which he gathered up and preserved
with reverent fidelity, "I am no longer the same. Did you but
know what I experienced, surely, if it could once be known,
there is no pride that would resist it . . . The fire of love which
burns in my soul is so great, no earthly fire could compare with
it, and it seems to renew in me the purity and simplicity of a

[1] Sup., Part I, Trat. 2, § 5.

little child, so that I feel as though I were no more than four years of age. This love of God, too, how it increases the love of our neighbour! Surely it would be the greatest earthly happiness to die for another soul!"

It was very shortly after this[1] that our Lord one day again appeared to her, in company with His Blessed Mother and St. Mary Magdalen, and asked her this question, "Daughter," He said, "what dost thou desire? *My will, or thine?*" Catherine wept when she heard the words which seemed to question the reality of the surrender she had already made; and she replied, like St. Peter, "Lord, Thou knowest all things; Thou knowest that now I have no will and no heart but Thine." As she said this, she felt within her soul the same sweetness as St. Mary Magdalen felt when she wept at our Lord's feet; whereupon she fixed her eyes upon her. Our Lord, seeing that, and knowing the inward desire of her soul, said these words to her, "Behold, dear daughter, from this time forward I give thee Mary Magdalen to be thy mother, to whom as to a loving mother thou mayest at all times flee for special comfort; for unto her specially have I committed the care of thee." When she heard that, she gave our Lord most humble thanks, and turning herself to the Saint with great humility and reverence, she besought her to take her under her motherly protection. And from that time she began to cherish a tender devotion to that blessed Saint, and always called her her mother.

The question seems naturally to suggest itself what was the significance of this gift to Catherine of the patronage of St. Mary Magdalen at this particular moment. The incident comes in, interrupting, as one may say, the regular course of a chain, each previous link of which is clearly connected. When we remember, however, that the entire series of these wonderful favours was manifestly intended (as the sequel will show) to be the introduc-

---

[1] Probably two days later, which would bring it to the feast of St Mary Magdalen. In the Legend, the visit of that Saint seems to break the series of revelations in an unaccountable manner, which is, however, explained by a little attention to the respective dates.

tion to her public career, the appearance of her on whom the Breviary Office bestows the quite exceptional epithet of the "*Apostolorum Apostola,*" will be seen to have an exquisite appropriateness.

For the rest, the separate visions we have related above, which in reality make up but one narrative, when compared and fitted one into the other, give us a clearer comprehension of the spiritual sense of that great and signal favour, the gift, namely, to our seraphic mother, St. Catherine, of the Heart of her Divine Spouse. Not that we would presume to explain, far less to explain away, the mysterious exterior sign which was the pledge and token of that surpassing favour. To students of Holy Scripture there will readily occur more than one parallel in the prophetic writings, where spiritual graces are both represented and communicated by the means of such outward symbols. But the exterior sign itself was not the favour, it was not the grace which Catherine had asked from God. What she asked and what she obtained, sealed to her by the outward sign of that magnificent gift, was that thenceforth she might love only what her Lord loved, and will only what He willed. In this, and in this alone, she was to find THE PERFECTION OF CHARITY. In this one page of her life, therefore, the page which presents her to us as the bride and client of the Sacred Heart, we find a summary of her whole spiritual doctrine.

But we have not yet come to the end of the mystic favours of this eventful year. She seemed to pass the whole month of August in a continued ecstasy,[1] during which time she received many wonderful revelations. The narrative of these exhibits to us at one and the same time her unbroken union with God, and the exquisite tenderness of her conscience. On the 3d of August, being the eve of the feast of St Dominic, she was praying in the church and meditating on the glory of the great patriarch of her order. About the hour of compline, F. Bartholomew Dominic chanced to enter the church, and Catherine, to whom he acted as confessor in the absence of F. Thomas, begged him

---

[1] Latin Sup, Part 2, Trat. 1, § 10

to hear her, as she had something to communicate. " Perceiving
her countenance all radiant with joy," he says,[1] " I accosted her,
saying, ' We have certainly some good news to-day ; I see you
are quite joyous.' Then Catherine began to speak to me of our
holy father, St. Dominic. ' Do you not see him, our blessed
father ? ' she said ; ' I see him as distinctly as I see you. How
like he is to our Lord ! His face is oval, grave, and sweet, and
his hair and beard are the same colour ! ' " [2] Then she declared
to him how in a vision she had beheld the Eternal Father producing from His mouth His Beloved Son ; and as she contemplated Him, she beheld St. Dominic coming forth, as it were,
from His breast. And a Voice declared to her, saying, " Behold,
daughter, I have begotten these two sons ; one by nature, the
other by adoption ; " amazing words, which He presently deigned
to explain as follows : " As this My natural Son in His human
nature was ever most perfectly obedient to Me even to death,
even so was this My son by adoption obedient to Me in all points
even from his childhood to his dying day, and directed all his
works according to My commandments, and kept that purity both
of body and soul which he received of Me in baptism, clean and
unspotted until the end of his life. And as this My natural Son
spake openly to the world, and gave a most clear testimony to
the truth that I put in His mouth, even so did this My son by
adoption preach the truth of My Gospel, as well to heretics and
schismatics as also among my faithful people. And as this My
natural Son sent out His disciples to publish the Gospel to all
creatures, so doth this My son by adoption now at this present,
and shall hereafter from time to time send out his children and
brethren under the yoke of his obedience and discipline. And
so for this cause is it granted to him and his, by special privilege,
that they shall have the true understanding of My words and shall

[1] Process., 1330.
[2] St. Dominic had auburn hair, as we know from the description given of him
by B. Cecilia His likeness to the person of our Lord has always been a
tradition in the Order, and is corroborated by an examination of his only
known portrait, that preserved at Sta. Sabina, and a comparison of its features
with those which tradition assigns to our Divine Saviour.

never swerve from the same. And as this My natural Son ordained the state of His holy life in deeds and words, to the salvation of souls, even so did this My son by adoption employ himself wholly, both in his doctrine and in example of life, to deliver souls from the snares of the devil, which are error and sin. For it was his principal intent when he first founded his order, to win souls out of the bondage of error and sin, and to bring them to the knowledge of truth, and to the exercise of a godly and Christian life, for which cause I liken him to My natural Son." [1]

As Catherine was declaring these things to her confessor, it chanced that her own brother, Bartolo, who was in the church, passed by, and his shadow, or the noise he made in passing, attracted Catherine's attention, so that for a moment she glanced aside to look at him   Instantly recovering herself, she broke off her words, and began to weep in silence.   F. Bartholomew waited for a time till she should speak again, but finding that she remained silent, he bade her continue.   "Ah, wretch that I am !" she said, "who will punish me for my fault?"   "What fault?" he asked.   "How !" she replied, "did you not see, that even while our Lord was showing me His great mysteries, I turned my eyes to behold a creature?"   "Nevertheless," said the confessor, "I assure you the glance of your eye, of which you speak, endured so short a time I did not perceive it."   "Ah, father," she said, "if you knew how sharply our Blessed Lady rebuked me for my fault, you would surely weep and lament with me."   And so saying she would speak no more of her revelations that day, but she retired to her chamber sorrowing and doing penance for her sin; and she declared afterwards that St. Paul had also appeared to her, and reproved her so roughly for that little loss of time, that she would rather suffer all the shame of the world than abide such another rebuke at the apostle's hand.   "And think," she added, "what a confusion and shame that will be which all wicked and unhappy sinners shall suffer at the last day, when they shall stand before the majesty of God, seeing that the presence of only one apostle is so dreadful and intolerable.   I assure you, father, that

---

[1] Fen., Part 2, ch. xxv. ; Leg., Part 2, ch. v.

his words and countenance were so terrible to me, that if I had not had the comfort of a beautiful Lamb[1] shining with light that stood by when he spoke to me, I think my heart would not have been able to abide the same, but would have died for very sorrow."

F. Bartholomew, who on this occasion received the saint's confidence, related the whole matter afterwards to Raymund, and has besides given the narrative with every particular in his deposition. He says that Catherine wept over her offence for three hours, until at length St. Paul appeared to her again, saying, "Daughter, God has accepted thy tears, be more careful in future." And thus it pleased our Lord from time to time to put her in mind of her own frailty, specially after receiving such great revelations which might otherwise have moved her to pride.

When the feast of the Assumption came, it found Catherine so prostrate with sickness that she was unable to leave her bed. She was not then in her own home, but staying in the house of one of her companions, probably Alexia. Unable to go to the church as she desired, she took comfort in being able to see from the window of her chamber the distant walls of the Cathedral (which is dedicated to the Mother of God); and uniting in spirit with the Divine offices which were being celebrated there with great pomp on that high festival, she was permitted to hear the melody of the sacred chant as though she were present in the church; so that at the moment when the celebrant entoned in the Preface the words "*Et Te in Assumptione Beatæ Mariæ*," &c., she beheld the Sacred Virgin herself, and entered into a sweet colloquy with her.[2]

As she lay on her couch her companions from time to time

[1] Fen., Part 2, ch. xxiv. A curious typographical error has here crept into Fen's English version of this passage, where the shining *Lamb* stands as "a goodly bright *lamp*."

[2] Sup., Part 2, Trat. 6, § 6. This is the solitary occasion when the Duomo of Siena appears mentioned in the life of St. Catherine, to whom, however, it must have been dear and familiar, and whose gilded bust is now to be seen over one of the three doors of the great entrance.

caught the sound of the words she was murmuring to herself. They were simple enough. "O sweetest Jesus!" she repeated again and again; "Son of God," and then after a little pause, "and of the Blessed Virgin Mary!" "This ejaculation," says Father Fen, "was her matins and her evensong." Sometimes she prayed to her Spouse that He would deliver her from the bondage of the body and take her to Himself. "Not so, My daughter," was the reply, "I desired indeed to eat the last pasch with My disciples, yet I awaited the moment fixed by My eternal Father." Then she requested that if she must still live in this wretched world He would deign to make her participate in His sufferings. "If I cannot be with Thee now in heaven," she said, "suffer at least that on earth I may be united to Thee in Thy Passion."

Her petition was indeed granted. At this time she began to suffer both in her soul and body something of those pains which our Lord had endured both in His life and death. She often declared that the interior cross which He endured out of His desire for the salvation of souls, surpassed all His other sufferings : and this torment of desire she shared to her life's end. Many things also she at this time declared to Father Thomas concerning the Passion of our Lord, which he carefully committed to writing, and afterwards delivered to F. Raymund. Thus she interpreted those words of our Lord in the garden of Olives, "Father, let this chalice pass from Me," as signifying His will to be delivered from that same torment of desire by the hastening of His Sacred Passion, rather than as a prayer that He might not suffer. She also declared that the pains which our Lord endured for our redemption were so great, that it would have been impossible for any man to endure the same without dying a thousand times. "What man," said she, "would have believed that those thorns of His crown should have pierced through His skull into His brain? Yet so it was. Again, who would have thought that the bones of a man should have been drawn asunder and disjointed? And yet so the Prophet David saith : 'They numbered all my bones.'" And the dislocation of His bones, especially those of the Breast,

she understood to have been the most grievous of all His bodily
pains. These and other meditations on the Sacred Passion appear
to have occupied her during the three days succeeding the feast
of the Assumption. On the 18th of the same month, being once
more able to go to the church, she approached the altar in order
to communicate: and as the priest, holding the sacred Host,
repeated the words, "*Domine non sum dignus*," &c., she heard a
Voice that answered, saying, "But I am worthy to enter into
thee." When she had received, her soul was so overwhelmed by
what it experienced that she scarcely found strength to return to
her cell, and there lying down on the planks that formed her bed
she remained for a long time motionless. Then her body was
raised in the air, in the presence of three persons who beheld it,
remaining so without support. After which, being again lowered
on her couch, she began in a low voice to say such sweet and
admirable things that her companions as they listened could not
refrain from tears. She prayed for many persons by name, among
others for her confessor who was in the Friars' Church, thinking
of nothing just then calculated to move him to special fervour.
But suddenly, as she prayed unknown to him, he felt his heart
touched by a devotion to which he had until then been a stranger.
Shortly after, it happened by chance that one of Catherine's companions came to speak with him, and said, "Father, Catherine
was praying much for you at such an hour." Then he understood why at that hour he had felt so unusual a devotion. He
proceeded to inquire more closely what it was she had said, and
found she had asked of God for him and for others the promise
of their eternal salvation. She had been seen also to stretch forth
her hand as she prayed, saying, "Promise me that you will grant
it." Then it seemed as if she had felt some sharp pain, which
forced her to sigh, exclaiming, "Praised be our Lord Jesus
Christ!" as she was used to do when she felt any bodily suffering.
F. Thomas soon after went to see her, and desired her to relate
to him the whole matter. She obeyed, and when she came to
that point where she prayed for certain special persons, she said
to him: "Father, when I prayed for you and for others, that our

Lord would vouchsafe to grant you everlasting life, it pleased His goodness to give me an assured comfort in my heart that indeed it should be so. With that I besought Him that He would grant me some token of the certainty thereof; not that I doubted anything of His promise, but because I was desirous to have some memorial of the same. Then He bade me stretch out my hand; and I did so, and He put into my hand a nail, and closed the same so fast within my hand that I felt a great pain as if there had been a nail stricken into it with a hammer. And so (Our Lord be blessed for it!) I have now in my right hand one of the marks of my sweet Spouse and Saviour, sensible to myself, though invisible to others." [1]

This beginning of her stigmatisation, which was to receive its completion five years later, caused her excruciating pain; whilst at the same time the abundance of supernatural communications which were vouchsafed to her, utterly broke down her natural powers and reduced her to a state of extreme weakness. At length, towards the close of the year, these sufferings reached their crisis. Not to speak of that terrible torture which resembled the dislocation of the bones of the breast, and which Raymund assures us *never left her*, she was enduring another kind of anguish, which they who have even partially experienced it, can in some degree comprehend. The revelation was being made to her in a sensible manner how deeply the Divine Spouse of her soul loved her, and not her alone, but all mankind. She understood, and that so clearly that it seemed to her she had never known it before, the truth expressed in those words, "God *so* loved the world as to give us His only-begotten Son, that the world by Him might be saved;" [2] and again those other words which tell us that " He

---

[1] This prayer of Catherine for her confessor is very commonly related, as if the confessor in question were F. Raymund. A reference to the original Legend, however, will show that this was not the case, and that the whole narrative belongs to a date much earlier than his acquaintance with her. He relates it throughout as of a third person, and says distinctly that he (the confessor) left this account in writing, from which it is evident that the father referred to was F. Thomas della Fonte.

[2] John iii. 16.

died for all."[1] A God to love us! A God to die! Truly might the Apostle say, "the charity of Christ *presseth us.*" After all it was no new truth or revelation;[2] only what she had learnt from infancy in her Creed: but who does not know that there are times when old truths assume such a life and reality that they seem to be new; so that we contemplate them with amazement as though until that moment we had never understood their sense. So it was with Catherine at this moment. She doubtless exclaimed with her favourite Apostle in rapturous wonder, "He hath loved *me* and hath given Himself for *me!*"[3] And unable to bear that great excess of love, the heart of the Saint was literally broken, and the links that bound her to life snapped in twain.

It was a Sunday about the hour of tierce, and F. Bartholomew Dominic was preaching, as he tells us, in the Friars' Church, when the news was brought that Catherine was in her agony. Many of the brethren, and a great number of other persons, at once hastened to her house, and Father Thomas della Fonte, who had been summoned to assist her, went accompanied by F. Thomas Caffarini. They found her, apparently in extremity, attended by Alexia, Catherine Ghetti, and some others of the Sisters of Penance. They began with tears to recite the prayers for the dying, and as the news spread from mouth to mouth, they were soon joined by F. Bartholomew Montucci, the director of the Sisters, who brought with him a certain lay brother named John, and, as soon as the sermon was over, by Bartholomew Dominic himself. He says so great was the multitude that flocked to see her, that her chamber was full, and the street leading to her house crowded by persons going thither, so that he found no small difficulty in effecting his entrance. But before he came she had, as it seemed, expired. "Those who had been with her from the first assured me," he says, "that she drew her last breath a considerable time before I arrived." At the sad spectacle all broke forth into vehement weeping; and the sorrow of brother John in particular was so great that he ruptured a vein in his breast, thereby increasing the general consternation. But

---

[1] 2 Cor. v. 15.   [2] *Ibid.* v. 14.   [3] Gal. ii. 20.

F. Thomas, full of faith in the sanctity of Catherine, made him take her hand and apply it to the place, and he was at once completely cured. Then the neighbours flocking to the house began to condole with the distracted mother, and to prepare all things for the burial.

For four hours she had lain to all appearance dead, when, with a sigh, Catherine once more opened her eyes and looked around her. She was living indeed, but what had passed in that mysterious interval? Those who were with her, and who scarce ventured to believe their eyes for joy, beheld how, for three days and nights, she wept without ceasing, as though plunged in bitter sorrow, and they gathered from her words that she had been admitted into a blissful state, whence she had returned once more to recommence a life of labour and suffering. F. Bartholomew examined her as to the reality of her death, reminding her, however, that there could be no certainty on a point touching which the great Apostle professed himself ignorant. At a later period Raymund of Capua interrogated her on the same subject, pressing her to explain the facts as commonly reported. She could only answer him with her tears, but at last she exclaimed, "Oh, lamentable case, that a soul that had once been delivered out of this darksome prison and had tasted the fruition of that joyous light, should ever have been constrained to leave it and return to earth! Father," she continued, "you ask the truth from me, and it is this: The desire I felt at that time to be united to my sweet Spouse was so great that it could not be resisted, and seeing as I did by my own experience how great was the love our Saviour bore me, and what intolerable pains He suffered for my sake, I was wholly overcome with the force of such inestimable kindness, and my heart, not being able to endure the strength of so much love, brake in sunder; for which cause, my soul was delivered out of this mortal body, and had the fruition of His Divine Majesty, howbeit, alas, but for a little time. . . . I saw the pains of hell and of purgatory so great that no tongue of man is able to declare them. I saw also the bliss of heaven and the glory of my Divine Spouse, which only to think

of fills my soul with a loathing for all things that are in the world
And when I had conceived a certain hope that now I was past
all pains and cares, and had come to a state of everlasting gladness, our Lord said to me, ' Daughter, seest thou these unhappy
sinners and transgressors of My laws : on the one side, what joys
they have lost, and on the other side, what pains they have found ?
For this cause have I showed these things to thee, because I will
have thee return to the world to declare to My people their sins
and iniquities and the great peril that hangeth over them if they
will not amend.' When I heard that I should return to the world
again, I was struck with a marvellous great fear and horror.
Whereupon our Lord, to comfort me again, spoke thus sweetly
unto me : ' Daughter, there are a great number of souls in the
world which I will have to be saved through thy means; and
that is the cause why I send thee thither again. Wherefore go
thy way with a good will, and be of good comfort. From this
time forward My will is that thou shalt change the order of thy
life. Thou shalt no more keep within thy cell, but shalt go
abroad into the world to win souls. Thou shalt travel, thou shalt
go from city to city as I shall bid thee ; thou shalt live with the
multitude and speak in public ; I will send some to thee, and I
will send thee to others, according to My good pleasure ; only be
thou ready to do My will.' While our Lord spoke these words
to me, of a sudden my soul was restored to the body, which
when I perceived, I wept for very sorrow for three days and three
nights, and never ceased. And yet to this day I cannot possibly
refrain from weeping when it comes to my mind how I was
deprived of that passing great joy and felicity, and sent back to
this dark prison. Therefore, Father, when you and others understand what a blissful state of life I have foregone for a time
(God knows how long !) and that I have resigned it by God's
ordinance for the good of souls, you must not wonder if hereafter you see that I bear a passing great love to them that have
cost me so dear, and that to win them to God, I alter the manner
of my life, and converse more familiarly with them than I have
done hitherto."

This was Catherine's own statement of what had passed in her soul during that mysterious suspension of the faculties of life. Caffarini, in the *Leggenda Minore* (Part 2, chap. vi.), examines it very precisely, and sums up his conclusions under twelve heads. 1. That Catherine's mystic death was caused by the pain she felt in contemplating the Passion of Christ and by her ardent love, and that it lasted four hours. 2. That during that space of time she beheld the joys of the blessed, and the sufferings of purgatory and hell. 3. That believing herself in the possession of eternal bliss, our Lord bade her look on the punishment due to sinners. 4. That He commanded her to return to earth for salvation of many souls. 5. That after this she felt her soul, as it were, restored to the body. 6. That for sorrow she wept three days. 7. That remembering these things she could not refrain from weeping still. 8. That these high and secret things of God cannot fitly be declared in our imperfect language. 9. That after this glimpse of eternal bliss, she longed to suffer more, knowing that it would increase her crown. 10. That she bade her confessors not marvel if henceforth she bore a great love to souls. 11. That the souls of her neighbours became her glory and her joy. 12. That from that time she ceased not to labour for their salvation. Here then was the last degree, not indeed of her spiritual life, but of her preparation for that providential mission which she was to exercise in the world for ten brief years. She had seen,—"whether in the body, or out of the body, we know not, God knoweth,"[1]—the bliss of heaven and the woe of hell. As in her childhood she had "beheld the King in His beauty and had seen the land afar off,"[2] so now she had gazed on Him nearer, and, as it were, face to face; and almost touching the goal of her longing desires, she had turned back at His bidding, and once more opened her weary eyes on a world lying in wickedness, that by this sacrifice she might advance His kingdom on earth, and be an instrument of sanctification to countless thousands. No wonder, then, that henceforth the love of souls became her glorious passion, that their salvation stood to her in the place of

---

[1] 2 Cor. xii. 2.   [2] Isa. xxxiii. 17.

meat and drink, that no one thing could render tolerable to her her prolonged separation from "Him whom her soul loved," save the labour of winning them to love Him also: no wonder that Catherine, to use her own words, "bore henceforth so passing great a love for them that had cost her so dear," a love so rapturous that in its holy excess she was wont to pray, "that God would place her in the mouth of hell that she might prevent sinners from going thither."

The memory of all these marvellous graces is still religiously preserved in the church within whose walls so many of them were bestowed. A tablet affixed to the great pilaster that supports the Chapel *Delle Volte*, marks the spot where took place the mysterious exchange of hearts; another is pointed out against which she is said to have been accustomed to lean when in prayer; the very pavement of the chapel has been protected by a flooring, through an opening in which, however, you may still see the bricks so often trodden by the spouse of Christ, though of these many have been given away as precious relics to various monasteries, specially to that of St. Caterina in Magnanapoli at Rome; while all around are pictures and frescoes, on which the first artists of Siena have vied one with another in depicting the mysterious scenes which we have described. We leave to others the task of enumerating the master-pieces left here by the pencils of Salimbeni and Sodoma. But over the door of the chapel appears one sacred work of art which we cannot pass without a word of notice. It is the painted crucifix attributed to Giotto, and which, if indeed as ancient as tradition affirms, must have stood there in Catherine's time.[1] On it, day after day, her eyes must have rested in loving veneration as she passed through the door to her accustomed place of prayer. The pilgrim who comes here full of

---

[1] Carapelli, in his *Corso Cronotastico*, assigns Catherine's mystic death to the beginning of the year 1371. But a little attention to the narrative as it stands in the Legend shows that it cannot be separated from the events of the July and August of 1370. Moreover, we know for certain that in the December of that same year and the February of the year following, she was engaged in matters which properly belong to her active mission; so that it seems scarcely possible to fix a later date for the above event than the autumn of 1370.

her beloved memory, as he gazes on that sacred image whereon the artist has left the solemn expression of antique piety, can hardly fail to hear within his heart the echo of her oft-repeated words : "Bathe yourself in the Blood of Jesus crucified. Hide yourself in the open wound of His Side, and you will behold the secret of His Heart   There the sweet Truth will make known to you that all that He did for us He did out of love.   Return Him love for love!"

CHAPTER X.

THE year 1370 which had proved so important an era in Catherine's spiritual life, was destined not to close before bringing her the first-fruits of those magnificent promises which had been made to her in the hour of her mysterious agony. The narrative we are about to relate is given by three different writers, by all of whom the extraordinary facts were carefully examined, while to two of them the person to whom they refer had been well known from a child, and they were present in the city when the events narrated took place.

There lived at that time in Siena a young man named Andrea di Naddino de' Bellanti, belonging to a good family, who, at the age of twenty, had already rendered himself infamous by his crimes. He was devoured by a passion for drink and gambling, and had quite given up all religious practices, being accustomed publicly to mock at those who frequented the Sacraments. He was such a notorious swearer that it was said of him that he uttered a blasphemy at every step he took ; and to crown the catalogue of his misdeeds, having on one occasion lost a large sum at play, he entered a church, and seeing a picture of our Lord on the Cross, in his mad rage he deliberately and many times over stabbed it with a poniard. He is also said to have trampled on the Crucifix, and to have thrown an image of our Lady into the fire, as though to revenge himself for his ill-luck. In the month of September of this same year he fell ill, and his sickness being soon pronounced mortal, he was visited by his parish priest, who exhorted him to prepare for death by repentance and a good confession.

But Andrea, according to his usual custom, drove the good man out of the room with horrible curses His family, distressed at his unhappy state, applied to several other pious persons, who conjured him to have pity on his soul and be reconciled to God even at the eleventh hour But it was all in vain. He took the exhortations of his neighbours in very evil part, and would not suffer the subject of confession to be named in his presence At last, on the 15th of December, the feast of St. Lucy, his parents bethought them of calling in Father Thomas della Fonte, the confessor of Catherine, "who," says Caffarini, "was then just beginning to appear in public." But Father Thomas succeeded no better than his predecessors in softening the heart of the miserable youth, who seemed dying in a state of utter impenitence. For three days and nights the good father never left him, and devoted himself unweariedly to the thankless task, but still with no result. At last, seeing the case was hopeless, he was returning the third evening to his convent, when passing by Catherine's house he entered, and knocking at her chamber door, found her praying and in ecstasy, as was usual with her at that time of day. Not wishing to disturb her, he told some of her companions to watch until she should return to consciousness, and then to tell her of the great danger of this poor soul on the verge, as it seemed, of a miserable eternity, and to desire her, in his name, to pray for Andrea's conversion.

It was the fifth hour of the night when Catherine returned from her ecstasy, and the Sister who was with her at once gave the message left by her confessor. No sooner had she heard the sad case and the obedience given her, than she set herself to pray with great earnestness, continuing even until the dawn of day to beseech our Lord that He would not suffer that soul to be lost which He had redeemed with His most precious Blood. But our Lord made answer, and said that the iniquity of that wicked man was so heinous in His sight, that the cry thereof pierced the heavens and called for justice, for he had not only in words most horribly blasphemed the holy name of God and of His saints, but also thrown a picture into the fire on which was painted the death and passion of our Saviour Christ, together with the images of our Blessed Lady and other saints by which and other like impieties he had deserved everlasting damnation. When Catherine heard that, she fell down prostrate before our Lord, and said, "O Lord, if Thou look narrowly to our iniquities, who shall be able to stand? Wherefore camest Thou down from heaven into the world? Wherefore tookest Thou flesh of the most pure and unspotted Virgin Mary? Wherefore didst Thou suffer a most bitter and reproachful death? Hast Thou done all these things, O Lord, to this end that Thou mightest call men to a strict and rigorous account for their sins, and not rather that Thou mightest utterly cancel their debts and take them to mercy? Why dost Thou, O merciful Lord, tell me of the sins of one lost man, seeing Thou hast borne upon Thine own shoulders the sins of the whole world that none should be lost? Do I lie here prostrate at Thy feet to demand justice, and not rather to crave mercy? Do I present myself here before Thy Divine Majesty to plead the innocency of this wretched creature, and not rather to confess that he is worthy of everlasting death and damnation, and that the only refuge is to appeal to Thine endless mercy. Remember, O dear Lord, what Thou saidst to me when Thou didst first will me to go abroad, and to procure the salvation of many souls. Thou knowest right well that I have none other joy or comfort in this life but only to see the conversion of sinners unto Thee. And for this cause only I am content to lack the joyful fruition of Thy blessed presence. Wherefore, if Thou take this joy from me, what other thing shall I find in this vale of misery wherein to take pleasure or comfort? O most merciful Father and God of all comfort, reject not the humble petition of Thine handmaid; put me not away from Thee at this time; but graciously grant me that this my brother's hard heart may be softened and made to yield to the workings of Thy Holy Spirit." Thus did she continue in prayer and disputation with our Lord from the beginning of the night until the morning dawned: all which time she neither slept nor took any rest, but wept and wailed continually, out of the great compassion she had to see that soul perish; our Lord ever more alleging His justice, and she craving for mercy. At last, our Lord being as it were overcome by her importunity and prayers, gave her this gracious answer, "Dear daughter, I can no longer resist thee in this matter. Thy tears and prayers have prevailed and wrested out of My hands the sword of justice. This sinful man shall for thy sake find such grace and favour as thou requirest for him."[1]

Meanwhile a strange scene had been passing in the chamber of the dying man. Through the long hours of that terrible night he had been unable to sleep, but as the grey light of morning dawned—at the very moment when Catherine's prayer received a favourable answer—his wife, who was watching by his side, was amazed to hear him cry aloud, saying, "Send quickly for a priest, for I will indeed confess." "How now," said his wife, "what is it you ask for?" "I ask for a priest," he said. "Look in that corner," and he pointed with his hand, "do you not see our Lord Christ who commands me to confess, *and near him that Mantellata whom they call Catherine?*" And in truth at that moment our Lord had appeared to him, saying, "Dear child; why wilt thou not repent of thine offences against Me? Repent and confess, for behold I am ready to pardon." Which words so pierced the heart of the dying sinner that he could hold out no longer, but sending for a priest, confessed all his sins with great sentiments of contrition, made his will, and so passed out of this world with every token of God's mercy.

On the morning of the 16th of December the news ran through the city that Andrea de' Bellanti had died penitent and fortified with the last Sacraments. Men could not believe their ears, for he was known to every one in Siena for his riches and his vices. They knew that all through his illness he had been vainly urged by his friends both to confess and to make disposition of his worldly goods, which last matter he could not bear so much as to hear mentioned, but now they heard of the wise and excellent way in which he had drawn up his will and distributed his wealth, a thing no less astonishing to them than the fact that he had died

[1] Fen, Part 3, ch. xi.

as a good Christian. It was not long before the good news was carried to Father Thomas, who was stupefied with astonishment. No one knew better than he what had been Andrea's disposition the evening previous to his death ; what then could have brought about so wondrous a change in the course of a few hours ? As soon as he had said Mass, he determined to lose no time in ascertaining if Catherine had received his message, and hastened at once to the Fullonica. In reply to his inquiries, Catherine informed him that she had done his bidding, and had prayed for the poor sinner, who, she assured him, had obtained the Divine mercy, and having confessed his sins with true contrition, had escaped eternal perdition. "And how do you know with such certainty the particulars of his death and conversion ?" asked F. Thomas. Constrained by obedience, yet not without reluctance, she related to him how the matter had come about. Amazed at what he heard, and not yet satisfied that she might not be-the sport of some illusion, he questioned her more closely, "Had Andrea, then, been guilty of such atrocious misdeeds ?" he asked. "Yes," replied the saint, "he was an habitual and most sacrilegious blasphemer; and over and above his other crimes he had, out of pure malice, dared to stab and trample upon the Crucifix." "And do you know at all what he was like ?" continued the confessor ; "if you can, describe him to me ;" for he well knew that Catherine had never been to Andrea's house, nor so much as once seen or spoken to him. Then she began to describe to him the countenance and person of the dead man, the size of the room in which he died, and its rich furniture ; nay, the very colour of the drapery which covered his bed, and that as exactly as if she were looking at it all with her bodily eye. "For," she said, "Our Lord deigned to show me the form and countenance of that poor man, whom before that time I had never once beheld "[1]

[1] All the additional circumstances of the narrative are given in the Processus by F. Bartholomew of Siena, and by F. Thomas Caffarini, and also by the latter in his Supplement (Part 2, Trat. 2, § 8). It must be remembered

This wonderful conversion became noised throughout Siena, where Andrea was universally known. It created a great sensation, and impressed on those who heard it unbounded confidence in Catherine's power with God, and her special readiness to exert it on behalf of souls. And this impression was confirmed by another extraordinary incident which happened a few weeks later. One day in the February of 1371, when Catherine was again staying in the house of Alexia, it chanced that two famous criminals condemned to death were carried in a cart through the street towards the place of execution.[1] "Their sentence was, that by the way as they were carried, they should be pinched, now in one part of the body and now in another, with hot irons or pincers, and so in the end put to death. Which pain was so intolerable that they (who were before in a desperate state, and might by no persuasions be brought to repent them of their manifold offences) blasphemed God and all His saints, insomuch that it seemed that the temporal torments that they were now enduring were but a beginning and way to everlasting torments. But our merciful Lord, whose provident goodness disposeth all things sweetly, had otherwise determined

that both these witnesses were in Siena at the time, and Caffarini, as he says, "had known Andrea from his cradle." F. Raymund, on the other hand, wrote from hearsay, not having been acquainted with Catherine till some years later. In the Supplement, however, Caffarini gives the date 1367; and we should have accepted it in preference to that of 1370, assigned by Raymund, but for the irrefragable authority of the Necrology of San Domenico, in which occurs the following entry: 1370, *Andreas Naddini mortuus est die deci- maseta Decembris et sepultus ad pedes scalarum claustri in Sepulcro suorum.* In the MS. of the Processus preserved at Siena occurs a marginal note in contemporary writing, which runs as follows: *Andrea di Naddino Bellanti, un singolare ribaldo   Al padre suo gli fu tagliato il capo.* (An extraordinary rascal, his father had his head cut off.)

[1] In the Chronicle of Agnolo di Tura (*Rer Ital. Script.*, tom. xv p. 220), we find the following entry.

"1371.   *Uno trattata fu scoperto in Suna a di 26 di Gennajo e funne pre- miati quattro che lo scupersero, e fu lo dato l'arme   E poi a di 8 di Ferrato, furono attanagliati due in sur uno carro, per lo Senatore di Siena*" There can be little doubt that these were the two criminals on whose piteous suffer- ings Catherine that day gazed for them. When they were come near to the house, Alexia, hearing a great concourse and noise of people in the street, went to the window to see what it might be, and seeing the horrible manner of the execution, she ran in again and said to the holy maid · "O mother! if ever you will see a pitiful sight, come now" At these words, Catherine went to the window and looked out, but as soon as she had seen the manner of the execution, she returned forthwith to her prayers again, for, as she declared afterwards to her confessor, she saw a great multitude of wicked spirits about those felons, who burnt their souls more cruelly within than the tormentors did their bodies without, which lamentable sight moved her to double compassion. She felt great pity to see their bodies, but much more to see their souls ; so that, turning herself to our Lord, with great fervour of spirit, she made her prayer to Him after this manner: "Ah! dear Lord, wherefore dost Thou suffer these Thy creatures, made to Thine own image and likeness, and redeemed with the price of Thy most precious Blood, to be thus led away in triumph by the cruel enemy? I know, O Lord, and confess that these men are justly punished according to the measure of their offences. So was the thief also that hung by Thee on the Cross, whom, notwithstanding, Thou tookest to mercy, saying that he should be with Thee that very day in Paradise. Thou didst not refuse Peter, but gavest him a friendly and comfortable look, though he like an unkind man had thrice refused and denied thee. Thou drewest Mary Magdalen to Thee with the cords of love when she had estranged herself from Thee by her manifold sins. Thou tookest Matthew the publican from a sinful trade of life in the world, to be an apostle and evangelist. Thou didst not refuse the woman of Canaan, nor Zaccheus the prince of publicans, but didst most sweetly accept the one and invite the other. Wherefore I most humbly beseech Thee, for all Thy mercies hitherto showed unto man, and also for all those also that Thine infinite goodness hath determined to show hereafter, that Thou wilt vouchsafe to look down upon these wretched creatures, and soften their hearts with the fire of Thy Holy Spirit, that they may be delivered from the second death." Our Lord heard the prayer of His spouse, and granted her such a grace, that she went in spirit with those two thieves towards the place of execution, weeping and lamenting for their sins, and moving them to repentance. Which thing the wicked spirits perceived well enough, and therefore they cried out upon her, and said : " Catherine, leave off to trouble us   If thou wilt not, we will surely enter into thee and vex thee." To whom the holy maid made answer · " As God wills, so will I   And therefore I will not cease to do what lieth in me for the relief of these poor wretches, because I know it is the will of God that I should so do." And so continuing her prayer, she procured them a singular grace and favour, as the effect declared, for when those thieves were come to the gate of the city, our Saviour Christ appeared to them, showing to them His precious wounds all streaming down with blood, and inviting them to repent of their former life, which if they did, He assured them that all was quite forgiven   At this strange sight their hearts were suddenly so altered, to the great wonder of as many as were present, that they turned their blasphemy into thanksgiving ; and showing themselves to be heartily sorry and contrite for their sins, desired earnestly that they might have a priest to hear their confessions.   That done, they went forward cheerfully towards the place of execution, where they showed likewise great tokens of joy and comfort, for that they had to pass by a reproachful death to a glorious life. All the people saw this strange alteration, and were much astonished at it, because they understood not then the cause thereof, which afterwards came to light in this way· The priest that heard the felons' confession went soon afterwards to visit F. Thomas, and in talk declared unto him how wonderfully God had wrought with them   F. Thomas began forthwith to suspect the truth, and asked Alexia what Catherine was doing at that time when the thieves were led through their street towards the place of execution.   She declared the whole process of the matter, as she had seen and heard it in her own house, whereby F. Thomas saw a very great likelihood that the thing had been wrought, as he had supposed, by the prayer and intercession of the saint. However, for more assurance he took an occasion afterwards to ask the holy maid herself. And she, to the honour of God and for the satisfaction of her confessor, declared unto him particularly how everything had passed. Within a few days after this was done, certain of the Sisters that were present while Catherine was praying, heard her say these words in her prayer: "O Lord Jesu, I most heartily thank Thee that Thou hast delivered them out of the second prison." And being afterwards asked the meaning of these words, she answered that the souls of those culprits were then delivered out of purgatory, and taken to paradise. For, having by her charity delivered them from the everlasting torments of hell, she never ceased to pray for them until she saw that they were also passed the temporal pains of purgatory and received into everlasting bliss." [1]

We have now to speak of one of Catherine's supernatural gifts of a kind differing from any yet referred to. Her power over evil spirits formed one of her special prerogatives, and is singled out for notice in the collect of her Office. Between her and the great enemy of souls there was an unintermitting war. She was ever robbing him of his victims, and in revenge he ceased not his efforts to vex and torment her. Though never permitted after her one sublime victory, in which she had mastered his assaults, again to disturb her soul, yet he was continually directing his attacks against her body. Sometimes she was raised in the air and cast into the fire, at other times when travelling on some errand of mercy she would be hurled from her horse with great violence.

[1] In their version of the above narrative, F. Ambrogio and his English translator have fallen into the error of supposing Catherine's confessor herein alluded to, to be none other than Raymund of Capua. A reference to the story, however, as he himself relates it in his Legend, will show the mistake. He says expressly, "The priest who accompanied these criminals gave these details to *Father Thomas, Catherine's confessor.* Later, I also received from Catherine, in confidence, the particulars of what took place, and found them in every circumstance *conformable to what Father Thomas had written.*"— Leg., Part 2, ch. vi. And in fact if, as we suppose, the incident took place in 1371, this was before the coming of Raymund to Siena.

On one such occasion when Raymund and others of the brethren were present, both she and her horse, without any seeming cause, were cast down a steep precipice. But she arose unhurt and smiling, and dispelled their alarm, saying, "Take no heed, it is only the work of Malatasca," the name she commonly applied to the evil one.

The mastery which she wielded over the unclean spirits becoming known, Catherine was constantly receiving applications from the friends of possessed persons to come to their relief; but however disposed to help her neighbours in other kinds of suffering, her humility shrank from being required to exercise this power, she evaded such requests whenever she could, and it needed no little adroitness to obtain her assistance.

One story of a deliverance wrought through her means we will quote from the English Legend. There was in Siena a certain notary, named Ser Michel di Monaldi, he was a pious worthy man, and had resolved to dedicate his two daughters to the service of God in the Convent of St. John the Baptist. The nuns of this convent were Augustinians, and occupied themselves in the education of young girls. Monaldi was a benefactor to their community, to whom he acted as a sort of temporal father, and the two children were therefore gladly received by the nuns, to be educated by them until such time as they might be old enough to take the religious habit. "But they had not been long in the convent when one of them, whose name was Laurentia (a child of eight years old), was, by the secret judgment of God, possessed with a wicked spirit. The whole monastery was much disquieted, and by common consent they sent for her father, and bade him take back his daughter. After the child was thus taken out of the monastery the wicked spirit uttered many wonderful things by her mouth, and answered to many dark and hard questions. And (which was most strange) he spoke commonly in the Latin tongue. He disclosed also many secret vices of divers and sundry persons, to their great reproach and slander. The father and mother, and others of their kindred, being much afflicted, left no means unsought for the relief of the child. Among other

things wherein they hoped to find help and comfort, was the
relics of saints kept in many places in the city, to which they
resorted daily with all diligence, and among others to the tomb
of B. Ambrose of Siena, who had been in his lifetime a Friar
Preacher, and to whom Almighty God had granted a singular
grace in casting out devils, so that his mantle or scapular being
laid upon those that were vexed with unclean spirits very commonly chased them away. They brought the child, therefore,
and laid her down upon the tomb, and placed these relics over
her; the father and mother in the meantime earnestly praying
our Lord by the intercession of that holy saint to take mercy
on their child. But their prayer was not then heard, which
happened not for any sin that they had committed, but because
it was otherwise disposed by the provident wisdom of God,
who put in the hearts of certain of their friends to counsel
that they should repair to the holy maid for the release of
their child. Sending to her, therefore, they prayed her in
most earnest manner that she would do her best to help their
daughter, to which she made answer that she had enough to do
with the wicked spirits that from time to time molested herself,
and therefore prayed them that they would hold her excused
The parents, whose hearts were very heavy for their innocent
child, would not take that excuse, but took their daughter, and
went with her to Catherine's lodging, and came to the house so
suddenly that she could not possibly escape by the door without
their getting a sight of her. Which when she saw, she found
means to convey herself out by a window, and so hid herself for
that time that they could not find her. At last, when they had
tried all ways, and saw that they could by no means come to her
speech (for she had given charge to as many as were about her
that none should move her in that matter), they resolved to go to
Father Thomas, her confessor, and to entreat him that he would
command her in virtue of her obedience to keep the child with
her for a time. Father Thomas was much moved with their
pitiful suit, and therefore assured them that he would do his best.
But because he knew well that if he spoke to her himself she

would of humility make one excuse or other, so that he should not be able to move her any further, he devised this stratagem He waited a time late in the evening when he knew that she was abroad, and then took the child that was possessed and put her into Catherine's chamber, whither he knew she would come that night, leaving word with the rest of the Sisters that they should tell her when she came home that he commanded her, in virtue of obedience, to suffer that child to remain with her all that night until the next morning. And so he went his way, and left the child with them. When she came home and found the child in her chamber, she asked the Sisters who had brought her thither. They said that Father Thomas, her confessor, had left the child there ; and declared, moreover, that he desired her, in virtue of obedience, to take charge of the child till the next day. When she heard that she made no more resistance, but set herself at once to prayer, and caused the child to kneel down and pray with her. And so they continued together all that night, fighting against the wicked spirit, until at length, a little before day, he was constrained by the force of her faithful prayer to depart, and to leave the innocent child without doing any harm to her body Which, when one of her Sisters, called Alexia, perceived, she ran to Father Thomas and told him that the child was delivered He, likewise, being very glad of the joyful news, went to the father and mother, and brought them with him to Catherine's chamber, where, when they saw the child delivered indeed, they wept for joy, and glorified Almighty God that had given such power to His humble spouse But the holy maid knew that the wicked spirit had not quite forsaken the child, and therefore entreated the father and mother that she might remain there with her a little time, which they willingly granted. She then began to instruct the child, and exhorted her to give herself to continual prayer. And she charged her that she should in nowise depart out of the house until her father and mother came thither again to fetch her home, which points the child carefully observed. Meantime, as the holy maid had occasion to go home to her own house about some necessary business (for all this was done not in

her own house, but in the house of Alexia), she left the child
with a servant, and gave her charge to have a care of her.   When
she had passed the whole day in her own house about necessary
business, and night was come, she desired Alexia to give her her
mantle, for she would return with her to her house   To that
Alexia answered that it was very late, and that it would be evil
thought of if women (especially religious persons) should be seen
abroad at that time of night.   'O Alexia,' said she, 'we must
needs go, for that wicked wolf is about to take my little lamb
away from me again.'   And with that they went both together,
and found the child indeed strangely altered, her face all red and
her wits utterly distracted.   When the holy maid saw that, she
exclaimed in holy indignation : 'Ah ! thou foul fiend of hell,
how durst thou thus to enter again this poor innocent?   I trust
in the goodness of my dear Lord and Saviour that thou shalt now
be cast out in such sort that thou shalt never dare to enter any
more.'   And with that she took the child into her chamber,
where she continued for a certain time in prayer.   But the wicked
spirit was so obstinate that she was fain to persevere even until
the fourth hour of the night before she could expel him   At last,
constrained by the force of her prayer and by virtue of the charge
that she gave him in God's behalf, he said these words to her :
' If I must needs depart out of the child, I will enter into thee.'
Whereunto she made answer and said, 'If it be God's pleasure
(without Whose licence I am well assured thou canst do nothing),
our Lord forbid that I should be against His holy will in anything.'
Which words, proceeding from a humble and resigned spirit, so
struck the proud fiend that he lost all the strength that he had
before against the innocent child.   Howbeit, in passing out
he rested awhile in the child's throat, which was perceived by a
great swelling that he made in that place, which the holy maid
seeing, she made the sign of the cross over the child's throat, by
virtue whereof the wicked spirit was thoroughly dispossessed in
such sort that he might never return to disquiet the child again
And the next day she sent for the father and mother, to whom
she said, ' Take your child home with you, in God's name, for

from this day forward she shall never be troubled more with that wicked spirit.' They took their child with glad hearts, and led her to the monastery whence she came, where she lived a very blessed life under that rule and discipline, and was never molested more to her dying day. Which thing was so joyous to Ser Michel, her father, that he could never tell it afterwards but that he wept for joy. And he honoured the holy maid in his heart as if she had been an angel of God."

It may easily be understood that facts of this kind, when once known, could not fail to bring Catherine's name before the notice of her fellow-citizens. "People began to resort to her," says F. Bartholomew Dominic, "more than they had done before, coming even from distant parts of the country to see and speak with her." In short her public life may be said to have fairly begun. She came to be regarded as one to whom recourse might be had in desperate cases, and whose prayers were never known to be left unanswered. One of the first who was moved by these reports to seek her out and ask her counsel, was Donna Onorabile Tolomei, wife to Francesco Tolomei, the head of the noblest family of Siena, one which boasts of having given a long line of illustrious citizens to the republic, and no fewer than fourteen saints to the Order of St Dominic. Onorabile, or Rabes, as she was commonly called, was a virtuous and religious matron, though not without plenty of family pride and a certain infirmity of temper. Her tale of sorrow was soon told. She was the mother of several sons and of two daughters, all of them given up to the vanities of the world. Giacomo, or James, the eldest son, led a life of ferocious crime. Whilst yet a child he had killed two men with his own hand, and such was his pride and cruelty, that though still a mere youth he was feared by all men. He had two sisters, one named Ghinoccia, and the other Francesca; Ghinoccia in particular was passionately addicted to the world and its pleasures, and carried her love of dress to an extremity of folly, filling the house with her perfumes and cosmetics. Rabes feared for the souls of her children, and specially of her daughters, whose giddiness and levity seemed even to threaten the loss of their good name. And inasmuch as she herself feared God, and desired nothing so much as the conversion of her children to a better life, she conjured the Saint to come with her to her house and see these young girls and give them some pious exhortation. It was probably the first time that Catherine had ever set her foot within one of the great houses of Siena. The Tolomei Palace still stands, a venerable building, ancient even in Catherine's time, and bearing in every part the tokens of belonging to the proudest family of the republic. Rabes introduced her to her two daughters, and then left them together. One little phrase which occurs in the narrative, as it is told by Caffarini in the *Leggenda Minore*, suggests a fact which possibly moved the heart of the Saint as she gazed on those young faces to a deep and singular interest. Does the reader remember that compliance with a foolish fashion in her early childhood (the dyeing of her hair to a fictitious appearance of fairness), which all through Catherine's innocent life weighed upon her conscience, and which she even regarded as a deadly sin? As she looked on the two maidens now before her, she beheld the revival of that same fashion. Dressed in the extravagant modes of the fourteenth century (and few centuries could boast of extravagances more preposterous), the raven hair of the two Italian girls was pomaded and powdered in the vain attempt to make them appear like English blondes. Catherine, as she looked at them, silently raised her heart to God, and that done, addressed them a few words of gentle remonstrance. It did not take many minutes for her to win their hearts and touch their consciences; her words, but far more her presence and the sweet odour of that perfect charity, tore away the veil from before their eyes, and wrought in them a change which was in truth "a change of the right hand of the Most High." Detesting the vanities which until then they had clung to, they cast all their cosmetics into the gutter, says Caffarini, and cutting off their (artificially) fair hair (*tagliati è loro biondi capegli*), they placed themselves at the disposal of Catherine, and declared themselves ready to begin an

entirely new life. It was one of those conversions in which
souls cannot stop half way, and before many days were over,
Ghinoccia and Francesca had asked and received the habit of
the Sisters of Penance. Ghinoccia, in particular, who had
formerly been the most given to worldly excess, was now the one
most disposed to the practice of penance, and both embraced a
rule of life as austere as it was edifying.

While all this had been going on, James, their eldest brother,
had been away from Siena. When he learnt the change that had
come over his sisters, he raged like a madman, and cursed all
those who had had any part in it. the friars, the sisters, and
Catherine above all, and ended by swearing he would tear from
their backs the religious habit which they had had the folly to
assume Rabes, who knew her son's violence, and dreaded what
he might be capable of doing, sent a private message to Catherine,
to warn her of the gathering storm. The Saint contented herself
with requesting F. Thomas to go and talk to the youth, saying,
" You may say such and such things to him from me, and I on
my part will pray for him to God "

There was a younger member of the family, named Matthew,
who at this juncture was the only one who had the courage to
face his ferocious brother. " Brother James," he said, "you do
not know this Sister Catherine. She is a wonderful woman. If
once she sees you, she will turn you also and make you go to
confession." " To confession !" he exclaimed, "I defy her and
all of them ; you may be sure of this, I will cut the throats of all
those priests and friars before they bring me to confession "
" Well, brother," replied the boy, "you will see my words will
come true, and that holy Sister will bring you to the grace of
God." James replied only by fresh curses, and on reaching Siena,
went at once to his father's house, where he threatened all manner
of horrible revenge, if his sisters, and Ghinoccia in particular, were
not made to lay aside the religious habit. Rabes, who knew his
violent nature, did what she could to calm him, and succeeded
so far as to get him to harm no one that night. The next morning she sent for F. Thomas, who came in company with F.

Bartholomew of Siena; and both spent several hours endeavouring to make him hear reason, but in vain. All this time Catherine was in prayer, and as the event showed, her prayers prevailed where the eloquence of the good fathers was of no effect. For when they had done their utmost and saw that they gained nothing, they were about to take their leave, when suddenly, and contrary to all expectation, the young man, as if touched by the hand of God, began saying of his own accord that he was well content to leave his sisters to serve God in the holy rule which they had chosen. The friars could not believe their ears, but their astonishment increased when James went on to say that he desired to be confessed and absolved from his sins, that he might serve God with them. In fact, he made his confession that same day, and the raging wolf was now as gentle as a lamb. Rabes and all her family rejoiced at the unaccountable change, whilst F. Thomas and his companion hastened to Catherine's house that they might bring her the good news. They found that she was in an upper chamber absorbed in prayer, and so were obliged to remain until she was able to see them. But one of her Sisters coming in to entertain them meanwhile, F. Thomas began to relate what had taken place. "It is no news to us," replied the Sister. "Catherine, from whom I have just come, has told me the whole matter." Then they all went up together to the Saint's chamber, who received them very courteously, and before they had had time to speak, expressed her joy at the conversion of Master James. "We are indeed bound to thank God," she said, "the wicked enemy thought to have got a little lamb of which he had some hope, but through the unspeakable mercy of God he lost a great prey of which he had full possession. He laid a snare for Ghinoccia, but he has lost James. May our Lord be blessed who turns all things to the comfort of His servants." Ghinoccia and Francesca persevered in the holy life they had embraced, and died a few years later in great repute of sanctity. James married, and became another man, showing so good and exemplary an example as to be the admiration of his neighbours. Towards the end of his life he put on the habit of a Dominican Tertiary and died in

1406. Matthew, as we shall see, became in time a Friar Preacher and one of the faithful disciples of our Saint.

It is not to be doubted that the connection thus formed between Catherine and the members of the Tolomei family must have brought her into relation with many other noble houses, and that by this means she became more fully cognisant of the troubles which infested not Siena only but all Italy. Her circle of friends was, moreover, becoming enlarged in another way. In a former chapter we have spoken of the heroic services she was in the habit of rendering to the sick, and of her visits to the Leper Hospital. There were other hospitals in Siena which she was wont to frequent; one was the *Casa della Misericordia*,[1] whose rector was one Master Matthew di Cenni di Fazio; the other was the great hospital of La Scala. Matthew was a man of noble birth, who in his youth had led a dissolute life, but who, together with his friend Francis Lando, was won over to better things through the means of a certain Father William Flete, an English Augustinian hermit. At the time of which we speak, Master Matthew was one of the notabilities of Siena, known to everybody, and everybody's friend; for his genial sympathetic nature won him the confidence of young and old. Between him and Catherine an intimate friendship soon sprang up, and lasted till her death. At La Scala also she came in contact with a group of excellent men who may be said to have made up the pious society of Siena. This noble hospital, which still exists, boasts of being one of the most ancient charitable institutions in Europe. It was founded in 832 by a poor shoemaker, and takes its name from three marble steps which were discovered when digging out the foundation, and which are supposed to have belonged to an old temple of Diana. Hence it was called "The Hospital of Santa Maria della Scala." Here Catherine often came, and a little room was assigned to her use. A stone is still shown on which she is said to have lain down to rest, and above it is the inscription. "*Here lay the spouse of*

---

[1] The *Misericordia* was founded in 1250 by B. Andrew Gallerani, called the first Tertiary of St. Dominic. A descendant of his, Louis Gallerani, was one of St. Catherine's disciples.

Jesus Christ, the Seraphic Mother, St. Catherine of Siena Laus Deo ! " whilst among the relics of the Fullonica is the lanthorn she carried with her when called forth on some errand of charity during the night. Caffarini in his Supplement speaks of her habit of attending the sick in the hospitals, and specially notes the fact of her serving them at night, which explains why she may have required the use of a little room in which to rest. "Whenever there was question of serving God or performing any works of charity," he says, "she readily quitted her cell to employ herself for the good of her neighbours, as our Lord commanded her after her three years of retirement. She was not afraid of serving the sick in the hospitals, even at the most fatiguing hours of the night ; nor did she shrink from those miserable creatures who were suffering from the most repulsive maladies. She once bestowed her whole care on an unhappy woman who for years had lived an abandoned life, and who now lay dying on a wretched bed, where she complained that she could find no one to assist her, or give her the kind of food she liked. Catherine resolved to take care first of the body and then of the soul of this poor creature. She prepared her the necessary food, and waited on her day and night, while at the same time she encouraged her to repent and have confidence in God's mercy."[1] But La Scala, besides being an hospital, was the rendezvous of a certain Confraternity which assembled in some subterranean vaults or catacombs, and was known by the name of "*The Company of the Discipline of the Virgin Mary, under the Hospital.*" This company was far more ancient than the hospital itself, and traced its origin to those first Christians of Siena who, converted to the faith by the martyr St. Ansano, assembled in these catacombs for the secret exercise of their religion. When the great hospital was built at a later period, the vaults were not destroyed, but included in the fabric and still assigned to the use of the company. Here the brethren had their own chapel and rooms in which they assembled and took the discipline.

They met on all festivals, and on every Friday in the year made

[1] Sup., Part 2, Trat. 3, § 6.

a long meditation, heard Mass, and approached the sacraments. Besides this they carried on a great number of good works, attending the hospitals both in and out of the city, and assisting the poor, the sick, orphans, and pilgrims, from their large revenues. This Confraternity was the very life and centre of the piety of Siena. It numbered among its associates a noble army of saints and saintly personages, and in St. Catherine's time we find in the Catalogue of the Brethren, the names of F. Raymund of Capua, F. Thomas della Fonte, F. Thomas Caffarini, F. Bartholomew of Siena, F. Bartholomew Montucci, Gabriel Piccolomini, Stephen Maconi, and the two Augustinians, F. John Tantucci, and F. William Flete, to which must be added that of Don John of the Cells of Vallombrosa; all in due time to be numbered among Catherine's friends and disciples. By all the members of this holy company Catherine was regarded with affectionate reverence, and accepted rather as a mother than as an associate; and when they assembled on festival days to sing the divine office in their chapel, Catherine would assist and share their devotions in the privacy of her little chamber. A fresco may still be seen at Siena, which represents St. Catherine with her mantle extended, whilst under its folds kneel four of her disciples, clad in the penitential garb of the Company of Mary.

Here, then, we probably see the first beginnings of that Spiritual Family which gradually gathered round the Saint, and which little by little drew into itself all those souls of predilection, who in a sad and evil day preserved in Siena and the other cities of Tuscany "the sweet savour of Christ." Whether seculars or religious, men or women, Dominicans or members of other religious orders, they all called her mother, and stood to her in the relation of spiritual children. It mattered little that she who was looked up to as their head was at this time but twenty-four years of age; of her, if any one, it might be truly said, that, "Venerable age is not that of long time nor counted by the number of years, but the understanding is grey hairs, and a spotless life old age." [1] Her very confessors regarded themselves

[1] Wisd. iv. 8, 9.

in no other light than her "sons," and whilst she rendered them the most implicit obedience in the discharge of their sacred office, it is impossible not to see that they were no less her disciples than the others. "People often said," writes F. Raymund, "that it was from the friars she learnt her wonderful doctrine, but the contrary was the case; it was they who learnt from her." And as the circle widened and extended, it came about necessarily and naturally that Catherine often had to communicate with those who sought her advice and direction at a distance. Hence the origin of that marvellous correspondence of which we possess but very imperfect fragments, but which, incomplete as it is, furnishes us with by far the most precious materials for forming a knowledge of her real character. As she herself did not as yet possess the art of writing, she was dependent on the assistance of others, to whom she dictated her letters with wonderful ease and fluency. Nor is it possible to doubt the originality of these compositions; on every page, in every word there is impressed the mind and heart of Catherine, wonderful in variety, adapting itself to the rank, the circumstances, the spiritual needs of each one whom she addresses; now burning with zeal, now melting with tenderness, supplying a body of spiritual direction of which the distinguishing feature is practical good sense, and a course of meditations, in which she is content to build up the faith of her disciples on the Eternal Truths.

Before going further in the course of our history, therefore, it will best answer the purpose we have in view if we pause for a brief space, and introduce to the reader a little more particularly the Spiritual Family of St. Catherine, confining ourselves, for the sake of brevity, to those most closely associated with her, and whose names will most frequently recur in the following pages.

CHAPTER XI.

CATHERINE'S SPIRITUAL FAMILY.

AND first, we will say a few words of those who may most properly be called St. Catherine's companions, the members, namely, of that religious body to which she belonged, the Mantellate, or Dominican Sisters of Penance. From the time she quitted the solitude of her cell, it had been her custom always to have one or other of them in her company. Of Alexia we have already said something, and she will often reappear in the course of our narrative. Catherine, as has been seen, loved her dearly, and on that account she did not spare her. From various little words that are dropped in her letters, it would seem that at the period of their first acquaintance, the Saint considered her friend a little open to that feminine weakness, an unguarded tongue. "Make a tabernacle in your cell," she says, "so as not to be going about everywhere gossiping; only go out when called by necessity, or charity, or obedience to our Prioress. . . . Watch the movements of your tongue, and do not let it always follow those of your thoughts; regulate your time well, watch at night, after you have slept as much as you require, and in the morning go to church before occupying yourself in frivolous things. Do not change your rule of life too often; after dinner take a little time for recollection, and then occupy yourself in some manual work. At vesper time go where the Holy Spirit may call you, but be sure you return and take care of your old mother, and see she has all she requires, for that is your plain duty. From this time until I return, try to do as I say." Alexia often succeeded in getting Catherine to take up her abode for some time

together in her house,[1] and on one occasion the Saint spent an
entire winter with her. The way it came about was this. Alexia's
father-in-law, Francesco, an old man above eighty, was still living,
and made his home under her roof. For years he had neglected
his religious duties, and resisted every effort which his daughter-
in-law made to put the affairs of his soul in better order. At
last she bethought her that if she could secure that Catherine
should come and stay with her for some months, her conversation
during the long winter evenings might produce the desired result.
The Saint consented, but owned that the task was a difficult one.
At last, however, the hard heart was touched, and he said. "I
am determined to confess, but first of all I must tell you, that
I entertain such a hatred against the prior of a certain church
that I daily seek means of killing him." But Catherine said
such moving things to him on the subject that he finished by
exclaiming, "I am ready to do whatever you order me ; you
need only speak." So she said to him, "I wish that for the love
of our Lord Jesus Christ, and in order that He may pardon you,
you should forgive the prior and be reconciled with him." He
promised, and on the morrow, at dawn of day, he took a falcon
of which he was very fond, and went alone to the church where
the prior lived. The latter immediately fled ; but the old man
charged a canon to go and tell him that he did not come to
injure him, but on the contrary, to bring him good news. The
prior learning that he was alone and unarmed, first caused several
persons to come into his apartment and then permitted his visitor
to be introduced ; who bowed to him and said, "The grace of
God has touched my heart, and I am come to offer to be reconciled with you ; and to prove that I am sincere, I entreat you to
accept this falcon, of which I am extremely fond" Peace was
soon concluded, and the old man returned to Catherine "I

---

[1] Where was this house ? Some writers suppose Alexia to have occupied
a portion of the Saraceni Palace during the lifetime of her father-in-law. It
stands in the Via del Casato di Sotto, not far from the Piazza del Campo. It
was possibly from the windows of this palace that Catherine beheld the
criminals on their way to execution.

have obeyed your orders," said he, "and I will obey you again." The Saint told him to go and confess to Father Bartholomew. His general confession occupied three days, and when he had received absolution, his confessor was at a loss what penance to assign him, because he was very aged, and although noble was poor. So he gave him a trifling penance, and said, " Return to her who sent you, and what she gives you, I give also." Catherine bade him rise every morning at dawn for a certain period, and go in silence to the cathedral, reciting each time a hundred Paters and Aves, and gave him a cord with a hundred knots on which to reckon them. He accomplished the whole with fidelity, and after a few years spent in the exercise of religion and charity, made a peaceful end.

This story must not be confounded with that of the conversion of another of Alexia's relations, Nicolas Saraceni. This old knight resisting all his wife's exhortations that he would attend to the affairs of his soul, she came as a last resource to Catherine and asked her prayers. Catherine promised not to forget him , and soon after appeared to Nicolas in his sleep, and desired him to give heed to his wife's counsel. Awaking in terror, he told the latter what had happened, and promised to go and talk with the holy virgin, who had no difficulty in sending him to confession. When he came from the church, she inquired if he had confessed all his sins. "Yes," he replied, "all that I could remember." On which she reminded him of one thing that had happened many years before in Apulia, which was known to no living man and which he himself had forgotten Filled with wonder he owned it to be true, and having finished his confession according to her direction, he was accustomed to tell the story to her honour, and say in the words of the Gospel, "Come and see one who told me all things that I have done . is not this a prophetess ? "[1]

Another of the Sisters was Cecca, or Francesca, the widow of

[1] On the margin of the MS. of the *Leggenda Minore* (translated by Stephen Maconi) is written this note . "I, brother Stephen, was not only familiarly acquainted with this Master Nicolas, but his wife was my near relation."

Clement Gori, of whom Raymund often speaks in the Legend, calling her Francesca of Gori. Her husband was of noble birth, and her three sons were Dominican Friars. They all died holy deaths before her, and as it would seem in the service of the plague-stricken. Her daughter Justina was a nun at Montepulciano. Alexia and Cecca frequently acted as Catherine's secretaries, and when they had finished writing what she dictated, they generally added some little message of their own, by which we are able to identify the writers. They were on specially familiar terms with F. Bartholomew Dominic of Siena, who held among them the place of a brother. So in the letters addressed to him on occasion of his frequent absences, there is often a playful and affectionate word from *Alexia grassotta*, or *Cecca pazza*. In one letter we read, "Alexia recommends herself to you a thousand times; she is astonished at not hearing from you. May God bring us where we shall all meet face to face!" And Alexia, who is acting as the scribe, adds from herself, "Alexia the negligent would very much like to put herself into this letter, that she might be able to pay you a visit." Of Lisa Colombini, Catherine's sister-in-law, we have elsewhere spoken. Through her, no doubt, it was that Catherine became so well known, both to other members of the Colombini family, and to those numerous Gesuati whom we learn from the Processus were to be found among her disciples. St. John Colombini, Lisa, Matthew, and the blessed Catherine Colombini were all four first-cousins, being children of four brothers. B. Catherine, who had been first converted to a holy life by the exhortation of St. John, her cousin, had a great love and devotion to our Saint, with whom she was on terms of intimate friendship. As she lay on her deathbed, we read that there appeared to her St. John Colombini, and St. Catherine of Siena, and recognising them with immense joy, she exclaimed, "O Blessed Catherine. O John, father of my soul, my sweetest patrons, I am coming to you!" and so expired.[1] Lisa had also a brother, who seems also to have been one of the Saint's disciples. In the same letter quoted above she says, "I send you this letter

[1] Fasti Senensi.

by the brother of her who is my sister-in-law[1] according to the flesh, but my sister in Christ." Of the other Mantellate, it will suffice to mention Giovanna Pazzi, a member of a branch of the noble Florentine family of that name, Jane di Capo, and a certain Catherine of the Hospital. It may illustrate the familiar and pleasant terms which existed among all these good Sisters, when we say that they not only gave each other nicknames, a habit from which no Italian could perhaps abstain, but at times were guilty of something very like a pun, so that Giovanna's family name is occasionally transformed from Giovanna *Pazzi* to Giovanna *pazza*, that is, mad or foolish Jane.

From the sisters let us now turn to the brethren of this happy society, three of whom have already been frequently mentioned. And first we must glance at the holy, though unlearned F. Thomas della Fonte, who acted as Catherine's chief confidant and director from her childhood until the year 1374, when in his simple humility he resigned his charge into the hands of Raymund of Capua, making over to his keeping all the notes which during fifteen years he had kept regarding his holy penitent. They filled four closely-written quires, and are among the chief materials from which Raymund afterwards composed the Legend; but with the exception of a few pages which have been embodied in the *Leggenda Minore*, no fragment of the original work has been preserved.[2] F. Thomas Antonio de Nacci Caffarini was, next to him, the oldest of Catherine's Dominican friends. Unlike his namesake he was a man of considerable learning, and seems to have assisted the Saint in her studies of the Sacred Scriptures. So we gather from one of his letters addressed to Catherine which has been preserved, and in which he replies to her inquiries as to the right reading of the 130th Psalm.[3] For ten

---

[1] *Mia cognata secondo la carne, mia sorella secondo Christo*, Letter 209 M. Cartier has a mistranslation of this passage, rendering *cognata* as *cousine*, but Lisa was not cousin, but sister-in-law to Catherine, as the word really means.

[2] According to Echard and Quetif (Script. Ord. Præd., tom. 1 696), this work bore the title of *Singularia et mira Sanctæ Catherinæ Senensis*.

[3] *Lettere dei discepoli di S. Cath.*, No 1.

continuous years he enjoyed her society and confidence, and during that time often acted as her confessor. Hence he became acquainted with many secrets of her interior life, which he has preserved in the Supplement to the Legend, so often quoted in the foregoing pages. But the one who has left us the most life-like portrait of the holy virgin is undoubtedly Father Bartholomew Dominic, or, as he is commonly called, Bartholomew of Siena He also frequently acted as her confessor, and seems to have lost no opportunity of searching and examining her spirit. Sometimes when she bitterly reproached herself with faults which none but her own eyes could detect, or charged herself with being the cause of all the evils that happened in the world, he either was, or feigned himself to be, incredulous of her sincerity. "How can you say such things sincerely," he asked, "when it is plain you have a great horror of sin?" "Ah, father," she would sorrowfully reply, "I see you do not know my misery. The most contemptible wretch on earth that had received the graces I have received would be on fire with the love of God. She would spread such fervour abroad by her words and example that men would everywhere leave off sinning. But I who have received so much, I am only a cause of ruin to those whom I ought to save, and so I am doubtless most guilty before God." He testifies to her wonderful love of suffering, and describes her as fastened to the Cross by three distinct kinds of torture, in her head, breast, and side. Yet never could he detect a shade of melancholy on her placid and smiling countenance, and if others pitied her she would not merely be cheerful, but gay. He also testifies to her wonderful prophetic spirit. Father Thomas della Fonte and he determined one day they would put her to the test on this point. Going together to her chamber, therefore, they desired her to tell them what they had been doing at two and three o'clock that morning. She replied evasively, "Who knows better than yourself?" Her confessor said, "I command you to tell, if you know, what we were doing at that time." She was obliged to obey, and humbly bowing her head, she replied, "You were four together in the cell of the sub-prior, and there you conversed together a long time" She named all who were present and the subject on which they had spoken. Father Bartholomew was amazed, but he thought she might know from some of the persons present, so he determined to try her again. On the morrow he went to her, and said, "Then you know, Mother, what we do?" She answered, "My son, know that my Divine Saviour, having given me a spiritual family, leaves me in ignorance of nothing that concerns them." "You know, then, what I was doing yesterday evening at such an hour?" "Without doubt," she answered, "you were writing on a certain subject. My son, I watch and pray for you continually until I hear the matin bell of your convent. I see all that you do, and if you had good eyes, you would behold me as I do you."[1] He experienced also on another occasion this power which Catherine had of knowing what was passing at a distance. Being sent at one time to Florence to discharge the office of Lector he was attacked by scruples on the subject of a supposed irregularity in his ordination, which gave him such trouble that he left off saying Mass. One day being in the church of Santa Maria Novella, he was revolving these things in his mind in bitter grief, and thinking how Catherine would surely comfort and give him light could he but see and speak with her, he called on her to help him in his anguish as though she could actually hear him At that very moment Catherine, who was praying in the church at Siena, was observed by her Sisters to give signs of extraordinary emotion. When they came away her companions asked for an explanation "My son Bartholomew, at Florence," she said, "was at that moment being tormented by the enemy." She had prayed earnestly for him, and at the same time Bartholomew was unexpectedly summoned to the presence of the Bishop, who, inquiring the cause of his trouble, was able to dissipate it in a few words. Another incident somewhat similar in its character to the one just narrated is related by Raymund of Capua. It

---

[1] Caffarini in his Supplement tells this story a little differently, and adds that the matter on which the two religious were engaged was the registering of her own miraculous favours.

happened during his residence at Montepulciano, "where,"
he says, "as there was no convent of Friars, and I had with me
but one companion, I was often glad to receive visits from the
religious of neighbouring places. It happened once that Father
Thomas della Fonte, Catherine's confessor, and Father George
Naddi, professor of theology, proposed coming to see me from
the convent of Siena, in order to converse and consult with me.
In order to travel more quickly they took some horses which
were lent them by their friends. Arrived within about six miles
of Montepulciano, which is situated among the mountains, they
imprudently halted to rest themselves, when some of the people
of the place, perceiving the two travellers alone and unarmed,
resolved on waylaying and robbing them. Going on before,
therefore, to the number of ten or twelve, they awaited the arrival
of the luckless friars in a solitary place. As they approached,
the robbers rushed out of their ambush, dragged them from their
horses, stripped them of their clothes and everything which they
carried, and then led them into the depth of the forest, where
they held council whether it would not be best to kill them and
conceal their bodies, so as to leave no trace of their crime.

"F. Thomas seeing his danger, was lavish of his entreaties and
promises to observe silence, but without effect; and when he saw
that the robbers were leading them further and further into the
entangled forest, he comprehended that God alone could succour
them, and began to pray. Knowing how agreeable his spiritual
daughter was to God, he said interiorly : "O Catherine, servant
of God, help us in this peril." Scarcely had he uttered these
words in his heart, than the robber nearest him, who appeared to
be charged to kill him, said: "Why should we kill these poor
friars who never did us any injury? it would be indeed an
enormous crime ! let us suffer them to go ; they are good-hearted
men, who will never betray us " All accepted this opinion so suddenly advanced with such unanimity, that not only they allowed
the religious their lives, but even restored to them their garments,
horses, and all that they had stolen, except a little money, and
suffered them to go at liberty · they arrived at my house on the

same day, and related all these circumstances. When Friar
Thomas returned to Siena he certified, as he wrote to me, that at the
same moment in which he had invoked her assistance, Catherine
said to one of her nearest companions . " Father Thomas is calling
me, he is in great danger," and rising immediately she went to
pray in her oratory.   It cannot be doubted that it was at that
moment by the efficacy of her prayers that a change so wonderful was produced in the dispositions of the robbers, which she
could only have known in the spirit of prophecy, being then at a
distance of four and twenty miles.[1]

It often happened that Bartholomew was called away from
Siena either to fill the office of Lector, as at Florence, or to
preach in the surrounding towns and country districts. Five of
Catherine's letters to him were written whilst he was giving what
we should now call a mission at Asciano, near Siena, in which
she took a peculiar interest, sending some of her other spiritual
sons to help him in his work.   He was also Lector at Pisa for
some time, and during his stay in these places helped to spread
abroad her fame.

Good Master Matthew, the rector of the *Misericordia*, has
already been made known to the reader, but a few particulars
must be added touching the manner of his first introduction to
Catherine.   He and his friend, Francis Lando, went once to see
her in ecstasy, as others were accustomed to do when they could
obtain permission from her confessor.   It was a visit of pure curiosity, and as she was quite abstracted during the whole time, they
did not hear her speak a single word.   But the spectacle so powerfully impressed them, and such a devotion filled their hearts, that
they felt like new men.   Coming away, they said one to another :
" What is this ?   If only to see her once, without her saying one
word, thus moves us to compunction, what might we not hope for
if she admitted us to the number of her spiritual children ! "   They
therefore returned with a far more serious purpose ; and when
they had once listened to her prudent words, and saw the sweet
courtesy of her manners, yielding to the charm which none could

---

[1] Legend, Part 2, ch. ix.

resist, they gave themselves to her as to their mistress and Mother.

Next on our list of Catherine's disciples comes one different in character and position from any yet named, Neri di Landoccio dei Paglieresi, a man of good family, well skilled in letters, and a writer of graceful verses, which have earned for him no mean repute. We know neither the time nor the occasion of his first introduction to Catherine, but it seems to have been about the year 1370. When once she had accepted him as her disciple, he never separated from her, but accompanied her on all her journeys, and was the first of the three noble youths who acted as her secretaries. He had the true poetic temperament, a gift of doubtful value to its possessor, and which in his case was linked with much sorrow. "The lover, the poet, and the madman," says Shakespeare, "are of imagination all compact;" and Neri during one brief period in his life knew what it was for a tortured imagination to overmaster reason. Sensitive in the extreme, and ever trembling on the verge of religious despondency, Catherine had to be always lifting him out of his natural tendency to sadness and discouragement, and infusing into him her own strong and high-hearted hope. We have her first letter to him, written on one of the occasions when F. Bartholomew Dominic was preaching at Asciano, whither Neri had accompanied him and was assisting him in his work. It was in the early days of his friendship with Catherine, and in reply to his request to be received among her disciples, she wrote as follows : " You ask me to receive you as my son ; I am unworthy to do so, for I am only a poor sinner ; yet I both have received you, and will do so with all affection. I promise to answer for you before God for any faults you may have committed, only, I conjure you, satisfy my desires ; conform yourself to Christ crucified, and separate yourself utterly from the world." [1]

In another letter, written a little later, she tries to calm the troubles of his conscience. Neri's habitual mental trial was this ; that he could not realise that God had forgiven him his sins.

[1] Sup., Part 2, Trat. 1, § 3

" Let the trouble of your soul (she says) be destroyed in the hope of the Blood. True self-knowledge by humbling you will increase light. Is not God more ready to pardon than we to offend ? Is He not our Physician, and are not we His sick children ? Has He not borne our iniquities, and is not sadness the worst of all our faults ? Yes, it assuredly is so, my dear son. Open your eyes then to the light of faith. See how much you are beloved of God, and beholding His love, do not be troubled because you likewise see the ignorance and coldness of your own heart, but let self-knowledge only increase your humility and kindle your love. The more you see how badly you correspond to the great graces bestowed on you by your Creator, the more you will humble yourself, saying, with holy resolution, ' That which hitherto I have failed to do, I will do now.' Remember that discouragement will make you entirely forget the teaching that has been given you ; it is a leprosy which dries up alike both soul and body. It chains the arms of holy desire, and prevents our doing what we would ; it renders the soul insupportable to itself and agitates it with a thousand phantoms It takes away all light, natural and supernatural, and so the soul falls into a thousand infidelities, not knowing the end for which God created her; *that He created her, namely, to give her life eternal !* Courage, then, and let a lively faith and firm hope in the precious Blood triumph over the demon who would trouble you " (Letter 274).

This beautiful letter contains the sum of all Catherine's instructions to this holy, but much tried soul. He proved himself worthy to be her son; yet, as we shall see, even to the end the same dark shadow dogged his footsteps and caused him a lifelong martyrdom. Neri had a great talent for friendship, and succeeded in bringing not a few of his friends to join the number of Catherine's disciples. Among these was Gabriel di Davino Piccolomini, a married man, whose son Giovanni at the instance of the Saint took the Dominican habit. Gabriel belonged to that noble family of Siena whose boast it is to have given to the Church four cardinals, fourteen archbishops, twenty-one bishops, and two popes, of whom one was destined to pronounce the canonisation of St. Catherine. No less illustrious in the career of arms, the family records are full of the great deeds of those warlike Piccolomini who headed the armies of the republic as well as those of foreign states. Gabriel shared this military spirit, and his chivalrous character longed for the proclamation of another crusade that he might take the Cross and strike a blow for Christendom. Herein was his great bond of sympathy with Catherine, whose heart responded to any note of true generous enthusiasm, and who would gladly have armed all her spiritual sons and sent them to fight against the infidels. When she wrote to Gabriel, therefore, she clothed her spiritual exhortations in military language, and spoke to him of arms and the battlefield, of courage and the love of glory. She told him to strike hard at his spiritual enemies with the sword of patience, to put on the cuirass of true charity, blazoned with the vermilion coat of arms of Jesus crucified. "I speak to you of these arms," she says, "that you may be the better ready when the standard of the Holy Cross is raised. I want to make you understand which are the best weapons; begin to make use of them now when you are still among Christians, that they may not be rusty when you march against the infidels"

Gabriel's brave honest nature made him embrace the cause of Catherine as a true champion : he opposed himself with loyal fidelity to all calumnies raised against her, and to use the language of the Process, "could not abide any who were wont to speak against the holy virgin." He led a most holy life, and was present on many occasions when the extraordinary powers of the Saint over the bodies and souls of men were most strikingly manifested. He was buried in the church of San Domenico "*sub picturis B Katerinœ de Senis,*" as though to mark his fidelity to her, even until death.

Another of Neri's friends has left the history of his first acquaintance with Catherine written by his own hand, and his testimony regarding her is perhaps one of the most valuable of any that has been preserved. This was Don Francesco Malevolti, who, like Gabriel, belonged to one of the noblest stocks of Siena. He describes himself at the age of twenty-five as being "hot-tempered and audacious on account of his family and nation," and was living a worldly life, intolerant of any kind of restraint. "Among the companions whom I loved the best," he says, " there was one noble youth of Siena, named Neri Landoccio dei Paglieresi, with whom I spent the greater part of my time, both because he was virtuous and agreeable, and also because he was a composer of most beautiful verses, in which kind of thing I then greatly delighted. After we had been intimate for some time, Neri having heard of the fame of the glorious virgin Catherine, went to see her without my knowing it, and so had become greatly changed, and, as it were, a new man. And pitying me on account of the dissolute life I was leading, for he loved my soul more than my body, he often begged me to go with him and speak to her. I gave little heed to his words, however, only laughing at them, and so some time passed without my granting his request. At last, not wishing to vex him, because of the singular friendship that united us, I told him one day that I was willing to gratify him; though in my secret soul I went out of no kind of devotion, but rather in derision, resolved, if she spoke to me on the subject of religion, and particularly of confession, to give her such an answer that she would not venture to speak to me again. But when we came into her gracious presence, I had no sooner beheld her face than there came upon me such an awful fear and trembling that I almost fainted; and though, as I have said, I had not the least thought or intention of confession, yet at the first words she spoke, God so marvellously changed my heart that I went at once to confession and became the very opposite of what I had been before. After that I visited her several times, and left off all my miserable habits, and instead of frequenting as formerly places where there was singing and dancing, I now fled from them, and found my delight in visiting churches, and conversing with the servants of God. However, though I often went to her house and took great pleasure in her admirable doctrine, and speedily corrected

my vicious habits, yet being still weak, and not fully established
in the right way, it chanced once that I fell into a grievous fault,
which none but God however could possibly have known. The
next time I went to her house, before I had even come into her
presence, she sent for me, and dismissing all those who were
present, she made me sit down beside her and said, 'Tell me,
when were you last at confession?' I replied, 'Last Saturday,'
which was true, that being the custom with all of us who conversed with her. Then she said, 'Go to confession directly!'
I replied, 'Sweet Mother, to-morrow is Saturday, I will go then.'
But she only replied by saying, 'Go, and do as I bid you.' I
still pleaded for some delay and refused to go, when with her
face all bright and kindling, she said to me, 'How, my son, do
you think I have not my eyes always open upon my children?
You can neither do nor say anything of which I am ignorant.
And how can you suppose that to be hidden from me which you
have just been doing? Go then at once and wash yourself from
this misery.' Confused and full of shame I obeyed her commands at once; and this was not the only occasion when she
manifested to me not only my secret acts, but also my thoughts
both good and bad, and that always in very modest and humble
words

"Another time much later than this, after her return from Avignon, I had fallen back into something of my old way of life; and
going to see her, she received me like a kind and sweet mother
with a joyful countenance, which greatly encouraged my weakness.
But one of her companions who was with her complained somewhat of me, saying that I had very little stability. She only
smiled, however, and said, ' Never mind, my Sisters, for he cannot
escape out of my hands whatever way he may choose to take;
for when he will think that I am far enough away, I shall put such
a yoke on his neck that he will never be able to get out of it
again.' What this prophecy meant and the manner of its accomplishment will be seen in a future chapter.

Two of Francesco's worldly companions, Neri Urgughieri and

Nicholas Ughelli determined to present themselves to the Saint, and show themselves proof against her influence. But no sooner had they entered her presence than all their boldness vanished, and they found themselves unable to speak so much as a word. Catherine sweetly reproached them for the injurious language they had used against her. "Madam," they stammered, "you have but to command us, and we will do your bidding." At her desire they presented themselves to F. Thomas, aud made a confession of their whole lives.

Very different from these brave and accomplished gentlemen is the next of the little company for whom we must solicit the reader's indulgent patience. Ser Christofano di Galgano Guidini, or, as he is more commonly called, Christofano di Gano, has contrived to make himself better known to posterity than many men of more genius than he. In fact, genius he had none, and what happy fatality put the thought into his head of becoming an author can never now be known. He was a man of low birth, a plain notary and man of business, who lived in the world of matter of fact, and was equally insensible to the poetic as to the humorous. He had the fidelity and the plodding perseverance of a terrier dog, nothing ever turned him from his purpose. So the thought having once suggested itself to him of writing his memoirs, he carried it into effect as a grave and solemn duty. Never surely did a man sit down to such a task who had less to say about himself, and never has it chanced that memoirs so barren of interest on all points save one should have enjoyed the fame accorded to his. It is thus he introduces his work to his readers.

"In this book shall be written certain memoirs of me, Ser Christofano di Gano, notary of Siena, who live at Uvile,[1] in the Popolo di San Pietro, of my doings And because it is only lately that I began to write my memoirs, they will not be very long. To which memoirs, written by my hand, entire faith may be given, by reason that they are true, as is everything contained

[1] The Porta Ovile, on the north-west extremity of Siena.

in this book ; and to make them of greater faith, I have set to them
by sign—

Jesu,
my sign.

Christofano,
the aforesaid
notary.

In the name of God, Amen.

"Memoirs of certain of my doings, done by me, Ser Christofano di Gano di Guidini, notary of Siena, who am now living at
Uvile, in the house which belonged to Abra di Cione Barocci,
who bought it of Chimento di Niccolo. This book and these
memoirs I have written with my own hand in memory of my
doings. However, as I have said above, it is only a short time
ago that I began to write and keep memoirs of my doings, and I
have not written them all, as many do, but only a part. And
first, it will be manifest to any one who sees this writing that I,
Ser Christofano di Gano aforesaid, am of low extraction." He
then proceeds to relate his early history: how his father married
his mother, who had a hundred florins for her dowry, which was
never paid , how his father died of the plague in 1348, after
getting into debt and leaving nothing behind him ; and Christofano at the age of two was left to his mother's care and in great
poverty. They went to live at Rugomagno with her father,
Manno Piccolomini, who did his best for the boy, had him taught
"Donatus," that is his Latin grammar, and got him placed as
"repeater" [1] to the children of Ristoro Gallerani. In this
employment he got six florins a year and his expenses, and was
able meanwhile to learn the notary's business. So he plodded
on, scraping together an education as well as he could, and
getting various small employments, till at last he came to live in
Siena and to have business at the Palazzo, and in short to get
on in the world, as a steady painstaking man of his calibre was

---

[1] That is, he helped the children to repeat their school lessons.

pretty sure of doing. We will now let him continue his own story.

"At the time when I began to live in Siena God put forth a new star in the world. This was the venerable Catherine, daughter to Monna Lapa of Fontebranda, a tertiary to whom I was introduced by Neri di Landoccio and Nigi di Doccio, two of her spiritual sons.[1] Both then and afterwards I heard things from her which it is not possible for a man to utter, and such as none who had not heard them would believe possible from a woman. Wherefore, listening to her holy teaching, I became pretty intimate with her, and so God touched my heart to despise the things of the world, and I had a mind rather to leave the world than to defile myself with it. But my mother, fearing I should choose some other state of life, began to beg me and to get others to beg me to marry. For her sake, then, I began to consent to take a wife, and among others that I thought of, there were three, the daughter of Francesco Ventura, and the one I now have, and another, whose name I do not at this moment remember

"Catherine was not then at Siena, with whom I could have taken counsel, and though things had gone some way, yet I would do nothing till I had written to her. She was then at Pisa; so I wrote to her, telling her how I had a conscience of leaving my mother, that my word was given too far to go back, and asking her to advise me which of the three I should take; how one had been married before, though her husband had not lived long, and other things I do not now remember. Catherine having received my letter replied to it, and out of reverence to her, and also because her reply contains some remarkable things, I will here give it. Outside was written, 'Given to Ser Christofano di Gano, notary of Siena,' and inside as follows."

He then gives the letter, which is printed at length in Gigli's Edition (No. 240) Catherine had believed him called to another

---

[1] With all his matter of fact, Christofano makes a rule of omitting all dates which would be of the least value. We do not therefore know in what year he made Catherine's acquaintance; it might have been at any time between 1368 and 1375

state of life, but seeing the line matters had taken, with her usual prudence she does not seek to argue with him, but only to confirm him in his good resolution, whatever state he might be led to enter. "Since it is so," she says, "I pray the Sovereign Truth to extend His holy hand over you, and to direct you in the state which may best please Him. In all states and in all your works fix your eye on Him, and seek His honour, and the salvation of His creatures. As to the choice of a wife, it is painful for me to have to occupy myself in this matter, which is more suitable to seculars. However, I cannot oppose your desire, and examining the conditions of the three you name, I find them all good. If you do not object to take the one who has been married before, do so, otherwise take the daughter of Francesco Ventura. I pray the Supreme Charity to shed on you both the plentitude of His grace."

"And now," continues Christofano, "before we say more of the holy spouse of Christ, Catherine, let us make here three tabernacles." We shall follow his example, and for the present quote no further from this singular biography, though we shall frequently be indebted to its notices of Catherine's disciples and friends ; we will only here observe that he does not seem to have taken either of the two ladies above spoken of, and after asking Catherine to choose his wife for him, he ended, quite naturally, by pleasing himself. We have presented our readers with a poet among St. Catherine's disciples; the little society could likewise reckon in its ranks a painter. The Vanni of Siena were a family of artists. Andrea Vanni was not perhaps the most illustrious of their number, nor was he so entirely devoted to his art as to neglect the career of a statesman. In fact, Catherine's acquaintance with him came about through his political connection with her brothers. In 1368 he was one of the leaders of the popular party, and took part in the revolution which resulted in the overthrow of the "Twelve." After that time he held office in the "Mount of the Riformatori" and attained the first post in the Government, being one of the "Defenders" in 1370, conjointly with the Saint's brother Bartolo. In 1373 he was Gonfalonier of

Justice, and in the same year went as ambassador to Pope Gregory XI. at Avignon, in company with two other Sienese of noble birth, to solicit the Pope's return to Rome. In 1376 he was Rector of what was called the "Opera del Duomo," a sort of standing committee for finishing the Cathedral of Siena; for which office his knowledge of art rendered him much better fitted than for political life. At last in 1379 we find him Captain of the people, holding that dignity for the two months of September and October. This was a post of much dignity and importance and could not be held by a foreigner. The Capitano was in fact at the head of the magistrates in time of peace, while in time of war it was his duty to guard the *Carroccio*, or great car on which the standard of the republic was borne to battle; and in his red toga, red cap, red shoes, and red stockings, with golden cords and other ornaments, he made no little display before the eyes of the people.

Some of Andrea Vanni's despatches have been preserved, which do not impress us with much idea of his powers as a man of the pen. One of them is written under the pressure of money difficulties, which he complains of bitterly, inasmuch as he affirms he has made sacrifices for his country and neglected his shop and his business to attend to the affairs of the Commune. He was a great friend of Christofano di Gano, for whom he is believed to have painted a portrait of Catherine which has not been preserved. One of her letters is addressed to him when Captain of the people. Another is written to him whilst holding some other office during the season of Advent, probably the months of November and December. Neither of the letters have anything very special in them, and they are chiefly directed to reminding Vanni to go to his duties like a good Christian at least once a year. She also exhorts him to be a just magistrate, and in her Advent letter asks him to make it a sweet Advent by keeping the coming feast of Christmas close to the crib of the humble Lamb. "There you will find Mary, the poor traveller, adoring her Son: she has no riches, nothing suitable in which to wrap Him, no fire by which to warm Him, the Divine Fire; only the

HEAD OF ST. CATHERINE OF SIENA.

From the Painting by Andrea Vanni.

beasts who bend over His little Body and warm Him with their breath." Is it fanciful to suppose that Catherine, as she wrote these words, did not forget that she was addressing a *painter* (indeed, she addresses her letter "To Master Andrea Vanni, *painter*"), and that she drew her picture of the crib of Bethlehem as it would commend itself to his artist's eye?

Some of Vanni's pictures are yet to be seen at St. Francesco *fuori dell' Ovile*, and elsewhere   His fame, however, chiefly rests (at any rate to the lovers of St. Catherine) on that portrait of the Saint, attributed to his pencil, which is still to be seen in the Church of San Domenico.   It was painted as far back as 1367, as appears from the inscription on the spot.   In 1667 it was taken from the wall it originally occupied, and transferred to its present position.   It was before this picture that the Blessed John Dominic received a favour, the account of which he gives in his letter to his mother, Paola.   Having asked to be received into the Order of Preachers when seventeen years of age, he was on the point of being rejected in consequence of an impediment in his speech which seemed to make him useless to their community. However, he overcame them by his prayers, and being at Siena and feeling a great wish to preach, he suffered much on account of his incapacity, to remedy which he twice had an operation performed on his tongue, but without success.   One day, however, being in the church, he prayed earnestly before this portrait of the Saint that she would obtain from her Divine Spouse that his tongue might be loosed, that so he might announce the Word of God.   His prayer was granted, and he lived to become one of the greatest preachers of his Order.

Many copies, good and bad, have been made of this picture, and it is the original from which almost all the engravings have been taken which profess to be the portraits of St. Catherine.   It is much injured by time, and has evidently been retouched, for on the extended hand of the Saint there now appears the sacred stigma.   This could not certainly have been represented by Vanni in 1367, nine years before that mysterious favour was granted to the Saint.   However, the outline and general character of the figure and features are undoubtedly genuine. She is represented in abstraction of mind, in which unconscious state a devout disciple kneels and reverently kisses her hand, a circumstance which often actually took place, and gave rise to many murmurs.

We will pass briefly over the names of some other of Catherine's devoted followers, such as Anastagio di Monte Altino, who wrote her life in verse, Jacomo del Pecora, the knight of Montepulciano, who wrote two poems on her, and after becoming acquainted with her gave up all he possessed, and followed her as a disciple, and Peter Ventura Dei Borgognoni, who was brought to Catherine by his sister, that she might say something to the profit of his soul, and who was thoroughly gained at his first interview. For Catherine asking him how long it was since he had been to confession, he replied, "A few days ago." "Not so," she said, "it is seven years since you have been." Then she reminded him of all the chief sins of his life, and sent him at once to wash them away in the Sacrament of Penance. A somewhat more particular notice is claimed by the good hermit, Fra Santi, a native of Teramo in the Abruzzi, and a friend of many saints, among others of St. John Colombini, and B. Peter Petroni. "He was holy by name and by life," says F. Raymund, "and having quitted his parents and country for God's sake, had settled in Siena, where for more than thirty years he led a solitary life, never speaking of himself, and following the direction of holy and pious religious. In his old age he found the precious pearl of the Gospel, our blessed Catherine. For her sake he gave up the quiet of his cell and the manner of life he had been so long used to in order to labour for others; and he constantly affirmed that he found more peace and profit to his soul in following and listening to her than he had ever found in solitude. He suffered from a disease in the heart, and the Saint taught him to bear his continual sufferings not only with resignation, but even with joy." It is not to be supposed by this account that Fra Santi abandoned his hermitage, though he often quitted it to accompany Catherine on her journeys. On the contrary, his cell had more than once the privilege of affording her a place of quiet retreat. In company with some of her religious Sisters she would often visit the holy old man in his hermitage, finding in his little oratory a welcome change from the noise and bustle of the city. It is remarkable that Catherine had a great love for hermits, and numbered several among her disciples. There were an extraordinary number of hermits in the Sienese territory, all of them, as Father Thomas Angiolini tells us, supported at the expense of the Republic. And as by far the most distinguished of these was a countryman of our own, whom we desire to make well known to English readers, we will not omit mention of him in this place, but in consideration of the interest which attaches to his name will give him and his companions a chapter to themselves.

CHAPTER XII.

THE HERMITS OF LECCETO.

ABOUT three miles from Siena are still to be seen the remains
of the monastery of Lecceto, a venerable sanctuary which
derives its origin from a few hermits who fled from persecution
in the fourth century, and being found here by St. Augustine as
he passed through these parts, received their rule from him about
the year 391. Landucci, the Augustinian chronicler, claims them
therefore as the true founders of the " Hermits of St. Augustine."
Their retreat was a thick wood of oaks (*Sylva Ilicitana*), whence
the name of Lecceto is derived. It was called by many titles, all
indicative of its sylvan solitude, as "The Shady Hermitage,"
"The Hermitage of the Wood;" while attached to it, at a little
distance, was another retreat known as "The Hermitage of the
Lake." It was in old time a woody wilderness, so overgrown
with bushes that they were only cleared with immense labour.
In St. Catherine's days the great oak forest still offered the charms
of solitary retreat to the good hermits, among whom she counted
not a few of her most devoted disciples. One of these was the
prior, Master John Tantucci, a member of the noble family of that
name settled in Siena. He was commonly called John III., as
being the third prior of that name who had governed the convent.
He was a man of genius and learning and had finished his theological course at the University of Cambridge,[1] where he graduated

[1] Father Ambrose Ansano Tantucci, O P., of the same family, who, in 1754,
edited the *Supplimento* of Caffarini, has gone sadly astray in his English
names, and tells us that John III was Doctor in the "then famous university
of *Cantonberi*" (!) Burlamacchi, a little happier, but not entirely accurate,
and possibly victimised by a printer's error, calls it "*Cambudge*" From
other authorities. however. we know that he graduated at Cambridge.

as Doctor. The manner in which this "great learned Doctor"
(as Father Fen calls him) first became known to Catherine is remarkable; and as this story has been admirably told by Francesco
Malevolti, it shall here be quoted at some length. The precise
date at which the events he relates took place is not given; but
they must belong either to 1373, or the year following. "There
were," he says, "at that time in the city of Siena two religious,
very influential and of great renown. One was called Brother
Gabriel of Volterra, of the Order of Friars Minors, Master of
Sacred Theology, of whom it was said that there was no man in
the whole Order so mighty for learning and preaching as he was;
and who was at that time Minister Provincial The other was
called John III., also a Master of Sacred Theology; he was of
Siena, of the order of Augustinian Hermits. These two powerful
masters used sometimes, when speaking together, to murmur
against the blessed Catherine, saying, 'This ignorant woman goes
about seducing persons with her false expositions of Holy Scripture, and is leading other souls along with her own to hell; but
we shall take such order in the matter that she shall see her error.'
So after many conversations of this sort they resolved to go both
together on a certain day, and with difficult theological questions
to shut up her mouth and put her to shame. But the Holy Spirit
who spoke by that holy virgin took care to dispose things otherwise. When the appointed day came, they went with their companions to Catherine's house. Now it so happened that when
they arrived, our Lord so disposing it, many persons of both sexes
were at the moment with her, having come together to listen to
her holy words. There was Brother Thomas della Fonte, and a
certain Brother Matthew Tolomei of the same Order, and Nicholas
Mimi, a great servant of God, and Thomas Guelfaccio, a Gesuat,
all men of good report. and Neri Landoccio, already named, and
Gabriel Piccolomini, and many others whom I cannot remember.
Likewise Donna'Alexia, Donna Lisa, and Donna Cecca of Clement,
and others, all Sisters of Penance; I also, though unworthy, was
among the rest. And as we stood there listening to the admirable
words of that holy virgin, she suddenly broke off her discourse,

and becoming as it were all on fire, with her face quite resplendent, she lifted her eyes to heaven, and said, 'Blessed be Thou, O sweet and Eternal Spouse, who findest out so many new ways by which Thou leadest souls unto Thyself!' We all stood amazed and attentive, observing her words and gestures, and Father Thomas, her confessor, said to her, 'Tell me, daughter, what does all this mean that you have just said? Let us understand something about it.' Then like an obedient daughter she replied, 'Father, you will presently see two great fishes caught in the nets.' She said no more, and we were standing in great surprise awaiting what would come next, when lo! one of the companions of the virgin who lived in the house with her came in, and said to her: 'Mother, Master Gabriel of Volterra of the Friars Minors, with a companion, and Master John III., of the brethren of St. Augustine, with a companion, are below, and wish to see you.' She went at once to meet them, and behold, they themselves came up and entered the room where we were. When therefore Catherine had shown them great respect and made them sit down, and the rest of us stood near (as they said they did not wish to speak to her in private) these two masters, like raging lions, full of the purpose they had conceived, began to put forth the most difficult theological questions to that meek and tender virgin, thinking to find her defenceless and forsaken by her most sweet Spouse. So when Master Gabriel had said what he thought good, the same was repeated by Master John, who added another most difficult question, both intentionally perplexing the matter, believing that she would remain quite vanquished, so that they might afterwards have occasion of giving vent to their malice and ill-will. But the Holy Spirit, who forsaketh not those who put their trust in Him, gave his handmaid such wisdom and strength that she would have been able to have overthrown, not these two only, but ten thousand such as they, had they been there. And so when these masters had proposed their questions, she stood for awhile with her eyes lifted up to heaven, they meantime awaiting her reply. At last with her countenance all beaming with Divine zeal she turned to them; and though she bore herself towards them with great reverence, yet she broke out in words to this effect: 'Oh! confounded, confounded, be this inflated science of yours, which does yourselves so much harm and to others so little good whilst you use it as you do! What does such a saint say in such a place, and such a one, and such a one?' And thus she continued bringing forth many examples to them. At last she concluded, saying, 'How can *you* understand these things? *you* who only seek after the husk of truth that you may please creatures and win praise from them? and on this only have you set your hearts, but, my Fathers, do so no more for the love of Jesus crucified.' Wonderful to relate, these two great pillars were forthwith cast to the earth; these two wolves became tender lambs, so immediately were they changed to the contrary of what they had been before. The first-named, Master Gabriel, had previously lived in such pomp that in his convent out of three cells he had made for himself one; and furnished it in such sumptuous style as would have been superfluous for a Cardinal. There was a fine bed with a canopy and curtains round about it, all of silk; and so many other precious things that reckoning with them the books, they were worth not less than a hundred ducats. But this man, touched by the Spirit of God at the words spoken to him by His handmaid, was suddenly stricken with such fear, that taking the keys from his girdle in the presence of us all, he cried out: 'Is there any one here who for the love of God will go and give away all that I have in my cell?' At once there rose up Nicolas Mimi and Thomas Guelfaccio, and taking the keys they asked him, 'What do you wish us to do?' And he answered, 'Go to my cell, and whatever you find there give away for the love of God, so that nothing may remain except my Breviary.' So they went, and perfectly fulfilled all he had charged them with, for they distributed the books among the other brethren who were students in the convent, and all the rest they gave to the poor, leaving nothing in the cell save what might suffice for one poor observant Brother. Master Gabriel himself, though he was Minister Provincial of the Order, went afterwards to the monastery of Santa Croce at Florence, where he lived in great fervour, and appointed himself to serve the brethren in their refectory at meal time, and exercised many other acts of humility.   Master John III. did as much, and even more ; for though he had not so much to distribute, yet he also only reserved to himself his Breviary ; and at once forsaking all the things of this world, and his hermitage also, he followed the holy virgin Catherine wherever she went, even as far as Avignon, and from thence to Rome and many other places even to the time of her departure.   And he was one of the three confessors deputed by the See Apostolic to hear the confessions of those who by the means of the said holy virgin should be brought to salutary penance."

Thus much for the conversion of John III., but he was not the only or the most illustrious disciple whom Catherine possessed in the hermitage of Lecceto.   Among the holy solitaries of that oak forest was Father William Flete, the English " Bachelor," as he was commonly called by the Saint and her companions "This excellent religious," says Caffarini, in the third part of his Supplement, " chancing to pass through Tuscany, had become enamoured of that beautiful desert ; and having obtained leave from his superiors, he determined there to abide with the sole thought of giving himself to the things of God, and not caring to pursue after the honour of the Doctorate or the advantages he might thereby attain."   In fact, he was as unlike to Master John in his natural tastes as could well be supposed, though they were probably fellow students at Cambridge.   The author of the *Miracoli* informs us that his devotion to Catherine began even before he had seen her, and that their acquaintance had in it something of a supernatural character.   " There is," he says, " in the Wood of the Lake, a hermitage of St. Augustine, about four miles from Siena, in which is an English brother, called ' The Bachelor.'   They call him ' The Bachelor of the Wood of the Lake,' and he has been there more than twelve years.   He is a man of great learning, and venerable for his holiness and love of solitude   He often lives in the caves which he has himself made in the most obscure and savage parts of the forest : and there he takes his books, flying from the conversation of men.   He goes as he likes from the church to the forest, and from the forest to the church. He is a man of wise counsel, the friend of God and of a most holy life, speaking little, and only when necessity requires. He has never seen Catherine, nor she him; but they know each other through the instinct of the Holy Spirit, so that they speak of each other with great reverence and respect." This account agrees with that of Christofano di Gano, who says that "he was a man of great penance, held in reverence by many people; that most of his time he abode in the forest, only returning to his convent in the evening, and that he never drank anything but vinegar and water."

Though F. William may not have known Catherine personally at this time, yet they probably corresponded. His determination not to leave his solitude without necessity prevented his going often to Siena, but in spite of his recluse habits he was a member of the Company of La Scala, and had had something to do with the conversion of Master Matthew, so that he could not have kept so absolutely in his caves as the above anonymous writer (whose accuracy is not always to be trusted) seems to have imagined. But if he could not come to visit Catherine, she was not prevented from visiting him. Lecceto, it must be remembered, was one of the holy places of Siena, visited as a sanctuary by Popes and Princes, and by many saints, among others by the holy Father, St. Dominic. Catherine, as we know from the Legend, was fond of making such pious pilgrimages, and on a certain feast of St. Paul, F. Thomas della Fonte, and F. Donato of Florence, who were going to Lecceto, came to her house and proposed that she should accompany them. Catherine who was just recovering from a prolonged ecstacy, which had lasted three days and three nights, was still so absorbed in the thought of the wonderful revelations she had received, that when the two friars tried to rouse her, saying, "We are going to visit the hermit who lives out in the country,[1] will you go with us?" she, hardly

[1] Leg., Part 2, ch. v. We know that the hermitage of Lecceto is here meant, for Raymund speaks of "a venerable religious of the *Order of Hermits*, who resided in the country."

conscious of what they said, answered "Yes." But no sooner had she uttered the word than the exquisite tenderness of her conscience reproached her with it as with a falsehood. Her grief restored her to perfect consciousness, and she mourned over the fault for as many days and nights as she had been in ecstacy.

Though Catherine did not accompany the brethren on this occasion, yet it is certain that she did visit Lecceto later, and that more than once. The wild beauty of the spot and the shadow of its mighty oaks had no less charms for her than for the English hermit, for Catherine had a true sense of natural beauty, as is apparent from a thousand passages in her writings She therefore often came to the Wood of the Lake; and when she did so she occupied a little room near the church, used as a chapel, where may still be seen her portrait, and over the door the following inscription · "*Siste hic, viator, et has ædes (erectas a B. Joanne Incontrio,*[1] *Anno* 1330) *ubi Seraphica Catherina Senensis Sponsum receptavit Christum, venerare memento*"

From the time of their first meeting, F. William became one of Catherine's most attached disciples ; she contrived to interest him in all her affairs, and he often acted as her confessor. It was in the January of 1376 that he wrote down from her dictation, and probably in the above-named chapel, that spiritual "Document" before alluded to, which throws much light on her interior life. There is no doubt, however, that if F. William had a fault, it was his excessive love of solitude, and Catherine did not fail to tell him of it. His continual absence from the convent and habit of abiding in the woods with his books gave trouble to his Prior. "I must tell you on the part of Our Lord," writes Catherine to him, "that you ought to say mass in the convent [2] more than once a week if the Prior wishes it · I would even say that you should celebrate there every day if that is his desire. You will not lose grace by sacrificing your consolations, you will

[1] A saint of Lecceto

[2] He generally said mass in one of the grotto chapels, of which there were many.

rather gain more in proportion as you give up your own will. If we would show our hunger for souls and our love of our neighbour, we must not be attached to consolations, we must listen to other people's troubles, and have compassion on those who are bound to us by the bonds of charity; it is a great fault if you do not do this. For example, I would have you show compassion for the troubles and difficulties of Brother Anthony, and not refuse to listen to him, and Anthony in like manner should listen to you. I beg of you to do this for Christ's sake, and mine; it is the way to keep up true charity between you: otherwise, you will give the enemy occasion to sow discord." Then she concludes with one of those touches so characteristic of her style; "I pray that you may be united *to the Divine Tree*, and transformed in Christ crucified." (Letter 128.) She did not forget that she was writing to one who would probably read her letter under the shadow of those mighty ilex trees he loved so well. Father William, however, stood in need of having the salutary lesson repeated more than once. In another letter (124) she reads him a very profitable lecture on the indiscretions into which even the most perfect souls may fall, such as half-killing themselves by excessive austerities, judging others who do not follow the same way as themselves, and liking to choose their own times, places, and modes of consolation. Such persons always say that they want consolation, not for their own sake, but to please God better, but she exposes the delusion and holds up before him another rule of perfection. "In truly perfect souls," she says, "self-will is dead, and in nothing do they see the will of man, but only that of God. Such souls have a fore-taste of life eternal. . . . But I do not see this perfection in you, and it makes me sad. God has given you great lights; He has called you first to abandon the world, secondly, to have a great love of penance, and thirdly, a desire for His honour. *Do not hinder your perfection by spiritual self-will.*" F. William took all her exhortations in good part, for he reverenced her as truly a saint. Christofano says that he held her in such respect that he would touch her very garments as though they were holy relics.

"He used often to say to us," says the same writer, "You none of you know her, the Pope himself might think it an honour to be one of her sons. Truly the Holy Ghost dwelleth in her!"

The testimony of one who had so many opportunities of knowing Catherine, and who enjoyed her most intimate confidence, is doubtless of the greatest value, and fortunately this testimony has been carefully preserved.   F. Tantucci, in his translation of the third part of Caffarini's *Supplimento*, observes that "after Catherine's death, F. William Flete drew up a compendious legend of the prodigious virtues of the Saint in the form of a sermon, or panegyric.   Our author (Caffarini) declares that both whilst living in Siena and also at Venice he had often seen this sermon, *but not being now to be found, we must suppose that from the scarcity of copies it has been lost.*"   This supposition is happily incorrect, for the *Sermo in reverentiam Beatæ Katherinæ de Senis* is one of the great treasures of the Communal Library of Siena, and an authentic copy of this precious manuscript is in the possession of the writer.   The original is in the handwriting of the fifteenth century, and is adorned with a miniature   The panegyric was composed in the year 1382, as is stated on the title-page,[1] thus disproving the statement of Tantucci and others, that F. Flete died in the same year with St. Catherine.   Had the good father ever seen the sermon he would have corrected his account of it in another point also, and would certainly not have called it a *compendious* legend.   Brevity was not the soul of F. William's wit; but we pardon his prolixity and disposition to illustrate the life and character of his beloved mother by copious quotations from every one of the books of Holy Scripture, for the sake of the genuine and original evidence which he renders to her sanctity, the more valuable as it was given many years before Raymund's Legend had seen the light.

In the first place, then, we discover from his own words the

---

[1] *Sermo in reverentiam Beatæ Katherinæ de Senis, compositus in Anno Domini* MCCCLXXXII, *per. magni Servum Dei Anglicum qui vocatus est frater Guglielmus de Anglia de Ord. Heremit S. Augustini.*—Cod. T. ii. 7, a. c, 17.

precise meaning of what Christofano di Gano tells us concerning his reverence for *her clothes.* "Not only the person, but the very garments of this holy virgin," he says, "gave out a most exquisite perfume ; and so did the things that she merely touched ; and we who were intimate with her were sensible of this fragrance which came forth from her clothes, like the sweet odour of a field which the Lord hath blessed. . . . How often have I seen her praying, prostrate with her face on the earth, for sinners, for the Church of God, for the sovereign Pontiff and all prelates, and for the reform of all the evils which afflicted the spouse of Christ ; and when she thus prayed she suffered incredible pains, a very agony in every part of her body. It was the same when she prayed in ecstasy, raised above the ground in the air, as we have many times beheld her. At such times she underwent a mysterious passion ; her bones seemed to crack and to be disjointed, and her heart to be torn and rent by the fervour of her supplications ; she would be bathed in so profuse a sweat that her Sisters were sometimes forced to change her clothes even more than once, whilst blood would flow from her mouth in the extremity of her suffering. If on coming to herself she perceived this, she would cover it with her foot, lest it should be observed by any one. These raptures were chiefly after Holy Communion, when often as we looked fixedly on her we beheld her face changed, now into the likeness of our Lord, now into that of an angel or seraph, which caused us no small terror. . . . And from these ecstasies Alexia and Lisa were forced generally to rouse her. Her life was doubtless a miracle, one long-continued martyrdom for the Church of God. What she suffered when she attempted to eat is known only to God ; and all this she endured for sinners, for whose salvation she would gladly have died, had it been needed, a hundred times a-day. Her thoughts were always intent on heaven, seeking how to draw other souls thither. Her heart, inflamed with the love of her Spouse, became transformed into the very likeness of the Object beloved. Some one once said to her, 'Mother, have you a home of your own?' To which she answered sweetly, 'Yes, I have a home ; it is in the wounded

Side of Christ crucified, my Spouse.' Another time I said to her, 'Mother, how can you live in such continued sufferings?' She glanced upwards, saying, 'I live, yet not I, but Jesus Christ liveth in me.' Wonderful were her labours for the Church and for souls. How many blasphemers, obstinate sinners grown old in vice, and those who had never named the name of God, or obeyed His Church, were by her means converted and brought to penance ! She despised no one, she rejected no one, not even the greatest sinners. She welcomed all who came to her, sometimes prostrating and kneeling to them, at other times pressing them to her heart. She suffered many to kiss her hand, she, the border of whose garments they were not worthy to touch Some in their pride and ignorant malice took offence at this, but indeed, she beheld the souls of those before her, and often took no note of their bodies. Many came to her from the most distant countries, and to all she was a star of consolation. No one in affliction ever went to her without receiving comfort. When she arrived in any place, the joy of the people was universal only to think that Catherine of Siena was present among them ; and when she left them they would ask for her blessing and rejoice to think that their country had been so honoured. Such was our mother, vituperated in life by evil tongues, even among the number of her familiar companions, worn out with labours and fatigues, pressed down by the burden of the Church which she bore upon her shoulders ! Woe to us, her children, unworthy of the name ! Woe to us, because we can no longer have recourse to that most sweet mother ! What teaching she would give us, how to live, and how to direct our souls ! She used to say, 'Let us begin afresh every day !' How she would warm the tepid and rouse the negligent, for to her every heart was open. Alas, we can no more run to her as we used to do, saying, 'Let us go, let us go and see our sweetest mother !' Never more shall we read those letters dictated by the Holy Spirit ; never more shall we be fed with the food of her familiar words, never never more ! O holy mother ! where is now that place in my own home of Lecceto where you used to feed your sons with the pasture of your words;

alas, alas! we were not worthy of your presence! we shall never see you more!"[1]

Such are some of the words in which F. William has left recorded his love for his holy mistress, and they need no comment. Among the other brethren of Lecceto who regarded themselves as her spiritual sons must be named, besides B. Anthony of Nizza, a certain F. Felix, of Massa, of the noble house of Tancredi, who is numbered among the Beati of Lecceto, and who accompanied the Saint on her journey to Avignon; and F. Jerome of Siena, to whom Catherine dictated a letter in ecstasy. This letter we shall quote on account of its singular beauty, both of teaching and language. If we are to gather from it any idea of the character of him to whom it was addressed, we should conclude that F. Jerome was a tender and loving soul, somewhat addicted to sadness and to a too sensitive affection towards his friends. Catherine seeks therefore to win him to an exclusive love of God, the only worthy object of our tenderness, in Whom, as she says, "nothing is wanting. Know then, my son Jerome," she continues, "we must be stripped of the love of self, and of the love of the world, and of all sadness; for sadness dries up the soul and hinders us from knowing the infinite goodness of God. For when a soul contemplates its Creator and His goodness it cannot help loving Him, and would rather die than do anything contrary to Him whom it loves. We love what He loves, and hate what He hates, because love makes us one with Himself. And this love and this desire inspire us with a *passion* for the Eternal Truth, so that we cannot love anything but Jesus crucified. Think how our Lord delivered Himself for us on the tree of the Cross, as though His love for us was an intoxication,

---

[1] The above passages do not in the original follow one another consecutively, but are scattered in various parts of the voluminous and verbose panegyric which fills seventy-two closely written pages. It has been a work of labour to sift the soil and extract the golden grains, which, when found, however, well repay the trouble expended on the search. I have also thrown in a few sentences extracted from F. Flete's letter to F. Raymund preserved in MS. in the same library. For a further account of our illustrious countryman and his writings, see Appendix B.

a folly ! *This* is the pasch I desire to eat with you Now, then, understand what I say. I know you love the creature only spiritually, in God. But sometimes from one cause or another, as you know very well, we love spiritually but find in this affection a pleasure and a joy, so that our less spiritual nature finds its part also. If you ask me how you can detect when this is, I reply, ' If you see that the person beloved fails you in anything, is no longer on the same terms with you, or seems to love another better than you, and if then you are chagrined and disturbed, and your own love grows less in consequence, *then be sure your affection is imperfect.* The Eternal Truth once said to one[1] of His servants, ' Daughter, act not as those who draw a vessel full of water out of a fountain, and drink from it when they have taken it out ; the vessel is soon emptied, and they do not see it. But you, when you fill the vessel of your soul, making of your affection only one thing with the love with which you love Me, you will not withdraw the vessel from Me, who am the true Fountain of living water ; but you will preserve in it the creature you love, as you keep the vessel in the fountain , and drinking from it there, it will never be emptied. And so neither you nor the creature you love will be ever empty, but you will always be filled with Divine grace, and so will never fall into trouble and regret. He who loves in this way when he sees one whom he loves change, and perhaps avoid him, does not trouble himself, for he loved his friend for God and not for himself, though indeed he may naturally feel a certain emotion when he sees himself separated from what he loves Such is the rule I would have you follow if you would be perfect, and may you ever abide in the sweet and holy love of God ! " (No. 132.)

Lecceto still exists much as it was in St. Catherine's time. A well, the waters of which she is said to have blessed and rendered drinkable, is still shown, with the ancient oak near the door of the church where the first hermits hung their bell. In the portico may still be seen the fine old paintings of heaven and hell, the works of mercy, and the Seven Sacraments, which date as far back

[1] Herself, of course.

as 1343, and are by a pupil of Ambrogio Lorenzetti. The place now belongs to the Seminary of Siena. Fifteen of the choral books of the brethren may be seen in the Communal Library of Siena, adorned with beautiful miniatures, which seem to indicate that the good hermits were lovers of art At St. Leonard's, or, the Hermitage of the Lake,[1] nothing now remains but the church, the convent having been wantonly destroyed in 1783 by the family who bought the place on the expulsion of the hermits. The church however was spared, and contains some precious frescoes; and under it is a cave or subterranean vault in which the blessed Agostino Novello is said to have lived for the greater part of his life, doing penance, and dying there in 1309. The spot was no doubt familiar enough to William Flete, who came to this place when he desired even more retirement than he could command at Lecceto. It is remarkable, however, that in spite of his efforts to bury himself in the wilderness and be hidden from the know-ledge of men, the fame of F. William's sanctity reached his native land, where he was held in great reverence, and his opinions on certain matters had its weight, as we shall see hereafter, even in the councils of the realm. He is said by Landucci to have foretold the apostacy of the English nation from the faith, and is numbered by him among the illustrious men of his Order.

These, then, were some of Catherine's disciples, for it would take us too long to enumerate them all. How dear they were to the Saint and she to them may be judged by their words and hers; she prayed for them continually, one by one and by name, and in her Dialogue she recommends them all to God in a touch-ing prayer: "O Lord," she says, "I pray for all those whom Thou hast given me, whom I love with a special love, and whom Thou

---

[1] The lake from which this hermitage derives its name received the waters of the Bruna, to keep which within their assigned bounds the Sienese con-structed a wall, the remains of which still exist The lake, however, burst its boundary and overflowed the country round, causing much loss of men and cattle. It was into this dangerous lake that Peter Ventura once rode his horse by accident, and was delivered, as he states in the Processus, by invoking St. Catherine. It is now dried up, and the land it occupied is brought into cultivation.

hast made one thing with me.   For they are my consolation, and for Thy sake I desire to see them running in the sweet and narrow way, dead to self-will and pure from all judgment and murmuring against their neighbour.   O sweetest Love! let not the enemy snatch any of them from my hands, but may all attain to Thee, O Eternal Father, to Thee who art their final end!"[1]   And she received an intimation that this prayer on behalf of her children was indeed granted.

[1] Dialogo, ch. viii.

CHAPTER XIII.

CATHERINE'S PORTRAIT.

WHO does not know the value which attaches to a genuine portrait? Could such be found of the saints we love the best, we feel that the silent study of their features would help to put us in communication with their souls, and that we should know and understand them better if we could but once set them before us in their living natural reality. It is often our misfortune that the very veneration which the saints inspire in their biographers, makes war on the fidelity with which their characters are transmitted to us; by which I do not mean (as the reader may well believe) to throw discredit on the miraculous facts which are delivered to us regarding them; but only that there is a way of presenting us with the extraordinary, which conceals from us the everyday reality; we learn something of the saint or the heroine at the sacrifice of knowing little or nothing of the woman. It is a vice which in its degree attaches to most biographies, in which the ordinary rule seems to hold good of regarding as a disrespect to the persons who are their subjects, anything which sets them on a level with ourselves, and displays them to us in their everyday aspect of flesh and blood. No greater error can surely be committed, and specially in treating of God's saints. The tie between them and their votaries is perhaps the sublimest form of friendship. We do not merely venerate, but we love them; and we desire to love, not abstractions, but realities. No fear that we shall venerate them less because we know them as they were; no fear that we can be the losers by becoming familiar with their countenances, the tone of their voice, their ordinary ways, gestures, and phrases; with their human infirmities, if such they had, or with a thousand things which may be trifles to an indifferent eye, but which to those who truly love reveal the character and the heart.

Willingly would we present our readers with the *Vera effigies* of our beloved Mother. That which stands as the frontispiece of this volume is probably the nearest approach which can now be given of a true portrait. Two likenesses exist of St. Catherine of Siena; one is the celebrated painting by Andrea di Vanni, which has already been spoken of; the other is the almost equally celebrated marble bust which claims to be the work of Jacobo della Quercia, and to have been carved by him from a cast taken after death. A careful comparison of these two portraits will show certain points of general resemblance. In both we observe the length of the nose, the great width of the head at the line of the eyes, and the distinctly cut chin. In both there are indications of a magnificent development of that portion of the head which rises above the eyebrows. In the profile of the bust we observe also that straight line from the top of the forehead to the extremity of the nose which gives a certain classic character to the features. Add the *attitude* of the head, gently but not extravagantly bent, the attitude at once of meekness and of thought, and you will recognise the general outlines which seem to have been faithfully reproduced by Francesco Vanni, the author of the engraving of which our frontispiece is a fac-simile. Gaze at it, dear reader, and bear in mind that she whom it represents was never for a moment free from a wearing bodily pain; you will detect in it something of the languor of suffering, and of that calm tranquillity which no provocation ever disturbed; but do not call it sad, for those eyes could have rested on you with unutterable tenderness, and those lips could always command a smile which carried joy and comfort into the hearts of those who beheld it. Raymund tells us that the beauty of Catherine was not excessive. But few persons when they think of the saints represent them as possessed of that kind of beauty which can be depicted by the brush or the chisel. We think of them with the light of faith beaming from their eyes, with purity on their smooth unruffled brows, and every feature sweetened by charity. We think of them as we think of our own mothers, who in the eyes and to the memory of their children are always beautiful; and we try to picture them as they were transfigured in moments of prayer and communion even before the eyes of men; a faint foreshadowing of that heavenly beauty which will rest on their countenances when we behold them standing in the eternal light.

Catherine always wore the habit of her Order, a white habit and veil, and a black mantle. In one of the narratives of her life she is represented as only wearing sandals on her feet. At her belt she carried her rosary, from which we have seen her breaking off the silver cross, to give it as an alms. It is a little singular to find that she always wore a ring, from which she also sometimes parted at the call of charity. It was a poor exterior enough, but scrupulously clean and neat, for in the matter of cleanliness, as in so many others, she resembled her father St. Dominic. Nor did the poverty of her dress conceal that air of majesty and power which made some say that they trembled when they gazed at her. Yet the pervading charm of her appearance was one which carried consolation into the saddest heart. "No one ever approached her," says Pius II. in the Bull of her Canonisation, "without departing from her wiser and better." And one of her disciples adds, "At her mere presence the temptations of the enemy disappeared; the sun in its meridian splendour does not more instantaneously scatter the darkness; . . . all the world recognised her as the image of the virtues, the perfect mirror of Christian purity. Never did I hear an idle word come forth from her lips, but she turned all things, even those most trifling, to our spiritual profit." [1]

Those of her disciples [2] who wrote their impressions of her in verse while she was yet living, have multiplied phrases which give us to understand how irresistible was her power over their hearts. "She draws souls as the magnet draws iron," they say, "always

[1] Stephen Maconi.
[2] Anastagio di Mont 'Altino and Jacomo del Pecora.

kind, always full of clemency.   She keeps her eyes turned
heavenwards, bathed in pious tears, while she is ready to pour
out her heart's blood at the call of charity. . . . She is ever
joyful and smiling, and counts her own sufferings as nothing,
though she has always the sharp knife in her side, yet she makes
light of it with her Spouse; and recreates herself cheerfully,
praying the while for those who have need of pardon. . . . From
the crown of her head to the sole of her feet, she is full of Christ,
and sings His glory day and night. . . . And when she names
the sweet name of Mary, she seems wholly united to her.   O
dearest, sweetest, most venerable Mother, I see thee at the foot
of the altar without so much as a drachm of life left in thee, yet
rising in thy spirit to venerate thy Lord, and with thy countenance
wholly transfigured!   It is surely a seraph that I look upon, dyed
in the Blood of the Lamb!". . .

In fact, there was an ever springing fountain of joy in
Catherine's heart which habitually found expression in her words
and countenance.   At times this joy could take the form of play-
fulness, and in the frank and happy intercourse which existed
between her and her spiritual children there was nothing of
restraint.   They gathered about her and gave her the tenderest
and most familiar titles; "*Nostra dolcissima mamma*" was the
ordinary name by which they addressed her.   However distant
she might be from them, she followed them with her heart, we
had almost said with her eyes, for all they did or thought lay
open to her gaze.   "Truly, Mother," said Stephen Maconi, "it
is a dangerous thing to be near you, for you find out all our
secrets"   "My son," she replied, "know that in the souls God
has confided to me, there is not so much as a speck or the
shadow of a fault which He does not show me."

She was never idle; when not engaged in prayer or in works
of charity for the souls and bodies of others, she was always to
be found either reading or working.   Burlamacchi bids us take
notice of the thimble that was in the bag of eggs, mentioned in
one of the anecdotes of her life, as a proof that she was accustomed to use her needle.   But we know as much from other

circumstances. She mended and patched the mantle of her clothing, and made the vestments and altar linen of her chapel. In fact, she was skilful in all a woman's best accomplishments; she could wash and cook, make bread, or tend the sick, with those same hands that were to be sealed with the mysterious Stigmas.

Judging from her letters we should say that her reading was extensive for the times in which she lived, for she quotes not only from the Holy Scriptures, but from the Fathers, and the Lives of the Saints, and her illustrations betray a varied knowledge which it is not necessary to regard as all derived from supernatural sources. Ignatius Cantu asserts that she was familiar with the poetry of Dante; nor would this have been in any way surprising, for Dante was popular reading in the fourteenth century, and we have distinct evidence that he was studied by some of her disciples.[1] Although, therefore, no passage in her writings affords any evidence of the fact, it is quite possible that she may have been acquainted with the works of the great Florentine, who had visited Siena, and learnt in that city the terrible tidings of his exile and disgrace. That Catherine herself had some claim to the title of a poet is more certain; her first written composition is declared by the best Italian critics to be in verse; and she possessed all the other gifts which ordinarily accompany poetic genius; a great sense of natural beauty, and the habit of seeing in exterior forms the symbols of Divine truths. Hence one of her disciples tells us that "she sought God in all that she saw. I remember" (he says) "how when she saw the flowers in the meadows, she would say to us, 'See how all these things speak to us of God! Do not those red flowers remind us of the rosy wounds of our Jesus?' And if she saw an ant-hill she would say, 'Those little creatures came forth from the mind of God. He took as much care in creating the insects and the flowers as in creating the angels!' And when we heard her speak thus, we neglected everything to listen to her, and often even forgot so much as to eat, neither

[1] " *Se mi po'ete mandare quello pezo di Dante che vi lassai, si me lo mandate.*"
—Letter from Gionta di Grazia to Neri Pagliaresi.

could we give a thought to our troubles or sufferings."[1]   Of her
love of flowers we have elsewhere spoken, and the singular skill
she displayed in their arrangement.   Some passages in her letters
could hardly have been written by any one who was not a lover
of flowers; nor must the reader think it too minute a criticism if
we say that the flowers which furnished her with her favourite
illustrations were no garden exotics, but the wild blossoms which
flourish so abundantly in the woods and meadows around Siena.[2]
Hear her describing our Lady as "the sweet field in which was
sown the seed of the Divine word.   In that sweet and blessed
field of Mary,[3] the Word made flesh was like the grain which is
ripened by the warm rays of the sun, and puts forth its flowers
and fruit, letting its husk fall to the earth.   It was so He did
when, warmed by the fire of Divine Charity, He cast the seed of
the Word into the field of Mary   O Blessed Mary !   It was you
who gave us the flower of our sweetest Jesus !   That flower
yielded its fruit on the Holy Cross, because there it was that we
received the gift of perfect life; and it left its husk on the earth,
even the will of the only Son of God, who desired nothing but
the honour of His Father and our salvation."[4]   But Catherine
had not only a sense of natural, but even of artistic beauty.   As
a citizen of Siena, it would have been hard for her not to have
inherited a taste which was as indigenous with the Sienese, as the
oaks and olives in their soil.   She had artists among her disciples,
and she lived exactly at the time when painting, sculpture, and
architecture were cultivated in their purest forms and their most
religious spirit.   From her infancy she had daily frequented the

[1] Letter of Stephen Maconi.

[2] "Under the shade of these woods may be found three kinds of the
anemone, the hellebore, lilies, geraniums, veronicas, and potentillas, also
eight species of orchis. . . Of the multiplicity of plants which are to be
found growing wild in the meadows, *not a few are the admiration of flower
fanciers.* . . . Some of the trees, natives of these parts, produce an odori-
ferous wood "—*Siena e il suo territorio,* 1862.

[3] *Ego flos campi.*—Cant. ii. 1.

[4] Letter 46.   The *husk,* in the original, *guscio.*   St. Bernard uses the
same expression, but applies it to the Blessed Sacrament, *cortex sacramenti.*
See Harphius, *Theol. mys. Lib.* 1, p. 2, chap. liv.

church which boasted and still boasts of possessing the greatest artistic treasure of Siena.[1] She was no stranger to the works then being actively carried on by the *Opera del Duomo*, and in her many visits to the hospital of La Scala[2] she must have seen the glorious cathedral growing under the hands of the workmen, directed as they were by the choicest artists of the age. A passage occurs in one of her letters to Nicolas d'Osimo in which we seem to behold her watching the builders at their work, and giving to all she saw a spiritual interpretation. "Is there anything better or sweeter for us," she says, "than to build the edifice of our soul? But to do so we must find the stone, and the architect, and the workman. Oh ! how good an architect is the Eternal Father ! in whom dwell the treasures of infinite wisdom He is *He who is*, and all things that are proceed from Him. . . . He has given His Son as the foundation-stone of our edifice, which is based on Him and cemented by His Blood. . . . Then the Father, considering all things in His wisdom, power, and goodness, *has made Himself the artist*, creating and building our souls in His own image and likeness. *The artist works by the power that is in him ; by his memory, in which are the forms of all that he desires to produce ; with his understanding which comprehends, and with the hand of his will which executes.* Now when we had lost grace by sin the Eternal Word came to unite Himself to our nature ; He made Himself the artist, and even the Stone of our soul, as St Paul says, ' The rock is Christ.' Yea, and He made Himself the workman also, and the builder of the edifice, for in His charity He has given us His life and His blood, as a builder mixes the lime and prepares the cement, so that nothing may be wanting. Let us rejoice then and give Him thanks that we have

[1] The celebrated painting of the Madonna, by Guido of Siena, which is in the Church of San Domenico, and which according to the inscription attached to it claims to have been painted in 1221, that is, nineteen years anterior to the birth of Cimabue ; a claim which, if established, would give to Siena the honour of founding a school of art earlier than that of Florence. Since the year 1859, however, critics have been found to question the real date of the inscription, and have so thrown doubt on this venerable tradition.

[2] The hospital occupies one side of the Piazza del Duomo.

so good an architect, so excellent a stone, and a workman who gives His own blood for the cement of our edifice, and makes it so firm and strong that neither hail, nor wind, nor tempest can overthrow it unless we give our consent." (Letter 40.)

This singular passage is certainly not a hastily written collection of far-fetched metaphors. When the Saint beheld the Eternal Father, as the Great Artist, creating our souls in His own image and likeness; and goes on to describe every human artist as drawing out of his memory the forms which he desires to produce, she evinced a comprehension of the real nature of art as exact as it is profound, and explains what we mean when, in a certain loose sense, we attribute to the true artist something of the creative faculty. He draws from within the ideas of those forms which he outwardly fashions; even as the Eternal Word, the First and Mighty Artist, possesses within Himself the archetypes of all created forms.

Catherine then, as we judge from this passage, was a lover of art, and understood its meaning. Of her musical taste, and of the traces it has left in her writings, we have elsewhere spoken. She had a sweet voice, that "excellent thing in woman," and often recreated herself with singing, and lastly, she had that most bewitching of gifts, a grace and facility in speaking, so that those who listened to her were never weary; but again and again declare in their depositions that they could have listened to her for ever.

We cannot now reproduce the charm of that eloquence which owed half its magic to the tones that uttered it, and the living energy from which it flowed. We have nothing but dead written pages which bear the same relation to the spoken word as does a lifeless picture to the living countenance which it portrays. Yet taking her letters in our hands and putting from us for the moment all thought of her supernatural gifts, we are overwhelmed both with the extraordinary beauty of her language, and the amazing compass of her mind. You rise from their perusal fresh and vigorous, as though you had been brought in contact with an intellect whose predominant features were its strong good sense, its absolute freedom from affectation, and a certain straightforward clearness, which is sometimes tinged with a sense of humour, a thing indeed inseparable from genius; and we hold it certain that apart from all supernatural illumination Catherine was a woman of true genius, and one not often surpassed. Her mysticism always has a daylight about it, and is expressed with such lucidity that after reading in the Dialogo her explanation of the different kinds of ecstasies, their whole phenomena appear to be rendered comprehensible even to the most ordinary intelligence. Then her mind was possessed of an exquisite skill in adaptation and an almost endless variety in its powers of illustration. I will not say that we never find her repeating herself, or that there is not a frequent recurrence of the same words, phrases, and reflections; but for all that, her style is never "cut and dried;" she does not write to a monk as to a man of the world, or to a noble lady as to one of her own sisters. She always remembers some little circumstance in the position or history or character of those whom she addresses, and introduces it with a happy grace. Thus in writing to the King of France, she does not forget his surname of "the Wise;" in addressing another prince, she remembers that he is a descendant of St. Louis; to the knight and the man of arms she can discourse of lances, spurs, and even of war-steeds, and to the man of science of mirrors and the stars.

Catherine had a true vein of enthusiasm in her; a noble word could fire her, and set her in a glow. Thus we understand the animation she displays whenever she names the holy war, and that ardent desire which she shared with St. Dominic of laying down her life for God. F. Bartholomew Dominic tells us that sometimes when they were speaking together, she would point to her white habit and exclaim, "Ah, how lovely it would be if it were dyed red with blood for the love of Jesus!" This enthusiasm was accompanied with a certain energy, almost vehemence, of expression when there was question of the offence of God. Her intense faith realised in so sensible a manner that the Church was the Body of Christ, and that the Pope was His Vicar, that those who set themselves to divide and contemn the

Church and its appointed Head were to her, by a rigorous logic, members of the evil one; and she expressed this by calling them "incarnate devils." So too, regarding priests, as by their office, earthly angels, she did not shrink from telling those who degraded their high dignity that they were not men, but demons. To appreciate such language aright we must measure it by the faith out of which it sprang, and if after so doing there still seem something of excess, this, it is to be presumed, is no more than to say that she was a real woman, and not a shadowless ideal. "She spoke the truth openly," says William Flete, "and where God's honour was concerned, she never cared about pleasing or displeasing any one." In her very prayers there appeared the same amazing energy, when she wrestled with God for the grace of pardon for some hardened sinner, "with strong crying and tears, and groanings unutterable," watering the ground even with a bloody sweat, her whole frame shaken, and as it were, torn to pieces with a mysterious agony.[1]

But we have not yet made acquaintance with the real Catherine; to do so we must try and set before our minds what she was to the poor sinful souls whom she rescued out of their misery by thousands and tens of thousands. Who shall find words with which to depict that great sea of charity, whose ample floods were ever pouring forth their tide for the salvation of sinners? In this too she was the true daughter of that great and glorious Father whose habitual ejaculation in his hours of prayer was, "What will become of sinners!" To quote once more the words of Anastagio di Mont' Altino, which are precious from their unmistakable genuineness: "You may see her kindly and suppliantly embracing now this sinner and now that; she takes them by the hand, and calls them to her if they would hide themselves from her, and if any conceal his thought, or is silent about

[1] F. Ambrose Ansano Tantucci, in his notes on the Supplement, has thought it necessary to say a word to justify these and other exterior signs of Catherine's emotions from the charge of excess, and he refers to St Thomas, who speaks of the violence caused at times by the movements of the Holy Spirit—St. Th 2da., 2dæ, Quest. 175, aits 1, 2.

it, she knows it nevertheless; and if it is evil she bids him drive it away. . . . Her words were like thieves which snatched souls from the world and drew them to Holy Mother Church. She stood like a rock, all joyous and transformed in the likeness of her Spouse, and turned on us her pure vermilion countenance irradiated by that Sun ; then, bathed in tears, she would reprove our sins, and teach us the bitter price at which the soul is cleansed."

What is here conveyed in the language of poetry is repeated by others in sober prose. When any sought her presence weighed down by the sense of sin, and feeling incapable to achieve their own deliverance, she welcomed them to her heart as a sister would welcome a long-lost brother; she lavished on them a tenderness which she drew out of that heart which God had given her, the Heart of Christ with which her own had become identified. She would not hear of the misgivings of fear or the despair of pardon But she would bid them lay their sins and their penalties on her shoulders, and think of nothing but reconciling themselves with God Her beautiful soul, stainless as the driven snow, came in contact with every hideous form of sin, and it is not to be doubted that the contact was an agony. The presence of sin made itself sensible to her exquisite organisation, as an insupportable and pestilential odour, yet she never shrank from sinners The hardened and impenitent indeed she knew how to reprove and even to terrify, but there was no depth of iniquity from which she ever turned away if there was any hope of winning it to better things. Thus, besides the unnumbered conversions which she effected among criminals of every class, she did not refuse to seek out the most abandoned of her own sex, and to use her most winning eloquence in order to touch their hearts. We read how one night she returned to herself after a long abstraction in prayer in which it had been made known to her that a certain woman in the neighbourhood, fearing the anger of her husband whom she had betrayed, was on the point of committing suicide. She at once sent two of her companions to Fontebranda, desiring them to find the woman out and bring her with them to her ; they obeyed, and were in time to prevent the dreadful deed ; and by means of Catherine's prudent interference the scandal was put an end to, and the husband and wife were reconciled. "Listen to me, beloved daughter," she writes to another unhappy outcast, "if you will but cast away your sins by a holy confession, and a firm resolution to return to them no more, the tender goodness of God 'has already spoken the word, ' I will no more remember thy offences.' It is true, those who here expiate their sins by penance He will not punish in the next life. Surely it cannot be hard to you to have recourse to our sweet Mother Mary, the Mother of compassion and of mercy. She will lead you into the presence of her Son, and showing Him the breasts that nourished Him in His infancy, she will move Him to show you mercy, and then like a daughter and a slave redeemed by His Blood, you will enter within His Wounds, and the fire of His ineffable charity will consume all your miseries and wash away all your faults. He will make a bath of His own Blood in which to purify you ; believe it well ; our sweetest Lord will not despise you if you come to Him." (Letter 373.)

With words like these did this soul of unspotted purity address itself to those encrusted with the filth of vice. Often enough her presence sufficed without her words to pierce them with compunction and draw them weeping to her feet. Nor is this to be wondered at ; for the true servant of God is a tabernacle in which is ever dwelling the hidden Christ As the priest who bears the Holy Mysteries to the dying, carries through the unconscious crowds the presence of One who is among them and they know it not, and who yet, little as they suspect it, is diffusing, it may be a grace and a blessing as He passes by ; so the faithful soul united to her God is a true Ciborium, and bears His Presence into the world that forgets Him, and sheds around her the perfume of His charity. In this indwelling presence of God in the soul lies the true power of sanctity, for it is not the poor fallen child of Adam who effects in another soul its resurrection to a life of grace, but, "the Spirit of Christ that worketh in her." Hence it is that the saints, and Catherine among the rest, did far more by their prayers than their exhortations. What they did they did in virtue of their union with God, like the little child whose fingers indeed hold the pencil, which is nevertheless guided by the master's hand. And this is to be remembered lest any should mistake the significance of those narratives in which Catherine is presented to us, converting souls by her mere presence ; for such marvels are not told of her "as though wrought by her own strength or power," [1] but rather to glorify Him who made her heart His abode, and thence sent forth the rays of His power, as from a Tabernacle.

Here, then, is a rude and imperfect outline of the portrait of St. Catherine, as we see her standing surrounded by her disciples. We could not, when sketching that little group, omit the central figure ; and now, perhaps, we shall better understand their mutual relations. Glancing over the names and quality of her devoted followers we see how greatly her acquaintance with the state of society, both in Siena and elsewhere, must through their means have become extended. Vanni, for example, had visited the Court of Avignon, and could tell her something of the condition of affairs in that luxurious capital ; and the longing eagerness for the restoration of the Holy See to Italian soil, which had prompted his journey, found a ready echo in her heart. From the Tolomei and the Malevolti and other noble families she must have become familiar with many a history of family feud and civil discord ; while the Friars, who, like F. Bartholomew, were going hither and thither preaching and giving missions, would bring back sad and terrible tales of the spiritual desolation which they found in the scenes of their ministrations, and the scandals that had penetrated even into the sanctuary. What kind of reports could those have been which Bartholomew brought from his long sojourn at Asciano ; and which prompted her to dictate a letter to Berenger dei Arzocchi, the parish priest of that place, in which she hints at ecclesiastics who out of avarice sell spiritual graces, and spend their money in feasting and fine equipages ; and that other letter addressed to the parish priest of Semignano which is probably

[1] Acts iii 12.

the most terrific castigation an unworthy minister of the altar ever received from the lips of man or woman?

From men of business and of the world, like Christofano and Master Matthew, she must have heard much of the ruin of families, and the stagnation of trade caused by those "rapacious locusts," the roving Free Companies, and the danger constantly threatening the safety and prosperity of peaceable citizens. Yet existing authorities, whether civil or ecclesiastical, seemed powerless to apply any remedy to all these frightful evils, and Catherine, as she poured out her soul in prayer for her country which she loved like a true Italian, and for the Church of God which she regarded as none other than the Sacred body of her Divine Spouse, must often have cried out in the language of the prophets: "How long shall I see men fleeing away, and hear the voice of the trumpet? How long shall the land mourn, and the herb of every field wither? Woe to the pastors that devour and tear the sheep of the pasture! For behold! the city of Thy sanctuary is become a desert: Sion is a waste, and Jerusalem is desolate. And the house of our holiness and of our glory where our fathers praised Thee is burned with fire, and all our lovely things are turned to ruins." [1]

But before the great thoughts which were working in her soul could begin to be accomplished, she herself was to be subjected to a new discipline of persecution. "When God would exalt a work,' says Saint Vincent of Paul, "He first humbles the workman," and the wonderful career of Catherine of Siena offered no exception to this Divine law. Let us see in what manner this came about, and admire the Providence which watches over Its chosen ones, and guards the souls most richly gifted by grace, from "the moth of pride," by covering them over with "the black garment of humiliation."

[1] Jer. iv 21, xii 4, xxiii 1; Isa lxiv. 10, 11.

CHAPTER XIV.

THE STRIFE OF TONGUES, 1372.

IN the beginning of the year 1372 Catherine received from our Lord the intimation that the wonders of her life were about yet further to increase. The promise of graces greater than any she had hitherto enjoyed was accompanied by a warning that the prodigies which God was about to work in her would give rise to murmurs on the part of men, and of some even of her own followers. Hers was not intended to be a merely splendid career in the judgment of the world, nor one the sufferings of which should be sweetened by the love and confidence of all good souls. Like her Divine Master she was to be a stone of stumbling and a rock of offence even to her own brethren.

"One day," says Raymund, "as she was praying in her little chamber, our Lord appeared to her, and announced to her the new kind of miracle He was about to operate in her. 'Dear daughter,' He said, 'henceforth thy life will be full of prodigies so amazing as that ignorant and sensual men will refuse to believe them. Many even of those who are now attached to thee will doubt thee, and believe thee to be deceived. My grace infused into thy soul shall overflow into thy body also, and thou shalt experience its effects, and no longer be able to live, save in a manner wholly extraordinary. Thou shalt be exposed to many labours, and gain many souls, but thy conduct will scandalise many, and they will contradict and publicly accuse thee. Nevertheless, fear nothing ; I will be ever with thee, and will deliver thee from the tongue that speaketh falsely. Follow with courage the path that I shall show thee, and by thy means I will save many souls from hell, and conduct them to My kingdom.' Catherine listened with reverence, and when she heard the words repeated, 'Fear nothing, for I am with thee,' she answered humbly, 'Thou art my God, and I Thy little handmaid; may Thy holy will be accomplished in all things, only forsake me not, but incline to my assistance.'"

When the vision had ended, she reflected within herself what change it should be that was thus graciously announced to her. And she became sensible of such an increase of spiritual grace as had for its inevitable result a yet further suspension of all her natural powers. At length it pleased God to inspire her with the thought of receiving as often as she could the Blessed Sacrament of the Altar, in which she might be granted the fruition of her love, not so as she would enjoy it in the bliss of heaven, yet so as to satisfy her in some sort during her time of exile. With the permission of her confessor, therefore, she began to communicate almost daily,[1] unless hindered by sickness; and when unable from any cause to do this she suffered so greatly as to be even in danger of death. Moreover, this heavenly food satisfied and supported not only her soul, but her body also; so that ordinary food became no longer necessary to her, and the attempt to swallow it was attended by extraordinary sufferings. This fact seemed to her family and those about her so incredible, that they readily enough decided it was a deceit of the enemy, and her confessor ordered her to take food daily, and give no heed to any visions which might seem to prescribe the contrary. She obeyed, as she invariably did, but the obedience reduced her to such a state that they feared for her life. Then he examined her and drew from her the fact that the Blessed Sacrament so satisfied her as that she neither desired nor was able to take any other food; nay, that the mere presence of the Blessed Sacrament, or of the priest who was privileged to touch It, in some sort refreshed her and supported her bodily strength. As he still hesitated, in doubt what to think, Catherine said to him with her customary sweetness and respect, "Father, I would ask you to tell me one

---

[1] Raymund distinctly says she did not actually communicate every day, though this was currently reported —Leg.. Part 2. ch. xi.

thing : in case I should kill myself by over-fasting, should I not be guilty of my own death?" "Yes," said he. "Again," said she, "I beseech you resolve me in this : which do you take to be a greater sin, to die by over-eating or by over-abstinence ?" "By over-eating, of course," he replied. "Then," she continued, "as you see by experience that I am very weak, and even at death's door by reason of my eating, why do you not forbid me to eat, as you would forbid me to fast in the like case?" To that he could make no answer, and, therefore, seeing by evident tokens that she was near the point of death, he concluded by saying · "Daughter, do as God shall put in your mind, follow the guidance of His Holy Spirit, and pray for me, for I see the things that our Lord works in you are not to be measured by the common rule "

The account which Raymund has given in his Legend is confirmed by the testimony of many of her disciples. Caffarini, who often sat with her at table, says that she forced herself to swallow a few herbs, but that it cost her such pain that she used to call it "going to execution," and was obliged afterwards to reject whatever she had taken. He says he had seen the green twigs she introduced into her throat for that purpose. Francis Malevolti, who on one occasion spent four consecutive months in her company, gives a precisely similar account both of her efforts to eat and the suffering it occasioned. The anonymous author of the *Miracoli*, who wrote during her lifetime, says that this extraordinary kind of life began with her so far back as the year 1370 ; and speaks as follows : "This holy virgin always has with her two or three Sisters who wear the same habit, and who never leave her ; and not for her own consolation, but theirs, she sits down with them to table. Her companions do not eat meat, but only herbs, vegetables and fruit, with bread and wine, and other coarse food, cooked or raw. She takes something into her mouth, according to what may be on the table, sometimes a morsel of bread as big as a nut, sometimes a leaf of salad, or an almond, or other such things, and in like quantities. She swallows nothing that she puts into her mouth, but when she has masticated it, rejects it into a little vessel, rinsing her mouth with some cold water. And this she does only once in the day." Stephen Maconi gives the same account, and says that she usually waited till the others had finished to take even this small amount of nourishment, saying gaily, " Now, let us go and do justice on the miserable sinner." Often the artificial means she was obliged to use to reject what she had swallowed caused her to vomit an abundance of blood.

Sometimes her confessor would compassionate her, and advise her to let men talk, and not to torture herself by the effort to eat. "No, no," she would say; "it is better to expiate my sins here. I ought not to shun the occasion which God gives me of making satisfaction for them in this life. If we did but know how to use His grace, we should profit from everything. Whether in favourable events or in contradictions, we should always say, 'I must reap something from this.' Did we but do this we should soon be very rich."[1]

This strange and unwonted manner of life gave matter of great offence to most of her friends. " They were in the valley," says Raymund, " and they presumed to judge concerning what was on the summit of the mountain." Some accused her of pride, as seeking to appear better than our Lady and the apostles, nay, even than our Divine Lord Himself, whom Holy Scripture declares did indeed both eat and drink. Others alleged the rules of spiritual life which forbid religious persons to practise any singularity. Some said that all virtue is in the mean, and all extremes are to be suspected And others again in plain terms declared she was a mere hypocrite, who made up for the denial she practised in public by plenty of good cheer in secret. If any of these slanders reached her ears, or were uttered in her presence, Catherine would reply with unruffled sweetness and patience. "It is true indeed," she would say, "that our Lord sustains my life without food, but I know not why this should offend you. Truly I would eat with a good will if I could. But Almighty God for my sins has laid on me this strange kind of

---

[1] Legend, Part 2, ch. iv.

infirmity, so that if I eat, I am forthwith in peril of death. Pray for me therefore that He will vouchsafe to forgive me my sins, which are the cause of this and of every other evil."

Yet she did not fail to suffer intensely; for Catherine had by nature a keenly sensitive disposition, and the injurious suspicions which were daily expressed in her presence caused her a secret anguish. This was rendered yet more intense when she perceived that in spite of what had passed between them, her confessor himself began to waver. Caffarini tells the story in his Supplement, and relates how one morning, meeting F. Thomas, the Saint observed that he was preoccupied and troubled, and asked him what ailed him. He endeavoured to evade her question, but she, who knew all that was passing in his mind, refused to be so put off. "You may tell me without fear," she said, "for indeed I already know all about it." Then he told her the various things that were gossiped about the city, and how he began to fear that he had not the light requisite for guiding so extraordinary a case, or discerning by what spirit she was led. The Saint paused, and then with great humility replied: "Father, let me pray, and ask God to make us know if you have hitherto directed me aright or not;" and then she told him exactly who the persons were who had suggested his doubts, though she had never either seen or spoken to them. The night following she prayed, kneeling without any support and with such intense fervour that, though it was winter time, her person and the very floor of the room where she knelt were bathed in a profuse sweat. And even as she prayed, the trouble passed from the mind of her confessor, and her own soul too was filled with a wonderful calm and assurance. At break of day she sent for him, and bade him give thanks to God for delivering him from his doubt, adding, "When I saw that you, who know the very secrets of my heart, were beginning to doubt by what spirit I was led, I too began to doubt, and to entertain great fears, but God in His goodness has been pleased this night to reassure both you and me."

Still neither were the murmurs of the world silenced, nor did any change take place in her condition of body. One day, in the

month of September 1372, as she knelt weeping over her sins, our
Lord appeared to her, and bidding her weep no more, extended
His hand over her head, and pronounced the customary formula
of absolution For many days after she felt the touch of that
Divine Hand, and the unspeakable joy of her soul was such, that
from that date until the Feast of the Ascension in the year follow-
ing—a space of nearly eight months—the suffering occasioned by
the attempt to take food greatly increased. From September until
Lent she could only retain the smallest quantity. From Ash
Wednesday, which fell that year on the 8th of March, until
Passion Sunday even this was impossible, and from Passion
Sunday until Ascension Day, a space of fifty-five days, no kind of
food passed her lips. And during the whole of that time she
suffered incredible pain, yet neither her weakness nor her sufferings seemed to diminish her activity in all good works. For
though she had become so feeble that those about her expected
every hour to be her last, yet if there were any occasion for winning
a soul to God, or doing any other good work for His glory, she
would rise and go about without any sign of weariness.

A few days before the Feast of the Ascension her sufferings
greatly increased, and believing herself unable to endure them
much longer, she turned to God, saying, "O Lord, how long is it
Thy blessed will that I should endure this torment?" And she
was given to understand that it would cease on the coming
Festival. During the three Rogation days her extreme state of
weakness prevented her from going to the church and receiving
Holy Communion, the only food which for two months had sustained her life. Caffarini says that our Lord took pity on her,
and deigned that an angel should bring her the Sacred Host in a
precious veil, which so comforted and refreshed her that she
revived, but during those three days spake no word to any living
creature The rest of the story shall be told in the graphic words
of F. Bartholomew. He says, that on going to see her the eve
of the feast, he doubted if she would live till morning. "The
bell rung for Compline and we all rose to depart. 'O Mother,'
I said, 'are you about to leave us?' 'I know not,' she replied,

'but either I shall go to God, or, if I recover, I shall live in some unusual way.' At daybreak (May 25th, 1373) she called Alexia, saying, 'Give me my shoes and mantle.' Alexia, astonished but rejoicing, did as she was bid, and they went to the church together. Catherine went to Communion with the other Sisters and remained in ecstasy, making her thanksgiving till the brethren came into the church to finish grace after dinner, according to the custom of the Order. Having finished grace in choir, many went into the nave of the church to look at Catherine Then rising from her prayer gay and joyful, she comforted them all by her sweet manner of receiving them. 'To-day is the feast of our Lord,' she said, 'I think our sweet Lord wishes me to eat with you to-day for your consolation.' These words filled them with joy, and six of the Friars went home with her, to dine with her at her own house, but as nothing had been provided, the brethren sent back to the convent for some beans dressed in oil that had been cooked for the community. They all then ate with her, rejoicing, and many devout people hearing what had happened rejoiced also; and coming in to visit her, she was obliged for their satisfaction to take food and wine several times in the course of that day." [1]

Nevertheless the hard judgments passed on her conduct did not cease. F. Bartholomew in his deposition mentions the letter written to her some time later by a certain person of high reputation for piety, named Elbianco, in which he remonstrated with her for her unusual manner of life. The letter fell into the hands of F. Raymund, who was at that time her confessor, and was by him shown to Bartholomew. Whilst they were conferring about it, Catherine observed their trouble and asked the cause. When she heard it she not unnaturally claimed her letter, and as they hesitated about giving it to her, she said, "If you will not give it to me, at least tell me what concerns me in it." Raymund

---

[1] We have followed the account of Caffarini and F. Bartholomew. If any one will compare their joint narratives with the brief and imperfect account given by Raymund in the Legend, it will be seen that they wrote as eye witnesses, whereas he only gathered his information from hearsay.

accordingly read it to her. She listened calmly, and then gently reproved them both for the indignation they had expressed. "You ought," she said, "to thank him who has written me this letter. Do you not see that he has given me precious advice? He fears lest I should fall into the hands of the enemy, and wishes to warn me of my danger. I must have that letter, and shall certainly write and thank the author of it." In fact she did so; and seeing that Raymund was not convinced by her words, she gave him a severe look, and reproved them both for seeing evil where there was nothing but good.

Her reply is preserved,[1] and is as follows: "I thank you heartily, my dear Father (she says), for the zeal you have for my soul. It seems you are astonished at what you hear of my way of life, and I am sure you have no other motive than a desire for God's honour and my salvation, and that you fear for me lest I should be deceived by the enemy. This fear does not at all surprise me, and I assure you if you feel it, much more do I tremble for myself, so greatly do I dread the delusions of the evil one. Nevertheless, I trust in God's goodness, and I am on my guard against myself, knowing that from myself I can hope for nothing. I take refuge in the Cross of Jesus Christ, and fasten myself to it, being persuaded that so long as I am nailed there with the nails of love and humility, the devil cannot harm me; not for my merits, but for those of Jesus crucified.

"You tell me I ought to pray God that I may be able to eat; I assure you before God that I use every effort to do so, and that once or twice every day I force myself to take food. I have constantly prayed to God, and I do and will pray that He will grant me grace to live like other people, if such be His will. I assure you I have thoroughly examined this infirmity, and I think that in His goodness He must have sent it to correct me of the vice of gluttony. I deeply regret not having had strength enough to correct it from the motive of love. I do not know what remedy I can now make use of, but I would beg you to pray the Eternal Truth, if it be for His glory, that He would enable me

[1] No. 305.

once more to take food. I am sure He will not despise your prayers; and I entreat you to send me the remedy you name, and I will certainly try it. I would also ask you not to judge lightly of what you have not examined before God. I will conclude."

The gentle reproof contained in the last phrase of this humble letter must, we would hope, have touched the heart of the person to whom it was addressed.

But the trials to which the Saint was exposed from the hard judgment of others were by no means confined to their strictures on her abstinence from food. It has been said that at the same time that this suspension of her ordinary powers became more habitual, her longing for Holy Communion greatly increased. It grew in very truth to be the life of her life, the daily bread of body and soul. Most wonderful, indeed, are the things that are told us of the Communions of Catherine, and of the favours she at such times received. We do not speak of them in this place, as they will more fitly form the subject of a separate chapter.[1] It was not so much these mysterious favours which formed matter of criticism, as the frequency of her Communions; a point on which endless discussions arose, many even of her best friends withholding their approval. Among the Mantellate themselves there existed a strong difference of opinion on the subject. There are indications of a sort of jealousy which had sprung up about this time on the part of the elder Sisters against Catherine and her younger companions. Why should these young ones affect to be holier than their seniors? Who was Catherine Benincasa that she should gather disciples about her and set up for being a Saint? So the matter was carried to a director of the Tertiaries,

---

[1] In order to preserve the chronological order of Catherine's life, it has been thought best as a general rule not to introduce incidents attested by Raymund of Capua until we reach the period when he first became known to the Saint. It is the mixing up of facts which occurred before and after that time which has confused the order of events, as given to us in the Legend. On this account, therefore, we defer the subject of Catherine's favours in Holy Communion to a later chapter, in which will be thrown together the testimonies of all her confessors and disciples on this interesting subject.

whom Raymund does not name, but only calls "an unenlightened religious."[1] He sided with the malcontents, and this is less surprising when we remember that such frequent Communion was not then a common thing even with the devout. Soon both Friars and Sisters were split into two parties. The one affirmed that these frequent Communions were presumptuous, and tended to irreverence; whilst the other as warmly took Catherine's part. Father Thomas stoutly defended his penitent, and in reply to the arguments and censures which he daily had to encounter, appealed to the practice of the early Christians, as recorded in the Acts of the Apostles, and to the authority of St Denys the Areopagite, who declares that in the primitive Church the faithful communicated daily. His opponents were not at all disconcerted, but alleged on their side a saying attributed to St. Augustine,[2] "To communicate daily, I neither blame nor praise." When this was repeated to Catherine, and by no less a personage than a learned bishop, she listened with her usual sweetness, and gave the matter a pleasant turn by replying, "If St. Augustine does not blame me, my lord, why should you?" Her confessors, who were familiar with the doctrine of St. Thomas, that they who find in themselves an increase of devotion and reverence towards the most Holy Sacrament by frequent Communion may safely receive it oftener, gave testimony that in her case she did increase, as in devotion, so also in charity, humility, and godly patience: they said, too, that when hindered from Communion, she languished as one sick of some bodily infirmity. Yet for all that many of her own religious sisters were not afraid of using every effort to prevent her communicating, on the plea that it troubled the Fathers, that it gave offence, and other like pretences. On this matter, Raymund has made some sad and humiliating disclosures. It seems that some of the elder sisters, moved by their miserable

---

[1] This could not have been F. Bartholomew Montucci, who is generally spoken of as holding that office, a man of great piety, and one of Catherine's most devoted friends.

[2] In reality it is from Gennadius, *De Eccles. Dogm. in cap. quotid.* 13. *de consec. dis.* 2. See Liguori on Frequent Communion.

jealousy, so worked on the Prior of San Domenico, and certain
of the friars who had espoused their side, that at last it was
determined that Catherine should be deprived of Communion,
and that the faithful confessor who had directed her for so many
years with consummate prudence should be removed. When
she next approached the altar rail, therefore, she was driven away
before the eyes of the public, and obliged to retire in confusion.
Catherine bore the trial with unruffled patience, and never uttered
a word of bitterness or complaint. But this was not all On the
rare occasions when she was now permitted to communicate, they
required her to finish her prayers directly and quit the church; a
thing which was wholly impossible in her case, as she could never
receive Communion without falling into an ecstasy, and remaining in that state some hours. The Fathers who had taken this
affair into their hands seem to have considered it in the light of
an intolerable nuisance Low and vulgar minds will regard even
the sublimest mysteries from a low and vulgar point of view.
We can fancy the old sacristan fidgeting about with his keys in
his hand, unable to shut the church doors because Catherine
Benincasa was so long at her prayers. That was the limit of his
view of the subject, and he found many among his brethren
whose comprehension of the matter did not rise to a higher level
than his own. So at last, one day, losing patience, they took her,
all in ecstasy as she was, and carrying her off in a rough and
brutal manner, they flung her out on a heap of rubbish outside
the church doors, which they then proceeded to lock behind her.
There she lay, cast out as if she had been some vile reptile, with
her senses the while all rapt in God. Her companions, bathed
in tears, gathered about her to protect her from the rays of the
midday sun, and so waited the moment when she would return
to herself. And this happened not once, but often.[1] At such
times the passers-by would kick her contemptuously ; one miserable woman satisfied her malice by kicking her in the church,

[1] This is clear from the Legend Raymund gives several instances of
persons, both men and women, who kicked and otherwise maltreated her,
and of the judgments that fell on them —See Leg , Part 3, chap. vi.

and then publicly boasted of what she had done. Catherine knew all this, but she never spoke of it except to excuse the authors of these strange excesses. One man, unhappily a religious, was not content with grossly insulting the Saint in the presence of her companions, but went so far as to take from her some money, bestowed on her for charitable purposes Catherine gave not the smallest sign of trouble. She forbade her companions to speak evil of the miscreant, or to cause him any pain. She possessed her soul in patience, and by patience she at last over-came Surely, in the sight of the angels, this is the sublimest page in Catherine's life. To many it is given, in a certain sense, to taste of the sufferings of their Divine Master, but compara-tively few enjoy the privilege of sharing His humiliations. Catherine in her ecstasy, flung out of the church by rude hands, and lying in the broad thoroughfare under the scorching sun ; kicked and spat upon by brutal men and spiteful women ; but unmoved in her patience, always calm, always sweet, always silent ; —what a spectacle is this ! What a reflection of the ignominies of Jesus ! And having reached that depth of profound abjection, can we wonder that she should soar upwards from it to the sublimest heights of charity?

About this time (probably towards the end of the year 1373),[1] Catherine became aware that an old woman named Andrea, her-self one of the Sisters of Penance, was dying by inches of a terrible cancer. As her malady made progress it caused such disgust to those about her, that scarcely any one could be found to visit or tend upon her. When Catherine heard this, she understood that our Lord had reserved the poor forsaken sufferer for her loving care ; and going to her at once with a cheerful countenance, she offered to remain with her and assist her as long as her illness might last. The charity thus generously

[1] Carapelli places it at the beginning of that year, but when we remember in what a condition Catherine then was, it seems more likely to have been some time after May We consider then the events here alluded to as occupy-ing the latter half of 1373 and the beginning of 1374, immediately before her first visit to Florence.

offered was as generously accomplished; day after day Catherine
lavished on her patient the tenderest care; in spite of the repulsive nature of the services she had to perform, she never
showed any sign of disgust or repugnance, or adopted any of
those precautions which others had made use of in the tainted
atmosphere of the sick-room, lest by doing so she should give
pain to Andrea's feelings. Once when the intolerable stench
almost overcame her courage, she reproached herself for this as
for a weakness, and bending over the bed she even applied her
lips to the wound, until she had triumphed over the revolt of
nature. But wonderful to say her charity elicited no gratitude
from her who was its object. Andrea's ears had no doubt been
poisoned by the malicious slanders before mentioned. The
tongues of some of the Sisters had already been busy tearing in
pieces Catherine's good name, and getting up a party among the
friars against her and her confessor, and this explains the otherwise incomprehensible fact that the sick woman should have had
her mind filled with the most injurious suspicions of the holy
virgin. She persuaded herself that Catherine's heroic perseverance in doing what no one else would consent to do was part and
parcel of her affectation of holiness, a would-be superiority to
other people, for it was there that the devil of jealousy had found
entrance among the Sisters; and at last her diseased fancies
so completely blinded her that whenever Catherine was out of
her sight she imagined her to be engaged in something sinful.
Though Catherine knew well enough the judgment which Andrea
passed on her, she did not show herself one whit less loving or
serviceable than she had been before But the more charity she
bestowed, the more was the malice of the old woman stirred
against her, so that not content with her unjust suspicions, she
went so far as to communicate them to the other Sisters, to
whom she accused Catherine as guilty of a breach of chastity.

The matter was too grave to be passed over without examination, and the Sisters, with their Prioress at their head, after
questioning Andrea, summoned Catherine before them to answer
to the charge. Catherine listened to their reproaches in humble

silence, and when she had to speak, said no more than these
words, "Indeed, my good Mother and Sisters, by the grace of
our Lord Jesus Christ I am a virgin!" And however much they
pressed her she would give no other answer save again and again
to repeat, "Indeed, I am a virgin." Then she went back to the
author of this malicious slander, and waited on her humbly and
charitably as before, yet not without feeling a pang in her heart
when she thought of the infamy attributed to her. Retiring to
her own chamber she opened her grief to Almighty God: "O
Lord, my sweetest Spouse," she said, "Thou knowest what a
tender and precious thing is the good name of those who have
vowed their virginity to Thee, and Thou seest the efforts made
by the father of lies to hinder me in this charitable work which
Thou hast appointed me to do; help me therefore in my innocence, and suffer not the wicked serpent to prevail against me."
When she had thus prayed a long time with many tears, our
Lord appeared to her holding two crowns in His hands, one in
His right hand of gold, all decked with precious stones, another in
His left hand of very sharp thorns, and said these words to her:
"Dear daughter, it is so, that thou must needs be crowned with
these two crowns at sundry times; choose thou, therefore,
whether thou wilt rather be crowned with the sharp crown of
thorns in this life, and have that other reserved for thee in the
life to come; or else, whether thou like better to have this goodly
golden crown now, and that other sharp crown to be reserved for
thee in the life to come?" To this demand the humble virgin
made answer after this manner: "Lord," said she, "Thou
knowest very well that I have resigned my will wholly to Thee,
and have made a full resolution to do all things according to Thy
direction, and therefore I dare not choose anything, unless I
may know that the same shall stand with Thy most blessed will
and pleasure. Nevertheless, because Thou hast willed me to
make answer concerning this choice, that Thou hast here made
unto me, I say thus: That I choose in this life to be evermore
conformed and made like to Thee, my Lord and Saviour, and
cheerfully to bear crosses and thorns for Thy love, as Thou hast

done for mine." With that she reached out her hands with firm courage, and taking the crown of thorns out of our Lord's hands, she put the same upon her own head with such a strength and violence that the thorns pierced her head round about insomuch that for a long space after she felt a sensible pain in her head by the pricking of those thorns, as she declared afterwards to her ghostly Father. Then our Lord said to her: "Daughter, all things are in My power; and as I have suffered this slander to be raised against thee by the devil and his members, so is it in My power to cease the same when I will. Continue thou, therefore, in that holy service that thou hast begun, and give no place to the enemy that would hinder thee from all good works. I will give thee a perfect victory over thine enemy, and will bring to pass that whatsoever he hath imagined against thee, it shall all be turned to his own greater confusion." Catherine, much comforted, returned to her charitable labours, giving no heed either to the malice of her enemy or the injurious gossip of the neighbours. But when the rumours that were spread abroad reached the ears of Lapa, her anger was past control. She needed no proof of her daughter's innocence, knowing more than the world did what manner of life she led ; and bursting into her presence, she began with her accustomed vehemence : "How often have I told thee that thou shouldest no more serve yonder wretched old crone? See now what reward she gives thee for all thy good service. She has brought a foul slander upon thee among all thy Sisters, which God knows whether thou wilt ever be able to rid thyself of so long as thou livest. If ever thou serve her again after this day, or if ever thou come where she is, never take me for thy mother; for I tell thee plainly I will never know thee for my daughter." Catherine listened as she spoke, and at first was somewhat troubled. But after a little time, when she had recovered her usual calm, she went to her mother, and kneeling down before her with great reverence, she spoke as follows : "Sweet mother, think you that our Lord would be pleased with us if we should leave the works of mercy undone because our neighbour shows himself unthankful towards us? When our

Saviour Christ hung on the Cross, and heard there the reproachful
talk of that ungrateful people round about, did He because of
their cruel words give up the charitable work of their redemption?
Good mother, you know very well that if I should leave this old
sick woman, she were in great danger to perish of neglect; because
she would not find any one to come near her and do such service
as is requisite to be done about a woman in this case; and so
should I be the occasion of her death. She is now a little deceived
by the ghostly enemy, but she will hereafter, by the grace of God,
come to acknowledge her fault and be sorry for the same." With
such words she pacified her mother's mind and got her blessing;
and so returned again to the service of the sick woman, about
whom she did all things with great diligence and love, never showing either in words or countenance the least token of discontent
or displeasure. So that the sick Sister was much astonished and
withal ashamed for what she had done, and began to have great
sorrow and repentance for the slander that she had raised against
her. Then it pleased our Lord to show His mercy towards His
faithful spouse, and to restore her again to her good fame after
this manner:—One day the holy maid went to the sick Sister's
chamber to serve her, as she was wont to do, and as she was
coming towards her bed where she lay, Andrea saw a marvellous
goodly light coming down from heaven, which filled all her
chamber, and was so beautiful that it made her utterly to forget
all the pains of her disease. What that light might mean she could
not conceive, but looking about her here and there she beheld the
maiden's face gloriously transformed, the majesty whereof was so
strong that she seemed to her rather an angel from heaven than
any earthly creature. Which brightness the more the old woman
beheld, the more did she condemn the malice of her own heart
and tongue in slandering such an excellent and holy creature.
At last her heart being quite softened, with much sobbing and
weeping she confessed her fault to the holy maid, and besought
her pardon. When Catherine saw her repentance and submission, she took the old woman in her arms and kissed her,
and spoke very sweet words unto her, saying, "Good mother, I

have no displeasure in the world against you, but only against our enemy the devil, by whose malice and subtilty I know all this is wrought, but rather I have to thank you with all my heart, for you have reminded me to have a more careful guard to myself, and so doing, you have turned the malice of the fiend to my greater good and benefit." With such kind speeches she comforted the sick Sister, and then she set herself to do all such services as were wont to be done about her. And when she had done all, she took her leave very gently (as her manner was), and so retired to her chamber, to give God thanks. In the meantime the old woman, who had a great care to restore the innocent virgin to her good name again, when any of those came to her before whom she had made that slanderous report, took occasion openly to confess, with many tears, that whatever she had at any time reported against that holy maid she had been induced to report it by the craft of the devil, and not by anything she ever saw or knew in her. She affirmed, moreover, that she was able to prove that the holy maid was not only free from all such suspicion, but also endued with singular graces of God, and that she was, indeed, a most pure and holy virgin. "Thus much," said she, "I speak not upon hearsay or opinion, but upon my certain knowledge."[1]

But the enemy of souls was not thus to be vanquished, and returning to the attack, he endeavoured once more to overcome the Saint's heroic courage by exciting within her a revolt of the senses. One day as she uncovered the dreadful wound to wash and dress it, the infected odour which arose from it was so insupportable that it seemed impossible for her to repress the disgust which it occasioned. But full of holy indignation at her own delicacy, she turned against herself, saying, "O wretched flesh, dost thou then abhor thy fellow-Christian! I will make thee even to swallow that of which thou wilt not abide the savour," and collecting in a cup the water in which she washed the wound, she went aside and drank it. This action became known, and her confessor questioned her about it. Catherine answered him

[1] Fen., Part 2, ch. xi.

with some embarrassment; at last she owned the truth, and added, "I assure you, father, never in my lifetime did I taste anything one half so sweet and delightful." The remainder of the story must be given in the words of the Legend. "The next night following, our Saviour Christ appeared to her, and showed her His Hands, Feet, and Side, and in them imprinted the five Wounds of His most bitter Passion, and said unto her: 'Dear daughter, many are the battles that thou hast sustained for My love; and great are the victories that thou hast achieved through My grace and assistance. For which I bear thee great good-will and favour. But especially that drink that thou tookest yesterday for My sake pleased Me passing well, in which, because thou hast not only despised the delight of the flesh, but cast behind thy back the opinion of the world, and utterly subdued thine own nature, I will give thee a drink that shall surpass in sweetness all the liquors that the world is able to bestow.' With that He reached out His arm, and bringing her lips to the Wound of His sacred Side, 'Drink, daughter,' He said, 'drink thy fill at the Fountain of Life!' Catherine obeyed; she pressed her lips to that Sacred Side, and drew from the wounded Heart of her Lord the liquor of life, as from the fountain of everlasting salvation!"

Meanwhile the story of her heroic charity could not be concealed. Andrea herself proclaimed to all comers the spotless innocence of her whom she had formerly calumniated, and the marvellous act of self-devotion which she had witnessed with her own eyes.[1] From that day, says Caffarini, she was called by all

---

[1] The story of Andrea is given in the earlier chapters of the Legend. Nothing, however, is to be concluded on that account as to the actual date of the occurrence, for Raymund grouped together events without the slightest regard to the order of time. F Angiolo Carapelli, who has made a serious study of the chronology of St. Catherine's life, assigns it to the year 1373 And on examination, many things will be found to support the accuracy of this statement. The calumny, so incredible at a time when Catherine's reputation for sanctity stood universally respected, would not unnaturally win belief at such a crisis as has been described in the above chapter, and by the very class of persons whom we have seen so maliciously disposed against her. Then her words to her Lord, "Thou knowest that *I have resigned my*

men "the Saint," and the fame of her virtue, spreading abroad like a sweet perfume, was carried beyond the bounds of her native place into the remotest cities of Tuscany

will wholly to Thee," seem to bear evident reference to that exchange of wills, which it is impossible to date earlier than 1371. And lastly, from the expression used both by Caffarini and Bartholomew, we infer that it was at that time "her fame spread *through Tuscany;*" whilst naturally enough, the very next event following is her summons by the General to Florence, which we know took place in 1374

CHAPTER XV.

THE PLAGUE, 1374.

" IN the May of 1374, at which time the Chapter of the Friar Preachers was being held at Florence, there came thither, by command of the Master General of the Order, a certain Sister of Penance of St. Dominic, named Catherine, daughter of Giacomo of Siena. She was of the age of twenty-seven, and was reputed to be a great servant of God; and with her came three other Sisters wearing the same habit, who held her company and took care of her, and from whom I, hearing of her fame, went to see her, and make her acquaintance." Thus writes the anonymous author of the *Miracoli;* and his words just quoted afford us the only existing notice of this first visit of Catherine to the city of Florence. No allusion to the fact is to be found in the pages either of the Legend or of any other original biography; we are left entirely in the dark as to the cause and duration of this visit, so that in the absence of all certain information on the subject, it may be permitted for us to venture on our own surmises.

She was summoned thither, as it appears, " by command of the Master General of the Order." That office was then held by F. Elias of Toulouse. Considering what had gone before, and the contradictory opinions which must have reached the General's ears regarding this celebrated woman, we can imagine it a very likely explanation that he summoned her to Florence in order that he might by his own personal examination satisfy himself as to her real spirit; and this appears the more probable, when we learn from the same writer that the injurious gossip spoken of in the last chapter had preceded her to Florence, and was there busily caught up and propagated. For he tells us that a dear friend of hers in that city expressing his sorrow at hearing that there was much murmuring against her singular way of life, not only on the part of the laity, but also of religious, she replied, "That is my glory; that is what I desire, to be well spoken against all my life; never you care about it! I am sorry for them, but not for myself." It seems then most probable that the hub-bub which had been going on at Siena, involving as it did not Catherine alone, but also her confessor and the other fathers who had stood her friends, must have come to the knowledge of Father Elias, and necessitated his interference. The great theo-logical Order of the Church, which glories in the title of the "Order of Truth," could scarcely be indifferent as to the real character of one wearing their habit, who was proclaimed on one side to be an Ecstatica and a Saint, living without corporal food, nourished by the Holy Sacrament of the Altar, to whose super-natural glance the secrets of hearts were manifested, and whose prayers had never been known to be offered without avail; and who, on the other, was stigmatised as an impostor and a hypocrite, who not only went astray seduced by the enemy, but was leading all the weak heads of Siena after her.

Whatever may have been the cause, the fact of her visit appears certain, and if there is any truth in the above surmise, we must suppose that the result of the investigation of the General and the Fathers of the Chapter proved perfectly satisfactory. It was the first journey that Catherine had ever taken so far from her native place. No doubt she must have contrasted the splendour of the great republican capital with the more homely beauties of her own little city. All things in Florence were then peaceful and prosperous, and there was nothing to indicate the outbreak of that terrific storm which two years later was to bring her back in a far different capacity. There can be no doubt, however, that the ties she formed during this, her first visit to Florence, and the impression she left on the minds of the people, had much to do with their future appeal to her mediation; and we may almost certainly conclude that the "dear friend" spoken of above can have been no other than Nicolas Soderini, the brave and virtuous citizen whose friendship for her began at this time, and lasted until death. In fact, his house was always her home in Florence, and in it is still to be seen a little chamber said to have been that occupied by Catherine, on the wall of which is painted a crucifix, before which she is supposed to have prayed. Soderini had been introduced to Catherine by her brothers, who, it will be remembered, were then living in Florence, and whom, being unfortunate in business, he had assisted with money[1] According to the "*Archivio di Magistrato*," they occupied a house near the *Canto a Soldani*, in a street running into the *Piazza d'Arno*. Bartolo's children were at Siena with their grandmother, but Catherine would have found here her niece Nanna, the daughter of the elder brother, who soon became dear to her. After she left Florence she often wrote to this young girl, and one letter is preserved which shall be quoted here for the sake of its sweet motherly tone, betraying that it was written by one remarkable for her tender love of children, and who knew how to adapt her style to the capacity of a child.

"Dearest daughter in Christ, I desire to see you avoiding everything which can hinder you from having Jesus for your Spouse. But you will not be able to do this if you are not one of His wise virgins, who have their lamps full of oil and light. Do you know what that means? The lamp is our heart, for our heart should be made like a lamp You know a lamp is broad at the top and narrow at the bottom ; that is the shape of our heart, which we must always keep open to heavenly things and good thoughts . . . but the lamp is narrow at the foot, and so we must shut our hearts up and keep them closed to things of earth. In this way our hearts will be like a lamp : but then we must have oil, for you know, my child, that without oil a lamp is of no use. Now the oil represents that sweet little virtue humility, for the spouse of Christ must be very humble, and mild,

---

[1] "As to Benincasa's affair, I can say nothing about it, not being in Siena. I thank Master Nicolas for his charity to them."—Letter 115.

and patient. . . . If we are patient and humble we shall have oil in our lamp; but that is not enough, the lamp must be lighted. Now the light is holy faith, but it must not be a dead faith, but a holy living faith; you know the Saints tell us faith without works is dead. We must try then to apply ourselves to virtue, and abandon our childish ways and vanities, and live, not like silly girls in the world, but like faithful spouses of Jesus, and so we shall have the lamp, the oil, and the light. But remember our sweet Spouse is so jealous of His spouses,—I could never tell you how jealous He is !—If He sees you loving anything beside Himself, He will be angry, and if you do not correct your faults, He will shut the door, and you will not be able to enter when the nuptials are celebrated. It was so with the five foolish virgins . . . they had not brought the oil of humility, and it was said to them, 'Go and buy oil.' There is an oil which the world sells, it is the oil of flattery and praise, and so it was said to the foolish virgins, 'You have not chosen to buy eternal life with your good works, but you chose to buy the praise of men, and all you have done was done for that; go now, then, and buy that praise, but you cannot enter here.' Beware then, my child, of the flattery of men; do not seek for your actions to be praised, for if you do the door of eternal life will be closed."

Catherine left Florence some time in June, and returned to Siena to find the city suffering from the twofold calamity of famine and pestilence. Neither of these scourges were new things in Siena, which had been wellnigh depopulated by the plague in the very year of Catherine's birth. But never before had it been known to rage with equal violence. It attacked persons of all ages, and a single day often sufficed to begin and end its fatal course. A panic seized the population; and whilst the more wealthy sought safety by flight, the poorer sort were thus abandoned in their misery, with none to help them. It will be remembered that when Catherine had left the city in the month previous it was under sorrowful circumstances. Many of her own sisters, and of those friars whose very footsteps in old time she had kissed with loving reverence, had turned their backs on her, regarding her as something half-way between a mad-woman and an impostor. She had received scorn and insult precisely from those who were most bound to protect her; and, true woman as she was, it is not to be believed that she could have been wholly insensible to such cruel injuries, or that the memory of them could have been quite effaced by subsequent applause. But now when she saw the gaunt faces of her fellow-citizens, and heard the doleful sound of the dead-cart as it went from house to house gathering the bodies of that day's victims for burial, there was but one thought in her heart, "This time is for me."

Her first ministrations were needed in her own family. Her sister Lisa (of the hospital) was one of the first victims. Then Bartolo, who had accompanied Catherine back to Siena to see his mother, was carried off by the pestilence. Francis Malevolti tells us that Catherine at this time lost *two* of her brothers, "both honourable merchants," and his statement is explained by a passage in the disposition of Peter Ventura. He tells us that Stephen had gone to Rome on occasion of the approaching Jubilee, and that one night, Catherine, who had received a revelation of his death, called her mother and said, "Know, dear mother, that your son and my brother has just passed out of this life," and some days later the fact was confirmed by persons who came from Rome bringing the sad tidings.[1] But this was not all : out of eleven of her grandchildren whom Lapa was bringing up in her own house, most of them the children of Bartolo, eight died. Truly in that hour of cruel bereavement she must have sighed for the death from which she had formerly shrunk, and bitterly bemoaned herself in the desolate house once filled with the gay voices of so many innocent children. But Catherine, to whom they were all so dear, buried them with her own hands, saying as she laid them one by one in their last resting-place, "This one, at least, I shall not lose." Then she turned her thoughts to those outside her home, and resumed her old habits of heroic charity. Terrible indeed are the accounts left by

[1] Process., fol. 199.

historians of this awful time. In some streets not a creature was left alive to answer the call when the dead-cart stopped at their door. Sometimes the priests and those who carried a bier to the grave fell lifeless while performing this last act of charity, and were buried in the yet open sepulchre. The public tribunals were closed, and the laws no longer remained in force. The victims were of all ranks. Two of the "Defenders" died within a day or two of each other. At the great Hospital of La Scala, the Rector, Galgano di Lolo, gave his life in discharge of the duties of his office.[1] The charity and the resources of the Confraternity of the *Disciplinati* were taxed to the uttermost, and not a few of them in like manner died martyrs of charity.

Once more, therefore, was Catherine to be seen in the hospitals, and the most infected parts of the city, assisting all no less with her charitable services than with her prayers "Never did she appear more admirable than at this time," says Caffarini; "she was always with the plague-stricken; she prepared them for death, she buried them with her own hands. I myself witnessed the joy with which she tended them, and the wonderful efficacy of her words, which effected many conversions. Not a few owed their lives to her self-devoted care, and she encouraged her companions to perform the like services." For herself she was insensible either to fear or the repugnances of nature. *She had died and*

---

[1] The office of Rector of La Scala was one of great dignity and importance. The person who filled it was by right a member of the high Consistory, and, moreover, appointed the governors of a great many other hospitals which depended on this one, not only in Siena, but even in other towns of Tuscany. He was also protector of several other charitable institutions in the city. Some of the governors were bound to be Sienese gentlemen. Besides the ordinary work of a hospital, La Scala received and educated foundlings, lodged pilgrims, and distributed alms to the sick and needy outside its walls, and in time of famine it distributed a great quantity of grain. Its revenues were very large. Among its sacred treasures is the Holy Nail that transfixed the left hand of our Lord on the Cross. Here is also preserved the Sienese standard which was carried at the great victory of Montaperto to which was given the title of the "*Manto di Maria;*" and a picture representing our Lady covering the city and its inhabitants with her mantle in token of her protection.—*Diario Sanese,* ii. 95, 96.

come to life again, and in whatever sense we understand that incident, she had come to regard this world as we also should regard it were we true to our profession of faith; as those could not fail to regard it to whom the last things and the eternal truths had by earnest meditation become realities. What were the chances of life or death, sickness or danger, to one who (as we may say) had *seen eternity?* What should they be to those who verily believe in it? "How can you endure such cold?" asked her confessor one day, as he saw her setting forth to her daily fatigues, scantily protected from the bitter winds to which Siena is so much exposed. "A dead body feels nothing,"[1] was her reply, and truly in her total insensibility to the claims of nature she might fitly have been said to have been dead. That heroic act of her early life by which she had chosen suffering as her portion in this world, was no empty profession; in virtue of it she accepted pain, fatigue, humiliation, and the frustration of many hopes with an equal mind and with an utter indifference to everything save the discharge of duty. Caffarini tells us that her disciples would sometimes express their wonder at her patience and courage; but in reply she would only laugh, and say, "If people knew how sweet it is to suffer for God, they would covet the opportunities of having something to bear as a piece of singular good fortune." In the same place he relates how a certain priest, having come from Florence for the purpose of testing her sanctity, in his presence uttered the most injurious reproaches against the holy virgin, who, lying on her bed of boards (for she was at the time very weak), listened to it all with a countenance so sweet and unmoved, and with such a heavenly joy and serenity, that when the speaker left her presence, he could only say that "she was pure unalloyed gold."[2] It was in this spirit, therefore, that she took on herself during this frightful time labours and duties, at the thought of which flesh and blood might well have shuddered; and whilst we are told that the unhappy citizens shrank from encountering one another in the streets, where men, to use the expression of Tommasi, "were

[1] Burlamacchi's notes to the Legend.   [2] Process., 1270, 1271.

daily falling dead like ripe apples from the tree," there was one form from which they did not shrink, but welcomed it as the harbinger of comfort; for they recognised in that attenuated, white-robed figure, "Catherine, the spouse of Christ," she whom they were wont to call "the Mother of Souls."[1]

For by this time her fellow-citizens had come to understand who and what she was. In their intolerable sufferings she possessed the power of consolation. She could give them sympathy, for they had not lost more than she. They had seen her burying the little ones whom she loved so tenderly; and mothers, therefore, who had lost their treasures, could bear to listen to her when she told them not to grieve.

It was precisely at this time that she made her first acquaintance with him who during the remainder of her life was to enjoy her entire confidence. This was Father Raymund of Capua, a Friar Preacher eminent alike for his learning and virtue, who for four years had filled the office of confessor to the nuns of St. Agnes of Montepulciano, where he wrote the life of that saint. He was a member of the Neapolitan family Delle Vigne, to which had belonged the celebrated chancellor of Frederick II. Early called into the Order of St. Dominic in some remarkable manner which he alludes to, but does not narrate, he suffered much from weak health, on which account the physicians forbade his keeping the fasts of the Order. This greatly afflicted him; and making it a matter of special prayer, he obtained strength enough not only to keep the obligations of his rule, but even to fast on bread and water on the vigils of all our Lady's feasts.[2] After preaching and lecturing on Sacred Theology in various cities of Italy, he was made Prior of the Minerva at Rome in 1367, and in that capacity presented his community to Urban V. when that Pontiff visited the eternal city. He was remarkable for his great devotion to the Blessed Virgin, and composed a treatise on the Magnificat in

---

[1] Process. Dep. of Bart. de Ferrara.

[2] He relates this story himself in a letter to Philip, Cardinal of Ostia, written in defence of regular observance, and by way of proving that on this head physicians are not the only authorities to be consulted.

her honour, as well as the Office used on the feast of the Visitation. Several years before he became acquainted with Catherine, the same most Blessed Virgin had made known to the Saint that she would one day obtain for her a confessor who would give her more help than any she had yet consulted. The first occasion on which she saw him was the feast of St John Baptist, when the high mass for the day was sung by F. Bartholomew Dominic, assisted by F. Raymund of Capua and F. Thomas della Fonte. After the conclusion of the high mass, Raymund said his own low mass, at which Catherine likewise assisted; and it was then that she heard a Voice saying, "This is My beloved servant, this is he to whom I will give thee."[1] From that day she placed the direction of her conscience in his hands. No doubt Raymund was well aware of the difference of opinion which existed among some of the friars regarding her. He had probably been consulted on the subject by them, and the visit of F. Thomas della Fonte and F. George Naddi to Montepulciano, mentioned in a former chapter, may have had some connection with the same affair. It is even possible that his superiors had despatched him to Siena with a view of settling the disputes which were dividing the community of San Domenico, as one to whose character and experience all would yield. These, however, are only conjectures; what is certain is, that a complete confidence was established between him and F. Thomas, equally honourable to both parties. F. Thomas put him in possession of his long experience in the guidance of this soul; of the notes he had taken day by day of her supernatural graces; and in particular of all the wonderful favours granted to her in Holy Communion.

Raymund, who was a man of much greater learning than F. Thomas, hesitated not in the favourable judgment which he at

---

[1] (Latin) Supplement, Part 2, Trat. 6, § 17. I quote the original as referred to and explained by Carapelli, in preference to Tantucci's translation, which is in this place obscure. See also letter of Stephen Maconi, and Catherine's letter to Raymund of Capua, No. 134 If the whole circumstances of the foregoing narrative are borne in mind, the change of confessors and final appointment of Raymund to that office become clear and intelligible

once formed on the question. "I first became acquainted with Catherine," he says, "when I went to Siena as Lector; and I used my best efforts to procure her the privilege of receiving Holy Communion, so that when she desired to approach, she more confidently addressed herself to me than to any other Father in the convent." This simple and unpretentious statement reveals to us that up to that time the difficulties which had been raised on the subject of Catherine's communions had by no means been dissipated. But Raymund's reputation and influence were of sufficient weight to prevent any interference between him and his new penitent, and from that time Catherine had no more disturbance on the subject.

Still the plague raged with ever increasing violence. Raymund perceived the terror that it everywhere inspired, and knowing, as he says, "that zeal for souls is the spirit of our Holy Order," he devoted himself to the aid of the sufferers. He, too, visited the sick and the hospitals, and in particular he went very often to the *Casa della Misericordia*, the Rector of which establishment, Master Matthew,[1] he loved entirely for his virtue's sake. Both he and Catherine were, in fact, in the habit of calling at the *Misericordia* every day to confer with Matthew upon matters connected with the relief of the poor

One day, then, as Raymund was going his rounds visiting the sick, having to pass the gates of the hospital he went in to see how Master Matthew was. The rest of the story must be given as it stands in the pages of the English Legend.

"When he entered, he saw the brethren busily occupied carrying Master Matthew from the church towards his chamber. With

---

[1] Master Matthew was appointed Rector of the *Misericordia*, August 1, 1373 In the *Leggenda Minore* the date 1373 is given for his attack of the plague and its appearance in the city The author of the *Miracoli* gives 1374, and the correctness of the latter date is confirmed by the Sienese Chronicle of Neri di Donato and the Necrology of San Domenico. We must remember that, according to the Sienese method of computation, the first three months of 1374 would be reckoned as 1373. The plague may also have first appeared in that year, but historians are unanimous in giving the later date as that of its greatest ravages.

that he asked him cheerfully how he did.   But Master Matthew
was so feeble and so far spent that he could not give him one
word to answer.   Then he asked them that were about him how
that sickness came to him.   And they made answer that he had
watched that night with one that was sick of the plague, and
about midnight took the sickness of him; since which time, said
they, he has remained, as you see, without colour, strength, or
spirit.   When they had brought him to his chamber, they laid
him down upon his bed, where, when he had rested a little while,
he came to himself again, and called for Raymund, and made his
confession to him, as he was wont oftentimes to do.   That done,
Raymund tried to cheer him.   'Master Matthew,' said he, 'how
do you feel?   Where is your pain?'   'My pain,' he said, 'is in
the groin, so that is seems as if my thigh were ready to break in
sunder; and I have so vehement a headache, as though my head
would cleave in four parts.'   With that he felt his pulse, and
found, indeed, that he had a very sharp fever.   Whereupon he
caused them to send for a physician, who, when he came, declared
that he saw evident tokens of a pestilential ague, and also of
approaching death.   'Wherefore,' he said, 'I am very sorry, for
I see we are like to lose a very dear friend, and they of this house
a very good Rector.'   'What,' said Raymund, 'is it not possible
by your art to devise some kind of medicine that may do him
good?'   'We will see to-morrow,' said he; 'but to tell you truly,
I have small hope of doing him any good, the disease is too far
gone.'   When Raymund heard these words, he returned towards
the sick man again with a heavy heart.   In the meantime it came
to the ears of Catherine that Master Matthew was dangerously
sick of the plague.   When she heard that she was much troubled;
for she knew him to be a very virtuous man, and therefore loved
him greatly; and forthwith went in great haste towards his house.
And before she came into his presence she cried out with a loud
voice, saying: 'Master Matthew, rise!   Rise up, Master Matthew:
It is no time to lie now sluggishly in your bed.'   At that word
and at that very instant the pain and headache and the whole
disease quite forsook him, and he rose up as merry and as sound

in his body as if there had never been any such disease upon him. And when he was ready he honoured the holy maid, and gave her most humble thanks, saying that he knew now by experience in his own body that the power of God dwelt in her and wrought strange things by her. But she could not abide to hear any words that tended to her own commendation, and therefore she went away. As she was going out, F. Raymund came towards the house, and meeting her in the gate, looked very heavily, for he knew nothing of all this that was done in the house, but came directly from the physician. When he saw her there, being as it were overcome with sorrow, he said to her. 'O mother, will you suffer this good man that is so dear to us, and so profitable and necessary to many others, to die after this sort?' To that she made answer very humbly, showing, indeed, that she had no liking of such words. 'O father,' said she, 'what manner of talk is this that you use to me? Do you take me to be a God that you would have me deliver a mortal man from death?' 'I pray you,' said he, 'speak these words to those who are strangers to you, and not to me who knows your secrets. I know well enough that whatever you ask of God heartily He will grant you.' With that she bowed down her head a little and smiled; and after a time, looking up to him again cheerfully, she said these words: 'Father, be of good cheer, for he shall not die this time.' When Raymund heard these words, he was much comforted, for he knew well what grace was given to her from above. And so he went into the house to comfort his friend, supposing that the thing had been yet to do that was already done. When he came in he found him sitting up in good health, declaring to them that were about him the manner of the miracle that had been wrought upon himself. For the further confirmation whereof the table was laid, and they ate together that morning, not such meats as sick men use to eat, but raw onions and such other coarse meats as cannot be digested save only by those in perfect health. And as they were eating they took great pleasure to recite the wonderful things that it pleased God to work by the holy maid.

" In the course of this same plague the hermit Fra Santi caught

the contagion, which, when Catherine understood, she caused him
to be taken out of his cell, and to be brought to the *Misericordia*,
where she came to him with some other of her Sisters and nursed
him, providing for him all such things as she thought necessary
And to comfort him with words also, she put her head close to
his, and whispered him softly in the ear, saying: 'Be not afraid,
however you feel, for you shall not die this time.' But to the
rest that were there she said no such thing, but rather, when
they entreated her that she would pray to God for his recovery,
she gave them but a doubtful answer, which made them very
sad, for they all knew him to be a holy man, and therefore both
honoured and loved him tenderly. The disease increased hourly
more and more, and they despairing of his life gave over the
charge of his body, and looked only to the health of his soul.
At last, when he was in extremes, and they all stood about him
with great heaviness, looking only when he would give up the
ghost, the holy maid came to him again, and said in his ear ·
'Be not afraid, for you shall not die at this time.' The sick man
both heard and understood that word, though before it seemed
that he was past all sense And he took comfort in it, crediting
the word of the holy maid that sounded in his ear rather than the
throes of death that gripped him by the heart. However, he
showed no token of amendment, and therefore they, not understanding what she had said, provided lights and other things for
his burial, looking still when he would depart out of this life. At
last, when it seemed that he was even passing out of the world,
Catherine came to him again, and spake these words in his ear
'I command thee, in the name of our Lord Jesus Christ, that
thou pass not at this time.' At that word he took comfort of
spirit and strength of body, and rose up in his bed and called for
meat, and ate in the presence of them all; and after that time
lived many years, and was one of them that were present with
the holy maid in Rome when she departed out of this life "[1]

Besides these cases of her power with the sick, Raymund had
experience of the same in his own person. "When the plague

[1] Fen, Part 4, chap. iii.

was raging in Siena," he says, ' I resolved to sacrifice my life for the salvation of souls and not to avoid any plague-stricken patient whatever. It is certain that the malady is contagious , but I knew that our Lord Jesus Christ is more powerful than Galen, and that grace is superior to nature. I also saw that many had taken flight, and that the dying remained without assistance ; and as the blessed Catherine had taught me that charity obliges us to love the soul of our neighbour more than our own body, I was desirous of assisting as many sick as I could, and I did so by God's grace. I was almost alone in that vast city, and had scarcely time to take a little food and sleep. One night as I rested, and the time approached to rise and recite my office, I felt a violent pain in the part which is first attacked by that malady, and soon discovered the fatal swelling which declares its presence. Greatly alarmed, I dared not rise, and began to think of my approaching death. I longed to see Catherine before the disease made further progress, and when morning came, I dragged myself with my companion to Catherine's residence ; but she was absent, having gone out to visit a sick person I decided to wait, and as I could no longer support myself, I was obliged to lie down on a bed which was there, and besought the persons of the house not to delay sending for her. When she came, and saw my excessive suffering, she knelt down by my bed, placed her hand on my forehead, and began to pray interiorly as usual , I saw she was in an ecstasy, and I thought that there would soon result some good both for my soul and body. She remained thus during nearly an hour and a half, when I felt a universal movement in every limb, which I thought was the prelude to some dangerous crisis; but I was in error, for I began at that moment to improve ; and before Catherine had recovered the use of her senses, I was completely cured, there only remaining in me a certain weakness, a proof of my illness, or an effect of my want of faith. Catherine, aware of the grace that she had obtained from her Spouse, came to herself and caused them to prepare for me the ordinary nourishment common to the sick. When I had taken it from her virginal hands, she ordered me to sleep a little   I obeyed, and on awakening I found myself as well as if nothing had happened to me.   Then she said to me, 'Now, go and labour for the salvation of souls, and render thanks to the Almighty God who has delivered you from this danger.' I returned to my ordinary work, glorifying the Lord who had bestowed such power on His faithful spouse."   At the same time and in the same manner she effected the cure of F. Bartholomew, though he had been lying sick of the plague for a considerable time.   Simon of Cortona was also cured by her, as he himself relates in his deposition.

Raymund relates other miracles, such as the cure of one of the Sisters of Penance, who lived near the *Misericordia*, and devoted herself to Catherine's service, and who was crushed under a falling building.   The neighbours drew her out of the ruins, and found her not dead, but in horrible anguish and past medical aid. "As soon as Catherine heard it," he continues, "she was filled with compassion for one who was her Sister, and who had made herself her servant.   She went immediately to visit her, and exhorted her to patience.   When she saw her suffering so excessively, she began to touch the places of which she complained; the patient willingly consenting, because she knew that those blessed hands could not fail to do her good.   As soon as Catherine touched any place, its pains vanished: then the sick woman showed her the other parts that were tormented, so that she might apply the same remedy, and Catherine lent herself to this charity with so much care that she finished by completely healing her.   In proportion as her virginal hand glided over the bruised body, the pain disappeared, and the sick woman, who before could not move a single member, little by little recovered the power of motion.   She kept silence whilst Catherine was present lest she might alarm her humility, but afterwards she said to the physicians and neighbours who surrounded her : 'Catherine, Lapa's daughter, has cured me by touching me.'"

Another cure, attested by all Catherine's biographers, was that of Sister Gemmina, one of the Mantellate, who, being attacked by a quinsy and in danger of suffocation, by an extraordinary effort contrived to get to Catherine's house, and said to her, "Mother, I shall die, if you do not help me!" Full of pity, Catherine applied her hand to the sufferer's throat, and at once the malady left her.

But pestilence was not the only scourge which at this time afflicted Siena; terrible civil disorders were likewise preying on the lifeblood of the republic She was reaping the inevitable fruits of revolution. No government found itself strong enough to repress the licence which universally reigned; and while the Riformatori were capable of any oppressive act towards the weak, a powerful miscreant had every chance of escaping just punishment.

Geri, Lord of Perolla, had an only daughter, to whom when dying he left his castle and estates in the Tuscan Maremma. Her kinsman, Andrea Salimbeni, under pretext of a friendly visit, seized the castle, and dyed his murderous hand in the blood of the innocent girl. He then applied himself to sack and ravage the adjacent territories; but such an excess of brutality did at last rouse the indignation of the senator, who prepared to avenge the crime. An armed force was despatched against Andrea. he was taken with twenty-eight associates, and committed to prison on the 23d of April 1374. A few days later, sixteen of the more insignificant criminals were executed, but the senator feared to proceed to extremities against Andrea and his more powerful comrades; and so the real authors of the bloody outrage were spared When the *popolani* learnt this, they assembled in vast numbers, and marching to the doors of the *Palazzo Pubblico*, demanded vengeance. Galgano, the captain of the people, deserted by his colleagues and powerless to resist the armed multitude, came forth and declared that he made over to their leader, Nocci di Vanni, a saddler by trade, the right and authority to do whatever he might deem best for the public good. The stern tribune seated himself on the bench of justice and commanded Andrea to be brought before him. Then in few words sentence was given, and the miserable man was borne forth into the Piazza, and there summarily beheaded.

The Salimbeni and all their adherents, furious at this act of popular justice, flew to arms; Cione Salimbeni, thinking it a good opportunity for gratifying his ambition, seized several fortresses belonging to the republic, and soon the whole mountain region was plunged in war, if such be not too dignified a word to be applied to the ruffianly hostilities of these bandit chieftains. Agnolo Salimbeni, the head of the family, and a man of chivalrous honour, seems on this occasion to have acted in a way which earned him the confidence of the citizens; for they made over to him the command of some of the strongest castles, a circumstance which excited against him the jealousy of Cione, and became the origin of a feud which was only extinguished three years later through the efforts of St. Catherine. But while such anarchy raged throughout the country, the fields were left uncultivated, and the miserable peasantry took refuge within the city walls from the violence of the roving brigand bands. Famine soon came to increase the horrors of pestilence, and Catherine and her companions had to feed as well as to nurse the destitute citizens. To this year must probably be assigned an incident which is related in the Legend, and which we shall quote from its English version. Catherine, as it seems, was at that time staying, according to her wont, in the house of Alexia. "It chanced that year that there was such a scarcity of corn in the city and country, that the people were constrained to eat bread made of musty corn that had been kept long time in underground caves, because there was none other to be got for money. Of such corn Alexia had made provision for herself and her family for that year. But before her store was spent, the harvest-time was come, and she heard that there was new corn to be sold in the market, whereupon she thought to cast away the little portion that was left of the musty corn, and buy new. But before she did it, Catherine being in the house with her, she chanced to break her mind to her, and to tell her what she was about to do. 'What will you do?' said she; 'will you cast that away that God hath sent for the sustenance of man? If you will not eat of that bread yourself, yet bestow it upon the poor that have no bread to eat.' To that Alexia replied, saying, that she had a conscience to give such mouldy and unwholesome bread to the poor, she would rather buy new corn, and make them bread of that. 'Well,' said the holy maid, 'bring me here a little water and that meal which you intend to cast away, and I will make bread of it for the poor.' So Alexia did as she was bid. Then the holy maid took it, and made paste of it: and of the paste made such a quantity of bread, and that so quickly, that Alexia and her servant, who beheld her all the time, were astonished to see it, for they made as many loaves as would have required four or five times as much meal; and delivered them to Alexia to lay upon boards and carry to the oven. And (which was most marvellous) there was no bad savour in those loaves as there was in all other made of the same corn. But when they were baked and set on the table to eat, they that ate of them could find no manner of evil taste in them, but rather said that they had not in their life eaten better or more savoury bread. This miracle being spread in the city, her confessor came with certain other of his brethren to examine the matter, and found, in very deed, that there were two great miracles wrought, one in augmenting the quantity of the paste, and another in amending the evil quality and stench of the corn. And a third miracle was added soon after, which was, that whereas the bread was very liberally dealt out to the poor and none other eaten in the house but that, yet there remained ever more great store of it in the larder. And so it continued many days and weeks, which moved certain devout persons that understood the truth of the matter to take some of the said bread, and to lay it up reverently where it might be kept for a relic and perpetual remembrance of the great work that Almighty God had wrought by His dear spouse. Afterwards F. Raymund being desirous to be more particularly informed of the matter by the holy maid, prayed her that she would declare to him how the thing had passed. And she made him answer simply after this manner: 'Father, I had a great zeal that the thing that God had sent us for the relief of man should not be lost; and I had moreover a great compassion for the poor.   Whereupon I went to the hutch of meal with great fervour of spirit.   As soon as I was there, behold, our blessed Lady likewise was there with me, accompanied with a number of saints and angels, and bade me to go forward with my work as I had determined.   And she was so benign and charitable that she vouchsafed to labour with me, and to work the paste with her own hands ; and so by the virtue of her holy hands were those loaves multiplied in such sort as you have heard, for she made the loaves and gave them to me, and I delivered them to Alexia and her servant '   ' Truly, mother,' said F Raymund, ' I marvel not now if that bread seemed to me and others that tasted it passing sweet, considering that it was made with the hands of that most heavenly and glorious Queen, in whose sacred body was wrought and made by the Holy Trinity that living Bread that came down from heaven to give life to all true believers.' "

F. Thomas Caffarini mentions this incident in his deposition, and says he was one of those who had eaten of the bread thus made.   Father Simon of Cortona also declares that during this time of famine the Saint often multiplied bread in order to feed the poor, and that he was himself present on one such occasion

CHAPTER XVI.

CATHERINE AT MONTEPULCIANO, 1374

A RUMOUR of the heroic deeds performed by Catherine and her companion during the plague was not long in reaching Pisa, where it made a great sensation, specially among the nuns of a certain convent which Raymund does not name. They appear to have pressed her to pay them a visit, but not meeting with the success they desired, they put the affair into the hands of a personage no less important than Peter Gambacorta, the supreme head of the republic. The character of this celebrated man is variously represented by various historians, but if not free from the charge of ambition, it undoubtedly possessed many noble points. His father and uncles had distinguished themselves by their resistance to the usurpation of a certain Giovanni Agnello, who, secretly encouraged by the Emperor Charles IV. (the same whom we have seen so ignominiously defeated at Siena), had assumed the title of Doge, and aimed at becoming the tyrant of the republic. The Gambacorti had paid the penalty of their patriotism on the block; their estates were confiscated, whilst Peter and the surviving members of the family were driven into banishment. Before many years were over, however, a fresh revolution broke out. The Doge was deposed, and all the exiles recalled. Peter and his children, now reduced to the utmost poverty, returned to Pisa, and entered the city in triumph carrying olive branches in their hands. Amid the acclamations of the populace they proceeded to the Cathedral, and there, standing before the high altar, Peter gave thanks to God for his restoration to his native country, and solemnly swore in the name of all the

exiles "to live as a good citizen, forgiving and forgetting all past
injuries." When we remember the ruthless spirit of the age in
all that concerned the forgiveness of enemies, this act on the part
of one who had suffered such bitter injustice appears truly heroic ;
and indeed it was far above the comprehension of his partisans.
Instead of following so glorious an example, they proceeded to
celebrate their triumph by setting fire to Agnello's house ; and
the wind being high, the flames spread, and the entire city was
threatened with destruction. Then it was seen that Peter's promise was not an idle form of words ; he rushed from the Cathedral
into the midst of the burning flames, and interposed his own
person between the savage multitude and his fallen enemies ; all
day long he was to be seen battling with the fire, and driving back
the maddened mob ; and standing there alone like a true hero
he cried aloud to those who clamoured for the blood of Agnello,
"*I* have pardoned him, what right have *you* to revenge?"[1]

Such a man was worthy and capable of appreciating the character of Catherine ; and he was not unwilling to draw her to Pisa
at a moment when the political horizon was overcast, and when
there seemed no small likelihood of a breach between Florence
and the court of Avignon. So he sent her a letter pressing her
to come, to which Catherine's answer is preserved :—

"I received your letter," she says, "and was much touched by
it ; I know it is not my virtue or goodness, for I am full of
miseries, but your own kindness and that of these holy ladies
which moves you to write to me so humbly, begging me to come
to you. I would gladly comply with your wish and theirs, but
for the present must beg to be excused : my weak health will not
permit of it ; and, moreover, I see that just now it would be an
occasion of scandal. I hope, however, please God, that when
the time arrives when I can do so without offence, and without
giving rise to murmurs, I may be able to come, and then I shall
be at your command. Recommend me to those holy ladies and
beg them to pray for me, that I may ever be humble and subject
to my Creator."

[1] Sismondi, vol. vii ch xlviii.

The state of her health which she here gives as a reason for declining the invitation to Pisa was indeed more suffering than it had been at any former period. Possibly, she had exhausted her strength during the time of the pestilence, for we learn by a passage in the *Miracoli* that in the August of that same year she was attacked by grievous sickness. "On the feast of the Assumption, 1374," says the author of that memoir, "Catherine fell sick, and was brought to death's door, but there was no sign of pestilence in her malady. She believed herself dying, which caused her the most unbounded joy. It would be impossible to describe the rapture she felt at the thought that she was passing to eternal life, and the very joy she felt so comforted and restored her vital powers, that the danger passed. Whereat she conceived a great sorrow and began to pray to the Blessed Virgin that she would not permit her to remain longer in this life. Then our Lady appeared to her, saying, 'Catherine, my daughter, seest thou all that crowd of people who are behind me?' 'Yes,' she replied, '*Madonna mia,* I see them all.' 'Then,' continued our Lady, 'look and see which thou wilt choose. My Divine Son, desiring that thou shouldst live yet a little longer, will give thee all these souls to be brought to eternal life, besides those others whom He has already given to thee, if thy death is deferred for another time ; but if thou choose to die now, He will not give them to thee. Choose, therefore, which thou wilt.' Then Catherine replied again, '*Madonna mia,* thou knowest that there is no power in me to will or not to will, for my will is not mine, because I have given it to thy Son Jesus.' Then said our Lady, '*Know then that He has given thee all these souls that I have shown thee ;* and that He will call thee to Himself another time, when it shall please Him ' Our Lady disappeared, and Catherine found herself delivered from the sickness which she had been suffering Some time after she made known this vision to a person, who asked her, saying, 'Should you know any of those persons whom our Lady showed to you?' And she replied, 'Yes, if I were to see them, I should know them all.'"

The other reason she assigns for deferring her visit lest she should give occasion of complaint to her fellow-citizens is but an example of the difficulties which generally presented themselves in the way of her leaving Siena. In the present case, however, they were rather more serious than usual, for just then Peter Gambacorta was not in very good odour with the magistrates of Siena. He had encouraged the Prior of the Pisan knights of St John to seize possession first of the strong place called Rocca dell' Albarese, and then of the castle of Talamon, and to hold them in the name of the Church. Talamon, as has been stated before, was the key of Siena, and its occupation by the knights was a very sore point with the citizens. Catherine therefore was wisely anxious not to irritate them further, and besides, she was habitually reluctant, and not forward, when there was any question of producing herself before a world of strangers. So she remained at Siena during the remainder of that year and the beginning of the following; and whilst waiting for a more favourable opportunity for visiting Pisa, she undertook a less distant journey to the monastery of St. Agnes at Montepulciano It is here that Raymund of Capua had resided for three years as confessor to the nuns before coming to Siena. He tells us in his Legend that Catherine had a great love for these holy pilgrimages, and, naturally enough, has given a rather careful account of the two visits which she paid to the convent which was his old home, and which he still governed as Vicar of the Provincial. Moreover, he goes out of his way to relate to us the history of St. Agnes, which he had written during his residence there, and which he also related to Catherine. After hearing his narrative she conceived a great desire to go and venerate the body of the saint which was preserved there incorrupt, and having asked and obtained the permission of her superiors, she set out with her companions; Raymund and Father Thomas following her the day after Having reached the convent, Catherine at once proceeded to visit the holy body, attended by all the nuns of the community, as well as by the Sisters of Penance who accompanied her; and kneeling at the feet of St Agnes she stooped to kiss them, when in the sight of all present one of the feet suddenly

raised itself as if to meet her lips. At this spectacle Catherine
was much troubled and confused, and restoring the foot to its
former position, she prostrated in humble prayer. Next day
when the two confessors arrived they found no small discussion
on what had passed going on among the religious; some affirming
it to have been the work of God, and others disposed rather to
regard it as a deceit of the enemy. Raymund, as superior of
the nuns, thought it prudent to investigate the matter; and
calling the community together desired all to give their testimony
under a precept of holy obedience. "All present," he writes,
"declared that they had seen the incident occur as related; and
as there was one who had offered greater opposition than the
rest, I inquired of her more particularly whether the affair had
passed as had been represented. 'Yes,' she replied, 'I do not
deny it, I desire only to explain that the intention of St. Agnes
was not what you believe.' 'My very dear Sister,' I replied,
'we do not interrogate you concerning the intentions of St. Agnes,
being well aware that you are neither her secretary nor her confidante; we merely ask you whether you saw the foot rise?' To
that she assented; and I then imposed a penance on her for the
discourses she had indiscreetly held."

Some little time later Catherine returned to the convent bringing her two nieces, Eugenia and another whose name is not
preserved, both of whom took the religious habit in the community. "As soon as she arrived," says Raymund, "she repaired,
as at the first time, to the body of the saintly foundress with her
companions and some nuns from the convent; she did not place
herself at the feet this time, but approached the head; designing
by humility, as we presume, to avoid what had happened before
when she attempted to kiss the feet; or perhaps she remembered
that Mary Magdalen at first poured her perfumes over the Saviour's
feet and afterwards shed them over His head. She placed her
face on the ornaments of gold and silk which cover the countenance of St. Agnes, and there remained a long time; then she
turned sweetly to Lisa, the mother of her two nieces, and inquired
smiling. 'What, do you not observe the present that Heaven

sends us · do not be ungrateful !' At these words, Lisa and the others lifted their eyes and saw a very fine white manna falling like heavenly dew, and covering not only St. Agnes and Catherine, but also all the persons present, and with such abundance that Lisa filled her hand with it."

A letter is preserved, written by the Saint to Eugenia after her profession at the convent, which exhibits the motherly interest she felt in her niece In this letter she warns her against imprudent intimacies whether with priests or seculars. "If I ever hear of your contracting such intimacies," she says, "I will give you such a penance as, whether you like it or not, you will remember all your life." Then she speaks of the visits of strangers . "If they have anything to say, let them say it to the Prioress; do not you stir to go to them unless the Prioress send you, and then be as savage as a hedgehog And when you go to confession, confess your sins, and having received your penance, retire [1] Do not be surprised at my speaking thus, for the company of those most falsely called *devotees* corrupts the rules and usages of the religious life. Be on your guard, then, never to let your heart be tied to any one but Jesus crucified ; otherwise when you would wish to untie it, you will not be able to succeed without much difficulty. The soul that is fed on the Bread of angels sees that all these things are obstacles Seek rather all that will unite you to God, and the best of all means is prayer." She then gives her a long and beautiful instruction on the three kinds of prayer, namely, a recollection of the presence of God, vocal, and mental prayer Of vocal prayer, including the recital of the office, she says, "We should use it in such a way as that, when the lips speak, the heart is not far from God." She describes the diffi-

---

[1] "*Recevuta la penitenza, fugge*" The severe expressions here used may be understood as in part directed against the Fraticelli, a dangerous and insidious sect who at that time made it their business to find their way into the parlours of convents, for the purposes of spreading their pernicious doctrines among the nuns. St. Catherine had many encounters with these gentry, and her letters are full of allusions to them. Eugenia died young, like so many of her family. At the Chapter held at her convent in 1387, her name does not occur in the list of the community.

culties which often beset the soul in mental prayer, such as combats, weariness and confusion of mind; but warns her niece not on that account to abandon it, because by these struggles God will fortify the soul and make it constant; and if we gain nothing else we get to know our own nothingness; whilst God on His part will not fail to accept and bless our good resolutions. "Prayer of this sort," she says, "will teach you to love your rule, it will seal in your heart the three solemn vows of your profession, and engrave there the determination to observe them even until death. Let me then see you a precious jewel in the presence of God, and have the consolation of knowing that I have not lost my time"[1]

In the narrative of the visit to St. Agnes's body the reader will have noticed that the name of Lisa once more occurs. She had returned to Siena after her husband's death, and putting on the habit of Penance, thenceforth made her home with Lapa and Catherine. The three are named together in a document dated 1378, as taxed by the Commune for the sum of six hundred lire.[2] On Lisa were settled as her marriage dowry the farm and vineyard belonging to the Benincasa family at San Rocco a Pili.[3] Catherine often visited this spot, which is situated about five miles out of the city on the Grosseto road. Caffarini in his Supplement relates the circumstances of one of these visits, when Catherine came thither at Lisa's earnest solicitation to recruit her strength, she being at the time in a very suffering state. Having reached the farm, Catherine had so sharp an attack of her habitual pain in the side, as to be unable to leave the house all that day and the following night. Next morning, desiring to receive Holy Communion, she rose, and went to the little parish church hard by. But presently she bethought herself that

---

[1] Letter 159

[2] Burlamacchi's Notes to the Legend.

[3] Sano di Maco was Procurator to Lisa in a money transaction regarding this property, the document relating to which is preserved in the *Libro delle Denunzie di Dogano* (*Diario Sanese,* ii., 100). Gigli calls the parish *S. Rocco,* Grottanelli, *Santa Maria a Pili.* At present (he says) it bears the name of S. Bartolomeo.

she was perhaps guilty of presumption in thus approaching the altar without having previously been to confession She therefore presented herself to the priest for absolution, and at the moment of receiving it felt herself bathed anew in the Blood of Jesus. Rapt in ecstasy she communicated, and remained so abstracted, praying for her confessor and her disciples by name. Raymund and one of his companions were at that moment in the convent of Siena; but feeling a sudden and sensible visitation of Divine grace, they said one to another, "Catherine must be praying for us!" and found afterwards that it had been even so.[1]

The memory of St. Catherine is still preserved in this place, which is commonly called *Il Podere di Lisa*, or *Lisa's farm*, and bears an inscription, recording its connection with St. Catherine. It was long the custom for the Rogation Processions to make a station on the spot, when the priest would exhort the people to offer special prayers for a blessing on their parish, on this ground once sanctified by the footsteps of the holy virgin of Siena. [2] And here we may observe that these Rogation Processions were in Catherine's time ceremonies of great splendour and importance, at which all the clergy and citizens assisted, nor is it to be doubted that the Saint herself was accustomed to take part in these beautiful devotions of her native city. Each day the crimson banner of the Duomo led the way out of one or other of the city gates, the procession making a circuit of many miles to bless the fields and vineyards of the outlying territory. Those who were too old or feeble to undertake so fatiguing an expedition, waited at the gates for the return of the banner; none ever dreamed of absenting themselves altogether. One beautiful custom existed of holding the consecrated banner across the street at certain spots where, according to tradition, pagan monuments formerly stood, in order that all the people might pass under it, and so offer their protest against the worship of the false gods, and render their homage instead to the symbol of Christianity. On the first day the procession went forth through the Porta Camollia, saluting as they passed the ancient

[1] Latin Sup., Part 2. Trat. 6. art. 48.　　　[2] Diar. San. ii. 100.

image of our Lady which stood there, and being careful to take the road through the chestnut woods of Montagnuola, that the chestnuts might be well blessed. On Tuesday they took a southerly direction, going out of the Porta Pispini through the suburban parish of St. Eugenia; on Wednesday they issued forth by the Porta Tufi, through the beautiful fields whence are seen the mountain district and the peaks of Monte Amiata, together with the valleys watered by the Orcia, and the distant Maremma. Gigli, who preserves these details, tells us that the Sienese kept the Rogation days as solemn holydays, and even gives us to understand that they observed what St. Cesarius of Arles had prescribed regarding them, namely, that on these solemnities no man should either be bled or take medicine, unless in great danger; probably in order that none might thereby be prevented from joining in these devout processions.

One other locality must be named in the vicinity of Siena where Catherine often retired, it was the hospice belonging to the Dominican Fathers at St. Quirico in Osenna, twenty-four miles out of the city on the Roman road. It is situated on a hill between the Orcia and the Ombrone, and from it is dated one of the Saint's letters to F. Thomas della Fonte. In the peace and silence of that beautiful retreat she pours forth some of the most exquisite of her impassioned words. Yet she begins by accusing herself of caring so little for God's honour, and thinking so seldom of His teaching. "I ought to live dead to my own will," she says, "and yet I have not subjected it to the yoke of obedience half so much as I could and ought to have done." Then she proceeds to speak of that transformation of the soul in God which is wrought by this conformity of our will with His · "O Love! Sweet Love!" she continues; "enlarge our memory to receive, to contain, to comprehend all Thy goodness, for when we comprehend it, we shall love it, and by loving it we shall be united to it, and so, transformed in charity, we shall pass through the door of Jesus crucified, according to His words to His disciples, 'I will come, and make My abode with you.' You tell me in your letter," she adds, "that you have been to visit the body of St.

Agnes (at Montepulciano), and that you have recommended us to her and to all the religious, which much consoles me; and you say that you know not why, but that you have no wish to return thither. I reply, there may be many reasons for this; one is, that a soul really united to God, and transformed in Him, readily forgets itself and all creatures. May this be so with you."— (Letter 105.)

Catherine often returned to Montepulciano, and corresponded with the Prioress and other members of the community; and there are no tenderer allusions in her letters than those which refer to "her St. Agnes," as she calls the convent. At the time of her first visit in 1374 it was situated at some distance from the town, but a few years later the unsettled state of that mountain district rendered it necessary for the nuns to seek safety by transferring their residence within the walls; and as the requisite expenses were beyond their means, St. Catherine applied to Ricasoli, Archbishop of Florence, who had promised to give her the first alms she wished to bestow. "Since you are the father of the poor," she writes, "and since you have made me promise to address myself to you the first time I wished to bestow an alms, I will fulfil my promise, for there is a very pressing alms I want to make to the convent of St. Agnes. They must be transferred within the walls on account of the wars; but they want fifty gold florins to begin with, the town will do the rest. I beg of you, therefore, help them if you can."

The secret of Catherine's great love for this community lay in the revelation which had been granted her, that in heaven she should enjoy a degree of bliss equal to that of St Agnes; and that they should be companions throughout eternity. It is a beautiful, and perhaps an unique passage in the lives of the saints. It gives us a glimpse of something beyond even the hope that shattered links of human affection will be reunited and purified in another life. It reveals to us the saints in glory endowed with the capacity, in some unspeakable way, of drawing near one to another in God, bound by the ties of a new and unearthly friendship. Nor, as we may safely infer, could such a trait be found in the history of one the chords of whose heart did not respond to that note of sublimised human affection; Catherine on earth knew how to practise her own doctrine of never removing the vase from the fountain which supplied it, and there was reserved for her in heaven to drink from the abundant torrents of sweetness which water the courts of the eternal mansions.

It would seem that these journeys to Montepulciano in 1374 had a double object; and that, besides the family affairs which often took her to the convent, Catherine was also bent on the reconciliation of certain feuds for which her mediation had been solicited However, on this, as on many like occasions, her departure from Siena gave rise to jealousies and suspicions on the part of the magistrates. They had moreover some difficult business of the same kind on their hands just then which they despaired of bringing to a favourable issue without her help, and evil tongues, always busy with their criticisms on her doings, filled their ears with murmurs and complaints So at last the Signoria despatched her disciple, Thomas Guelfaccio, with a message bidding her return, as she was greatly wanted in Siena Catherine, however, was equally proof against their flattery and the fear of their displeasure. "You desire my return," she says in her reply, "and ask my advice how to obtain peace. I am incapable of the least good, but I shall bow my head whenever God wills me to obey you, for of course I must place the will of God before that of man At present I do not see that I can possibly return, for I have still an important business to negotiate for the nuns of St. Agnes, and I am here with the nephews of Messer Spinello, in order to make peace with the sons of Lorenzo. I regret the trouble my fellow-citizens take in judging me; it really seems as if they had nothing else to do than to speak evil of me and my companions. In my case they are right, for I am full of faults, but they are wrong in their judgment of the others. However, we shall overcome all things with patience."

It was at Montepulciano that two events took place which are related by Raymund in the Legend as "occurring in the beginning of their acquaintance." He had heard many marvellous things concerning her, which he hesitated to believe, and desired, as her confessor, to put them to the proof by some infallible test. 'I remembered," he says, "that we were living in the time of the third beast with the skin of a leopard, whereby is denoted hypocrites, and in my day I had met with plenty of persons, specially women, easily deceived like their first mother." The rest he resolved on was to desire that by her intercession she should obtain for him such a perfect contrition for his sins as he never before had, and that he might also have some token that the same had been procured by her means; for he was assured that the devil could not be the author of such contrition, and that it is not in the power of any man, but of God only, to touch and move the heart to conceive such sorrow. With this purpose, therefore, he went to Catherine, and asked her to do him a pleasure. "What is it?" she asked. "None other than this," he replied, "that you will pray to your Spouse for me, that of His mercy He will pardon me all my sins." She answered that she would cheerfully do what he asked, as one who felt no doubt of obtaining her request. "But," said Raymund, "this is not enough. I must have a full pardon and bull drawn after the manner of the court of Rome." She asked his meaning. "The bull I desire," he said, "is that I may feel a deep and true contrition." At these words she gave him a sweet and penetrating look which seemed to betoken that she had read the secret thoughts of his heart. "Have no fear," she said, "you shall have the bull you ask for." And so they parted, for it was towards evening, and the friars lodged at a house separate from the monastery. The next morning Raymund found himself too unwell to leave the house, and so remained in his apartments together with his companion, Brother Nicolas of Pisa,[1] the same who has before

---

[1] This brother Nicolas da Cascina finds honourable mention in the Chronicle of S. Caterina of Pisa as a man of signal virtue. He was a man of austere life, chastising his body, and often spending entire nights watching and praying in the church. He was as learned as he was humble, and a model of religious obedience. At his death, which took place on the vigil of Pentecost, the angels are said to have visibly assisted.

been named as having travelled from Pisa to Siena for the sole purpose of seeing the Saint. Catherine, understanding in spirit that he was ill, said to her companion: "F. Raymund is ill; let us go and see him." They went, therefore, and entering his apartment somewhat suddenly, she approached the couch where he lay, and asked him how he found himself. Then entering into discourse she began to speak of God, of His benefits to His creatures, and of their ungrateful return for all His goodness, with such grace and unction, that, as he listened, Raymund felt his heart moved as it had never been before. And all the time he never thought of the bull he had asked for, but was wholly carried away by the force and efficacy of her words. They pierced his heart like sharp darts, and wakened such a sense of his past sins as never in his life had he experienced until that moment. For he seemed to see himself arraigned, as it were, before the tribunal of God, and confessed in himself that he was worthy of everlasting punishment. Then when this terrible thought had lasted a good space, he seemed to behold our Lord as a pitiful Father, clothing His nakedness with His own robes, leading him into His house, giving him to eat at His table, and accepting him as one of His own servants. And so considering both the deformity of his sins, and the merciful goodness of our Saviour who received him again so lovingly, he burst into tears, and continued weeping and sobbing as though his heart would break. Catherine, who had watched the whole matter, and who understood well enough what was passing in his heart, when she saw the medicine begin to work, held her peace, and let him weep on undisturbed. At last he suddenly remembered within himself what had passed between them the day before, and turning to her he said · "Ah, daughter, is this the bull I asked for yesterday?" "Even so," she replied; then rising she touched him lightly on the shoulder saying, "Forget not the benefits of God," and departed, leaving him and Nicolas much consoled and edified.

He tells us of another token of her sanctity, which was given to him without his having asked for it, and at the same monastery. It happened that she was suffering much from her accustomed infirmities, and was lying on her little couch, when having received certain high revelations, she sent to Raymund, praying him to come at once that she might communicate the same to him. "When he heard the things that she reported, and reflected on the greatness of the same in comparison to what he had read of other saints, he said to himself, ' Is it possible that all this should be true that she saith?' And with that, looking steadfastly upon her, he saw her face suddenly transformed into the face of a Man, who likewise set His eyes steadfastly upon him, and gave him a marvellous dreadful look. The Face that he saw was somewhat long; it appeared to be that of a man of middle age, His beard was somewhat of the colour of ripe wheat, that is, between red and yellow, His countenance was very comely, reverend, and full of majesty. And for a little time he saw that Face only, and could see none other thing, which put him in such a fear and terror that, casting up his hands above his shoulders, he cried with a loud voice, and said, 'O Lord, who is this that looketh thus upon me?' ' It is He,' said she, ' that is.' And with that she came again to her own form."[1] "At the same moment," he writes, "my understanding was illuminated with an abundant light on the matter of our discourse. I had indeed been before incredulous, but our Lord had come and manifested to me His own Face, that I might no longer doubt Who it was Who spoke in her. As Thomas, after he had received the token which he had demanded, exclaimed, saying, ' My Lord and my God!' so I also, after this vision, exclaimed to myself, Verily, this is indeed the spouse and disciple of my Lord and God And I declare these things that my readers may understand that our Lord displayed His doctrine in her as in a vessel frail and weak indeed by nature, but by His power miraculously made strong."[2]

[1] Fen., Part I, ch. xxiv   [2] Legend, Part I, ch. ix.

(249)

CHAPTER XVII.

BEATI PACIFICI.

IN following thus far the course of Catherine's history we have chiefly been engaged with its domestic aspect, and have sought to unravel the narrative as it has been given to us by Raymund, supplementing it, where defective, by the abundant testimony of her other biographers and disciples. Her life, however, was something more than a series of charming stories and supernatural favours. The graces which were poured out on her with such magnificent profuseness were given to her not for herself alone, but for others. Called to a special work and a wholly exceptional mission, she was designed by God to be a chosen vessel to carry His name before princes and nations.[1] And that mission, as was fitting and natural, she began among her own people.

Surrounded, therefore, by the group of faithful disciples whom we have described in a former chapter, and to whose ranks fresh accessions daily flowed, Catherine accepted the work which Divine Providence presented to her, and applied herself to it with that earnestness mingled with simplicity which marked her whole career. If that career were strange and unprecedented for a woman to follow, this, at least, is worthy of remark, that there is no single example to be found of her ever taking on herself any duty (beyond those ordinary good works open to all devout women) without solicitation or command. On the contrary, there is abundant proof of the reluctance with which she invariably hung back from the efforts made on the part of the world to draw her from her retirement. But when the multitude sought

[1] Acts ix. 15.

her out in her humble chamber in the Fullonica, she did not refuse
to listen to their sorrows and to heal their discords, nor did she
hesitate to use the marvellous but unstudied eloquence both of
tongue and of pen which God had bestowed upon her, to deliver
His message to men of all conditions. Catherine was a true Italian
and a true Dominican also. She loved her country, and names it
in her letters with unmistakable tenderness, and she inherited
the traditions of an Order, one of whose chief works in the early
centuries of its existence had been the healing of party feuds.
Everywhere throughout Italy the friars appeared as the apostles
of peace; we need but mention the names of John of Salerno,
Latino Malabranca, and Bernard di Guido, to remind the reader
of those tales of wondrous and pathetic beauty which exhibit to
us the sons of St. Dominic in the character of the blessed peace-
makers. And surely no portion of their apostolic mission could
fall more fitly or gracefully than this to the share of a religious
woman. How could she come in contact with such a soul as
that of James Tolomei without conceiving a detestation for those
habits and social maxims so deeply rooted in the hearts of her
countrymen, that crime had ceased to be regarded as crime, and
a youth before he had attained to manhood could boast of the
blood which he had shed, just as some wild Indian might exhibit
and number up the scalps of his victims? "The hatreds of the
Middle Ages," says Capecelatro, " had a vigour and tenacity in
them unknown in our days, when base cowardice sometimes dis-
guises itself under the mask of gentle manners. The super-
abundant life of those times, when men seemed full of young
blood, and which when directed to Christian practice produced
such prodigies of charity, betrayed itself also in those deadly
hatreds which resisted even the instincts of faith then so powerful
in society. The customs of their old heathen and barbarian
ancestors had not entirely decayed, so that the supreme moment
of life, blessed and sanctified by the last offices of religion, was
often chosen as a time for securing that the dying sinner's thirst
for vengeance should last beyond the tomb. Horrible oaths
sealed these iniquitous compacts; the Almighty, the Father of

mercy and of pardon, was called to witness the work of blood, and sons believed themselves bound to discharge the infamous obligation as a sacred inheritance from their fathers."[1] Yet the men who made up such a society were Christians; they believed in God, and expected to be pardoned through the Blood of His Son; they probably from time to time recited their chaplet, and asked to be forgiven even as they forgave; and saw no inconsistency with such words upon their lips in handing on from father to son a legacy of revenge and homicide.

When such men heard of the holy maid of the Fullonica ("*La Beata Popolana*," as the citizens loved to call her—proud of her plebeian birth), they often enough came, now with one of her disciples, and now with another, to behold the prodigy of Siena. And when Catherine began to speak to such souls, she had in the most literal sense of the word to "lay again the foundation of penance from dead works . . . and the doctrine . . . of eternal judgment."[2] We will give one example of the kind of men with whom she had to deal, and of her method of addressing herself to their hearts. There were two nobles, Benuccio and Bernard, members of the haughty family of the Belforti. They belonged to the Guelph faction, and reckoned among their kinsmen not fewer than nineteen valiant warriors. They were the hereditary lords of Volterra, in whose historic annals the most heroic deeds of valour and patriotism were often enough mingled with tales of treachery and assassination. Bochino, the head of the family, was himself afterwards slain with many of his faction. His brother Pietro was married to Angela Salimbeni, one of that illustrious family with whom Catherine was on intimate terms, and Benuccio and Bernard were their sons. At her urgent request, it would seem, Catherine undertook to address the two brothers and remind them that they were Christians. But before we quote her words to the two warriors, let us hear in what terms she consoles Donna Benedetta, the wife of Bochino, when she was mourning over the loss of several much-loved children:— "My dearest mother and sister in Jesus Christ," she says, "is

---

[1] Storia di St. Cath., Lib. 2.   [2] Heb. vi. 1, 2.

it not sweet to you to think that the heavenly Physician came
into this world to heal all our infirmities ?   And like a good physician, He is often obliged to give us a bitter medicine, and even
to bleed us sometimes, in order to restore our health.   You know
a sick person will endure anything in hope of being cured
Alas ! why do we not treat the Physician of Heaven as we do
the physician of earth ?   He does not wish the death of the
sinner, but rather that he should be converted and live.   And
so He puts a bitterness into the things of sense.   And He bleeds
us too, when He takes from us our children, our health, our
worldly goods, or whatever else He thinks best.   Courage then ,
what He has done, He has done to heal, and not to slay ; and
since it is the sweet will of God, clothe yourself with patience.
As to the other son who is left to you, you must try not to look
on him as something that belongs to you, for that would be to
appropriate to yourself what is not really yours, but only lent.
You know I am speaking the truth, and because these things are
only lent, not given to us, we must be ready to give them back
to our sweet Master Who gave them and Who created them.
When I heard that He had called them to Himself, I rejoiced
at their salvation ; and though I pitied you, yet I rejoiced at the
fruit which you will draw from this affliction   Have courage
then, the time is short, our sufferings are light, and the reward
exceeding great.   May the peace of God be with you.   Catherine
the useless servant salutes you."

No doubt when Catherine compared the anguish of Benedetta
as she wept over her dead sons, with that which her kinswoman,
Donna Angela, endured when she watched the career of her own
living ones, she must have felt that bereavement was not the
worst sorrow   They were steeped up to their eyes in deadly
enmities, to lay aside any one of which would have been ac-
counted a blot on their scutcheon   This was that grievous " point
of honour," which the saints so fervidly denounced ; not honour
in its true and noble sense, but the false honour of the world,
which at that time held a man disgraced if he did not seek to
slaughter his enemy.

"My dearest sons," writes Catherine, "I desire to see your hearts and souls at peace with our crucified Jesus, otherwise you cannot be sharers in His grace. You know, my sons, that sin establishes a feud between man and his Creator. When the whole human race was at enmity with God through the sin of Adam, our merciful Creator desired to make peace with man, and sent us His only Son to be our Peace and our Mediator, and He became so by bearing all our iniquities in His own Body on the Cross. You see, then, that God has made peace with man, and that so perfectly that even if man revolt against Him, he can always find the precious Blood again in holy confession, which we may make use of every day if we choose . . . . But know this, we cannot love God except through our neighbour. Christ asked Peter if he loved Him, and when he said 'Yes,' our Lord replied, ' Then, feed My sheep.' As much as to say, it is very little to Me that you love Me, unless you love your neighbour. And this is the way of putting an end to the great feud we have with God. For our crucified Jesus came into the world to extinguish the fire of hatred between man and his brother. Yes, my dear children, I want to see hatred disappear out of your hearts. Do not act as madmen do, who by seeking to injure others only injure themselves. He who kills his enemy kills himself first, and with the same poniard, for he dies to grace. Fear the Divine judgments then, hanging over you, and promise me two things : Be reconciled both to God and to your enemies ; you cannot have peace with God unless you have peace with your neighbour ; and, then, come and see me as soon as you can , if it were not so difficult for me to do so, I would come and see you "

We do not know the result of this appeal, or whether the sweet echo of that word *peace* found an entrance into the heart of the Belforti , but having seen in what way she sought to win these turbulent spirits by her words, it may be well to show her gaining one such soul by the simple power of her prayers. The story is thus beautifully told in the old English Legend.

" There was in the city of Siena a gentleman called Nanni di

Ser Vanni,[1] who bore a great sway among the people, being a very fierce and warlike man, and also of a marvellous subtle and crafty wit in worldly affairs This Nanni, with the rest of his family and friends, maintained a faction and perpetual quarrel among certain other families in the city, who, dreading his power and policy, sought by all means and with great submission to make their peace with him. He made them answer that it was all one to him whether they had peace or no peace, and that for his own part he was very ready and willing to come to terms if they would win certain others to it, who were as much concerned in it as he was himself And thus he gave them very fair words, and put them in hope of peace; but in the meantime he dealt secretly with those other persons, bidding them stand stiffly to it, and in nowise to condescend to any conditions of peace. This matter came to the ears of Catherine, who seeing herein the occasion of working a charitable work, sought by many means to speak with him But whenever he understood that she was coming towards him, he fled from her, as a serpent is wont to flee from the enchanter that comes to charm him At last, by the importunity of a holy hermit, Brother William the Englishman,[2] they won so much of him that he was content to hear the holy maid speak, but yet with this protest, that whatever she said concerning the peace, he was fixed, and would not be moved. With this resolution he went to Catherine's house at a time when she chanced to be abroad. F. Raymund, by the providence of God, was there at that time, who, understanding that Nanni was coming, was very glad of it, for he knew that the holy maid had

---

[1] Mrs. Butler, in her life of St. Catherine, has confused Nanni di Ser Vanni with Andrea Vanni the painter. They were two totally distinct persons. She even imagines that Father William Flete's acquaintance with Nanni was formed on occasion *of having his portrait painted*, the last notion that would probably have occurred to the good hermit. Nanni really belonged to the noble house of Savini; Vanni was not his family name, but the Christian name of his father, and he bore it according to the Italian custom of those times, just as Stephen Maconi is called *Stephen di Corrado*, and Neri dei Paglieresi appears as *Neri di Landoccio*. For an account of the Savini family, see *Diar. San.* ii 162.

[2] *i.e.*, Father William Flete.

a great desire to speak with him ; so he went out to meet and entertain him until her return. When they were come into the house, F. Raymund led the way to the holy maid's chapel or oratory, where he caused him to sit down, and entered on such talk with him as he thought most convenient to protract the time. But after they had sat there a little while, and saw that she came not, Nanni thought the time long, and therefore began to break the matter with F. Raymund after this manner : ' Father,' he said, ' I promised Brother William that I would come here and speak with this holy maid ; but now seeing she is abroad about some other business, and I have at this present certain affairs that must needs be despatched out of hand, I pray you excuse me unto her, and tell her that I would gladly have spoken with her if she had been at home' F. Raymund was very sorry that Catherine came not. However, to gain a little more time, he took occasion to talk with him concerning the peace, and asked him how the matter stood between such and such persons. Whereunto he made answer after this manner : 'Father,' said he, ' to you who are a priest and religious, and to this blessed maid, of whom I hear report of great virtue and holiness, I will speak no lies, but tell you plainly and sincerely how the case stands between these men. It is true that I am he who hinders this reconciliation, though indeed it seem otherwise, because the matter is openly con- trived by others, but I alone privily maintain and uphold one side ; and if I would give my consent to the peace, the matter were ended. But to tell you my meaning in few words, my peace shall be made and confirmed with the blood of my enemies. This is my resolu- tion, and from this I will not be moved. Wherefore, I pray you, set your hearts at rest, and trouble me no more.' And with that he rose up and took his leave to depart ; but F. Raymund was very loath to let him go, and therefore, though he saw that he was unwilling to tarry, or to hear any more words of that matter, yet to gain more time, he asked him divers and sundry questions, and by that means kept him there so long that Catherine was come home and entered into the house before he could get out of the oratory. When Nanni saw her, he was sorry that he had tarried so long. But she was right glad to see him there, and bade him welcome after a very charitable and loving manner, and caused him to sit down again. And when he was seated, she asked him the cause of his coming. He answered her, and declared so much in effect as he had declared before to F. Raymund; at the same time protesting that concerning that matter of the peace he would have no talk, for he was absolutely bent to the contrary. The holy maid hearing that, began to exhort him to brotherly love and concord, and showed him withal what a dangerous and damnable state they were in that lived out of charity. But he gave a deaf ear to her words, which she perceived well enough, and therefore she sat still, and spake no more to him. But casting up her eyes and heart to God, she besought His grace and mercy for that hard-hearted man. When F. Raymund, who had evermore a diligent eye to the holy maid, had espied that, he spoke some words to Nanni to occupy him the while, nothing doubting but that she should work a better effect in him by that silent prayer than both he and she had done before with many words. And so indeed it proved; for within a little time after, he spoke to them both after this manner: 'It shall not be said of me that I am so hard and untractable that I will have my own way in all things and relent in nothing   I will condescend to your mind in some one thing, and then I will take my leave of you.   I have four quarrels in the city, of which I am content to put one into your hands. Do in it what you shall think good; make you my peace, and I will abide your orders.' With that he rose up, and would have gone his way; but on rising, being inwardly touched, he said these words to himself: 'O Lord, what comfort is this that I feel at this instant in my soul upon the only naming of this word "peace"!' And soon after he said again: 'O Lord, O God! what virtue or strength is this that holdeth and draweth me after this sort! I have no power to go hence. I can deny you nothing that you require me. O Lord! O Lord! what thing may this be that thus enforceth me?' And with that he burst out into weeping, and said: 'I am quite overthrown. I am not able to make any longer resistance' Then suddenly he cast himself down at Catherine's feet, and with marvellous great submission and abundance of tears, said these words : 'O blessed maid, I am ready to do whatsoever you command me, not only in this matter of peace, but also in all other things whatsoever they be. Hitherto I know well the devil has led me up and down fast tied in his chain, but now I am resolved to follow you whithersoever it shall please you to lead me ; and therefore I pray you for charity's sake be you my guide, and teach me how I may deliver my soul out of his bonds.' At those words the holy maid turned to him and said, 'Brother, our Lord be thanked that you are now, through His great mercy, come to understand in how dangerous a state you stood. I spake to you concerning your soul's health, and you made light of my words. I spake to our Lord touching the same matter, and He was content to hear me. My advice therefore is, that you do penance for your sins in time, for fear of some sudden calamity that may fall upon you, which finding you unprovided, may otherwise bear you down and quite overwhelm you.' Nanni was so inwardly stricken with these words of the holy maid, that he went forthwith to Father Raymund and made a general confession of all his sins with great sorrow and contrition And so, when he had made his peace with Almighty God, by the advice of F. Raymund and virtue of the holy Sacrament of Penance, he was content likewise to submit himself to the order of the holy maid, and according to her direction and arbitration to make a firm peace with all his enemies Within a few days after Nanni was thus converted, it chanced that he was taken by the governor of the city and cast into a strait prison for certain outrages that he had committed before. And it was commonly said among the people that he should be put to death, the which when F Raymund understood, he came to Catherine with a heavy cheer, and said, 'Lo, mother, so long as Nanni served the devil, so long did all things go prosperously with him. But now, since the time that he began to serve God, we see the world is wholly bent against him. This sudden alteration putteth me in great fear and doubt of the man, lest, being as yet but a young and tender branch, he should be broken off by the violence of this storm, and so fall into despair. Wherefore I beseech you heartily, good mother, commend his state to God in your prayers, and as you have by your mediation delivered him from everlasting death, so do you endeavour also to deliver him from this temporal and imminent danger.' To that the holy maid made answer, saying, 'Father, why take you this matter so heavily? Methinks you should rather be glad of it, for by this you may conceive a very sure hope that our Lord hath pardoned him all his sins, and changed those everlasting pains that were due to him for the same into these temporal afflictions. When he was of the world, the world made much of him, as one that was his own; but now, since he began to spurn at the world, no wonder if the world should likewise kick at him again. As for the fear that you have, lest he, being overcome with these calamities, should fall into despair, be of good comfort, and assure yourself that the merciful goodness of our Lord, that hath delivered him out of the deep dungeon of hell, will not suffer him to perish in prison.' And as she said, so it proved indeed, for within a few days after he was delivered out of prison; his life was indeed spared, but for that they set a great fine of money on his head. Whereof the holy maid was nothing sorry but rather glad. 'For,' said she, 'our Lord hath mercifully taken away from him that poison with the which he had before and might again have poisoned himself.'"

Nanni was not ungrateful to her who had delivered him from his miserable bondage; and as soon as he regained his freedom he made over to her by deed of gift his great castle of Belcaro, about four miles out of Siena, that she might convert it into a convent. And this, as we shall show, she did a little later, dedicating it under the title of Our Lady of Angels.

It was not long before Catherine acquired such a reputation for success in the reconciliation of long-standing family feuds, that appeals were made to her arbitration from all quarters. As at Montepulciano, so also at Asciano, Semignano, and other of the towns and villages in the vicinity of Siena, there are indications in her letters of her exercising the good office of an angel of peace ; reconciling enemies, and not unfrequently administering some well-earned rebukes.

At Semignano, a village about a mile out of Siena, two priests were themselves engaged in a deadly feud against each other, and St. Catherine was appealed to, to put a stop if possible to this frightful scandal   She wrote to one of them, and if her words are terrible in their severity, there is evidence that they were every whit deserved by the offender.   It is thus that she addresses him · " Priest ! whom the august Sacrament which it is yours to administer renders dear to me, I, Catherine, the slave of the servants of Jesus Christ, write to you in His Precious Blood, desiring to see you a vessel of election, bearing worthily the name of Christ, and applying yourself to live in peace with your Creator and to make peace between His creatures.   That is your duty, and you ought to fulfil it   If you do not do it, God will reprove you with severity.   Respect the exalted dignity of your state.   God in His mercy has appointed you to administer the fire of Divine Charity, I mean the Body and Blood of Jesus crucified.   Oh think, the angelic nature enjoys not that honour : do but consider, He has put His Word into your soul as into a sacred vessel.   You represent the person of Christ when you consecrate His Sacrament   Therefore, you should love and reverence your dignity with great purity and with a peaceful heart, tearing out from your soul every hatred and desire of vengeance.

" Alas ! where is now the purity of God's ministers !   You require a spotless purity in the chalice you make use of at the altar, and refuse to use one that is soiled , remember then, that God, the Sovereign Truth, demands a like purity in your soul. Woe is me ! on all sides we behold the contrary.   Those who should be the temples of God are the stables of swine : they carry the fire of hatred and vengeance, and an evil will in their souls. They forget that God sees them, and that His eye is ever over them, penetrating to the bottom of their hearts.   Alas ! Alas ! Are we brutes without reason ?   One would say so, when one sees how we abandon ourselves to our wicked passions.   The pride of man is now so great that he will not humble himself either to God or creatures. If any one injures him or threatens him with death, he will not pardon his enemy, and yet desires and expects that his own sins against God shall be pardoned. But he deceives himself; for with the same measure that he metes to others he shall be measured himself. . . . I wonder how a man like you, whom God has drawn out of the world and made an earthly angel by making him the minister of His Sacrament,—I do wonder how you can hate. I know not how you dare to celebrate, I declare to you that if you persevere in this hatred, and in your other vices, the wrath of God will burst over your head. Let there be an end of this, reform your life, and cast out from your heart all this misery, and, above all, this deadly hate I desire that you be both reconciled. What a disgrace to see two priests engaged in deadly hatred! It is a marvel to me that God does not command the earth to open and swallow you both up. But courage! there is yet time, have recourse to Jesus, and He will receive you if you will but go to Him. If not, you will be punished like the wicked servant, who, after he had been forgiven by his master, refused to forgive his fellow servant a paltry debt, and tried to strangle him. Then his master revoked his pardon, and bade them bind him hand and foot and cast him into the outer darkness. Our sweet Jesus left us those words as a warning to those who lived in the hatred of God and their neighbour. I will say no more; but reply to me, and tell me what is your will and intention. May you abide in the love of God!"[1]

Such a letter as the foregoing suggests the answer to a question which inevitably presents itself when we read of the kind of work which fell into the hands of St. Catherine. How was it that in a Christian land the word of a *woman* should have been needed

[1] At Semignano, the residence of the unhappy man to whom this letter was addressed, there now stands the magnificent villa of Cetinale, where Alexander VII was wont to spend his hours of learned retirement. In a chapel in this villa is preserved, among other relics, a bone of St. Catherine of Siena. She has a worthy claim to be venerated on that spot.

to bring men to penance? were there not Priests, Bishops, Pastors of souls? Alas! it must be said : at this precise epoch the deepest and deadliest of all the wounds which were lacerating society was the corruption of manners among the clergy. Most religious orders were in a state of relaxation, and the example of the court at Avignon had spread among the prelates of the Church, to say the least, habits of worldly ease and luxury which cried aloud for reform. Not to state this fact plainly would be to omit what alone explains, and we may say *justifies*, many of St. Catherine's acts and words ; a fact also which alone can enable us to comprehend how such events as the Great Schism in the fourteenth century, and the Protestant Reformation in the sixteenth, could ever have come about

This terrible wound of the Church lay open to Catherine's eyes, and we see by her writings that she had probed it to its depths. It formed one part of her lifelong martyrdom to know all that she did know of the lives led by those whom, in her intense and living faith, she could think of only as "the Ministers of the Blood." If to love God and see Him offended be anguish to a loving soul, what must it have been to see every abomination of desolation brought even into the sanctuary? It caused her a horror which inspired her most burning words. " How !" she exclaims, "God has not yet commanded the ground to open, or wild beasts to devour you . He still bids the earth yield you its fruits, and the sun to shed on you its warmth and light. The heavens still roll on in their course, that you may live and have time to repent; and all this He does out of love !" Again and again she reminds the priest and prelate to whom she bears the message of her Master that they are consecrated chalices, —channels to convey to souls the ever-flowing torrents of the Precious Blood ; and alas! reminds them, too, what kind of sacrilege it is to soil the sacred vessels of the sanctuary with the iniquities of avarice and sensuality. Hence she was ever praying for the *reform* of the Church; a word which has been laid hold of by some writers as indicating that the Saint of Siena may be claimed as one of those precursors of the so-called Reformation, among whom are to be numbered such luminaries as Huss and Wickliffe. One passage of her own writing will be the best answer to this extravagant theory, and sufficiently explains in what sense she makes use of a word destined in after ages to bear so questionable a reputation; "Strengthen yourself," she writes, "in the sweet Spouse of Christ. The more tribulation and sorrow abound, the more does the Divine Truth promise an abundance of sweetness and consolation; and this sweetness will be in the renewal of good and holy pastors, who like glorious flowers will offer to God the good odour of virtue. For this reform will only be in the ministers and pastors: *the Church herself has no need of being reformed, for the fruit she gives can never be spoiled nor diminished by the sins of her ministers.*"[1]

In addition to what has already been said of the demands made on Catherine as a healer of feuds, there were other sources of trouble and civil distraction which naturally arose out of a society seething with successive revolutions. In the purely political side of these matters Catherine took no part; nevertheless the tumults and popular changes of the republic always brought to her door some new work of charity. She was not one to harangue mobs, or take on herself the part of a politician, but when the excitement was over, she was ever at hand to soothe the susceptibilities which had been roused, and bring comfort to many a wounded heart. Thus, when in 1373 the populace clamoured for the blood of Vico di Mugliano, senator of Siena, who had earned their hatred by hanging a good many public malefactors and banishing others, Catherine was ready with her words of consolation to support his terrified wife, who in her dismay had sent her word that she had no other hope than in the holy virgin's prayers.

Daughter of the people as she truly was, she never shrank from giving her sympathy to the victims of the revolutionary government, whose leaders were not long in power before they showed themselves in the light of cruel tyrants. The state prisons were filled with unhappy beings, whose crimes were of no blacker

[1] Letter 90.

dye than those of Agnolo d'Andrea, condemned to death for giving a banquet to which none of the "Riformatori" had been invited. But even into those darksome dungeons the charity of Catherine penetrated. On a certain Holy Thursday, when full of the thought of the Passion of her Lord, the solemn celebration of which is just then commencing, her heart wanders away to those forlorn ones whom she had already doubtless visited; and she strives to render their sufferings more tolerable to them by reminding them of One, who for their sakes had suffered torture and imprisonment. "O my sweet Love, Jesus!" she exclaims, "did not *You* endure for us opprobrium and ill treatment? were *You* not bound and buffeted and scourged at the column, tied and nailed to the cross, drenched with ignominies, tormented with thirst; and for Your relief they gave You nothing but vinegar and gall, and You bore it all with patience, and prayed for Your murderers? O unutterable mercy! You not only prayed for them, but excused them, too, saying, 'Father, forgive them, for they know not what they do.' Oh, my children, it is impossible that you should not bear your misfortunes patiently; for in the memory of the Blood all bitter things become sweet, and all hard things easy. Remember that you have to die, and you know not when; prepare then by confession and Communion, that after death you may rise again to grace with Christ Jesus."

These victims, whether of justice or state tyranny, were the objects of her peculiar tenderness. She saw in them the likeness of her adorable Master, as He passed to Calvary loaded with chains to die between two malefactors. Hence she was no stranger to the "Giustizia," or place of public execution; many a time had she taken her place in the grim procession as it set out from the Piazza of the Old Market, and leaving the city by the Porta della Giustizia, made its way through the Val di Montone and ascended the little hill called the Corposanto a Pecorile, opposite to which was the church of St. Stefano, where the bodies of those executed were buried[1] Those who would venerate each footprint left by Catherine of Siena, should follow that track with

[1] See Grottanelli's notes to *Leggenda Minore*, p. 53.

a kind of awful reverence. She came thither not once, but often ; Simon ot Cortona tells us in his deposition that she converted, and brought to confession, many who were led to execution in a desperate state ; and Caffarini declares that he could not number the occasions when she gave help to the dying ; whether those who had been slain by their enemies, or those who paid the penalty of their crimes on the public scaffold. Of the first-named act of charity no example has been preserved, but one is recorded of the second, and by no other than her own pen.

A young knight of Perugia, named Nicholas di Toldo, was accused of having spoken against the Riformatori, and advised his friends in Siena to shake off their odious yoke. He was arrested and condemned to death. The sentence fell on him like a thunderstroke and drove him to the madness of despair. Of noble birth and full of gallant hopes, with all his passions unsubdued, he could not resign himself to give up his life while yet the young blood was coursing through his veins, and the world spread itself before him as a fairy land of enjoyment. He had never cared for his religious duties, never even made his first Communion, so that when that terrible decree had gone forth, there was nothing to brighten the path that lay before him. A day or two more in his miserable dungeon, and when next he should be restored to the light of day that bright sun in which he had revelled would shine only on the black cart that would be carrying him to the gallows. In his utter misery he bethought him of Catherine ; he had heard of her, but they had never met. Still, her name was in every one's mouth, and men said her power of consolation was something boundless ; so, forsaken of every other hope, the unhappy youth despatched a messenger, and implored her to come to him in his prison. She came, and when the awful scene was over, she wrote the following narrative to Raymund of Capua.

" I went to see him whom you know of, and he was so cheered and encouraged that he confessed at once to F. Thomas, and showed the best dispositions possible. He made me promise, for the love of God, that when the time of execution came I would be with him. I promised him, and I kept my promise. In the morning before the sound of the bell I hastened to him, and my arrival greatly comforted him. I took him to Mass, and he communicated for the first time in his life. He was perfectly resigned to God's will, and had no other fear than that his courage might forsake him at the last moment. But God in His goodness inspired him with such a love of His holy will that, penetrated with a sense of His adorable Presence, he kept repeating the words, 'Lord, be with me! Abandon me not, Thou art with me now, and all must go well with me! I die content!' Oh, how at that moment I longed to mingle my blood with his, and shed it all for our sweet Spouse Jesus! This desire increasing in me, and seeing my poor brother agitated by fear, I said to him 'Courage, my brother! we shall soon be at the eternal nuptials You are going to die washed in the adorable Blood of Jesus, and with His sweet Name upon your lips! I charge you forget it not, and I will wait for you at the place of execution.' Now think, my father, how his soul must have lost all fear; for his face was transformed from sadness to joy, and he said in a kind of transport, 'Whence comes such a grace to me as this, that the sweetness of my soul should wait for me at the holy place of execution!' You see what great light he must have had to have called the place of execution *holy.* Then he said : 'I shall go strong and full of joy, it seems to me as if I should have to wait a thousand years till I see you there ;' and he added other words so sweet that I was amazed as I beheld the goodness of God.

"I went then to the place of execution, where I ceased not to invoke Our Lady and St Catherine the martyr. But before he arrived, I knelt down and placed my own neck on the block, but alas! my desire was not fulfilled Oh, how I prayed that Our Lady would obtain for him at that last moment light and peace of heart, and for me, the grace of seeing him attain his end. My heart was so full, and the impression of the promise I had received so deep, that in the midst of all that crowd of people I saw no one. At last he came, and like a meek lamb he smiled when he saw me, and desired I would make the sign of the cross

on his forehead. I did so, saying, 'Depart to the eternal
nuptials ; soon, very soon, you will be in the life that never ends.'
He extended himself on the scaffold, and with my own hands I
placed his head under the knife ; then I knelt by his side, and
reminded him of the Blood of the spotless Lamb. His lips
murmured the words, 'Jesus and Catherine.' Then the knife
fell, and I received his head in my hands. I fixed my eyes on
the Divine goodness, and lo ! I beheld, as clearly as one beholds
the light of the sun, Him who is God and Man. He was there ;
and He received that blood. . . . He received it, and placed it
in the open Wound of His Side, in the treasury of His mercy. . . .
Oh, how lovingly He looked on that soul bathed in the blood
made precious by being united to His own ! Then Father, Son,
and Holy Spirit received him ; and he was inundated with a joy
that would have ravished a thousand hearts. And then I saw
him turn, as the bride does when she reaches the door of the
bridegroom ; she turns and bows her head to salute those who
have conducted her there, and to give them a last farewell.
Then all disappeared, and I felt a delicious peace, and the perfume of that blood was so sweet to me, that I would not suffer
them to wash away what had fallen over me. Alas ! miserable
that I am, still to be left to linger in this wretched world !"[1]

[1] The last paragraph, which in the letter (Let. 97) is very obscure, receives
a perfect explanation from the following passage in the *Leggenda Minore.*
It will be remembered that the writer is F. Thomas Caffarini, who was
present on this occasion.

"La quale disse poi al suo confessore, *e anco a noi altri,* che benche si
fusse grande moltitudine di gente, essa non vedeva neuno Ma ben vide Jesu
Cristo benedetto che in virtù della sua santissima passione accettò il sangue
di quello agnello ingiustamente sparto, con la sua volontà in tutto accordata
con la volontà di Dio, a portare pazientamente questo martirio. Unde in quello
punto introdusse quella benedetta anima nell 'eterno regno. *E prima che
intrasse si rivolse dietro, inchinandosi alla vergine in segno di ringraziamento.*
(Leg. Min., Part 2, chap. vii., p 94). The date of Nicholas di Toldo's death
is uncertain, but it occurred after the Saint had become acquainted with
Raymund of Capua (to whom the letter describing his death is addressed),
and therefore some time later than June 1374. It forms the subject of a fine
fresco by Sodoma, in the chapel of St. Catherine in the Church of San
Domenico.

At this most wonderful scene, F. Thomas Caffarini was personally present, and he has carefully described it in the Process. He says, at the moment when the axe fell, Catherine received the head in her hands, being in an ecstacy. Her eyes were fixed on heaven, and her eyelids motionless, and so she remained for a long space. The spectators were all in tears, and declared they were witnessing the death of a martyr rather than the execution of a criminal; while Catherine, heedless of all around her, was beholding in spirit the happy soul of him, whose blood was flowing over her garments, ascend to heaven, and before entering the eternal portals turn to give one last look of gratitude on her whose amazing charity had rescued him from perdition. "I saw it all," says Caffarini, "and never at the most solemn religious festival have I witnessed such devotion as there was displayed at his burial"

It must not be gathered from what has been said of Catherine's horror of feuds, or of her wondrous pity for criminals, that she was on the one hand deficient in that appreciation for brave men and brave deeds which finds a place in every woman's heart that is attuned to what is noble; or that, on the other hand, her compassion for the erring was akin to weakness. In the righteous cause of God or country, Catherine would have buckled on the sword of the combatants, and followed them with her prayers to the battlefield. Some of her letters addressed to knights and men at arms seem to ring with the very sound of the tourney. Perhaps there are no figures of speech in which she appears more entirely at home than with those of knighthood and battle. "Our King," she says, writing to the Prior of the Knights of St. John, "Our King, like a true knight, remained on the battlefield till all His foes were conquered. With His flesh all torn with scourges, He vanquished our rebellious flesh; by His ignominies, He overcame the pride, and by His wisdom the malice of the devil, and with His unarmed hands, pierced and nailed on the Cross, He has conquered the prince of this world. Our knight mounted on His battle-steed, the wood of the most holy Cross, and for His cuirass He took the flesh of Mary, that clothed in it He might receive the blows which should satisfy for our iniquities. The helmet on His head is that cruel crown of thorns that pierced to His very brain; His sword is that wounded Side which displays to us the Secret of His Heart, a gleaming sword, indeed, that should pierce our hearts with ardent love; and for His lance, He bears the reed given Him in derision. The gauntlets on His hands, and the spurs on His feet, are the rosy Wounds in the Hands and Feet of that sweet Word. Who armed Him thus? It was Love. What bound and nailed Him to the tree of the Cross? not the nails, nor the stones, nor the earth in which it was planted; they could not have held fast the Incarnate God. It was nothing but the bond of love, love for God's honour and our salvation. Oh, what heart could behold such a knight and such a chieftain, at one and the same time dying, yet a conqueror, and not be ready to overcome all his weakness, and go forth bravely against all his foes! It is impossible. Take then Jesus crucified for your model; dye your tunic[1] in His crimson Blood, and by Him you will triumph over all your enemies."

Nor, when occasion served, did Catherine shrink from reading a lesson to the magistrates of the republic, and telling them some honest truths which, had they proceeded from any other lips, might have sent the speaker to the dungeons of the Palazzo Pubblico. "My Fathers and Brothers in Jesus Christ," she says (writing to the 'Magnificent Lords Defenders of the people'), "I desire to see you true and faithful Christians, full of zeal for holy justice, which should shine like a precious jewel on your hearts; stripped of self-love, so that you may be able to apply yourselves to the general good of the city and not your own private interests. A man who thinks only of his own interests has very little of the fear of God; he does not observe justice, but breaks it in a thousand ways; he allows himself to be corrupted—sometimes for money, sometimes to please those who ask him to do them a service in an unjust way; sometimes also, to avoid the just punishment of his own faults, he will let off those on whom the stroke of justice should fall. And so he shares in the guilt and

---

[1] The tunic worn by the knights on state occasions was of crimson velvet.

deserves to suffer the same punishment which he has been bribed to spare another. Yet if a poor man were to do the thousandth part as much, he would punish him without mercy.[1]

" A wretch like this who is appointed to govern the city, and yet does not know how to govern himself, cares not to see the poor oppressed , he despises their rights, while he listens readily enough to those who have no rights to plead. But it is no wonder that such men commit injustice when they are cruel even to themselves, wallowing in sensuality like swine in the mire Proud and senseless, they cannot bear to hear the truth. They tear their neighbours to pieces and wring out of them unjust gains, and commit a thousand other offences which I will not weary you with enumerating. I wonder not that such as these fail in administering holy justice ; and therefore it is that God has permitted, and still permits, that we should suffer from chastisements and scourges, the like of which I verily believe have never been seen since the world began." [2]

Truly, there spoke the " Blessed Popolana," the " Daughter of the People," fearless and true, striking her blows home to guilty consciences, and appalling them with her clear, calm words ; the advocate of the poor, the lover of justice, the healer of discords and the champion of truth.

And here we close the first part of Catherine's history, to which for the most part belong those narratives which display her to us exercising her mission of charity within the walls of her native place or its immediate vicinity. Those who have trodden its streets best know how ineffaceable are the footprints which she has left behind her At every turn they are met by some memory of her who, belonging to a city so rich in Saints, still remains and will ever remain *the* Saint, by excellence, of Siena. They gaze at the grand old church as it stands on the summit of its grassy hill, and behold, it may be, in pious imagination the vision of

[1] This passage is aptly enough illustrated by the affair of Andrea Salimbeni, narrated in the last chapter. It was not, however, written on that occasion, but some years later.

[2] Letter 204.

beauty which first won the heart of Catherine to her Eternal Spouse. They descend to the fountain by the very path down which so many a time she came to draw water for those homely household duties she loved to discharge, and which, ever blended with tales of vision and rapture, remind us that her life was all the time the life of a sister and a daughter, perfumed through and through with the charities of home. They enter her house, and stand within her chamber; they see the little window and the hard brick steps beneath, where she rested her head. And in that sanctuary they kneel to do homage to the greatest of all the Divine works; the sanctity of which a human heart is capable when the will of God is substituted for the will of the creature: and they contemplate in amazement the close union which He, by His grace, renders possible between Himself and the frail mortal espoused to His Heart, in "the Perfection of Faith and Charity."

Part II.

ST. CATHERINE'S EMBASSIES.

PAPAL PALACE, AVIGNON.

CHAPTER I.

THE CHURCH AND ITALY, 1372–1374.

IN the year 1305, in the reign and at the solicitation of Philip
le Bel, Pope Clement V. transferred the residence of the
Popes from Rome to Avignon. Urgent as the causes may have
been which prompted this measure, its effects on Italy and the
Church at large were most disastrous. The six successors of
Clement were all Frenchmen by birth and sympathies; and
having purchased from Joanna of Naples the sovereignty of
Avignon, they established themselves in the fairest city of France,
and drew around them the most splendid and luxurious court in
Europe. The cardinals also were all but exclusively French;
and from their ranks were drawn the legates sent into Italy to

govern the States of the Church. Their indifference to the populations over whom they ruled, and their undoubted misgovernment and rapacity, brought the Holy See itself into contempt, and sowed the deadly seeds of hatred and rebellion. All good men lamented what in the writings of the times was stigmatised as the second Babylonish Captivity, and minds as widely apart in their sympathies as were those of Francis Petrarch and St. Bridget of Sweden alike sighed for the day of deliverance.

Urban V. was the first to conceive and attempt the execution of a project for returning to Rome. Deaf to the remonstrances of his French courtiers, he left Avignon in the May of 1367, and reached Rome in the following October. His progress was one long triumph When the rumour of his coming first spread through Italy it awakened high hopes and passionate rejoicing. Queen Joanna of Naples and all the maritime republics sent their galleys to conduct him to the Italian shores; and when he landed at Corneto, St John Colombini was waiting on the landing-place to receive him, surrounded by his followers, "the poor men of Siena," with rose garlands on their heads and olive branches in their hands. All the way to Viterbo they ran beside his litter, singing praises to God and telling the Pope how glad they were to see him When he entered Rome, the sad and melancholy streets of that long-deserted city put on its beautiful garments to greet him, and every house appeared garlanded with flowers. All the princes of Italy were there, taking part in the glorious procession. Nicolas of Este, Lord of Ferrara, headed his bodyguard; Ridolfo of Camerino bore aloft the standard of Holy Church; while walking at the Pope's bridle, in the character of Master of the Horse, was Amadeus IV., the brave Count of Savoy. Two thousand bishops, abbots, and ambassadors followed, and conducted Urban to the palace of the Vatican. It was a day of splendid promise, which ended in as bitter a disappointment During the three years that Urban remained in Rome he did enough to vindicate the wisdom of the step he had taken, but the calamities of a century could not be dissipated in three years, and a nearer view of the unhappy country, as it lay lacerated by its intestine wars, petty tyrannies, and the ravages of the Free Companies, so disheartened him, that in 1370, overcome by the entreaties of his French cardinals, and desirous, as it is thought, of stopping a renewal of hostilities between France and England, he returned to Avignon, to die.

Some writers, and among others Isidore Ugurgieri, have represented this visit of Pope Urban's to Rome as due to the representations of St. Catherine. But there is actually no ground for such a supposition. In the year 1367 she was only just emerging from her life of retreat, and though she must have heard not a little about the great event from the lips of the Colombini family, and though, doubtless, her own heart responded to the universal joy, yet it is quite certain that at that time she had as yet taken no part in public affairs outside her own city.[1]

The cardinals, on whom devolved the election of Urban's successor, regarded with dismay the possibility of a second departure from Avignon, and thought to secure themselves against such a danger by electing one who, while his virtues rendered him well worthy of their choice, seemed of all men the least likely to undertake a difficult and unpopular enterprise. Peter du Rogier de Beaufort-Turenne, who took the name of Gregory XI., was only thirty-six years of age, of blameless life, and enjoying a reputation, writes the Florentine ambassador, Lucius Coluzzi, "for prudence, modesty, circumspection, faith, goodness, and charity; and what is yet rarer to find in a great prince, for truth in his words and loyalty in his actions."

Despite his gentle and even timid character, Gregory was capable of great purposes, and from the moment of his accession one desire filled his breast. It was to bring about the pacification of Europe by the proclamation of a CRUSADE. The word falls dull and meaningless on the ears of our generation, or associates

---

[1] Ugurgieri in his *Fasti Senensi* (part 2, lib. viii., p. 143) affirms as a fact, that Urban V., desiring to reform the monastery of Monte Cassino, appointed as abbot Dom Bartholomew of Siena, at the recommendation of St. Catherine. Malevolti, the historian of Siena, likewise says that she wrote to this Pontiff, but if so, none of her letters to him have been preserved.

itself to the notion of a scheme of half-crazed enthusiasm. To regard it in that light, however, is to betray but an imperfect comprehension of history. Neither would it be at all accurate to suppose that the announcement of such a project in the fourteenth century burst on the world and took it by surprise, as the revival of an idea long obsolete. In fact, there was nothing at all new in it; it had been the cherished desire not of this holy soul or of that, but, in turn, of all the Sovereign Pontiffs. So long as the safety of Christendom was threatened on the side of the infidels, that is, for the space of about six centuries, those who successively filled the Apostolic See were ever seeking to raise a bulwark against their further advance westward, and persevered in unavailing efforts to rouse Christian kings and nobles to a sense of their terrific danger. What they desired, and were ever seeking to promote, was to oppose to the onward wave of barbarism the fair front of a united Christendom. The fratricidal wars between France and England were for a long course of years the great obstacle to the realisation of these hopes ; and we have but to turn to history to see what were the efforts of the Roman Pontiffs to put a stop to those miserable hostilities.

This project of the crusade, then, was the first thought which Gregory shared in common with Catherine. Indeed, most writers represent him as first moved to act in this matter by her persuasions , but such a supposition falls very far short of the truth. He was but following the constant tradition of the papacy when he proposed to raise the standard of the holy war, and thereby at one and the same time to check the advance of the infidels, and sheathe the swords which were drenching the fair fields of his native land in torrents of Christian blood Gregory was every way moved to take a keen interest in the last-named matter. A Frenchman by birth, he was not without a tie to England He had resided in that country, where he held the office of Archdeacon of Canterbury ; he was the intimate friend of William of Wykeham, to whom he seems to have sent the first tidings of his election to the papal chair ; and he gladly welcomed English prelates to his court, and was no stranger to their habits or language. It was but natural that to one of his gentle character the chief ambition which filled his breast should be that he might become a pacificator between two nations both equally dear to him. His first act, therefore, after his election in 1371, was to write letters to the king of England, the court of Flanders, and the doge of Venice, calling on them to come to the defence of Holy Church and turn their arms against the Turks. He bestowed on Raymund Berenger, Grand Master of Rhodes, the rich domain of Smyrna to be an outpost against the enemy; and to unite in one body the Christians of the East and of the West, he had it in his mind to call a congress in which to settle the plan of the crusade and raise the necessary means for its commencement. But at the very moment when the father of Christendom was thus concerting schemes for the pacification of Europe and the repulse of the common enemy, two of the maritime powers on whom he chiefly relied for the accomplishment of his purpose, took up arms against one another in a miserable quarrel. War broke out between Genoa and Venice; the navy of the former state was despatched against Cyprus, and thus the project of the congress for that time ended in smoke.

Still the crusade itself was not abandoned, and the design of the new Pontiff was well known throughout Europe. It was a thought which had long occupied the mind of Catherine, and she must have rejoiced with exceeding great joy when she understood that the Vicar of Christ was labouring for its accomplishment. Though far from believing that it owed its birth to her suggestion, we deem it almost certain that the projected Crusade formed the matter of their earliest communication, and that her letters of sympathy and encouragement on that subject were the first links of their mutual friendship.

But whatever may have been Catherine's enthusiasm for the holy war, not less urgent was her solicitude for the peace of Italy. How are we to condense in few words the unutterable woes under which that unhappy country was at this period writhing? Yet we must make the attempt, even though it should seem to transform the page of sober history into the semblance of some monstrous melodrama.

In the middle of the fourteenth century, then, Italy presented the spectacle of every variety of government. Her old republican institutions were falling into decay, and in many states the sovereign power had been seized by some fortunate adventurer who raised himself to the position of its tyrant. Thus, in the north, almost all Lombardy was bent under the sway of the Visconti. Bernabò Visconti, Duke of Milan, a great military genius, an astute politician, and a patron, moreover, of art and men of letters, had spent the greater part of his life in arms against the Church. Wholly indifferent to all religious obligations, he had grown accustomed to excommunication during the Pontificates of Innocent VI. and Urban V., and mocked at the censures of the Church with a profanity worthy of the age of Voltaire. Indeed, he seems to have united in his single person the brutality of the eleventh, the astute cunning of the sixteenth, and the scepticism of the eighteenth centuries. Muratori gives a summary of his game laws that casts those of our Norman tyrants into the shade. No man was allowed to kill or eat a wild animal under pain of death. His five thousand hunting dogs were quartered on the convents, and the monks were expected to keep them well fed and bring them to a monthly review. Those who failed to bring up their dogs in good condition were fined, flogged, or otherwise tortured. At the approach of his huntsmen the miserable peasants quailed in abject fear. None had the courage to rebuke the tyrant save two friars who, valuing their lives as nothing for God's sake, entered his presence and reminded him of death and judgment. Bernabò with a hideous laugh ordered them at once to be burnt alive. He had gradually obtained possession of his large dominions by a long course of cunning and treachery. One example may suffice as showing the origin of his war with Gregory XI., and aptly illustrating the anarchy which everywhere prevailed.

Gonzaga, Duke of Feltrino, governed the city of Reggio as feudatory of the pope. Este, Marquis of Ferrara, leagued with some

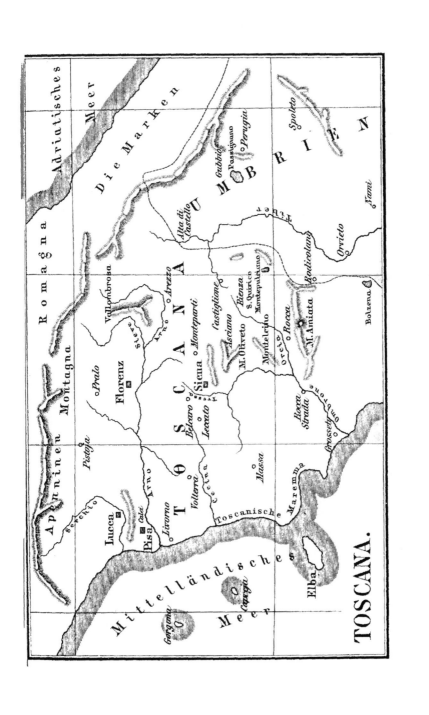

TOSCANA.

of the inhabitants to deprive him of his sovereignty; and having hired a company of German Free Lances, commanded by the celebrated Condottiere Lando, he loosed these ruffians against the unhappy city, expecting them to resign their conquest into his hands according to the terms of their mutual bargain. Lando soon made himself master of the place, but after frightful slaughter and the desecration of every sanctuary, he found it more to his advantage to listen to proposals made him by Bernabò, to whom he sold the city for 25,000 gold florins. The rights of Feltrino and of the Holy See were naturally as little regarded as the contract with the Marquis, for whom it is impossible to feel much sympathy when he found himself the dupe of a more sagacious scoundrel than himself; and it was by various achievements of a like character that Bernabò contrived to gain possession of other territories of the Church.

After fruitless appeals and embassies, Gregory at last pronounced against him sentence of excommunication. But to a man like Bernabò such a sentence only afforded matter for some grim pleasantry. When Urban V. had adopted a similar measure, Bernabò had met the Legates who were bringing the Bulls of excommunication on the bridge of Lambri, and required them to eat the parchment on which they were written, on pain of being flung into the river. Then he dressed the Pope's ambassadors in white garments, and paraded them through the streets of Milan; and when the Archbishop ventured a remonstrance against such acts, he answered fiercely: "I would have you to know that I am Pope, emperor, and king in my own domains, nor shall God Himself do here what is contrary to my will." When the news reached him of his fresh excommunication by Gregory XI., he dressed up a poor madman in some ridiculous vestments, and commanded him to excommunicate the Pope. In 1372, therefore, Gregory declared war against him: he obtained the support of the Emperor, the queen of Naples, and the king of Hungary; and took into his pay the English leader, Sir John Hawkwood. Bernabò did not feel himself strong enough to oppose an alliance so strong, or so redoubtable a general: he had recourse, therefore, to his usual weapon of cunning, and despatching ambassadors to Avignon, proceeded to bribe some of Gregory's counsellors, in order to obtain for himself a favourable truce. Meanwhile Cardinal Peter D'Estaing,[1] whom Scipio Ammirato calls "a man of large heart and wise head," was appointed Legate of Bologna. This was in the year 1372, and the letter alluded to in the last chapter, as the first of a positively political character which Catherine is known to have written, is addressed to him by her on hearing of his appointment. But as a French writer has well remarked, this letter shows her to be already in the possession of a political influence, not in its infancy, but fairly established. When the curtain rises to display her *public life* at last begun, we find to our wonder that in reality it must have begun long before. It is impossible to read her letter to Cardinal D'Estaing and for a moment to doubt that they were personally, and even intimately acquainted. Perhaps in a former visit to Italy he had passed through Siena, and visiting the holy maid of the Fullonica had conferred with her on what lay close to both their hearts—the peace of Christendom and the proclamation of a Crusade. It was certainly no stranger whom she addresses with that graceful play upon words impossible to render into English: "Scrivo a voi con desiderio di vedervi *legato* nel legame della carita, siccome siete fatto *Legato* in Italia, secondo che o inteso."[2] Observe, too, on this first page of her correspondence that beloved name of ITALY! and what has she to say to him?

"Son and servant, redeemed in the Blood of Jesus!" she cries, "follow His footsteps promptly and bravely: suffer not yourself to be held back either by suffering or pleasure; but apply yourself to root out the iniquities and miseries caused by the sins

---

[1] In St. Catherine's Letters, those to D'Estaing bear the title, "To the Cardinal Peter of Ostia." But this has been added by some later hand, and is an anachronism. D'Estaing afterwards became Bishop of Ostia, but he was not so at the time of his appointment as Legate.

[2] "I desire to see you bound with the bonds of charity, as I hear you have been made Legate in Italy." The significance, of course, is in the double meaning of the words *legato* (bound) and *Legato* (Legate).

which outrage the name of God. Hunger and thirst for His honour and the salvation of souls that you may repair so many evils; use the power given you by the Vicar of Christ in the sweet bonds of charity, without which you cannot discharge your duty. Be strong in Christ, then, and zealous, not negligent in what you have to do ; and thereby I shall know that you are a true Legate if you have a longing to behold the standard of the holy Cross at last displayed on high ! " In a second letter she urges him to restore peace to the distracted country "If possible, make peace," she says ; "is it not miserable to see us with arms in our hands, fighting one against another, whilst every faithful Christian should be ready to do battle only against the infidels ! The servants of God are overwhelmed with sorrow when they see nothing on all sides but deadly sin and perishing souls ; whilst the devils rejoice, for they have it all their own way. Peace—peace, peace, then, dear Father ; urge the holy Father to think more of the loss of souls than the loss of cities, for souls are dearer than cities to the heart of God " [1]

Meanwhile strange to say, Bernabò had bethought him of addressing himself to the holy virgin, of whose marvellous powers he had often heard. He believed that if he could only establish relations with her, it would patch up his reputation as a pious Christian, and stand him in good stead with the court of Avignon. He therefore stooped to try and gain the good graces of the " Popolana " of Siena, and in reply to his overtures received a letter which made him comprehend that there could be no fellow-ship between Christ and Belial It must have stung his brutal pride to the quick to have been told that "to glory in one's human power is a folly and a madness," and that " no man can properly be called the lord or master of anything here below, because he is only steward of the one real Master." Then she reminded him of the Blood of Redemption, and that he who holds the key of that Blood is the Vicar of Christ. How mad then is he who revolts against Jesus in the person of His Vicar ! " Do nothing I charge you, then," she says, " against your Head.

[1] Letter 24.

The devil will persuade you that you may and ought to punish the faults of wicked pastors. Believe him not, and lay not your hands on those who are the Lord's anointed. He reserves that right to Himself, and has confided it to His Vicar. Mix yourself no more up in these affairs, but govern your own cities in peace and justice; punish your subjects when they do amiss, but judge not the ministers of the Precious Blood. You can only receive It from their hands, and if you do not receive It, you are a dead, corrupt member cut off from the body of the Holy Church!" Then she adds a word of terrible warning "Think not because Christ appears to see nothing in this life that He will not punish in the next. When our soul departs out of our body we shall then know to our cost that He has indeed seen all." And she concludes by inviting him to repair the past by taking the cross and turning his arms against the infidels. "You must now come to the help of him whom you have hitherto resisted. The holy Father is raising the standard of the holy Cross—it is his one wish and desire. Do you be the first to solicit him to carry out his enterprise Truly it were a shame for Christians to leave the infidels in possession of what is our own by right. Be ready then to give your life and all that you have for the cause of Christ crucified." How great must have been the opinion in which Catherine was held even by such characters as the Visconti, may be guessed by the fact that not only did Bernabò endeavour to make her his friend, but that his wife, Beatrice Scaliger (or La Scala), the proudest, vainest, and most ambitious woman of her time, despatched a trustworthy envoy of her own to the holy virgin, whom possibly she thought to dazzle by so bewildering a condescension. The character of Beatrice, like that of the Visconti themselves, was that of a thorough *parvenue.* Her ridiculous assumption went so far that she insisted on being given the title of *Queen,* though her husband had never assumed the royal dignity. She demanded adulation from everybody, and no doubt expected it from the Saint; and even on her tomb, after death, there blazed the pompous words of courtly flattery, "*Italiæ splendor, Ligurum Regina Beatrix.*" Catherine replied to her humbly enough, addressing her with the homely title of "Reverend Mother in Christ," and requesting her to become the instrument of reconciling her husband to the Pope. Always happy in her mode of adapting her exhortation, she suggests to the haughty dame some wholesome counsel against the pride of wealth and the love of display, and tells her that she ought to look on herself as the appointed means for leading her husband to a better way of life, and keeping him in the paths of virtue; an idea which was probably the very last to suggest itself to Donna Beatrice as any part of her vocation. There was one other member of the Visconti family with whom Catherine was in correspondence, as is proved by a letter addressed by her to the Saint in 1375. This was Elizabeth, daughter to the Duke of Bavaria, and wife of Bernabò's eldest son. From this letter we learn what we should not otherwise have known, that Catherine contemplated a personal visit to Milan for the purpose of securing the Duke's adherence to the cause of the Crusade. "Your proposed visit here," writes the princess, "has filled us with a joy no tongue can tell, as we hope thereby to receive great consolation." It is needless to say the journey to Milan never took place, having probably been frustrated by the negotiations with Florence in which the Saint soon after became involved.

D'Estaing concluded a truce with Bernabò, a step prompted no less by the entreaties of Catherine than by Gregory's natural mildness of character, and his aversion to bloodshed. "Far be it from me," he replied to Bernabò's ambassador, "that I should be at enmity with any one." In a purely political point of view, however, the truce was a mistake; for had the allies pushed their advantage at that moment against the Visconti, their odious power would probably have been broken; whereas the moderation shown them, however creditable to the clemency which inspired it, met with no other return than renewed treachery. For the moment, however, the restoration of peace facilitated the prosecution of the Crusade, and the powers who had joined the league against Bernabò were naturally those whose support Gregory solicited for his cherished design. To them also

Catherine as naturally addressed herself. She was unavoidably drawn into the current of public affairs by the constant appeals made to her for advice and direction by men in high position. Thus, when in 1372 Gerard du Puy, the abbot of Marmoutier, and a kinsman of the Pope, was named Governor of Perugia and Apostolic Nuncio in Tuscany, his first thought was to write a letter to Catherine and ask her advice as to his future course We have her reply; and we gather by it that the Nuncio must have written, not in his own name, but rather in that of the Sovereign Pontiff. In this fact we possibly come on the first link of the chain which united the future lives of Gregory and Catherine She writes as follows:

"I have received your letter, my dear Father, and it gives me great joy that you should deign to think of a creature so vile as I am. I think I understand it, and in reply to the three questions you ask me *on the part of our sweet Christ on earth*, I think before God that he ought above all things to reform two great evils which corrupt the spouse of Christ. The first is the excessive love of relations; that abuse should be entirely and everywhere put a stop to. The second is a weakness which springs from too much indulgence. Alas! the cause of all these corruptions is that no one now reproves ! Our Lord holds in aversion three detestable vices above all others—they are impurity, avarice, and pride. And they all reign in the spouse of Christ—at least among her prelates, who seek after nothing but pleasures, honours, and riches. They see the demons of hell carrying off the souls confided to them, and they care nothing at all about it, because they are *wolves*, and traffic with Divine grace. It needs a strong hand to correct them, but over-compassion is real cruelty; only in order to reprove we must blend justice with mercy.

"I hope, by God's goodness, the abuse I first spoke of, the excessive love of relations, is beginning to disappear, thanks to the unwearied prayers of His servants. The spouse of Christ will be persecuted, no doubt, but she will, I trust, preserve her beauty. As to what you say of our sins, may God show you the abundance of His mercy. I; your poor little daughter, will take the penalty

of your sins on myself, and we will burn yours and mine together
in the fire of charity. As to the other point, in urging you to
labour for Holy Church, I was not so much thinking of temporal
things; the care of them is all very well; but what you ought
chiefly to work at in concert with the Holy Father is to use every
effort to drive out of the sheepfold those wolves—those incarnate
demons—who think of nothing but good cheer, magnificent ban-
quets, and superb equipages. What Christ gained on the wood
of the Cross they spend in guilty pleasures. I conjure you, should
it cost you your life, urge the holy Father to put a stop to these
iniquities. And when the time comes for choosing pastors and
cardinals, let not flattery and money and simony have any part
in their election, but entreat him as far as possible to regard
nothing but the good qualities of the persons proposed, and give
no heed whether they are nobles or peasants. Virtue is the only
thing which really makes a man noble, or pleasing to God. This
is the work I recommend you, my Father ; other works no doubt
are good, but this is the best. I recommend myself to you a
hundred thousand times in Christ Jesus." [1]

We may, I think, safely infer that in 1372, when this very
interesting letter was written, Catherine was not yet in direct
communication with the Holy Father. Had she been, it would
not have been requisite for her to say what she had to say through
the intervention of a third party. Equally evident is it that
Gerard had been deputed by Gregory to ask her opinion, and
the next step would easily follow of a direct communication
between Catherine and the Pope. In this light, then, the letter
is an important link in the chain of our present history ; but it
has also a melancholy interest of another kind   It gives us a
glimpse of what those disorders were which at various times drew
from the Saint such tremendous denunciations. Her language
no doubt was strong, and so was that of the prophets when they
declared, "Woe to the pastors who devour the sheep," and
"destroy the Lord's vineyard ;" so, too, was that of the Chief
Pastor when He unveiled the abomination of the Scribes and

[1] Letter 41.

Pharisees, and drove out from His sanctuary the miserable money-changers who had converted it into a den of thieves. It was language that could only find a place on the lips of one to whose loving faith the Church was Christ Himself, and the ministers of His sanctuary by their office, earthly angels; for such alone could measure the abyss of misery into which those would fall who should profane so sacred a calling.

In the meanwhile, advantage was taken of the interval of peace to urge on the prosecution of the Crusade, which was publicly proclaimed by the Pope in the beginning of 1373; and whilst Gregory was despatching fervent and eloquent letters to the Emperor, and the kings of Hungary and Bavaria, as well as to the knights of St. John in England, Bohemia, France, Portugal, and Navarre, Catherine, on her part, addressed herself to those personages of importance with whom she had been brought into communication during the course of late events, and among others to Queen Joanna of Naples.

As the name of this unhappy woman will often occur in our subsequent pages, a few words must here be devoted to remind the reader of her character and history. Not a few writers have sought to draw a parallel between her story and that of the no less unfortunate Mary Stuart, and the points of supposed resemblance between them are obvious at a glance. Both were Queens-regnant, both thrice engaged in the ties of marriage,[1] both charged with the assassination of one of their husbands, and both themselves the victims of a violent death. For the rest, those to whom the good name of Mary Stuart is wellnigh as dear as their own (and in spite of the freaks of our pseudo-historians such persons still exist) will feel a reluctance to see it so much as occupy the same page with that of Joanna of Naples.

We have no great love for tales of scandal, and no skill in their narration, but one incident in the history of this celebrated woman must be briefly touched on, as throwing light on some future passages in our story. After the death of her first husband,

---

[1] The above expression is not literally accurate, for Joanna was *four* times married.

Andrew of Hungary, whom she was accused of having caused to be suffocated, Joanna fixed her affections on Prince Charles of Sweden, who visited Naples with his mother, the celebrated St. Bridget. Charles was already married, but the infamous queen did not fear to press him to divorce his wife and accept her hand. St Bridget, trembling for the soul of her son, recommended him to God, desiring rather to see him die than fall a victim to so detestable a conspiracy. Her prayer was heard, for Charles fell sick and died a holy death, and was thus preserved from the terrific danger. Those who desire to know in what light the character of Queen Joanna was made known to the royal Saint of Sweden may read the awful vision which is described in the Seventh Book of her Revelations.[1]

However, at this precise time the measure of Joanna's iniquities was not full; she had not entirely lost all womanly reputation, and she had shown herself a zealous supporter of the Holy Father in the league against Bernabò. Her adhesion to the Crusade was of paramount importance, as the head of a great maritime state which, by its geographical position, held command of the southern Mediterranean, and was in the direct line to Palestine, half-way between west and east. So Catherine writes to her, and informs her that the Holy Father has sent letters to the Provincials of the Friars Minors and the Friars Preachers, "and to one of our Fathers, a servant of God,"[2] bidding them preach the Crusade, and seek out in all Italy those who should be ready to offer their lives for the faith. She conjures the Queen to join the holy cause of the Church, and prepare the necessary forces, and it would seem that her appeal received a gracious answer, for in her next letter Catherine thanks her for her reply which has filled her with joy, and reminds her in her felicitous style of the glorious title which she bears as Queen of Jerusalem. In fact, the sovereigns of Naples had assumed this title since the year 1272, in consequence of their descent from John of Brienne, one of the last kings of Jerusalem. Very beautiful are the words in which she

---

[1] St. Bridget, lib. vii. chaps. ii., xi.

[2] *i.e.*, Raymund of Capua.

takes this empty and unmeaning title, and makes it a text to
remind her to whom she speaks, that after the sovereignties of
this perishable world shall have passed away, there is awaiting us
another crown and another kingdom, and the heritage of the
eternal Jerusalem.   She also wrote to the queen-mother of
Hungary, begging her to use her influence with her son King
Louis, and get him to take the Cross.   "Persuade him to offer
himself to the Holy Father," she says, "and to assist him in his
project of the Crusade against those wicked infidels the Turks,
who, they tell me, are about to undertake fresh conquests.   No
doubt you have heard how they persecute the faithful, and possess
themselves of the dominions of the Church.   I have written to
the Queen of Naples and many other princes.   They have all
replied favourably, and have promised help in men and money,
and seem impatient to see the Holy Father raise the standard of
the holy Cross.   I trust in God he will soon do so, and that you
will follow their example."   In short, at this moment everything
seemed to promise success to the enterprise, when on the Tuscan
horizon there arose a little cloud.   Bernabò Visconti, unable to
meet the allies in the field, had adopted a policy worthy of himself.   Having by a feigned submission secured for himself excellent terms, he applied himself to work underground, after the
fashion of a mole, in order to destroy the power of the Sovereign
Pontiff in Tuscany, and foment all existing discontents.   It was
his cunning and slanderous tongue which first whispered into the
ears of the Florentines that the real object of Gregory was to
enslave Tuscany, and deprive her cities of their independence.
Unhappily, the folly of some of the Legates gave a colour of
probability to the suggestion.   In a former chapter we spoke of
the petty civil war that was being waged between the citizens of
Siena and some of her turbulent nobles, particularly Cione Salimbeni.   He was causing endless trouble and bloodshed to his distracted country, yet he found support and encouragement from
Gerard du Puy, the Legate of Perugia.   Bernabò failed not to
point to this fact in confirmation of his statement, and quoted it
as a fair sample of the future policy to be looked for from the

court of Avignon. Other steps as imprudent and impolitic on the part of the Legates were used with a like skill, and thus were sown seeds of disaffection, which needed but an accident to ripen into open insurrection. It will be seen in a subsequent chapter in what way this was at last brought about, and a storm raised which for ever swept away all hopes of the holy war.

CHAPTER II.

CATHERINE AT PISA, 1375.

IT was not until the February of 1375 that Catherine found herself able to comply with the renewed and pressing solicitations of her friends at Pisa that she would repair to that city; nor did she finally yield her consent until moved to do so by the express wish of the Holy Father, who committed into her hands certain important negotiations with the magistrates of the republic. In obedience to his commands, therefore, she set out, accompanied by Raymund of Capua, Master John III, F. Thomas della Fonte, Alexia, Lisa, and her own mother Lapa, who, foreseeing that her daughter's absence from Siena would be of some duration, refused to be left behind.

Her reputation, as we know, had preceded her, and the eagerness to behold the Saint of Siena was so great that the citizens gave her a public reception. In the crowd which on that occasion assembled to welcome her, there appeared, besides the Sisters of Penance, who were very numerous in Pisa, the Archbishop, Francesco Moricotti da Vico, and Peter Gambacorta, the renowned chief of the republic, who brought with him his daughter Thora, then a young maiden of thirteen.

Catherine was received as a guest by Gerard Buonconti, in a house which may still be seen in the street where stands the little Church of St. Christina.[1] Gerard and his brothers, Thomas, Francis, and Vanni, were already well known to the Saint. Their sister, Agnes, now became her disciple, and was afterwards one of the first companions of B. Clara Gambacorta. The three

---

[1] Baronto in his deposition calls the house "*Juxta Cappellam S. Christinæ.*"

younger brothers had at Catherine's solicitation taken the Cross ; Gerard, as a married man, being excused from joining them. The chamber which she occupied in his house is still shown, together with the Madonna before which she was accustomed to pray ; nor is it strange that these relics of her residence at Pisa should have been carefully preserved, for her visit was of some duration, and rich in incident.

Almost the first day of her arrival, her host, Gerard Buonconti, brought to her a youth about twenty years of age, on whose behalf he begged her charitable prayers. For eighteen months the poor sufferer had been subject to attacks of fever which had resisted all medical skill and reduced him to a miserable condition. Fixing her eyes on the young man, Catherine at once asked him how long it was since he had been to confession "Not for some years," was his reply. "Know then," she said, "that God thus afflicts you on account of this neglect , go, therefore, and wash away the sins that infect your soul, for they are the real cause of your bodily infirmity." Then sending for F. Thomas, she committed the youth to his care ; and when, having made his confession, he returned to the holy virgin, she gently laid her hand on his shoulder, saying, "Go, my son, in the peace of Jesus Christ, and in His name I bid thee have the fever no more," and from that moment he found himself entirely delivered from his troublesome malady.

One main motive which had determined Catherine on undertaking this journey was the hope that, by her influence, she might keep the cities of Pisa and Lucca faithful to the Sovereign Pontiff. The quarrel between the republic of Florence and the court of Avignon had already begun, and the Florentines were using every effort to draw all the other cities of Tuscany into a great league against the Church. The very first letter which has been preserved from Catherine to Gregory XI. appears to have been written shortly after her arrival at Pisa, and alludes to these affairs and to the difficulty in which the Pisans found themselves placed. " I beg of you," she says, "to send the inhabitants of Lucca and Pisa whatever paternal words God may inspire you to utter. Help them as much as you can, and encourage them to stand firm and faithful. I am here, using every effort to induce them not to league with the guilty parties who are in revolt against you; but they are in great perplexity, for they receive no encouragement from you, and on the other hand they are threatened by your enemies. However, as yet they have promised nothing. I earnestly beg of you, therefore, to write to Master Peter, kindly and without delay." (Letter 1.)

Master Peter, here named, was, of course, Peter Gambacorta, the Captain of the people, and first *Anziano* (or Ancient) of the republic. He was at that time in the enjoyment of undisputed power; and James Appiano, who eighteen years later betrayed and assassinated him, was then his chosen friend, and filled the office of chancellor. Peter's support and alliance was essential to the success of the contemplated Crusade. Pisa was the great naval republic of the Middle Ages, and though at the time of which we are speaking her power had been considerably broken by her wars with Genoa, yet she was still an important maritime state. With such traditions as adorned her history, it was not to be doubted that she would fling herself with enthusiasm into the holy war whenever it should commence in earnest. Of all the cities of Europe none was more closely linked than she was to the cause of Palestine, and none could boast of prouder achievements in the long struggle waged by Christendom against the infidels. As Catherine passed through the streets and visited the churches, with her heart and her thoughts full of the Holy Land, she would everywhere around her have seen its sacred memorials. That noble Cathedral, the glory of Italy, was a thank-offering for the success of the Pisan fleet, sent in 1063 to assist the Normans in freeing Sicily from the Saracen yoke. Breaking the chain that guarded the harbour of Palermo, the Pisan ships attacked the enemy and won a glorious victory; and returned home with six captured vessels and abundant booty. It was the best age of faith and of chivalry; and with the treasures thus gained the brave citizens resolved to raise a sanctuary to God which should be a worthy tribute of their gratitude. Then there was the Campo Santo, the beautiful cloisters of which were built to receive the earth brought from Mount Calvary in fifty-three Pisan ships by Archbishop Ubaldo Lanfranchi, in the days of Saladin. These cloisters were being decorated almost at the time of Catherine's visit with the celebrated frescoes which, even in their decay, still impress us with awe and admiration; some of them being the work of her own countryman, Simon Memmi. We are not left merely to conjecture whether she ever paid her devotions in this holy spot, and kissed the soil once watered by the Price of our Redemption : we have sufficient proof of the fact, were any needed, in the letter she afterwards addressed to "James and Bartholomew, hermits in the Campo Santo." (Letter 186.) Nor would she fail to have visited such churches as St. Sisto, erected to commemorate four victories, all gained over the infidels in different years on the feast of that saint; or St. Stephen's, where hung, and still hang, the banners and scimitars taken by the knights of St. Stephen from the Turks. Nay, a yet stranger memorial of that distant Eastern land, bound close to every Christian heart as by the tie of home, might be found in the camels, whose ancestors had been brought thither by crusading heroes, and whose uncouth forms would have met her eye as they passed through the streets, laden with water-skins, or carried their loads of wood in the pine forests outside the city walls [1]

Naturally, therefore, there was much in the very exterior aspect of Pisa which kept alive in Catherine's mind the thought of the Crusade. And as it happened, she found on her arrival in the city the ambassador of the queen of Cyprus, who was waiting there for a favourable wind in order to pursue his journey to Avignon. Eleanor, queen of Cyprus, was a daughter of the prince of Antioch, and governed the island for her son, Peter II., during his minority. The same island, which in the strange transformation of European policy is now held by England for

[1] Beckford describes the oriental appearance which these animals in his day imparted to the streets of Pisa. About two hundred of them may still be seen at the dairy farm of San Rossore in the suburbs; and are said to be descended from the same lofty ancestry.

the protection of the Turkish Empire, was then regarded as an outpost of Christendom, which Europe was bound to defend against the advancing Turkish hordes. Gregory, who was well aware of the importance of the island, as well as of the dangers by which it was threatened, had placed the queen under the special protection of Raymund Berenger, the grand-master of Rhodes. But as the inroads of the Turks were daily advancing nearer, Eleanor now despatched an embassy to Avignon to implore more efficient aid. The ambassador, whose name has not been preserved, sought an interview with Catherine; and we may well imagine how her heart kindled as she gave ear to the tales he had to tell. They brought in living reality before her the cause for which she would gladly have shed her blood; and listening to his narrative on that heroic soil, where all around her recalled the memory of the holy wars, she felt a renewed desire to see all brave and noble hearts rally to the defence of Christendom, and to do what in her lay to rouse them to embrace so glorious an enterprise. It would be impossible to quote all the letters she wrote during her residence at Pisa with the hope of infusing into the princes and nobles whom she addressed something of her own generous enthusiasm. Nor must it be supposed that she was content with mere pious exhortations on the subject. These letters bear evidence that in some directions her negotiations had obtained very substantial results. "Oh!" she exclaims, writing to F. William Flete, "could I but hear that word which all the servants of God are longing to hear: 'Go forth out of thine own home and thine own land; follow Me. and offer the sacrifice of thy life!' I assure you, my dear Father, when I consider that God is perhaps giving us at this time an opportunity of dying for His Name, I feel as if my soul would depart out of my body. The time seems fast approaching, and everywhere we find men in excellent dispositions; I suppose you know that we despatched Brother Giacomo to the governor of Sardinia with a letter about the Crusade. He sent a very gracious reply, saying he would come in person, and furnish for ten years two galleys, a thousand horsemen, three thousand foot-soldiers, and six hundred arbaletiers. Genoa also is full of enthusiasm; every one there seems ready to offer his person and his fortune. God will surely draw glory out of all this." (Letter 125.)

But by far the most singular episode connected with St. Catherine's efforts on behalf of the Crusade was the attempt she made to gain the adherence of Sir John Hawkwood and his company of Free Lances. This design, had it been crowned with success, would indeed have been a master-stroke of policy; at one and the same time ridding Italy of a terrible scourge, and securing for the Christian armies the assistance of the most skilful general of the time. It will not be a digression from the subject in hand if we here say a few words on the origin of these Free Companies and the position which they then occupied in society. A great change in the military system of Europe, especially in Italy, was taking place in the middle of the fourteenth century. The feudal custom of rendering personal military service was now often enough exchanged for the payment of sums of money, which were devoted by the sovereign to the hire of mercenary troops. This change brought with it two great evils: the people lost their military habits, and a new class of men were created, most formidable to society. These were the bands of foreign companies, known as Free Lances, or Companies of Adventure, composed of disbanded troops of all nations; indifferent as to the cause for which they fought, their only motive in bearing arms being the hope of plunder and the freedom of a lawless life. Very soon these mercenaries, when discharged from the service of a state or republic, began to gather together under leaders of their own, and to make war on their own account. This system of brigandage first began in 1343, when the republic of Pisa having disbanded a large body of German cavalry which had been employed in the war with Florence, the troops united into a free company under a chief known as "the Duke Guarnieri" (or Warner), and roamed over Italy, levying contributions from the peaceful inhabitants. A little later followed a yet more formidable body under the command of Conrad Lando, to whom the rich cities of Tuscany and the Romagna paid large sums in order to purchase immunity from their ravages. None of the foreign partisan chiefs or Condottieri, however, were so famous as the Englishman, Sir John Hawkwood, called by Italian writers Agutus.[1] The son of a tailor, he had served in the French wars under Edward III., from whom he received his knighthood; he was a man of true military genius, and Hallam calls him, "the first real general of modern times, the earliest master in the science of Turenne and Wellington." After the peace of Bretigni, a large number of the disbanded troops, who had hitherto found employment in the wars between France and England, gathered under Hawkwood's standard, so that he found himself at the head of a powerful army, with which he was engaged for upwards of thirty years waging war—sometimes in the pay of Bernabò Visconti, the tyrant of Milan, sometimes in that of Florence, sometimes of the Pope, and not seldom living on the contributions or plunder of the states through which he marched. Urban V. took vigorous measures for freeing France from the scourge of the Free Companies, and succeeded to a great extent in driving them out of that country; but in Italy the evil had taken a yet deeper root, chiefly owing to the decay of military spirit among the citizens of the northern republics. They were constantly engaged in petty wars one against another, and being unable to fight their own battles, were obliged to have recourse to these paid brigands. One great object which Gregory XI. had in view for urging the Crusade was, as we have seen, the hope of pacifying Italy by engaging in this enterprise all the restless spirits who filled the ranks of the Free Companies. He had very early addressed himself to Hawkwood for this purpose, and would appear to have received some vague promise, which however did not restrain the English chief from continuing his destructive raids; for in 1374, the very year in which Tuscany was ravaged by that famine which was the immediate occasion of the war between Florence and the Holy Father, Hawkwood's

---

[1] The Italian variations of Hawkwood's name are worth preserving Auguto, Aguto, Acuto, Haukennod, Hau Kennode, Hau Kebbode, Haucutus, Aucobedda, and Falcon' del Bosco!

Company appeared to increase the misery of the suffering population. Angelo de Tura di Grasso, the author of the "Annals
of Siena," thus speaks : "On the 12th of July 1374, the Company
which had been in Lombardy came into Tuscany to make trouble
between the Church and Messer Bernabò. They made a truce
for eighteen months, and all the cities of Tuscany bought themselves off, and their captain was *Messer John Acuto*"

We have now to see how it was that St. Catherine was brought
into communication with this redoubtable leader. In one of her
letters to Nicholas Soderini, which bears no date, but which
appears to have been written during her stay at Pisa, she says to
him, "The time is come for us to use our treasure in a sweet
merchandise. Do you know what I mean? Nothing else than
the sacrifice of our lives for God, by which means we may expiate
all our sins. . . . The flower is about to open and shed forth its
perfume. I am alluding to the Holy Crusade, about which the
Sovereign Pontiff, the Christ on earth, wishes to know our dispositions. If men are ready to give their lives for the recovery of
the Holy Land, he will help them with all his power. This is
what he says in the Bull which he has sent to our Provincial, to
the Minister of the Friars Minors, and to Father Raymund. He
recommends them to ascertain the favourable dispositions which
may be found in Tuscany and elsewhere, and to let him know the
number of those who desire to join the Crusade."

The presence in Tuscany at this very time of the English
commander and his well-disciplined Company suggested to St.
Catherine the idea of despatching F. Raymund to him with a
letter from herself. This letter appears in the old Aldine edition
of her epistles, with a heading (omitted in Gigli's edition) which
runs as follows: "To Messer John, Condottiere and head of the
Company which came in the time of the famine; which letter is
one of credentials, certifying that he may put faith in all things
said to him by F. Raymund of Capua. Wherefore the said F.
Raymund went to the said Messer John and the other captains,
to induce them to go over and fight against the infidels, if it
should happen that others should go. And before leaving he had

from them and from Messer John a promise on the Sacrament that they would go, and they signed it with their hands and sealed it with their seals." Then follows the letter :—

"Dear and well-beloved brothers in Christ Jesus, I, Catherine, the servant and slave of the servants of Jesus Christ, write to you in His Precious Blood, desiring to see you true knights of Christ, willing if need be, to give your lives a thousand times in the service of our sweet Jesus, Who has redeemed us from all our iniquities. Oh, my dear brothers, that you would enter a little into yourselves, and consider the pains and torments that you have endured whilst you were in the pay and service of the devil ! My soul desires now to see you quite changed, and enrolled under the Cross of Christ crucified ; you and all your comrades forming a Company of Christ, and marching against the infidel dogs who possess the holy places where the Sweet and Eternal Truth lived and died for us. I beg of you, therefore, in His name, that since God and our Holy Father give the orders to march against the infidels, and since you are so fond of fighting and making war, you will fight no more against Christians, for that offends God, but go and fight against their enemies. Is it not a cruel thing that we who are Christians, members of one body, the Holy Church, should attack and slaughter one another? Do so no more, but set out with holy zeal and with quite other thoughts.

"I am astonished that you, who, I am told, had formerly promised to go and die for Christ in the holy wars, now persist in carrying on war here. It is not a good preparation for what God demands of you, by calling you to those holy and venerable places. You ought to be now preparing yourself by the practice of virtue for the moment when you and your companions may give your lives for Christ. Then you would show yourselves to be brave and gallant knights. This letter will be given you by Father Raymund ; believe all he tells you, for he is a true and faithful servant of God ; and he will advise you nothing that is not for God's honour and the salvation of your own souls. In conclusion, my dear brothers, think of the shortness of time.

Abide in the sweet love of God!—Catherine, the useless servant."

The promise thus extorted from Hawkwood and his comrades was conditional on the Crusade actually taking place; and as it never did take place, the promise of course fell to the ground. Burlamacchi, however, in his notes to this letter bids us remark that Catherine's appeal was not entirely without fruit, for from that time Hawkwood only used his arms in just and regular warfare, entering into the pay first of Gregory, then of the Florentines, and finally into that of Urban VI, for whom we shall hereafter see him doing good service. I fear we must admit that these fluctuations between the service of the Church and the republic were not very honourable to the memory of the English chief; and that, in spite of his promises, he did not altogether abstain from private brigandage. However, Sir John Hawkwood was decidedly the most skilful, and perhaps not the very most rapacious of the Condottieri, "the greatest nor the worst" of the Free Lance captains. The Florentines, whom he served with a certain amount of fidelity during many years, regarded him with esteem and admiration, and on the occasion of his death in 1394, they decreed him a public funeral of extraordinary splendour. He lies buried near the chief entrance of the church of Santa Maria del Fiore, the cathedral of Florence, where may still be seen his equestrian portrait, painted by Paolo Uccello at the command of the magistrates. Another monument to his memory formerly existed in the parish church of Sybil-Headingham, in Essex (the birthplace of this singular man), rebussed with hawks flying through a wood, but it has long since been destroyed.

The great affair of the Crusade did not so entirely engage Catherine's attention as to hinder her charity from being claimed on behalf of many souls who gathered around her, attracted by the fame of her sanctity. In the letter from the Blessed John Dominic to his mother, which has already been quoted, he refers to what he himself witnessed at this time. "In the year 1375," he says, "I heard her at Pisa speak to many sinners, her words being so profound, burning, and full of power, that she at once transformed these vessels of impurity into vessels of purest crystal, as Jesus Christ did to St. Mary Magdalen, as we sing in the hymn of that saint."[1] We should have been glad if this illustrious writer had given us some more exact particulars of these conversions, but like too many of the Saint's biographers he contents himself with referring to facts instead of relating them. His account, however, corroborates that of Raymund, who speaks of the wonderful power which she exerted over those who approached her, and which was exhibited in a very special degree at this time. Many of those who came to see her would kneel down and kiss her hand, at which some took scandal. Among others there was a certain famous physician in Pisa named John Gittalebraccia, who determined on visiting Catherine that he might put her sanctity to the test. He came, therefore, in company with Peter Albizi, a very learned lawyer; and Master John, who was the younger of the two, began as follows: "We have heard, Sister Catherine, a great deal of your virtue and your knowledge of Holy Scripture, and have come to gather some instruction from your lips. I wish to know how you explain the passage where we are told that God *spoke* when He created the world. How could He speak? Has He a mouth or a tongue?" And he went on further in the same strain, putting a great number of similar questions; and then paused, awaiting her reply. Catherine, who had listened in modest silence, answered, "I wonder that you who teach others should say that you come to seek instruction from a poor little woman like me, whose ignorance you should rather enlighten. However, as you desire me to speak, I will say what God may inspire. It would be of very little purpose to me to know *how* God, Who is a Spirit and not a body, spoke in creating the world. What *does* matter both to me and to you is to know that Jesus Christ, the Eternal Word of God, took flesh and suffered to redeem us. It is necessary for me to believe in Him, and to meditate on Him, that my heart may be full of His love, Who died for the love of me." She continued for some time to

---

[1] In vas translata gloriæ
De vase contumeliæ

speak in this way, and that with so much fervour and unction, that at last Peter Albizi could not restrain his tears, and falling on his knees he begged her pardon for having tried to tempt her. Catherine knelt likewise, and begged him to rise; and then they had a long spiritual conference, which ended by his asking her to stand sponsor to his infant daughter. She promised to do so, and from that time both John and Peter became, her zealous champions.

But the unfavourable judgments which were passed on the Saint, in consequence of the exterior signs of respect which were shown by those who resorted to her, induced Raymund to make his own representations on the subject. "Why do you not forbid people who come to you to kiss your hand?" he asked. "The world says you like this sort of homage, and it causes scandal; are you certain that such things never cause in you a movement of vainglory?" Catherine replied with her usual frankness, "As to the first part of your question, my dear Father, I assure you I never observe what they do; I am too much engaged with the interior disposition of their souls, and I certainly do not like it; as to the second, *I marvel how any creature, knowing herself to be a creature, can find it possible to be moved to vainglory.*" [1] Noble words, which deserve to be numbered among the Saint's profoundest utterances.

Yet to one whose humility rested on a less solid basis, the admiration and popularity which Catherine excited at Pisa might truly have been perilous. She could not stir out of her house without gathering a crowd about her. Among other depositions in the process is that of the Cistercian Abbot, Baronto di Ser Dato. He was a novice of sixteen, in the Dominican Convent of Santa Caterina, at the time of Catherine's first visit to Pisa; but afterwards entered the Cistercian Order, and became Abbot of the monastery of St. Thomas at Venice. He deposes to having frequently seen the Saint in ecstasy, both in the church of St. Christina, and likewise in that of St. Catherine. One day when she was crossing the Piazza in front of the latter church, the

[1] Process, Dep. of Caffarini.

crowd of persons of all ranks and conditions who thronged about her was so great, that Baronto, wishing also to see her, and being quite unable to do so, bethought him of climbing the wall of an old tomb hard by, and was about to do so, when Catherine, knowing his purpose in spirit, though she could not so much as see him, nor he her, called out in a loud voice, bidding the by-standers prevent that young religious from climbing the wall, as it was unsafe. This proved to be the fact, and the incident soon became known throughout the city. He also relates that having some habitual indisposition he went to Catherine, and kneeling down, begged her to procure for him the same relief which she had obtained for so many others. But she replied, " My son, this infirmity will be profitable to you, and will be the means of your ultimate salvation ; were you to be cured of it you would fall into many sins ; you will never, therefore, be quite free from it, but it shall not so gravely incommode you as to hinder you in your religous duties." And her words proved true, for though he consulted many physicians, and took every possible means of restoring his health, he suffered from this malady in a less aggravated form to the end of his days. [1]

We will now pass on to give some account of two of Catherine's Pisan friends who were hereafter like her to find a place in the calendar of the Dominican Order. The first of these was Thora Gambacorta, destined to commence, that reform of the order, so long one of the cherished desires of Catherine's heart. She was born in 1362, and while still a child was espoused to Simon di Massa, whom, however, she never saw after her seventh year, for he went to serve in foreign wars, and died without returning to Pisa. During Catherine's stay in the city a great intimacy sprang up between her and the young girl, who two years later was left a widow. As soon as she found herself thus set free from worldly engagements, she resolved to dedicate herself to God. That in this resolve she was advised and encouraged by Catherine is evident from the letters addressed to her by the Saint, in which, after alluding to the cruel opposition

[1] Process, fol. 210

which Thora had to encounter on the part of her family, she counsels her " to enter the bark of holy obedience; it is the safest way, and makes a soul advance not in her own strength alone, but aided by that of the Order." (Letter 322.) In another beautiful letter she seeks to confirm Thora in her generous resolution, by setting before her the nothingness of the world and the infinite treasures we possess in God. "If our heart be stripped of the world it will be full of God, but if it is empty of God, it will be full of the world. We cannot serve two masters. Let us then free ourselves from the yoke of the tyrannical world and give ourselves generously to God, *all* to God, without division, without reserve, without pretence, for He is our own God, and beholds the most secret folds of our hearts. What folly to wait for a time that may never be ours! We are always deferring and delaying; if God presents one thing to us we take another, we fear more to lose some passing pleasure than to lose God Himself. And so He justly permits that the soul that loves earthly things with irregular affection shall become weary of them and insupportable to itself. Such a soul suffers from what it possesses, through fear of losing it, and it suffers from what it does not possess, desiring to obtain it; and so it is never at peace, because all things that are in the world are less than the soul. God, and God alone, knows, and wills, and can give us more than we know how to desire. In Him alone the soul can find peace, because He is the infinite riches, and wisdom, and beauty, and goodness; and He will fill to overflowing the holy desires of those who strip themselves of the world for His sake." (Letter 323.)

What wonder if such words, from such a teacher, bore fruit in the sanctification of her to whom they were addressed? Thora found courage at the age of fifteen to resist the entreaties, and even the violence of her father and brothers, and flying first to the Franciscan Convent of St. Martino took there the name of Sister Clara. But before her profession she was forcibly seized by her father and imprisoned at home for five months, at the end of which time she was released through the interference of

Alphonsus di Vadaterra, Bishop of Jaen, and formerly confessor
to St. Bridget.   He was one of the most influential religious of
the time, and had a special hold over the heart of Peter
Gambacorta, for in former days they had been fellow pilgrims to
the Holy Land.   His mediation obtained Clara's release, and
eventually her father founded the Dominican Convent of the
Holy Cross, into which she entered with four companions in the
year 1382, establishing there such strict observance, that the new
convent became the cradle of reform to the entire Order, in
which she is now venerated as the Blessed Clara Gambacorta.

Another beatified saint of the Dominican Order was likewise
gained to religion by Catherine during her residence in Pisa.
This was the Blessed Mary Mancini.   She was the daughter of
Bartholomew Munguto, and her baptismal name was Catherine.
She had been twice married, and was living as a devout secular
at the time of Catherine's coming to Pisa.   A strict friendship
sprang up between them , and we are told that on Easter Day,
the two being together in prayer in the chapel of the Annunziata,
attached to the Dominican Church of Santa Caterina, they were
in the sight of all the people covered by a beautiful and brilliant
cloud, out of which there flew a white dove.   Most writers tell
us that it was at this time that Catherine persuaded her friend
to enter the Third Order of Penance ; while others say that Mary
did so in consequence of a vision in which the Saint appeared
to her after her death.   She subsequently entered the convent
of the Holy Cross, and governed it as Prioress after the death of
Blessed Clara.

Meanwhile Catherine was still suffering from the same infirm
state of health which she had pleaded in the previous year as an
excuse for not coming to Pisa.   At no period of her life, indeed,
did her physical strength appear less equal to the demands of her
fervid and energetic soul.   "During her whole sojourn at Pisa,"
says Raymund, "her continual ecstasies so enfeebled her body
that we thought her at the point of death.   I dreaded losing her,
and considered what means I could take to revive her strength
when thus exhausted.   Meat, eggs, and wine she held in abhor-

rence, and yet more, any kind of cordials. At last I bethought me of asking her to let me put a little sugar into the cold water which she drank. But she answered a little quickly, 'Alas, Father, would you utterly quench the little life that is left in my body? for you know that all sweet things are like a deadly poison to me.'"

It was a difficult case; nevertheless, Raymund and their good host, Gerard Buonconti, set themselves to consider what they could find to give her some refreshment. "Then," says Raymund, "I remembered having seen in similar cases the temples and wrists of an invalid bathed in a certain red wine, called the wine of Vernaccia, which caused much relief. I proposed to Gerard that as we could give her nothing which she could take interiorly, we should try and administer this exterior remedy. He replied that he knew of one of the neighbours who had a cask of this kind of wine, and that he would at once send and procure some of it. The person whom he sent for the purpose described the exhaustion from which Catherine suffered, and in Gerard's name begged for a bottle of the wine. The neighbour, whose name I forget, replied, 'My friend, I would gladly give Master Gerard not a bottle only, but the whole cask: but it has been quite empty for the last three months; to make sure, however, come with me and see.' So saying, he led the way to the wine-cellar, and the messenger saw well enough that the cask was empty. Nevertheless, the good man, to make more sure, drew the wooden peg which served for drawing off the wine, when lo! an excellent wine of Vernaccia came forth in great abundance and flowed on the ground. The owner, greatly astonished, replaced the peg, and calling all the inmates of the house, asked who had put new wine into the cask. All declared that there had been no wine in it for the last three months, and that it was impossible for any one to have poured any into it secretly. The news spread through the neighbourhood, and every one regarded it as a miracle. Gerard's messenger, meanwhile, full of joy and wonder, brought back a bottle of the wine, and related to us what had happened; and Catherine's spiritual children rejoiced in the Lord, giving thanks to Him for His miraculous assistance."

A few days later, Catherine, being somewhat restored in strength, went to visit the Apostolic Nuncio who had just arrived in Pisa; but no sooner had she entered the streets than the whole city was in commotion. The artizans left their shops, and hurried out to see her. " Behold," they cried, " the woman who does not drink wine herself, and who has yet miraculously filled a cask with excellent wine !" When Catherine perceived the general excitement, and knew herself to be the cause of it, she was much distressed, and poured out her complaint before God " O Lord," she exclaimed, "why wilt Thou afflict the heart of Thy poor servant, and render her the sport of the whole world? All Thy servants may live in peace among men, save only me ! Who asked this wine of Thy bounty? For many years I have taken no wine, for Thy sake, yet now, behold, on account of this wine I am covered with confusion. I conjure Thee, then, of Thy mercy, cause it to dry up again as quickly as possible, so as to put a stop to all this talk and unseemly excitement." Then in answer to her prayer, our Lord worked another wonder greater than the first The cask had up to that time been filled with the very best wine, and although out of devotion many of the citizens carried some of it away to their own houses, yet the quantity in no way diminished. But now it suddenly changed into a thick sediment, and what had before been so excellent and delicious became nothing but disgusting dregs, quite unfit to drink In consequence of this, the master of the house and those who had drank of the wonderful wine were obliged to hold their peace, being ashamed to say any more about it Catherine's disciples were also much mortified, but she herself was never gayer or better satisfied, and gave thanks to God that He had delivered her from the observation of men, and turned their praise to her own confusion." [1]

But if Catherine had been revived for the moment by the solicitude of her friends, no remedy could really relieve the malady under which she was suffering. She was slowly dying the glorious martyrdom of the saints, burnt up in the sacred fire of Divine

[1] Leg , Part 2, chap. ii.

Love. Moreover, as the time was approaching when she was to be called to labours yet more responsible than any she had ever yet undertaken for the good of Holy Church, it pleased God that according to the law which appeared always to regulate the successive stages of her wonderful life, a Divine seal should be set on this fresh mission, and a new and surpassing grace bestowed on her to whom had already been granted the ring of Espousal, the Crown of Thorns, the exchange of Hearts, and a foretaste of the sufferings of the Passion

It was a Sunday; the fourth Sunday in Lent, which that year fell on the 1st of April. According to their custom, Catherine and her companions were assembled in the little Church of St. Christina to hear Mass, which was celebrated by F. Raymund. He administered Holy Communion to all the company, after which, as was usual with her, Catherine remained a long time in ecstasy. "The soul that sighed after its Creator," he says, "separated as much as it could from the body. We waited until she had recovered her senses, hoping to receive some spiritual consolation from her; when suddenly we beheld her, who until then had been lying prostrate on the ground, rise a little, then kneel and extend her hands and arms. Her countenance appeared all on fire, and thus she remained for a long time perfectly motionless Then, as though she had received a deadly wound, we saw her fall suddenly, and a few moments later she came to herself. She immediately sent for me, and said to me in a low tone, 'Father, I have to make known to you that by the mercy of our Lord Jesus Christ, I now bear His Sacred Stigmas in my body I replied that I had guessed as much from what I had observed during her ecstasy, and asked her in what manner it had come to pass. She replied, saying, 'I beheld our Lord fastened to His Cross coming down towards me surrounded by a great and wonderful light. Then my soul was all ravished with the desire to go forth and meet its Creator, so that by the very force of my spirit, as you might see, my body was constrained to rise. Then there came down from the holes of His Blessed Wounds five bloody rays, which were directed towards the same parts of my body, namely, my hands, feet, and heart. I understood the mystery, and cried out, saying, "Ah, Lord God, I beseech Thee, let no signs of those holy marks appear outwardly to the eyes of men!" And while I was yet speaking, those rays that were before of a sanguine red changed to a marvellous brightness, and so in the form of most pure light they rested upon those five parts of my body.' Then I asked her if no beam of light had reached her right side. She replied, 'No, it fell on the left side and directly above the heart; for the ray of light that came from the right side of our Lord did not strike me obliquely, but directly' Then I inquired if she felt any sensible pain in those places, on which, sighing deeply, she answered, 'I feel in those five places, but specially in my heart, so great and violent a pain, that unless Almighty God be pleased to work a new miracle, I cannot live.' These words filled me with grief, and I carefully examined whether I could see any tokens of such grievous suffering. So when she had finished what she had to say, we all went out of the church together to return home. On reaching the house she went at once to her chamber, and lying down on her bed soon became quite unconscious. All her disciples collected round about her, weeping bitterly to see her whom they loved so tenderly in this state, and fearing lest they should lose her. For though we had often before seen her in ecstasies which deprived her of the use of her senses, we had never before seen her apparently so near to death. Presently she came to herself, and when at last she was able to speak she repeated to me that if God did not come to her aid, she felt certain she should depart this life. When I heard that, I assembled all her spiritual children, both men and women, and besought them with tears that they would unite in offering their prayers to God that He would spare our Mother and Mistress to us yet a little while, and not leave us orphans before we were confirmed and strengthened in the path of virtue. They all assented, and going to her dissolved in tears, they said, 'O Mother! we know well that your desire is to be with your dear Spouse and Lord, our Saviour Christ. But our earnest petition is that you would take pity on us, your poor children, and not leave us thus comfortless and without direction. Your reward is safely laid up for you in heaven, and abideth your coming; but we are in danger of perishing a thousand ways in the tempestuous sea of this world. We know also, good Mother, that your dear Spouse loveth you so tenderly that He will deny you nothing that you ask Him. Wherefore, we all beseech you with one voice to make your humble prayer to Him that He will vouchsafe to lend you yet a little time of life among us, for our further instruction in this holy order of life wherein you have begun to train us We will pray with you also, but what are we, feeble wretches and sinful creatures ! We are unworthy to appear before His Divine Majesty, being, as we are, full of iniquity and subject to many imperfections. And therefore we pray you, dear Mother, that our suit may be offered up to Almighty God by you, who, for the tender love you have always shown to us, will solicit it more carefully, and obtain it more certainly.' Many such words we spoke to her, with great heaviness of heart, which we showed more by tears than by words. Then Catherine answered us, saying, 'It is now a long time, as you know, that I resigned my own will to God, so that I have no will of my own, nor do I wish or desire aught whether for myself or others save what is in accordance with His most blessed will. True, indeed, I love you all entirely, and no less true is it that He also loves you far more tenderly than I can do, and thirsts for your salvation more than I or all men are able to conceive, as He has shown by the shedding of His most Precious Blood His will therefore be done in this and in all things. Therefore I will not cease to pray, but only that His gracious will may be done, as may be for the best '

"On hearing these words we remained deeply afflicted, but God did not despise our prayers. On the following Sunday, having received Holy Communion, she again fell into an ecstasy, as before ; but this time, instead of being left prostrate by it, she seemed on returning to herself to have regained fresh vigour. I told them all that I trusted our prayers and tears had been accepted by God. But to be more certain, I asked her, saying,

' Mother, does the pain in your side, feet, and hands continue as before?' To which she replied, ' I think our Lord has granted your prayers. For not only are these wounds no longer a torture to me, but they seem even to strengthen and fortify my body, so that what before weakened me now gives me comfort; and therefore, I see that Our Lord at your entreaty has given me a longer time of affliction in this life, which I am glad of for the love I bear you.'"

We have little to add to Raymund's circumstantial narrative of this wonderful event. It took place when the Saint was twenty-eight years and six days old. The place where the miraculous favour was granted is marked in the Church of St. Christina by a little column and an inscription [1] The crucifix[2] before which St. Catherine was kneeling at the time was in 1563 removed from Pisa to Siena, with the consent of Angelo Niccolini, Cardinal Archbishop of Pisa; but so great was the devotion of the inhabitants to everything connected with her memory, that the removal had to be effected by night, and under the escort of an armed force.

[1] This inscription unfortunately contains a chronological inaccuracy which has caused some perplexity to St. Catherine's biographers. It states that she received the stigmas in 1375, *when she was on her way to Avignon.* One or other of these statements is necessarily mistaken. If the date is correct, she was not then on her way to Avignon, whither she did not proceed till the June of 1376 : if it was on her journey thither that the event took place, then the date 1376 should be substituted for 1375 But we know for certain that this latter supposition is impossible, for the chief witness and narrator of the event is Raymund of Capua, who did not accompany Catherine on her journey from Florence to Avignon, but preceded her thither some time before. Moreover, all the other witnesses concur in assigning 1375 (*i.e.,* the period of Catherine's first visit to Pisa) as the known date of her reception of the stigmas. P Gregorio Lombardelli, in his *Disputa a difesa della Sacre Stimate,* misled by the inscription which he too easily accepted as correct, has included among the witnesses present, all those whom he knew to have been her companions on her journey to Avignon, and among others Stephen Maconi, whose acquaintance with the Saint did not commence until after her return from Pisa, and who certainly therefore could not have been present on this occasion.

[2] This crucifix, the work of Giunta Pisano, is now preserved in the chapel of the Fullonica, Siena.

During the lifetime of the Saint the stigmas remained invisible, but it was not so after her death. P. Gregorio Lombardelli, in his learned " Defence of the Sacred Stigmas of St. Catherine," has collected the testimonies of several witnesses who actually beheld them. Among others he quotes a letter written to Raymund of Capua by F. Antonio of Siena, who was Prior of the Minerva at the time of Catherine's death, and who solemnly affirms that on the day of her obsequies the stigmas[1] were distinctly seen both by himself and other persons. On the foot preserved at Venice, in the Church of St. John and Paul, the stigma is said to be plainly marked. P. Frigerio of the Oratory, the author of an excellent Life of St. Catherine, writes in 1656, that he had seen the hand, which is kept as a sacred relic in the Convent of SS. Domenico and Sisto at Rome, and declares that on it, also, the stigma is plainly discernible. If by a stigma we are to understand an open wound or scar, this assertion is certainly not correct. Nevertheless, the precious relic does exhibit in the centre of the palm an appearance as though all the substance of the hand under the skin had in that part been pierced, or removed, so that when a lighted candle is placed behind it, a spot of light becomes distinctly visible, shining as it were through the thin integument.[2] Caffarini in his Supplement has an entire treatise on the subject of the stigmas, in which he enumerates the various ways in which they may be, and have been, received at different times and by different persons. He

---

[1] " The Blessed Anthony, of the illustrious family of the Counts of Elci of Siena, was Prior of the Minerva at Rome when Catherine died there, and kept account of all things which took place at her death and burial : and in a letter written by him to Raymund of Capua, he testifies to having seen with his own eyes her five sacred stigmas, which were manifest after death to whosoever chose to behold them " (*Sommario della disputa a difesa della Sacre Stimate.* Part I, chap x.) Although no reference to the stigmas is made by Pius II. in his Bull of St. Catherine's Canonisation, yet the fact is affirmed in the Office drawn up for her feast by the pen of the same illustrious Pontiff, in the Vesper Hymn, in which occur the following words : *Vulnerum forman miserata Christi exprimis ipsa.*

[2] In a photograph taken from the hand, and in the possession of the writer, the stigma appears very distinctly.

dwells on the thought that this crowning and stupendous favour
was granted to Catherine as a means of more entirely imprinting
on her the likeness of the sufferings of Our Lord; those sufferings
which she contemplated with such devout affection, and strove
to make her own by such generous and lifelong penance. And
he adds one fact, which is given by no other writer, but which
coming from his pen must be held as of undoubted authenticity,
namely, that she who in her younger days was wont to chastise
her own flesh with such rigorous severity, was accustomed in
later years to receive the same penance from the hands of her
companions, in order the more exactly to conform herself to the
humiliations of our Divine Lord.[1]   The office of the stigmas of
St. Catherine was first granted by Pope Benedict XIII. to the
whole Order of St. Dominic; and afterwards at the request of
the Dukes of Tuscany was extended to every part of their
dominions.   This feast is now kept on the 3rd of April.

At the time of Catherine's residence at Pisa the little Church
of St. Christina, which was the scene of the mysterious event just
spoken of, had for its curate a certain Ranieri, commonly known
among his fellow-citizens as Ranieri di Sta. Christina. After
Catherine left Pisa he decided on entering the Dominican Order.
and we have a letter addressed to him by the Saint on hearing
the good news of his approaching reception of the habit. In
Gigli's edition this letter (120) is addressed : "To Father Ranieri
in Christ, *of St. Catherine*, of the Friars Preachers at Pisa." The
old Dominican convent at Pisa is dedicated, it must be remembered, to St. Catherine the Martyr. Burlamacchi in a note to
this letter observes that in the Aldine edition of 1500, the words
stand, not '*of St. Catherine*' but '*of St. Christina,*' but that
Farri, who published a later edition of the letters in 1579,
substituted the words '*St. Catherine*' instead; and the last

---

[1] " *Caterina quante volte si fece dar la disciplina dalle compagne, e per tali
percosse si vedevano in lei i lividi segni.*" (Sup. Part 2, Trat. 7.) This treatise
is not included in F. Tantucci's Italian translation of the Supplement. It is
to be found, however, in the original MS. preserved at Siena, and an authentic
copy of it is in the possession of the writer.

reading was adopted by Gigli. "Whether of the two readings is correct," he continues, "I cannot guess." His perplexity would have been easily set at rest had he been acquainted with the ancient and very curious "*Chronicle of the Convent of St. Catherine in Pisa*," which has of late years been printed in the Second Part of the 6th Volume of the *Archivio Storico Italiano*. There we find entered the name of "Fra Ranieri *di Sta. Christina*," with the following notice : " Fra Ranieri *called of Sta. Christina*, by reason that when he entered our Order he was parish priest of the Church of St. Christina of Pisa He had before been chaplain of other churches in our city of Pisa, and received the habit of our holy Order on the Feast of St. Thomas. He was assiduous in the Divine Office, and sang well, with a good voice. He was also a skilful, acceptable, and indefatigable confessor."

It is evident that the Aldine reading is the correct one, and that Farri only blundered in seeking to amend it. And thus we come on the interesting fact that St. Catherine numbered among her disciples, and welcomed into the ranks of her own Order, the parish priest of the little church where during her stay at Pisa she made her daily orisons, and where she received the supreme favour of the stigmas.[1] The Chronicle contains no direct reference to St. Catherine's visit to Pisa ; but glancing further over its Catalogue of the brethren, we come on the name of Fra Niccolo Gittalebraccia, "whose family was very great and powerful in the time of the Lord Peter Gambacorta, and who was a great friend of the blessed Clara " And we learn in a note that " of this family was the famous physician, John Gittalebraccia, who lectured at Pisa in 1373 at a salary of 200 gold florins ;" and who, I need not say, was identical with our friend John, the companion of Peter Albizi, when he tried to puzzle the Saint with hard questions.

---

[1] Ranieri was certainly present on the occasion. P. Lombardelli, in his list of the witnesses, gives twice over the name of Ranieri (or Neri) dei Paglieresi, and it would seem that this error arose from the circumstance of a second person of the same name being present.

One other fact may be given to show in what light the reception of the stigmas of St. Catherine was regarded in her own time, and by those immediately surrounding her. Among the disciples whom she gained at Pisa was Giovanni di Spazzaventi di Puccetto, or, as he was more commonly called by his fellow-citizens, Nino Pucci. He was priest and chaplain of the Metropolitan Church, of great repute for holiness, and a large benefactor to the Certosa of Calci. He was also the founder of a pious Confraternity among his penitents and disciples, and chose for its title, "the Stigmas of St. Francis," in memory, as is commonly supposed, of the somewhat analogous favour granted in Pisa to the holy maiden of Siena, whom he regarded and venerated as his spiritual Mother.

THE ISLAND OF GORGONA.

CHAPTER III.

CALCI AND GORGONA, 1375.

ABOUT six miles to the east of Pisa, in a beautiful spot called the Valle Graziosa, stands the celebrated Certosa of Calci, the splendid buildings of which were raised in the seventeenth century on the site of a more ancient monastery which was founded in St. Catherine's lifetime, and the erection of which remained incomplete at the time of her coming to Pisa from the want of funds. Nino Pucci and the Gambacorta family had helped the monks with liberal alms; but their contributions did not supply the whole sum required. The Prior of Calci at this time was the Blessed John Opezzinghi, who had joined the ranks of Catherine's disciples; and we learn from the MS. memoirs left by Don Bartholomew Serafini of Ravenna (one of the witnesses

of the Process) that the Saint undertook to plead the cause of
the Carthusians with the Sovereign Pontiff, and that in consequence of her representations, Gregory gave them 1000 gold
florins towards the completion of their monastery She visited
Calci more than once, and made the brethren several fervent
exhortations, and her correspondence exhibits the close relations
which she kept up with these and other Carthusian disciples
between whom and herself there existed a sympathy the more
remarkable from the contrast which existed between their respective states of life Two inscriptions are to be seen at Calci which
affirm that it was owing to St. Catherine's good offices with
Gregory XI that the island of Gorgona was made over to the
Carthusians of Calci; if this statement is correct, it would serve
to explain the visit which she made to that island at the urgent
entreaty of the Prior, Don Bartholomew. The island of Gorgona
is about twenty-two miles from the shores of Tuscany, and is not
without its poetic and classic associations It finds a place in
the poem of Dante, who, after relating the terrific story of Count
Ugolino's starvation, denounces Pisa for the monstrous crime, and
calls on the two islands of Capreja and Gorgona to rise from their
deep foundations, and dam up the mouth of the Arno, that so
every soul in the guilty city might perish by the overflowing
waters.[1] Gorgona was a dwelling-place for monks as early as the
fourth century, as we learn from some verses of Rutilius Claudius
Numantius, which are quoted by Baronius in his Annals. St
Gregory the Great reformed their discipline, but in the fourteenth
century their descendants had become so relaxed that Gregory
XI. removed them and made over the island to the Carthusians

[1] Inferno, Canto xxxiii 82. "Cette imagination peut paraître bizarre et
forcée si l'on regarde la carte; car l'île de la Gorgone est assez loin de
l'embouchure de l'Arno ; et j'avais pensé ainsi jusqu'au jour, où étant monté
sur la tour de Pise, je fus frappé de l'aspect que de là, me présentait la
Gorgone Elle semblait fermer l'Arno Je compris alors comment Dante
avait pu avoir naturellement cette idée, qui m'avait semblé étrange ; et son
imagination fut justifiée à mes yeux. Ce fait seul suffirait pour montrer
combien un voyage est une bonne explication d'un poete."—*J. F. Ampère,
Voyage Dantesque*

of Calci. Don Bartholomew Serafini was appointed their first Prior, and through his exertions religious observance was rigorously established, and all inhabitants besides the monks excluded from the island. They remained there until 1425, when the attacks of the Saracen corsairs forced them to return to Calci.

It was certainly a bold proposal on the part of the Prior that Catherine and her companions should come and spend a day with him and his brethren in their island retreat; involving as it did a voyage of twenty-two miles for one as yet wholly unused to the perils of the sea. Indeed, he had to renew his request several times before it was granted, and was obliged at last to secure the powerful support of Father Raymund to back his petition. Catherine's consent was at last obtained, and our readers may think of the little company setting out in the early summer morning, and riding through the great pine woods which extend between Pisa and the seashore, till they reached what we now name Leghorn, then more often called "the Port of Pisa." There, from that shore, she for the first time beheld *the sea!* Perhaps she had before this caught its distant gleam from the hills about Siena, or from the peaks that rise above the Certosa of Calci; but not until now had she stood on its shores or beheld its big waves breaking at her feet. Now for the first time she lifted her eyes to the broad horizon of the purple Mediterranean, and felt its breath on her forehead, while its musical chant was sounding in her ears. She drank in that spectacle of the "*mare magnum et spatiosum,*" which as yet she knew only in the poetry of the Psalter. It left its impress on her memory and in her writings, stamping there two images, the one of trouble and restlessness—a fitting symbol of the inconstant world; the other of peace and immensity, which became to her the most familiar image of God; so that often afterwards she was heard in her hours of prayer and ecstasy murmuring the words, *O mare piacevole: O mare pacifico!*" And in her Dialogue we see her contemplating Him again and again under that aspect, and likening Him to the tranquil sea.[1]

---

[1] *Dialogo,* chaps. liii., liv. She also compares the unruffled surface of a

Gorgona is a lofty and picturesque rock rising precipitously out of the waves, in form not unlike a haystack; the landing is at certain times attended by some danger, but no misadventure befel the little party, who were about twenty in number. "The evening of our arrival," says Raymund, "the Prior lodged Catherine and her companions about a mile from the monastery; and the following morning he conducted all his monks to Catherine and requested her to favour them with some words of edification. Catherine refused at first, excusing herself on the grounds of her incapacity, her ignorance, and her sex, saying that it was meet that she should listen to God's servants rather than speak in their presence. Overcome at last by the earnest prayers of the Prior and of his spiritual sons, she began to speak, and said what the Holy Ghost inspired her in reference to the numerous temptations and illusions which Satan presents to solitaries, and concerning the means of avoiding his wiles and of gaining a complete victory, and all this she did with so much method and distinctness, that I was filled with amazement, as indeed were all her audience. When she had terminated, the Prior turned towards me and said with admiration, 'Dear Brother Raymund, I am the confessor of these religious, and consequently know the defects of each. I assure you, that if this holy woman had heard the confessions of all of them, she could not have spoken in a more just and profitable manner, she neglected none of their wants, and did not utter a useless word. It is evident that she possesses the gift of prophecy, and that she speaks by the Holy Ghost.'"

When they were about to quit the island and return home, Don Bartholomew begged the Saint to leave him her mantle as a remembrance.[1] She complied with his request, saying as she did so, "Father Prior, watch well over your flock, for I warn you

calm and crystal sea, which mirrors on its bosom the reflection of the heavens, to Faith, wherein we see and know the beauty and the truth of God (*Ibid*, clxvii.)

[1] This mantle he afterwards left as a precious relic to the Certosa of Pavia, where he died in 1413

the enemy is trying to cause some scandal " Then seeing him troubled, she added, " Have no fear, he will not prevail." Some of the monks accompanied their visitors on their return, and when Catherine had landed, they asked her blessing before starting home again. She gave it them, saying, " If any accident should befall you on the way, fear nothing, for God will be with you." As they approached the island a storm arose, the helm broke, and the vessel striking on a dangerous part of the coast filled with water. A monk who came down to their help was carried away by the waves, yet in spite of all this no harm befel any of them, and the vessel itself was uninjured It was not long, however, before Catherine's warning to the Prior received its accomplishment. " Some days later," says Don Bartholomew in his deposition, "the master of a boat from Pisa, laden with wood for our island, brought to one of the young monks bad news of his mother He asked leave to return to Pisa in the boat, and when permission was refused, he fell into melancholy and temptation. One day he came to me with a disordered countenance and demanded with great violence that he might be allowed to go to Pisa. I was reluctant to give consent, but seeing his excitement, desired one of the elder monks to follow him. The unhappy youth ran to his cell, and taking thence a knife tried to kill himself His companion, however, was in time to catch his hand, and calling for help, I went with all speed and endeavoured to calm him by promising that his request should be granted. But he began to say, ' No, no, it is the devil who is tempting me, and he is even now endeavouring to persuade me to throw myself from the top of the convent ' And as all the religious were agitated and terrified, I ordered the cloak that the Saint had given me on quitting the island to be brought, and placing it in the arms of the monk, he immediately recovered. I said, ' My son, recommend yourself to the prayers of Sister Catherine.' He answered, ' She is truly praying for me, otherwise I should certainly have been lost.' " Being at Pisa, after Catherine's departure, Don Bartholomew interrogated a possessed person, " Is that Saint in Siena as holy as persons think ? " he asked. " More holy," answered the possessed. Another religious asked him whether Catherine could deliver him? "*She* could do what *you* could not do," he replied, "because, although you are a good religious, you have not arrived to the same degree of perfection."

Catherine had a special love for the Carthusian Order, and corresponded with the General, Don William Rainaud, as well as with the monks of Pontignano and Belriguardo near Siena, and those of Milan, Rome, and Naples. Her letters to Don John Sabbatini at the Certosa of Belriguardo were written from Pisa, Gerard Buonconti acting as her secretary. There is also a curious letter written to another Don John of the Roman Certosa, to comfort him under his unreasonable affliction at not being permitted by his superiors to visit the Purgatory of St. Patrick.[1] Nor among Catherine's Carthusian disciples and correspondents must we omit the name of Francesco Tebaldi of Gorgona, whom she addresses as "my sweetest, my dearest, and my best beloved brother, whom I love as my own soul," and to whom she sent a copy of her Dialogue.

Catherine's residence in Pisa certainly lasted as long as six months, during which time her attention was directed to every variety of business. A rumour reached her that the Pope was about to raise F Elias of Toulouse to the dignity of Cardinal, and considering how this event might be made to advance the good of the Order, she at once wrote to Gregory, entreating him to appoint "a good and virtuous Vicar; our Order needs one," she adds, "for its garden has run very wild." She suggests his consulting on the subject with the Archbishop of Otranto, and Master Nicholas da Osimo, two of her own personal friends, to whom

---

[1] This is a cave or well in an island in the Lake of Dungal in Ireland, where, according to tradition, St. Patrick, finding it impossible to make the people believe in hell, traced a circle with his stick, when an abyss opened, out of which cries and groans were heard to issue. It was further said that the saint obtained a promise from God that those sinners who should spend an entire day in this cave should, on their repentance, be entirely purged from their sins. The spot is still visited in pilgrimage by great numbers of persons.

she writes more openly than she could venture to do in addressing the Pontiff. "I hear," she says, writing to the Archbishop, "that our General is to be made a Cardinal; I conjure you, think of the interests of the Order, and beg the Christ on earth to give us a good Vicar. Perhaps you could suggest Father Stephen della Cumba, who has been Procurator. He is a virtuous and energetic man, and has no fear; and just now our Order needs a physician who will not be timid, but know how to use the knife of holy justice. Up to the present time so much ointment has been applied that the diseased members have become corrupt. I have not named him in writing to the Holy Father, but only begged he would consult with you and Master Nicholas. If F. Raymund can be of any use in this matter, he will be at your command." (Letter 33.) She wrote in the same terms to Nicholas, but the report in question proved fallacious, and Elias remained in office, and lived, unhappily, to take part in the Great Schism.

We also find letters which belong to the same time, and which are addressed by Catherine to Peter, Marquis del Monte, who held the office of Senator of Siena; in which she calls his attention to a number of affairs, and requests that justice may be done on a certain offender who has been persecuting a convent of nuns. Peter held his office from the February to the August of 1375, the precise time of Catherine's stay at Pisa, a fact which shows that she took cognisance of the events which were meanwhile passing at Siena, and relaxed nothing of her vigilance over the interests of her native city. Meanwhile Catherine's prolonged absence was exciting great impatience among her friends at home. She exercised a power over the hearts of her disciples which had in it this great inconvenience, that they found it difficult to make themselves happy without her; and when she left them for any length of time, some of them were foolish enough to think and to say that she did not care for them, or that she cared more for others. Something of this sort reached the Saint's ears when she was at Pisa, and what is more, she had reason to think that no less a person than good Master Matthew had joined in the silly

gossip. So she wrote him a letter (142) in which we seem to
see that one cause of the discontent so often expressed arose
from a sort of jealousy on the part of those she did *not* take with
her, against those whom she chose as her companions. Sad
and humbling as it is to think that these petty feelings could exist
among the disciples of a saint, we cannot say that it was altogether
strange or unnatural; and perhaps it better helps us to realise
her life and its difficulties, when we see her dealing with the
ordinary infirmities of men and women of precisely the same
quality as other sons and daughters of father Adam. In her
letter to Matthew, St. Catherine says a good deal about sheep
and shepherds, and tells him that shepherds must not abandon
the sheep who are in real danger to go after those who only fancy
themselves so. "Look at the saints," she says, "whether they
travelled, or whether they stayed at home, you may be sure there
were always plenty of murmurs. Now, do you all be faithful
sheep; and do not suppose I am leaving the ninety-nine for one.
On the contrary, I can tell you this; for every one of those I am
leaving, I have ninety-nine known only to the Divine Goodness;
and this is what makes me endure for God's glory the fatigue of
the journey, the burden of my infirmities, and the annoyance of
scandal and murmurs. If I go, or if I stay, I shall do it to please
God, and not man. I have been delayed by sickness, but still
more because it is God's will; we shall return as soon as we can
Meanwhile you ought to rejoice to see me go, or stay; so calm
yourselves, and believe that all will be ordered by Providence,
if I am not an obstacle by my sins." (Letter 142.) In this letter
she speaks of sickness as the cause of her delay, but from another,
written about the same time to F. Thomas della Fonte, we find
that the Archbishop of Pisa had applied to the General of the
Order for permission to keep her a little longer.[1] By her words
we gather that some kind of a storm had been raging in the home

---

[1] This fact is worthy of notice, as showing that the Tertiaries were at that
time under the government of the Order, and that a strict obedience to her
religious superiors was required of Catherine, without whose permission she
undertook no journeys.

circle, and that Alphonsus Vadaterra, who was then at Siena, was one of those who had been agitating for her return. "The cross is our best consolation, my dear Father," she says, "let us make our bed upon it. I assure you I rejoice at all you say, and to hear that the world is against me ; I feel unworthy of so great a mercy, since what else are they giving me than the vestment which was worn by our Lord ? And then it is such a trifle—a trifle so small as to be next to nothing. May the sweet Word give us some good morsels ! I fear not to be faithful to obedience, for the Archbishop has asked our General as a favour to let me stay here a few days longer. Beg that venerable Spaniard, therefore, not to oblige us to return without necessity." [1]

But before Catherine returned to Siena, she was doomed to receive the tidings of events which filled her with the deepest affliction, and seemed to put a stop to all present hopes of the proclamation of a Crusade. Allusion has been already made to the intrigues set on foot by Bernabò Visconti, with the view of effecting a breach between the Pope and the Florentines, and to the partial success of his efforts. The famine, which had followed the pestilence of 1374, and spread through every part of Tuscany, had been the immediate occasion of fanning the smouldering embers of resentment into a flame. William Noellet, Cardinal of St. Angelo and Papal Legate of Bologna, whether actuated by an ill-will to the Florentines, or merely by the desire of protecting the interests of his own dominions, refused to allow corn to be exported from the States of the Church into Florence during the time of scarcity, although earnestly implored to give the starving people this relief. At the same moment when his refusal was causing the utmost suffering and exasperation, other sinister events occurred. The troops of Hawkwood, who had been taken into pay by Gregory, in order to carry on the war with Bernabò, were dismissed after the conclusion of the truce. And foreseeing that the leader of the Free Lances was not likely to leave the country without seeking to indemnify himself for his trouble by some acts of pillage, Noellet warned the Florentines that should

[1] Letter 106.

Hawkwood enter and ravage the lands of the republic, it would not be in his power to hold him back, he being no longer in the pay of the Church. In fact, the terrible bands appeared as was expected; laid waste the whole country, and even attempted to take possession of Prato, at the very gates of Florence.[1] So far from being pacified by the assurance of the Legate, the enraged republicans saw in the whole transaction only fresh and convincing proof of the Legate's treachery. Mad with rage, the Florentine rulers determined to take Hawkwood into their own pay, and heedless of their Guelph traditions, to declare war against the Sovereign Pontiff. A frightful revolutionary spirit seemed to awake among the citizens; they rose in insurrection, attacked the convents and churches, slaughtered the inquisitors in the public streets, and declared the clergy to be the enemies of the state; while the magistrates sharing in the popular excitement, passed a decree, in virtue of which the nomination to all benefices, as well as judgment in all ecclesiastical causes, was made over to the civil government.

When the tidings of these events reached Avignon, they deeply afflicted the gentle and fatherly heart of Gregory. He at once gave orders for the export of grain from the Romagna to the suffering districts; but Noellet refused so much as to read the Papal Brief, and persisted in his former odious prohibition. War seemed inevitable, and both parties began their preparations. Fresh troops were taken into pay by the Pope, while the Florentines, according to their custom, elected a body of Magistrates to whom was entrusted the management of hostilities. All the members of this body were in the present case chosen from the ranks of the most advanced Ghibellines; they were eight in number, and were commonly known as the "Eight of War," but the mob, with horrible pleasantry, conferred on them the title of the "Eight Saints," in mocking allusion to the deeds of blood and sacrilege which marked the beginning of their rule. Another committee was formed to propagate the revolt throughout the

---

[1] This was the event alluded to in the preface to Catherine's letter to Hawkwood, quoted in the last chapter.

rest of Italy ; and for this purpose envoys were despatched to a great number of cities, who, by a singular anticipation of the phraseology and even of the badge of modern revolution, displayed a blood-red flag inscribed with the ominous word " LIBERTY ! " " Fling off the yoke of the foreigner," they cried ; "the time is come. every man who takes up arms against the Church is the friend and ally of Florence !" These words betrayed the root from which the whole evil had arisen , the Popes, since their residence on the soil of France, had come to be regarded by the natives of the Italian provinces as *foreigners*, and the national jealousy of the Italians had thus been roused against their authority. The flame spread like wild-fire : Città di Castello was the first city to join the alliance, and her example was soon followed by Viterbo, Perugia, Narni, Spoleto, Urbino, and Radicofani. in short, before the close of 1375, eighty cities and strong places had joined the league, and taken up arms against their common mother.

These, then, were the tidings which reached Catherine and her companions while they were still at Pisa. When Raymund received the news of the revolt of Perugia he was overwhelmed with grief and horror " I went at once to Catherine," he says, "in company with F. Pietro of Velletri, penitentiary of St. John Lateran. My heart was drenched in grief, and with tears in my eyes I announced to her the sad event. At first she mingled her sorrow with ours, deploring the loss of souls and the great scandals which afflicted the Church ; but after a little, perceiving that we were too much dejected, she said, in order to calm us : ' Be not in haste to shed tears , you will have worse things to excite your lamentations , what you now mourn is mere *milk and honey* to what will follow.' These words, instead of administering comfort, awakened a deeper grief, and I said to her, ' Mother, can we possibly witness greater misfortunes than to behold Christians lose all love and respect for the Church of God , and many, fearless of her censures, even separating from her ? the next step will be to deny our Lord Himself ! ' Then she said to me : ' Now it is the laity who behave thus , but ere long you will find that

the clergy will also render themselves guilty.'   And as, in great
astonishment, I exclaimed, 'How!—will the clergy also rebel
against the Sovereign Pontiff?' she continued, 'When the Holy
Father will attempt to reform their morals, the clergy will offer
the spectacle of a grievous scandal to the whole Church; they
will ravage and divide it as though they were heretics.'   These
words overwhelmed me with emotion, and I asked, 'What,
Mother! will a new heresy arise?'   She answered: '*It will not
be an actual heresy, but it will divide the Church with all Christendom;* hence arm yourself with patience, for you will be obliged
to witness this misfortune.'"[1]

The course of our history will show the fulfilment of this
prophecy, which anticipated the origin and course of the schism
that was hereafter to break out with a precision truly extraordinary.   At this moment, however, the dangers which threatened
were of another kind; and the too probable success of the
intrigues by which the Florentines were seeking to draw into
revolt, not Pisa and Lucca alone but Siena also, made clear to
Catherine the new line of duty which lay before her.   The power
which God had given her over the hearts of men she was now
to use to hold them to their allegiance; and at once accepting
the burden, she turned her steps homeward, and arrived at
Siena some time in the month of August 1375.

[1] Leg., Part 2, ch x.

CHAPTER IV.

CATHERINE AT LUCCA, 1375

CATHERINE'S return to Siena was scarcely a return to rest,
nor indeed was her stay there of any long duration. The
grievous events related at the close of the last chapter were
rousing anxiety on the part of all good men ; and no one knew
where next the spirit of insurrection might be expected to break
out. Moreover, there was an additional sorrow in the reflection
that all the fault was not on the side of the rebellious people.
Though Catherine was ready to shed her life-blood in the cause
of the Sovereign Pontiff, and refused no labour that could avail
to win back the cities of Italy to their true allegiance, yet she never
dissembled the grave fact, that all the disasters which had taken
place had had their origin from "bad pastors and bad governors."
Hence, when at the close of the year she learnt the nomination
of nine new Cardinals, a pang shot through her on hearing that
seven out of the nine were Frenchmen and three of them near
relations of the Pope. Not that either condition was incom-
patible with their being worthy of their high dignity ; but the
moment seemed to demand the promotion of those only who
would secure the confidence of Gregory's estranged subjects, and
be the certain pledge of a sounder future policy. Hence in
writing to the Pope she refers to the event in a few prudent but
suggestive words, "It is said here that you have made some new
Cardinals. I think God's honour and your own interests require
that you should choose men of virtue ; otherwise you will incur
blame and do harm to the Church, and then we cannot wonder

if God sends us chastisements. I entreat you, do what you have to do courageously, fearing no one but God."

But soon came rumours that the danger was approaching nearer and nearer; the emissaries of the revolution were everywhere busy; and the little republic of Lucca was being sorely pressed —now by the threats, and now by the promises of the cities already in revolt. Catherine had already exerted herself with success in holding back Pisa from joining the league, and she now considered what steps could be taken to preserve Lucca also unshaken in its fidelity. And first she addressed a letter to the Magistrates of that city, the nervous eloquence of which fills us with amazement. "You fancy perhaps," she says, "that the Church has lost her power, that she is weak and ready to succumb, and that she can help neither herself nor her children. Believe it not: trust not to appearances, look within, and you will discover a strength in her before which no enemy can stand. What madness for a member to rise up against his Head! specially when he knows that heaven and earth will pass away sooner than the power and strength of that Head. If you say, 'I know nothing about all that; I see some of these rebellious members prospering and doing very well,' I reply, Wait a little, it will not be so always, for the Holy Ghost has said, 'Except the Lord keep the city, he labours in vain that keeps it.' Their prosperity will not last, but they will perish, body and soul, as dead members. God will not defend them if they turn against His Spouse. Never let yourselves be moved by servile fear; that was what Pilate did, when for fear of losing his power he put Christ to death, and so lost both soul and body.

"I entreat you then, my dear Brothers, all of you children of Holy Church, be firm and constant in what you have begun. Do not let yourselves be persuaded either by demons, or by men who are worse than the demons, whose office they fulfil. Keep faithful to your Head, and to Him Who alone is strong; and have no fellowship with those dead members who have separated themselves from the source of strength. Beware, I say, beware of allying yourselves to them; suffer anything rather than that;

fear to offend God above all things, and then you need fear nothing else.[1] As for me, I thrill with joy in thinking that up to this time you have remained firm in your obedience to the Church. I should be overwhelmed with sorrow if I heard the contrary, and I come on the part of Jesus crucified to tell you that on no account must you abandon what you have begun. If you are tempted to do so under the hope of preserving peace, be very sure you will only plunge into wars more bloody and ruinous than anything you have yet experienced. You know that if a father has many children and only one remains faithful to him, that one will receive the inheritance. But, thank God, you are not alone. There are your neighbours the Pisans, they will not abandon you, they will help and defend you until death against any attacks. Oh, my dear Brothers, what demon can hinder the union of two such members in the bonds of charity!" (Letter 206.)

But she was not content with despatching to them her written words of encouragement. Caffarini tell us she had received an express command from Gregory to repair in person to Lucca; and though only just returned from her former journey, she was ready to defy the murmurs of her own people in order to obey the orders of the Sovereign Pontiff, and to leave no means untried to confirm the wavering allegiance of the Lucchese. She set out, therefore, in the month of September, once more passing through Pisa on her way. A close connection subsisted between these twin republics, and at various times Lucca had been subject to her powerful neighbour, though at that moment she enjoyed her independence, and was governed by her own Gonfalonier and Ancients, chosen from patrician families. The two cities were but ten miles apart, but separated by that high ridge of mountains which, as Dante says, prevents the Pisans from beholding Lucca.[2]

---

[1] In these words St. Catherine almost anticipates the famous line of Racine, "Je crains Dieu, cher Abner, et n'ai point d'autre crainte."

[2]   .   .   .   .   . il monte
Per che i Pisan veder Lucca non ponno.
                              Inf. xxxiii. 36

Over those beautiful mountains Catherine now travelled, passing
on her way through the frontier town of Ripafratta, destined only
four years later to give to her Order a saint,[1] foremost in the
cause of reform; while all around her bristled castles and towers,
many of which may still be seen standing, the memorials of a
feudal age long since passed away. On reaching Lucca the warm
reception given her by the inhabitants suggested the consoling
hope that her mission would not prove ineffectual. She was
lodged at first in a house provided for her by F. Gilbert di Narni,
near the Church of St. Romano It is still pointed out in the Via
St. Romano She was afterwards entertained as a guest by a
noble citizen named Bartholomew Balbani, who lived in a villa
outside the city, and here Catherine was received with open
arms by Donna Mellina Balbani, who had assembled a little group
of pious ladies at her house, all eager to see and listen to the
saintly maiden of Siena. The names of this devout little company
are preserved in the letters addressed to them by Catherine after
her departure, but we possess no other notices regarding them.
F. Thomas Caffarini has left us a vivid account of the enthusiasm
which her presence caused among the Lucchese. "She was
received," he says,[2] "by the nobles and citizens with every
demonstration of honour. As she passed through the streets, all
those who had any petition to recommend, and who could find
no other means of obtaining an interview, were to be seen running to her and flocking about her. Persons of every age, sex,
and condition demanded to see her; and it was no wonder, for
her reputation had preceded her, and through all the country
round they spoke of her admirable holiness and prudence, and
the wonderful graces which God had granted to this young
maiden—destined to treat of such important affairs, though she
was no more than twenty-eight years of age Moreover He gave
manifest proofs of her sanctity when she was in St. Romano, the
church of our Order, where she used to repair for prayer and
Holy Communion. She was often seen there after Communion,

---

[1] Blessed Lawrence of Ripafratta, born 1359, professed 1379.
[2] Sup., Part 2, Trat. 6, § 7.

not only motionless and in ecstasy, but with her body raised from the ground in the ardour of her contemplation, and remaining so for a long time, supported, as it were, by an invisible hand." The Dominican Convent attached to St. Romano was founded in the year 1236. The church, however, which still exists, is much older, and dates from the eighth century. Modern restorations have left little of the ancient structure, nor does it contain any memorial of St. Catherine, unless we class as such the beautiful picture of her in ecstasy, together with her patron St. Mary Magdalen, by Fra Bartolomeo, formerly to be seen near the entrance door, but now removed to the museum.

In this church, or in that which stood in its site before the barbarians of the seventeenth century began their so-called restorations, wonderful scenes were witnessed. F. Francis of Lucca, a Friar Preacher, whose deposition is in the Process of Venice, declares that he often beheld her at this time, and saw her do many things which caused her to be regarded as a saint. Such multitudes of both sexes resorted to her, that even in the church she was often quite surrounded, in such sort that many who wished to see her could not get at her for the crowd. And he tells a story which is also related by Caffarini, from whose pages we shall quote the narrative.

During her residence in the city Catherine fell sick, and made known to a certain priest her humble desire of receiving Holy Communion, from which alone she hoped to receive any relief. The priest appeared willing to grant her request, but formed the guilty resolution of making this an opportunity for testing the truth of the common report that she could take no food save the Holy Eucharist. He therefore went to the church, and thence set out for Catherine's house, accompanied as usual with a number of the faithful, chanting psalms and bearing lights, whilst he carried in a small pyx an unconsecrated Host, which he determined to give her. Entering the house he approached the bedside of Catherine, but she neither moved nor gave the least sign of religious reverence, though the bystanders, according to custom, prostrated in worship, making acts of faith and adoration. Seeing

Catherine did not join in these, the priest went so far as to reproach her for her indevotion. Then the Saint, justly indignant at beholding the Sacred Mystery thus profaned, kindled with holy zeal, replied, "Are you not ashamed, Father, to bring me a piece of common bread, an unconsecrated Host, and with this ceremony to deceive all the people assembled here, and oblige them to commit an act of idolatry? If they stand excused of impiety, being ignorant of what you have done, I could not be excused, God having made known to me your fraud." Full of confusion the priest retired, troubled as much by her reproof as by the remorse of his own conscience. He sincerely repented of his fault, and always retained a great veneration for her whom, by his own experience, he had certified to possess such supernatural light.[1]

There is another sanctuary in Lucca which Catherine certainly visited, and which contains a sacred treasure, to which she alludes in writing to one of her Lucchese disciples. In a chapel attached to the cathedral is preserved the "Volto Santo di Luca,"[2] an ancient cedar-wood Crucifix, said to have been carved by Nicodemus, the disciple of our Lord. When he came to the face, says the old tradition, he desisted through fear and reverence, and was assisted by an angel who completed it, and thus gave the features that expression of majesty which is recognised by all beholders. It was brought to Lucca from Palestine in the eighth century, and is held in great veneration by the inhabitants who call it the *Santo Volto*, or, quite as often, the *Santa Croce*. It is under the latter term that St. Catherine refers to it, in a letter to be quoted presently. During Catherine's stay at Lucca she visited at their own houses several sick persons who could not come to her, and an incident which occurred in one of these visits of charity is related by Caffarini in the Supplement. "Happening one day," he says, "to hear that a poor woman lay

---

[1] Sup., Part 2, Trat. 6, § 7.

[2] In Latin "Vultum de Luca." This explains the customary oath of William Rufus, "Per vultum de Luca," rendered by many English writers as "*By the face of St. Luke.*"

in her agony and in imminent danger of losing her soul, she left the house without delay and hastened to find her out, though a torrent of rain was falling at the time. Catherine remained with the dying woman, consoling and assisting her till she breathed her last sigh. The rain meanwhile continued to fall so that in returning home she found the streets running with water, nevertheless she reached the house without being in the least wet."[1] Many other remarkable events happened at Lucca, which are unfortunately alluded to, but not related, by Caffarini. The same observation applies to the testimony of Dino and Leopard, two Lucchese merchants, disciples of Catherine, who are named in the Process as having witnessed marvellous, but unrecorded incidents.[2] No illusion occurs in the Legend to this visit of Catherine's to Lucca—a fact which is sufficient to illustrate how imperfectly the narrative of Raymund gives the real history of her life. He probably did not accompany her thither; and judging from the manner in which Caffarini appears as the chief authority for what relates to this journey, we should judge him on this occasion to have taken Raymund's place. Neri di Landoccio was also one of her companions, a fact which we learn incidentally from a line in one of his poems, one of those half revelations which tantalise us by what they leave untold, rather than satisfy by what they tell.

> " E non di vero gia mai si strucca
> In fin che tu non mi sarai ben certo
> *Di cio che mi promettesti a Luca.*"

What it was that she promised him at Lucca he does not say; but judging from his ordinary temptation to despondency, it seems probable that at this time she encouraged him by some powerful hope of his perseverance.

I will conclude this part of our narrative with a few extracts

[1] Sup., Part 2, Trat. 1, § 5.

[2] Included in the Process are the depositions of two other men of Lucca, F. John of Lucca, Dominican friar, and Thomas Thomasini, a bishop; but they bear no reference to her visit to the city. They are printed by Baluze in the fourth volume of his "Miscellanea."

from her correspondence with her Lucchese friends after her departure from the city. She seems to have spent about three months with her hospitable host, and returned to Siena towards the close of the year. The warm affection which Donna Mellina had conceived for her new friend left her inconsolable when the time came for their separation. It was an embarrassment to which Catherine was constantly exposed; those who were brought into close relations with her found in that wonderful mixture of strength with sweetness, and that unbounded power of sympathy, which sprang from her habit of loving all creatures in God, so great a support and consolation that they knew not how to live without it. Mellina was one of these, and together with her little circle of devout friends conveyed to Catherine a woful expression of the desolation they felt after her departure from among them. It was a great blank which nothing would fill up, and they knew not how to endure it. Catherine was indulgent, and wrote no fewer than five letters of consolation to her sorrowing friends. That to Mellina is of touching beauty, and is worth quoting for the sake of its exquisite lesson on detachment.

"I wish, my dear daughter," she says, "that I could see you transformed in the ardour of charity, so that no creature could separate you from it. You know that in order that two things should be united there must be no obstacle between them that would hinder their perfect union. Think, then, that God would have no other love come between Him and you, whether it be the love of yourself or of any other creature; for God loves us, entirely, generously, gratuitously, without obligation, and without being first loved by us. Man cannot thus love God; he is bound to love Him by duty, being always the object of the benefits and goodness of God. We should love nothing, therefore, whether spiritual or temporal, out of God. You will say, 'How can I obtain such a love as this?' I reply, only by drawing it out of the Fountain of Supreme Truth. There you will find the beauty and the dignity of your soul. In that Fountain the soul drinks deep; seeing and loving nothing in herself, but seeing all things reflected in the clear Fountain of God's goodness; loving all that she loves for His sake, and nothing apart from Him. When once she beholds how good God is, how can she help loving Him? And it was to this that He invited us when He cried, standing in the temple, ' If any one thirsts, let him come to Me and drink, for I am the Fountain of living water.' Let us then go to the Fountain of God's goodness, whence we can draw out the water of Divine grace; but to follow this path we must lay aside every burden. And therefore I will not have you love me, or any other creature, unless it be in God. I say this, because I see from your letter that you have suffered from my departure; but you must follow the example of our Lord, who did not allow His love for His Mother and His disciples to hinder Him from running to the shameful death of the Cross. He left them, though He loved them; He left them for God's honour and the salvation of His creatures. And the Apostles also separated, because they did not rest in themselves. They renounced their own consolation in order to glorify God and to save souls. No doubt they would gladly have remained with Mary whom they so tenderly loved; and yet they all went away because they did not love themselves, neither did they love their neighbour nor God for themselves; but they loved God for His own sake, and in Him they loved all things.

"And this is how you must love yourselves and creatures. Think only of God's honour and the good of souls. If the separation from those you love causes you sadness, do not let yourselves be cast down. Try not to be any more afflicted about me, for that would really be an obstacle, and prevent your being united with Jesus crucified, and resembling Him. God gave Himself generously to us, and He demands the like generosity from us: therefore renounce all affection which opposes charity That glorious affection unites, it never divides. It is like the mortar which an architect uses when he builds a wall of many stones; for the stones only form a wall when they are cemented together by mortar: without that they would all fall asunder.

"Perhaps you will remind me of our Lord's words to His

disciples when He said, 'A little while and you shall not see Me, and again, a little while and you shall see Me,' and you will ask me, 'Why say that God will have no ties of the heart, when here He speaks of them?' My dear children, *the bond of charity is not a tie.* If you put in place of it the tie of self-love, that, indeed, will separate us from God, and lead us to nothing. So now, have courage. I feel for your sorrow, but I show you the remedy: give your hearts wholly to God, and if indeed you desire to love me, unworthy as I am, I will tell you where you may always find me. Go to that sweet—that adorable Cross,[1] with the good and tender Magdalen, and there you will be able to satisfy all your desires!" (Letter 348.)

One more quotation, and we must take leave of Lucca, though not without regret and a wistful longing to know more of her relations with the place and its inhabitants who seem so heartily to have appreciated her. This time she is writing, not to senators or noble ladies, but to John Perotti, a poor tanner, and to his wife, who had sent her, as a *souvenir* from their city, one of those "Bambini," or images of the Infant Jesus, for the manufacture of which Lucca is still famous. The good couple had dressed the *Bambino* with their own hands; and in reward for their kind thought and simple piety, Catherine found time to write them a graceful letter of thanks. She reminds them that we should try not only to clothe the little image of the *Bambino*, but ourselves to be clothed with Jesus Christ. " I thank you with all my heart for your present," she says, "and as out of love and charity you have clothed the Child Jesus, I doubt not He will clothe you with the new man, Christ crucified, and in His sweet love I pray that you may ever abide." (Letter 302.)

Of Catherine's political negotiations at Lucca and their result, not a trace is to be found in the pages of her biographers. She barely alludes to the subject in her first letter to Gregory XI., in a passage which has been quoted in a former chapter [2]

Pisa eventually got entangled so far as to fall under the interdict,

---

[1] *i e.*, the Santa Croce of Lucca, spoken of above.
[2] See page 291.

but Lucca remained faithful. Neither city entirely escaped the same kind of trouble as that in which Siena became involved, by holding friendly communications with the Florentines after they had incurred the censures of the Church ; but they certainly took no open part in the hostilities carried on by Florence against the authority of the Sovereign Pontiff. Considering the power then exercised in Tuscany by the latter republic, this abstention could not have been persevered in without considerable firmness on the part of the weaker cities ; nor can it be doubted that this result was mainly owing to the counsels and influence of Catherine.

CHAPTER V.

STEPHEN MACONI, 1376.

AT the moment when Catherine was entering on a period in her life which was to be filled with fresh sufferings and heavy responsibilities, it pleased God to sweeten her path by the gift of a great consolation. He brought into the ranks of her spiritual family a soul who became dearer to her, perhaps, than any of her other disciples, and whose name for the remainder of her life was to be indissolubly connected with her own. Stephen Maconi was the son of Conrad Maconi and his wife Giovanna, a daughter of the house of Bandinelli. They were grandees of Siena, and as noble by character as by birth. We first hear of Stephen as the schoolfellow and close friend of Thomas Caffarini ; and their friendship not only lasted through the vicissitudes of school-life, but stood the test of separation. At fourteen Caffarini entered the novitiate of San Domenico, whilst Stephen remained in the world and was bred to arms ; yet in spite of the widely different careers which they embraced, nothing dissolved that tie of friendship, "which has remained unchanged," writes Caffarini in the concluding part of his Supplement, "for more than fifty years." Stephen's parents were proud of their son, and not without reason. In addition to a handsome person and bewitching manners, he possessed great natural gifts, and a heart as pure and innocent as that of a child. In this lay the secret of that gaiety and light-heartedness which made him so universally beloved, but it was not long before dark clouds gathered on his horizon. At a banquet at which were present certain members of the Rinaldini and Tolomei families, between whom and the Maconi there existed a kind of rivalry, a dispute arose on some point of honour. Stephen himself had good sense enough to desire that this unfortunate quarrel should not be suffered to ripen into a feud, but his companions were less reasonable, and urging him to support the honour of his family, they pledged themselves to stand by him to the end. Stephen, therefore, in compliance with the miserable customs of the time, raised a band of followers, and being joined by several of his relatives, they went about the city armed, and prepared for bloodshed. All this took place in the year 1374, when Siena was being ravaged by the plague, a circumstance which produced no sort of impression on the youthful partisans. Efforts were made by mutual friends to bring about a reconciliation, but without success; and so a year or more went by. At last some were found who advised Stephen to apply to Catherine and secure her mediation; for the continuance of the feud with two such powerful families would, it was feared, bring ruin on his house. But Stephen scorned the idea. "To what purpose would it be," he said, "to apply to a woman of no rank or authority; one who has managed to get a reputation for sanctity by sitting in the corners of churches telling her beads? Do you suppose that one like her will be able to succeed where so many illustrious gentlemen have failed?" At this time he had no knowledge of the Saint. "Although a citizen of Siena," he writes, "neither I nor any of my family had any acquaintance with Catherine before the year 1376. At that time I was carried away in the current of a worldly life, and had no thought of becoming known to her; but the Eternal Goodness, Who wills not that any should perish, saved my soul from the abyss by means of this holy virgin." It was through the entreaties of his mother that Stephen's pride at last yielded. She cast herself into his arms, and implored him to make peace at any cost, advising him to place himself in the hands of a certain Peter Bellanti, a friend of the family, and one well acquainted with Catherine, being probably a relative of that Andrea dei Bellanti whose conversion on his deathbed has been related in a former chapter. Stephen consented to be guided by his advice; and Peter, who had himself been reconciled to his enemies through Catherine's means, offered to introduce him to the Saint, and accompany him to her house. "We went therefore together," says Stephen, "and she received me, not with the timidity of a young girl, but like a sister who was welcoming a brother returned from a distant journey. Full of astonishment, I listened to the words she addressed to me, exhorting me to confess, and lead a Christian life. I said to myself, 'The finger of God is here.' When I had unfolded to her the object of my visit, 'Go, my son,' she said, 'leave the matter with me; I will do all in my power to obtain for you a good peace' And thanks to her efforts, we did indeed obtain peace in a manner truly miraculous." What this was he does not say, but the story is related at length in his life. Catherine, who, as we know, had great influence with the Tolomei, succeeded, though not without difficulty, in getting all the hostile parties to agree to meet in the Piazza Tolomei to be reconciled; but when the appointed day came, the Tolomei and Rinaldini kept away, and avoided meeting Catherine for some days after. She perceived their intention of escaping from their engagements. "They will not listen to me," she said; "well, then, whether they will or no, they shall listen to God." So saying, she left her house, and going to the Piazza Tolomei, where she had desired Conrad Maconi and his son Stephen to met her with the rest of his family, she led them all into the neighbouring church of St Christoforo, where, prostrating in prayer before the high altar, she was rapt in ecstasy. And suddenly there entered the church the Tolomei and the Rinaldini; they came, neither aware of the other's intentions, brought thither by God, and seeing the holy virgin raised in ecstasy, her face surrounded by light, the spectacle so struck them with compunction, that they laid aside their rancour, and agreed to place themselves entirely in her hands; nor did they all leave the church until a perfect reconciliation and mutual forgiveness had been exchanged between them [1] This occurrence took place in the beginning of the year 1376.

After this Stephen often visited her on business connected with

[1] Vita Steph. Maconi, lib i., cap. vi.

the reconciliation, and she asked him to help her by writing some letters from her dictation; for, says Dom Bartholomew, the author of his life, "this holy virgin being engaged in many affairs regarding the salvation of souls, in which, by reason of her sex, she could not always personally appear, was obliged to have re course to letters, and sometimes dictated to two or three secre- taries at one and the same time, and on different subjects" He gladly complied with her request, and whilst writing from her dictation felt a singular change working in his heart, as though called to be a new man. And the change soon became apparent to the whole city, exposing him to no little ridicule. There were plenty of mockers to whom the spectacle of a young man of rank and worldly reputation acting as the secretary of the poor dyer's daughter, was regarded as an excellent joke, and he was followed through the streets by some who spent their jests on his sudden conversion, calling him "*be-Catherined*," (Caterinato) the cant phrase with which the street wits of Siena were wont at that time to greet any who were known as disciples of the Saint.[1]

Stephen soon became thoroughly one of the "spiritual family," and endeared himself to all of them, no less than to her whom they regarded as their mother. Between him and Neri di Lan- doccio a strict friendship sprang up, which was perhaps all the closer by reason of the marked contrast of their natural char- acters. Where indeed could two beings have been found more unlike each other, than the gay young cavalier full of life and drollery, who even when writing on the gravest affairs could not restrain his love of banter, and the sensitive poet, the "*grazioso rimatore*," as Gigli calls him, who was ever trembling on the verge of despondency, and needing Catherine's strong and masculine direction to lift him out of himself?

But as is generally the case, each found a charm in the opposite qualities of his friend. Stephen by his raillery often drove away from Neri's soul the black clouds of melancholy; whilst Neri's graver and more thoughtful character was ever on the watch to guard the brilliancy of Stephen from degenerating into levity.

[1] It was the same witticism which had been expended on Fra Lazzarino.

Catherine loved them both; but Stephen was, or was supposed to be, the Benjamin of the "family," and like other Benjamins he had to pay for the privilege, real or supposed, of being his mother's darling, by incurring a certain amount of jealousy on the part of his companions. "She loved me," he says, "with the tenderness of a mother, far more than I deserved, so as to inspire some of her children with a kind of envy; she admitted me into her closest confidence, whilst on my part I studied her words and all her actions with the greatest attention, and sinner as I am, I can say on my conscience, that though for sixty years I have frequented the company of many great servants of God, yet never did I see or listen to any one who had attained such exalted perfection as she. Never did an idle word fall from her mouth; our most frivolous conversations she knew how to turn to our spiritual profit. She could never be satisfied with speaking of God and Divine things, and I believe could she have found any one to listen to her on those subjects, she would never have slept or eaten. If any one spoke in her presence of worldly things, she took refuge in contemplation, and then her body would become wholly insensible. Her ecstasies were continual, and we witnessed them a thousand times. Her body might then be seen raised in the air, contrary to the laws of gravity, as I myself can personally testify. Her whole life was a miracle, but there was one circumstance about it truly admirable. Nothing that she did, said, or heard, hindered her soul from being intimately united to God, and plunged as it were into the Divinity. She never spoke save of God or what referred to Him; she sought Him and she found Him in all things, and that by an actual and sensible love. Temptations and troubles vanished in her presence. Criminals condemned to death often sent for her; and when she had once visited them, they seemed no longer to think of the terrible destiny awaiting them. I myself remember often going to her in some interior trouble, and afterwards acknowledging to her that I had quite forgotten what it was. I would ask her to tell me, and she would do so, and explain it far better than I could have done myself. Nor is this surprising, for it is well known that she saw souls as we see faces; we could hide nothing from her. By her holy words she brought back an immense multitude of persons to the path of virtue, and led them to confess their sins; in fact, it was impossible to resist her.

"Sometimes sinners presented themselves who were so chained by their sins, that they would say to her, 'Madam, were you to ask us to go to Rome or to Compostella, we would do it directly; but as to our going to confession, do not mention it, it is impossible.' When she had exhausted every other method, she would say to them: 'If I tell you why you refuse to go to confession, would you then go?' They would accept this condition, and she would then say to them: 'My dear brother, we may sometimes escape the eyes of men, but never those of God. You committed such a sin, in such a place, and at such a time, and that is the reason that Satan troubles your soul and hinders you from confessing.' The sinner finding himself discovered would prostrate himself at her feet, acknowledging his fault, and with a profusion of tears confess without delay. This I can certify as having occurred to many. One among others who held a high position and enjoyed a great reputation throughout all Italy, told me: 'God and myself alone know what that holy woman revealed to me, I cannot therefore doubt that she is much greater before God than we can even think.'"

Stephen had personal experience of the Saint's wonderful powers in this respect. In the early period of their acquaintance he allowed himself to be drawn into some plots against the government, and attended the secret meetings of the conspirators, held in the vaults of La Scala. Catherine, who knew by revelation what was going on, sent for Stephen, and, severely reproving him, bade him take a discipline, and shed as many drops of his own blood as he had spoken words in the unlawful assembly. She also foretold that these holy subterranean vaults would one day be closed in consequence of the bad use made of them by seditious persons; a prediction which was verified in 1390. (Vit Steph. Mac., lib. v. c. 2.)

Such is the testimony which Catherine's favourite disciple has borne regarding "the holy memory," as he calls it, looking back on it through the long vista of thirty years. No wonder that the affection and confidence given him by such a soul weaned him from every other human tie, and that his intercourse with her seemed to satisfy every wish and desire of his heart. "The longer I was with her," he says, "the more I felt the love of God and a contempt of the world springing up and growing within me. Soon after our acquaintance had first begun, Catherine one day said to me, 'You will see, my dear son, that ere long your greatest earthly wish will be accomplished.' These words surprised me much; I did not know what I could desire in *the world*, I was thinking rather of quitting it entirely. I said to her: 'My very dear Mother, what is that greatest desire?' She replied, 'Look into your heart.' I said, 'Beloved Mother, I do not find any greater desire than that of always remaining near you.' She answered instantly, 'And it will be satisfied.' And, in fact, shortly after this conversation, events occurred which once more summoned Catherine away from Siena."[1] And in these fresh journeys Stephen was chosen to be one of those who should bear her company "I left my father, my mother, my brothers and sisters, and all my kindred with joy," he says, "so happy was I to remain in Catherine's presence, and to be admitted to her holy friendship." And it is of these new and important expeditions that we now have to speak.

---

[1] In his letter to Caffarini, from which the above extracts have been taken, Stephen says that he soon afterwards accompanied Catherine to *Avignon*, omitting all mention of their previous visit to Florence. Caffarini, however, with his usual accuracy, says in his Supplement, that Stephen went with her, "from Siena to Florence, and from Florence to Avignon, and thence to Genoa; after which he again returned with her to Florence."

CHAPTER VI.

CATHERINE'S FIRST EMBASSY TO FLORENCE, 1376.

IN the part which Catherine had hitherto taken in the affairs of Tuscany she had found means of combining an uncompromising zeal for loyalty with an earnest advocacy of indulgent measures towards the revolted cities and provinces. There were two objects which she sought to gain by her efforts and by her prayers: on the part of the rebels, an unconditional submission; on that of the Pontiff and his advisers, a policy of peace and reconciliation. Hence, while in her correspondence with her friends at Florence, she exerted herself to convince them that members of the Church when separated from its head must inevitably become dead and corrupt, and that no amount of wrongs endured can justify children in revolting against their Father, her letters to Avignon as constantly pleaded for pardon for the past and good government for the future. She uses every argument in her power to induce Gregory to adopt measures of pacification. She admits the just complaints which he might allege against the rebellious Florentines, but urges on him the magnanimous policy of forgiveness, as best befitting the Vicar of Him Who laid down His life for His sheep. What hope for the reform of scandals and abuses, what hope for the prosecution of the Crusade, if the Church were to plunge into war with her own children? Better far to admit their real grievances, and to appoint good and just governors; this is the summary of all her arguments, and still she reiterates the cry, "Peace, for the love of Jesus crucified, no more war, my sweet Father, but peace! peace!" Gregory, who had already taken a considerable body of troops into his pay, listened to St. Catherine's appeal, and in the beginning of 1376 despatched ambassadors to Florence, offering very moderate terms. If the Florentines would renounce their warlike programme and engage not to stir up Bologna to rebellion, the Pope would grant freedom to Perugia and Città di Castello. But such a proposal was by no means acceptable to the "Eight of war," whose power and consequence were entirely bound up with the prosecution of hostilities. Whilst, therefore, the Pope's envoys were actually negotiating these terms of peace with the citizens, the "Eight of war" secretly despatched their own envoys to Bologna, with instructions to rouse the populace to revolt; and the Legate of that city had to seek safety in flight.

This odious piece of treachery was naturally resented by Gregory, who saw himself mocked and betrayed at the very moment when he was condescending to the Florentines and soliciting peace. Catherine, however, did not yet despair, and whilst she continued to implore the Pope still to show clemency to the infatuated people, she addressed herself to one of the Florentine Magistrates whom she knew and trusted as an honest citizen, and faithful son of the Holy Church. This was Nicolas Soderini, who had been Gonfalonier of Justice in 1371, and at this time was one of the "Priors of Arts" in Florence, and a chief Magistrate of the republic. Catherine addresses him in just such plain common-sense terms as suited his straightforward character. "Can there be a greater misfortune than to lose God? We may form a powerful league, and be allied with many cities and great personages; but what good will that do us if we are not united with God? What blindness! It is God Who preserves all the cities in the world, and I revolt against Him! Perhaps you say, ' I do *not* revolt against God;' but I say, what you do against His Vicar you do against Him. Since the Vicar of Christ has such power that he can open or shut the gates of life eternal, what are we but dead members if we revolt against him? Without him we can do nothing. If you are against the Holy Church, how can you share in the Blood of Christ? For the

Church is none other than Christ Himself[1] Perhaps it seems
to you that it is you who have received the injury, but how can
those judge others who have themselves fallen into the same
fault? I beg of you, Nicolas, do your utmost to be just. It is
not for nothing that God has put it in your power to make peace,
it is to save you and all Tuscany. War does not seem to me to
be such a sweet thing that we need seek for it when it is in our
power to avoid it. Try and discharge the office of the Angels
who are ever seeking to make peace between us and God Do
your utmost, whether it pleases or displeases men; think only of
God's honour and your own salvation, and even if it cost you
your life, never hesitate to speak the truth, fearing neither men
nor devils." (Letter 217.)

Meanwhile things seemed approaching a crisis; on the one
hand the mad Ghibelline mob, encouraged by their "Eight
Saints," after slaughtering the inquisitors, seized the Papal Nuncio
and flayed him alive in the streets of Florence with circumstances
of unspeakable atrocity. The Pope replied to these enormities
by placing the city under an interdict, and excommunicating
the authors of the crime. The censures of the Church in those
days were no mere nominal punishment, nor were their consequences exclusively spiritual. In the present case the sentence
pronounced against the Florentines broke up their commercial
prosperity, and thus touched them on their tenderest point. To
preserve their important mercantile relations with England, they
despatched envoys to that country, declaring themselves entirely
innocent of the crime of rebellion against the Pope, and requesting that their merchants might take refuge in the king's dominions,
"till a more serene air of papal grace should smile upon them."
Richard II. received them kindly, and showed himself disposed
to grant their request, when letters were received from the Pope
explaining the facts of the case; declaring the Florentines excom-
municated for their crimes, and specially for the horrible murder
of the Nuncio, and requiring that the Bulls to that effect should
be published in the metropolis by the Bishop of London A

[1] *La chiesa non è altro che esso Christo*

singular alternative, however, was offered by these Bulls to the Florentines residing in England. If they were willing to become bondsmen, with all their goods and chattels, it would be lawful for the English who so received them to communicate and treat with them, and for the Florentines who consented to such an alternative to remain and dwell in the land. In short, strange as the condition appears, it was, and was intended to be, a way of escape from the extreme penalty, as it enabled the Florentine merchants to hold on until better times; and they unanimously agreed to accept the proposed condition.[1]

The injury inflicted on their commerce induced the Florentines to pause in their headlong career, and despatch envoys to Avignon to treat for peace. The envoys were accompanied by Donato Barbadori, a popular orator, who set forth the grievances of his fellow-citizens and the misdeeds of the Legates in a strain of impassioned eloquence, but without one word in acknowledgment of the treasons and atrocious acts of violence with which these grievances had been met. After some days' consideration, during which the Italian Cardinals pleaded for gentle measures, and the French for war, the final answer was given · the counsels of the French prevailed; the interdict was to remain in force, and war was declared.

When this news reached Florence, it raised a furious storm. The revolutionary party proposed to break with the Church altogether and establish a new religion; and, on the other hand, Count Robert of Geneva, appointed commander of the Papal forces, was leading into Italy an army of 10,000 Breton Free Lances. The danger was imminent, and in their extreme alarm the Florentines turned their thoughts towards Catherine, and the less insane members of the republic, with Soderini at their head, implored her to come to Florence and assist them in fresh

[1] See Thomson's "Chronicon Angliæ," by a monk of St. Albans, pp. 101-2, 109-11. These facts explain the statement of Scipio Ammirato, who says that the English made slaves of the Florentines residing in England. Tronci, the Chronicler of Pisa, says that it was because the Pisans did not dare to expel the Florentine merchants from their territory, that they fell under the interdict.

negotiations with the Pope; "for," says St. Antoninus, "they knew her to be most acceptable to his Holiness." She set out, therefore, in the month of May 1376, just two years after her first visit. Many of the citizens had seen her on that occasion, and formed their own opinion of her sanctity. Others knew her by report alone, and the events of her six months' residence at Pisa in the previous year could not fail to have reached the ears of many. It is thus that Scipio Ammirato, the Florentine historian, and one by no means to be reckoned among Catherine's adherents, speaks of the feeling of his countrymen regarding her. "The Florentines knew for certain that she had remained many days without any other food than the Blessed Sacrament, though that was impossible in the natural order; they were aware that she had passed most of her life in the most absolute solitude; they were convinced that it was by the particular design of God that she had exchanged the contemplative for the active life; and hearing that with no knowledge of Latin she yet explained the most difficult passages of Holy Scripture, and that she had learned to read by no human means, all her words and actions came to be regarded as divinely inspired Hence she was continually implored to reconcile enmities, to deliver the possessed, to console the afflicted, and to come to their help, all which she did with so much zeal and humility, that though some were not wanting who blamed her with little kindness, she was generally regarded, as well by men as women, as a true servant of God, and very dear to His heart." [1]

This passage is a valuable testimony from a purely secular writer, and shows in a clear manner how it was that Catherine was drawn out of her solitude and compelled to take part in public affairs, through the increasing fame of her sanctity, and its power over a believing people. She therefore prepared to depart. She had already sent Neri di Landoccio to Avignon, bearing a letter to the Pope, and had urged him to support its arguments with all his might. "Labour in the cause of charity," she writes to him, "and so you will be doing the will of God and

[1] Scipio Am., liv. xiii p. 711.

that of your poor mother, whose heart is just now very sad."
Some time in March she had likewise sent F. Raymund of
Capua and Master John III. to Avignon to prepare the way for
a pacification.[1] We learn this from Raymund's own words in
the Legend (Part III chap vi.) and from a letter written to him
by the Saint, in which she speaks of certain revelations made to
her "on the first day of April." She was then preparing for her
own part in the mission of peace. On that first day of April God
revealed to her admirable things, and explained to her "the
mystery of the persecution which the Church was then suffering."
He made her comprehend how it was that these scandals which
obscured the Church's splendour were permitted. "I allow this
time of persecution," He said, "in order to tear up the thorns
with which My Spouse is surrounded; but I do not consent to
the guilty acts of men. I do as I did when I was on earth: I
make a scourge of cords to drive out those who buy and sell in
My Temple, and with it I chastise those impure, avaricious
merchants who traffic with the gifts of the Holy Ghost." Then
Catherine beheld herself surrounded by many saints, among
whom were St. Dominic and St. John the Evangelist, together
with many of her children; whilst our Lord placed His Cross on
her shoulder and an olive branch in her hand, and commanded her
to bear it *all' uno popolo, ed all' altro ;* that is, to both the hostile
parties. "I am dying of desire and expectation," she concludes;
"have pity on me, and beg the Christ on earth not to delay."
(Letter 87.)

This, then, was her preparation for her first public mission, the
Cross laid on her shoulder, the olive branch placed in her hand!
This interesting passage does not appear to have been quoted by

[1] Capecelatro supposes Raymund to have accompanied Catherine to
Florence, and to have been sent thence by her. But these are Raymund's
own words : "The Florentines decided that I should *first* go to the Holy
Father on the part of Catherine ; and *then* they summoned her to Florence."
She did not go to Florence until the beginning of May ; and writes to
Raymund in the early days of April, her letter being addressed to Avignon.
St. Antoninus says she was at Pisa when she was summoned to Florence,
but this is allowed to be a mistake.

ıny of the Saint's historians ; but no more exquisite introduction
o her political life can surely be imagined.

She proceeded then to Florence, accompanied by some of her
ırdinary companions and disciples, and among others by Stephen
Maconi. and, as Raymund tells us, was met by all the principal
nen of the city with every mark of respect. In Francesco
Vanni's illustrations of her life, he represents them riding forth ın
tate to receive her, as she and her companions appear coming over
he hills, clad ın the garb of pilgrims. All the magistrates were
ıot strangers to her. With Buonacorso di Lapo and Charles
Strozzi she had probably made acquaintance the previous year,
vhen they came to Siena as arbiters to settle the difference
ıetween the Sienese government and the nobles. Nicolas
Soderini was also an old and long-tried friend, and he now
gladly received her and all her company ınto his house,[1] furnish-
ng them with all necessaries, and exerting himself to introduce
he Saint to those who might be likely to forward the business
ın which she came.

Immense difficulties stood in the way of any peaceful accom-
modation. The government of Florence was carried on by a
ıumber of separate committees of magistrates, a minute account
ıf which will be found given ın Capecelatro's history. It was a
system which seemed to have been devised with the express view
ıf promoting factions and misunderstandings ; at any rate it
ıffered singular facilities for the purpose. Moreover, like all the
Italian republics, Florence was torn by the contending parties of
Guelph and Ghibelline, and by the feuds of rival families. The
Ricci fomented the war, because they aimed at placing themselves on a level with the great Guelph family of the Albizi ; and
for that reason set themselves to oppose the efforts of the Saint
to promote peace by all the means ın their power. That in spite

[1] "Pursuing the quay along the river, the present Casa Molini and the
ıouses on the other side of the Piazza beyond belonged to the Soderini family,
who from the earliest times exercised great ınfluence ın the republic. It was
ıere that Nicolas Soderini received St. Catherine of Siena."—(Homer's
"Walks ın Florence," vol. ıı. p. 284.)

of every difficulty Catherine should have succeeded in gaining a hearing, and in softening the hearts of men inflamed with revolutionary passions, speaks volumes of itself. In a short time she was able to despatch a letter to Gregory, in which she assures him of the pacific disposition of the Florentines, while at the same time she ceases not to press upon him the necessity of three important measures—the conclusion of peace, the return to Rome, and the proclamation of the Crusade.[1] "Do not be discouraged," she says, "by the scandals and revolts of which you hear, give no ear to the devil, who sees the loss which threatens him, and who would do all in his power to dissuade you from returning to Rome. My Father, I say to you in the name of Christ, come, and come quickly. Remember you hold the place of the Sweet Lamb of God, whose unarmed hand slew all our enemies. He made use of no other weapons than those of love. He thought only of spiritual things, and how to give back to men the life of grace My dearest Father, with that same sweet Hand of His, I conjure you, come, and conquer all our enemies in the name of Christ crucified ; do not listen to those who would hinder you : be generous and fearless. Respond to the call of God, Who bids you return to the city of St. Peter, our glorious Head, whose successor you are ; come, and live there, and then raise the standard of the Holy Cross This will deliver us from our wars, and divisions, and iniquities, and will at the same time convert the infidels from their errors. Then you will give good pastors to the Church, and restore her strength ; for those who have hitherto devoured her have drained her of her life-blood, so that her face is become quite pale. Do not stay away because of what has happened at Bologna. I assure you the savage wolves are ready to lay their heads on your bosom like so many gentle lambs, and to ask mercy of you, as of their father. I conjure you, then, listen favourably to what F. Raymund and my other sons will say to you ; they come to you on the part of Jesus crucified, and are faithful children of Holy Church."

This letter explains St. Catherine's entire policy. Peace at any

---

[1] Letter 5.

cost, and the prevention of that worst of all scandals—the war
between a father and his children, the return of the Pope to his
own States, that he might govern them with justice and clemency
in his own name, and deliver them from the rapacity and cruelty
of his lieutenants; and, lastly, the Crusade,—to heal society,
wounded to the heart with faction and civil discord, and unite all
in a common cause, namely, the protection of Christendom from
the approaching hordes of the Turks. Her views were not the
views of a visionary enthusiast, but eminently practical, had there
been in any of the public men of the time the heart that could
have responded to such a call. She loved her country, and, like
a true Italian, held in horror the bands of mercenary foreigners
ready to be let loose on the fair fields of Tuscany; and so in her
next letter she failed not to remind the Pope that if he came, it
would be to little purpose if he brought with him his foreign
soldiers. "Keep the troops you have taken into pay," she says,
"but do not let them come into Italy; for, instead of settling
our difficulties, they will spoil all. Come like a brave and fearless
man, but, for the love of God, come with the Cross in your hand,
not with a great military escort." Unhappily, even as she was
writing the words, the Breton troops were already on their march.
Robert of Genoa left Avignon on the 27th of May, and his
soldiers, entering the Bolognese territory, at once commenced a
course of pillage and devastation, which furnished triumphant
arguments to those who desired nothing better than an irrecon-
cilable breach.

Catherine's stay at Florence during this second visit could
hardly have exceeded a month or six weeks, for she came thither
in the early part of May, and entered Avignon on the 18th of
June. During this time, short as it was, she was able to make
many friends. Of Nicolas Soderini I have already spoken; to
his name must be added those of Peter Canigiani, and his two
sons, Ristoro and Barduccio; of Don John of the Cells, the
hermit of Vallombrosa, whose acquaintance she had already
made at Pisa, and who had given her his hearty support in her
negotiations for the Crusade; of Bartolo Usimbardi, an illus-

trious noble, and his wife Monna Orsa, to whom she sent several letters which, oddly enough, are addressed to them in common with Francesco Pepin, the *tailor*, and his wife Agnes. She likewise formed ties of yet stricter friendship with some of the religious communities in and near Florence, specially with that of St Gaggio, whose Abbess, Nera ("My own dear Nera," as Catherine called her after her death), was tenderly loved by the Saint. In the intervals of her business with the citizens and magistrates, she resorted to various churches and monasteries, and it was probably at this time that she was often seen by Blessed John Dominic in the Church of Santa Maria Novella. Writing to his mother Paola, many years later, he reminds her of this circumstance. "I saw her at Santa Maria Novella in Florence, and I think you yourself must also many times have seen her there when she was in ecstasy, rapt out of her bodily senses, and remaining for a long time motionless as if dead." This is the wonderful feature in the character of Catherine; it had as many sides as a cut diamond, and each side reflected its own exquisite colour. Now engaged in weighty negotiations for the pacification of her country, and braving all human respect, as she lays before the eyes of the Pontiff the wounds inflicted by bad pastors, who had drained Italy of her life-blood; now instructing and reforming religious Communities that had fallen into decay, or building up others in the spiritual life; now beheld in her hours of privacy rapt in ecstasy and dead to things of self; and now giving rules of Christian life to persons as opposite in their calling and intellectual calibre as Ristoro Canigiani, the scholar and advocate, and Monna Agnes, the tailor's wife.

Her letters to Ristoro form a series by themselves, and contain a body of instruction for the sanctification of persons living in the world, which for their prudence and practical utility have never been surpassed. At the time that she was dictating these admirable compositions she was sending a good scolding to her female friends in Florence, who, after her departure from the city, had got themselves into a vexatious quarrel, all out of their love for her. They had undertaken to defend her against malicious

ongues, and they did not defend her wisely. So Catherine
writes a joint letter to them all. "I shall scold you well, my
dear daughters, for forgetting what I told you. I recommended
you to have nothing at all to say to those who might speak against
me. Now, remember I will not have you begin it all over again.
My faults are many, so many, alas! that I could not confess them
all. When any persons speak to you of them, tell them to have
compassion on me, and to pray to God that I may change my
life, He will punish my faults, and reward those who bear with
me for His love. As to Monna Paula, I will not have you put
yourselves in a temper with her. Try and think that she acts
like a mother who wishes to see if her daughter has virtue or not.
I confess sincerely I find nothing good in myself, but I trust that
God in His mercy will change and correct me. Courage, then,
and do not torment yourselves any more; let us all be united in
divine charity, and then neither men nor devils will be able to
separate us." (Letter 366.)

In another Letter (No. 367), addressed to "Three Florentine
adies," she gives some admirable practical advice on the folly of
choosing many spiritual advisers, and following the direction of
none. Nor in noticing her relations with her Florentine friends
can we omit an anecdote related by Caffarini in his Supplement,
though without indicating at what time the event occurred.
There was, he says, a certain noble lady living in Florence named
Donna Christofora, who had in her service a waiting woman
named Elizabeth. The latter had a most ardent desire to see and
speak with Catherine, whose fame resounded throughout Tuscany.
She wished to consult her on some interior troubles, but her state
of servitude rendered it impossible for her to undertake the
journey to Siena in order to satisfy her wishes. One night, however, Catherine entered her chamber after she had retired to rest,
and, sitting down beside her, consoled her with charitable words.
Elizabeth was able to explain all her troubles, which the Saint
entirely dissipated; and after a long and sweet conference she
disappeared, leaving the poor woman full of consolation.[1]

[1] Sup., Part 2, Trat. 5, § 4.

The notice in Blessed John Dominic's letter of Catherine's habitual visits to Santa Maria Novella has its special interest, as it enables us to fix with certainty one locality in Florence associated with her presence. Begun in the year 1279, this beautiful church was not completed at the time of Catherine's visit; its decorations were still in progress, and on one series of frescoes, only recently finished, her eyes must often have rested with pleasure, whether for the sake of the subject of which they treat, or of the hand that executed them. We allude to those scenes from the Life of St. Dominic, which were painted in the old chapter house [1] (as is supposed) by the Sienese artist, Simon Memmi. To so ardent a lover of her glorious Father as was St Catherine, it must have been a delight to have gazed at his noble form represented again and again as the Preacher, the Apostle, the Lover of Souls; she was one, too, who could relish the quaint device of her fellow-citizen, who has depicted the followers of sin and error as wolves dispersed and driven away by black and white dogs, the *Domini Canes,* and from those other grand and solemn representations of the Sacred Passion, of Judgment, Heaven and Hell, on whose faded colours careless eyes now come and gaze as on mere artistic curiosities, *she* received, perhaps, an illumination, a comprehension of the eternal truths, which rapt her in ecstasy, and drew her upwards to a region wherein the turbulent dissensions that raged outside those walls were for the time forgotten

We must also assign to this time spent in Florence certain visits which Catherine seems to have paid to various places in the neighbourhood of the city, where local tradition still preserves the traces of her presence. Thus in the Villa Petrognano in Val d'Elza, there is a fountain from which she is said to have drunk, and which is on that account held in veneration by the people. A little chapel is built over it, and an inscription commemorates the fact. At Pontorno another interesting tradition declares that she came thither at the time when the church bell was being

---

[1] Now the Capella degli Spagnuoli. The paintings are commonly attributed to Simon Memmi and Taddeo Gaddi, though the fact is disputed by Crowe and Cavalcaselle.

ounded, and that she cast into the melted metal her own ring.
The inhabitants bestowed on the bell the name of "Catherine,"
and consider themselves to have been frequently preserved from
empests by ringing it. Gigli, in his *Vocabolario*, mentions these
anecdotes, and also speaks of another inscription to be seen in the
Church of St. Antonio de' Fanciulli, in memory of her residence
near that spot, at the time of her embassy to the city. Of
Vallombrosa, and her relations with its austere hermits, we must
speak in a separate chapter.

Meanwhile the leaders of the more moderate party at Florence
were urging their colleagues to place the renewed negotiations for
peace in Catherine's hands. Soderini and Buonacorso di Lapo
were among those whose influence and persistency for the moment
won the day; and presenting themselves to the Saint they
besought her to save their city from destruction, by undertaking
to go to Avignon, and plead their cause with the Sovereign Pontiff
in a personal interview. One and all assured her of their sorrow
for what had passed, and their readiness to humble themselves in
any way that the Holy Father might require. Catherine's quick
discernment disposed her to doubt the perfect sincerity of some,
at least, of the speakers. "See, gentlemen," she said, "if you
really have the intention of submitting to the Sovereign Pontiff,
and if you desire me to present you to your Father as children
willing to humble yourselves, I will shrink from no trouble or
labour in bringing this business to a happy issue; but on no other
conditions will I go."[1]

They all declared that those were their true sentiments, and
that they desired nothing better than that she should so represent
the case to the Holy Father. On this understanding Catherine
consented to accept the difficult and responsible task; but before
starting she wrote to Raymund, expressing her ardent desire to
see that removal of scandals, and that renewal of fervour for
which she was ready to give her life. And she concludes with a

[1] *Per altro modo io non v'andarei.* The whole narrative, even to the very
words spoken, is given by the Saint herself in her letter to Buonacorso (Let
215), written from Avignon, and reminding him of what had passed.

touching message to the Holy Father, whom as yet she had never seen. "Tell the Christ on earth that when I have seen him I shall sing my *Nunc dimittis.*"

It was the beginning of June when Catherine and her companions left Florence. A manuscript by Buonconti, preserved in the Bandinelli family, informs us that the little party included the three Pisan brothers, Thomas, Gerard, and Francis Buonconti, besides Stephen Maconi, and three of the Saint's religious sisters. F. Bartholomew Dominic and Felix of Massa were also of the party. Raymund, Neri, and Master John III. awaited them at Avignon. We do not know with any certainty what route they took. Pius II, in the Bull of St. Catherine's canonisation, however, speaks of her having crossed "the Alps and the Apennines" in the service of the Church; and it is therefore most probable that she performed the journey by land. This is also in accordance with local tradition, which affirms her to have passed through Bologna on her way, where she visited the tomb of St. Dominic in the church of the Friar Preachers, and beholding their cemetery, is said to have exclaimed, "How sweet it would be to lie there!" In any case it was a journey which involved fatigue and even danger, and must have occupied some time. The date of her departure from Florence has not been preserved; but that of her arrival at Avignon is given by her own pen in a letter to Sano di Maco, then in Siena. "By God's grace," she says, "we arrived in Avignon twenty-six days ago, and I have already spoken to the Holy Father and to some of the Cardinals and other prelates of the Church, and have done a good deal in the affairs which brought us here. We reached Avignon June 18th, 1376." [1]

[1] Letter 214

.

CHAPTER VII.

THE COURT OF AVIGNON, 1376.

O N the platform of the great *Rocher des Doms*, which overlooks
the whole city of Avignon, rises a pile of buildings wherein
the fortress, the palace, and the cathedral are blended together
in strange and picturesque confusion. You ascend to the
cathedral, which is the most ancient part of the structure, by a
flight of steps known as the *Escalier du Pater*, from the circumstance of its numbering as many steps as there are words in the
Pater Noster. By the side of the cathedral stands the Papal
palace, which Froissart calls "the strongest and finest building in
the world." Begun by John XXII., it received additions from
each of his successors, and was only completed in 1364 by Urban
V , who added that tower of St. Lawrence, which was called by
the name of *Rome*, as though to keep alive the memory of the
widowed city in the hearts of her exiled Pontiffs.

The city of Avignon as yet formed no part of the dominions of
France. It had been purchased by Clement VI. for 80,000 florins
from Joanna of Naples, who ruled this part of the country as
Countess of Provence. During the long wars with England
which raged with short interruption throughout the fourteenth
century, the peace and security which were banished from every
other province found refuge here ; and, sheltered from the clash
of arms, the Avignon of the Popes became the home of the arts,
and the centre of a luxurious civilisation. Churches and monasteries, palaces and public buildings of all kinds multiplied ; the
unceasing chimes of its many bells earned for it the title of *la
ville sonnante*, while magnificent walls arose of squared stone,

flanked with nine and thirty grotesque towers; structures which time's destroying hand has as yet spared, and only imparted to them the mellow tint as of a faded leaf, which but augments their beauty.

Strange, indeed, that to such a capital there should have come such an ambassadress as Catherine Benincasa, the humble *Popolana* of Siena. On that June evening when her little company entered the city gates she found herself in an atmosphere entirely new to her. With all their vices, the capitals of Tuscany, with which alone she had hitherto been acquainted, cherished in their citizens a certain robustness of character which grew out of their republican institutions. If Siena cultivated the arts with passionate enthusiasm, and if the Florentine merchants were second only to those of England in their pursuit of wealth, yet greater even than their love of money, or of the arts, was their love of liberty; and the democratic forms so jealously cherished among them, fruitful as they were of many social evils, had at least protected them from courtly corruptions. But the character of a *Court* was precisely that most unmistakably stamped on the society as well as on the exterior aspect of Avignon; nor were the disadvantages of such a state of things diminished by the fact that the courtiers were for the most part ecclesiastics. We have elsewhere spoken of the abuses which prevailed in Italy, and which had been so unsparingly denounced by St. Catherine; of the luxury and worldliness too common among the prelates of the Church, and of the vices of the inferior clergy. But how could these abuses be remedied, so long as the city, which was now regarded as the capital of Christendom, presented such an example as we find portrayed in the pages of John Pino of Toulouse? As the modest band of pilgrims made their way through those streets of Oriental magnificence, they would have met the equipages of cardinals and prelates, the trappings of whose very horses blazed with gold, attended by crowds of servants in costumes of extravagant magnificence. Avignon had its ladies, too, the nieces and sisters of great prelates, who thought it no inconsistency to display themselves and their finery in those same streets, and whose nfluence at court was reported as often more powerful than it was edifying. Much has often been said by ecclesiastical histo-rians of the evils of nepotism; but at Avignon the abuse had taken a form which could hardly fail to give scandal. It was commonly said that the road to promotion was through the *salons* of these great dames; and those who desired a rich benefice were advised to pay their court to Miramonde de Mauléon or Énénonde de Boulbon (the nieces, respectively, of Clement V. and Innocent VI), or to some other lady as skilled in the "*gaie science*," is she was nearly allied in blood to eminent and illustrious pre-ates. Provence, it will be remembered, was the native soil of the muses of the Middle Ages, and these muses often bore but a doubtful sort of character. In any case it was unfortunate that the temporary capital of the Church should have been fixed in a region so given up to the influence of "singers, actors, cooks, mimics, and troubadours."[1] A motley crowd of such personages crowded thither day after day, and found liberal patronage at the hands of those who, in that soft and delicious climate, seemed to forget that life had any more serious end than amusement and enjoyment.

A residence was assigned to the use of Catherine and her companions, by order of Gregory, in the house of John de Regio Stephen Maconi calls it "a handsome house with a richly adorned chapel," but when purchased by Cardinal Brancaccio in the seventeenth century, and presented to the college of the Jesuits, nothing remained but a tower, in which, though the chapel had disappeared, a room was still shown as St. Catherine's so late as 1706 Two days after her arrival she was admitted by the Pope to an audience,[2] and for the first time the holy maiden of Siena and the Vicar of Christ met face to face

Gregory's appearance was the index of his character. Small in stature, of a pale and delicate complexion, Peter du Rogier de

[1] John Pino, Vita Div. Cath

[2] Capecelatro says he received her in public Consistory; but there is no expression in Raymund's account which seems to indicate that it was anything but a private audience

Beaufort-Turenne bore on his person none of the marks of commanding will or splendid genius.   He looked a man fitter to be loved than feared ; and distinguished, as he undoubtedly was, for modesty, fidelity to his word, and goodness of heart, he lacked that force of character which seemed needed for one who would stem the torrent of an evil time, or accomplish great and difficult achievements.   Yet in the councils of Divine Providence such an undertaking was reserved to Gregory XI., and it was from the poor dyer's daughter of Siena that he was to receive, if not the inspiration to resolve upon, yet undoubtedly the courage to execute it.   He could not have been insensible to the irresistible charm which has been attested by all who knew her ; and he probably felt the power of that great soul, the strength and grandeur of which one of her disciples has described by saying, that "you could not look at her without trembling."   There was, nevertheless, some difficulty in their holding any intercourse together, for Catherine spoke only in the Tuscan dialect, which to Gregory, unhappily, was an unknown tongue.   He himself addressed her in Latin, and Raymund of Capua acted as interpreter between them.   Still, even with this disadvantage, it did not take long for Catherine to win the Pontiff's entire confidence.   She pleaded the cause of peace with her lips, as she had already done by her letters, and that so successfully that Gregory placed the whole matter at issue with the Florentines in her hands.   "The Holy Father," says Raymund, "in my presence and by my mouth, committed the treaty of peace to Catherine's decision, saying to her, 'In order to show you that I sincerely desire peace, I commit the entire negotiation into your hands ; only be careful of the honour of the Church.'"

F. Bartholomew Dominic, who accompanied the Saint to Avignon, lets us know what Raymund does not notice, namely, that on first coming to the court Catherine had to encounter prejudices, not only on the part of the cardinals and prelates, but even of Gregory himself.   "Almost the whole court of Rome," he says, "rose up against her ; nevertheless, their minds soon underwent a wonderful change, so that those who were at first her perse-

cutors became her greatest benefactors." He names among
these the Lord (*i.e.*, Archbishop) of Bari, afterwards Urban VI.,
who at this time made his first acquaintance with Catherine.[1]

After leaving the presence of the Pope, Catherine held con-
ferences with some of the cardinals and others of his councillors,
and was able in a few days to give hopes to her friends at Siena
of a speedy and favourable termination of her enterprise. Writing
to Sano di Maco about three weeks later, she says, "I have seen
the Holy Father and several cardinals, and other lords of the
court, and the grace of our sweet Saviour has already done much
in the business which brought us here; therefore rejoice in Him,
and be full of confidence." And indeed the obstacles which had
hitherto opposed themselves to the conclusion of peace, and
which had rendered fruitless the previous embassy of Barbadori,
all yielded to the persuasive eloquence of the Saint; and her
mission would have been crowned with complete success, but for
the bad faith of the Florentines themselves. It had been agreed
before Catherine left Florence, that as soon as she had arrived at
Avignon, other ambassadors should be despatched to the Papal
court to treat for peace in a formal manner, on such terms as
she might have been able to secure. Weeks passed on, however,
and no ambassadors appeared. But instead there came rumours
of fresh taxes having been levied on the clergy; and Catherine,
who instinctively felt that the hindrance of her efforts came from
"Eight of War," addressed them a letter of remonstrance, which
gives us a clear idea of the situation of affairs. "I have great
cause to complain of you," she says, "if it is true, as is here
reported, that you have taxed the clergy; you have no right to
do so, and it would be a great obstacle in the way of concluding
peace, for the Holy Father when he hears it will be naturally
indignant. I have had an audience with him, and he listened
to me most graciously, through the effect of God's goodness
and his own. He expressed the most sincere wish for peace,
and seemed like a good father who, instead of regarding the
offences committed by his son, remembers only that his son has

[1] Process, 1337.

humbled himself for his fault, and is ready to show him mercy. No tongue could tell the joy which this has caused me. After my long conference with him, he told me that if things were as I said he was ready to receive you as his children, and to do whatever I might judge best. It seems to me that he cannot give any further reply until your ambassadors arrive. I wonder that they are not yet come ; I shall await their arrival, and will see both them and the Holy Father, and I will then write to you and say what are his dispositions. But I fear you will spoil all with your taxes and your new decrees. I beg of you not to do so, for the love of Jesus crucified, and for your own interest."

It would seem that this rumour about the new taxes was a false report, spread abroad by the secret malice of those who had no desire to see the Florentines admitted to terms of reconciliation. On the other hand, the non-arrival of their ambassadors gave the enemies of peace grounds only too plausible for casting discredit on the whole affair. Gregory himself understood that the Florentines were not to be trusted; and in speaking to Catherine he expressed his misgivings in words which were exactly justified by the event. "Believe me, Catherine," he said, "the Florentines have deceived you, as before now they have deceived me. You will see they will send no ambassadors, or if they do, the ambassadors will conclude nothing."   And, in fact, when at last Pazzino Strozzi, Alexander dell' Antella, and Michael Castellani arrived as envoys from the republic, it was plainly to be seen that the conclusion of peace was the last thing contemplated by those from whom they had received their instructions. In justice to the Florentines, however, it must be borne in mind that the parties at whose entreaty Catherine had undertaken her journey, were not the same as those who had despatched the envoys. The mischief arose from the vicious system of the Florentine government, which admitted of power being vested in several distinct bodies who were often of opposing views and interests, with no one supreme and responsible head. Soderini and the more moderate party in the republic had been sincere enough in soliciting Catherine to make their submission to the Pope; but after her departure their views had been overruled by the more powerful "Eight of War," whose only object was to prolong their own term of power, which would cease with the proclamation of peace. They had consented therefore to despatch the envoys, but with a purpose very different from that which Catherine had designed, desiring only to soothe the irritation which had been roused at the Roman court by their proceedings, but with no purpose of submission.[1]

As soon as they arrived in Avignon, Catherine requested an interview, in which after reminding them of the mission which had been intrusted to her by the Magistrates of Florence, she informed them that the Sovereign Pontiff had listened graciously to her representations, and had placed the matter in her hands. It was in their power, therefore, to obtain peace on the most favourable conditions. If they dared not trust themselves to the French cardinals who had caused the rejection of their former overtures, they might safely place themselves in the hands of one who was ready to give her life to restore peace to Italy. To this the envoys replied briefly and coldly that they had no instructions to treat on the subject *with her*, but only with the Pope, and on her reminding them of the pledge so solemnly given her at Florence before she would consent to undertake the mission, they only returned an abrupt and insolent refusal to have anything to say to her on the affairs of the republic.

An ordinary character, if placed in so mortifying a position as that in which Catherine now found herself, would have taken little further trouble in the cause of the treacherous Florentines; but no motive of self-exaltation or desire of renown had prompted her to enter on her present undertaking. A dead body is not more insensible to pain or pleasure, than she was to all those human considerations which have their root in self-love. She

---

[1] It is Scipio Ammirato, a partisan of the Florentines, who gives this explanation of their conduct. "The Eight," he says, "thought it necessary to send an embassy to the Pope to calm somewhat the jealous suspicions of which they were the object, *but they did not on that account renounce their projects of war.*" (Stor. Fior., lib. xiii. p. 699.)

desired peace, because in the continuance of hostilities she
beheld the loss of souls, and the offence of God, and the contempt and ingratitude of the rebellious Florentines produced
absolutely no change in her purposes regarding them. "Catherine
saw through their dishonesty," says Raymund, "and perceived
that the prediction of the Holy Father had been correct; nevertheless, she did not discontinue her solicitations to Gregory XI.,
but continued as before to plead that he would show them the
clemency of a father, rather than the severity of a judge." [1]

However, she expressed her opinion on the conduct of the
Magistrates in a letter to Buonacorso di Lapo. "Alas! my dear
brother," she says, "I am distressed at the means they are taking
here for asking peace from the Holy Father; they ask it more in
words than in truth. You remember that when I consented to
come here, you and the other Magistrates seemed repentant for
the faults committed, and ready to submit to the Holy Father in
order to obtain mercy. I said to you then, that if you really
meant to humble yourselves, and to allow me to present you to
your Father as contrite children, I would shrink from no trouble
or fatigue, but that otherwise I would not go. And you all
declared that you joyfully consented to these terms. That was
the only right way of acting, and if you had persevered in it you
would have obtained the most glorious peace. I do not say this
at random, for I know what the dispositions of his Holiness were
But now we have taken quite the wrong road, and are employing
the deceitful ways of the world, contradicting our words by our
actions, and so rather irritating the Holy Father than appeasing
him.

"When your envoys came here they did not act as they should
have done with the servants of God; and it is now impossible
for me to ascertain if you have spoken to them in the same sense
as you did to me, when giving them their credentials . . . If you
had trusted your interests with the servants of God, they would
have obtained an excellent peace for you from the Holy Father.
But this you have not done. I am sorry for it, because of the

[1] Leo. Part 2. ch. vi.

ffence of God, and the injury you do yourselves, and you do not ꝛe the terrible consequences which your perseverance in this line f conduct will certainly produce." The reader will not fail to otice that in this simple and straightforward remonstrance, not word appears expressive of a woman's mortified vanity; and so ꝛr was she from abandoning the cause of the people who had ꝛeated her so unworthily, that at her urgent solicitations Gregory greed to condescend to yet further overtures, in the hopes of ꝛinning back his rebellious children, and saving them from the orrors of war, as it were, against their will.

In the meantime, the extraordinary favour with which Catherine ꝛas regarded by the Holy Father was causing much perplexity in ꝛe court circles of Avignon. That one so wholly separate from ꝛe world should have been chosen to mediate between the greatest f the Italian republics and the Holy See, was in itself a difficult roblem, but the amazement of the French lords and ladies was ꝛcreased when they formed a close acquaintance with this wonder-ꝛl woman, and took notice of her indifference to the splendour ꝛhich everywhere met her eye, and the freedom of speech with ꝛhich she passed her judgment on the courtly crowds around her. ꝛn one occasion, soon after her arrival in Avignon, when she was onversing with the Holy Father (Raymund of Capua, as usual, cting as interpreter), Catherine expressed her sorrow at finding ꝛe Roman court, which should have been a Paradise of heavenly irtues, stained by so many grievous vices. The Pope, astonished t her words, turned to Raymund and asked how long they had ꝛeen in the city; and understanding it was only a few days, "And ow," he asked, "have you in so short a time been able to gain ꝛ much information as to the manners of the Roman court?" ꝛThen," says Raymund, "suddenly changing her attitude of pro-ꝛund humility and reverence, she raised herself with an air of ꝛajesty, and said, 'To the honour of Almighty God I will dare ꝛ say that I was more conscious of the infection of the sins com-ꝛitted in the court of Rome when I dwelt in my native city, than hose are who daily commit them.' The Pope remained silent, ꝛnd I have always remembered her words with astonishment;

nor shall I ever forget the dignity with which she feared not to speak to so great a Prelate."

Her wonderful knowledge of souls was never more signally displayed than at this time, and enabled her to detect the concealed profligacy which often lurked under the fair outside of those with whom she came in contact. No mannerism of piety could deceive the keen spiritual instincts of the Saint. "It often happened both to me, and others who accompanied her on her journeys," says Raymund, "that we found ourselves with her in companies altogether new to us, where we saw for the first time persons of honourable and respectable appearance, who were in reality addicted to every vice. Catherine knew the state of their interior directly, and would refuse so much as to look at them or answer them if they addressed her on spiritual subjects. And if they persisted she would say, ' First let us purify ourselves from our faults, and be delivered from the bondage of Satan, and then we will converse about God.' In this way she would soon rid us of the presence of these hypocrites, whom we afterwards discovered were plunged in incorrigible habits of sin."

It was in this way that she conducted herself towards some of the fair dames of Avignon who sought an interview with her to satisfy their curiosity, and who imagined it necessary to assume the airs of *dévotes* when they appeared in the presence of so holy a personage. But no pious grimaces could ever impose on Catherine. One day a lady presented herself at the house, who, to the unsophisticated eyes of Father Raymund, bore every semblance of respectability; her demeanour was so modest and her conversation so edifying, that it caused the good father no little surprise when he perceived Catherine resolutely turn her back, as though she would neither see nor be seen by her. On the departure of this visitor he ventured to remonstrate with the Saint for her apparent rudeness; but she soon explained the matter. "O Father," she said, "if you had been conscious as I was of the stench of sin that made itself sensible whilst that woman was speaking to us, I think it would verily have turned you sick." He took some pains to ascertain the real circumstances and character of the person in question, and found indeed that her life was a deplorable scandal.[1]

The Countess of Valentinois, sister to the Pope, and a person of real and unaffected piety, had succeeded in obtaining several interviews with Catherine, whose conversation inspired her with great esteem and veneration. Desiring much to be present on some occasion when the Saint should approach Holy Communion, she made known her wish to Raymund, who promised to satisfy her. On the following Sunday Catherine went to the chapel, and making her preparation for Communion, was as usual rapt in ecstasy. Calling Stephen Maconi, who was present, Raymund bade him go at once to the palace, and tell the Countess that Catherine would communicate that morning. The Countess was just about to hear Mass, but on receiving the message she at once set out for Catherine's residence, accompanied by a number of persons equally curious as herself, but considerably less devout. Among others was Elys de Turenne, wife of the Pope's nephew, a young and giddy woman of the world, and an utter stranger to divine things. While the Countess was praying with all earnestness, Elys was examining Catherine, whose ecstasy she supposed to be feigned in order to attract attention ; she perceived that the Saint wore nothing but sandals ; so, stooping down under pretence of devoutly kissing her feet, she drew out a large pin, and with it pierced one of them through several times so as to draw blood. Catherine, however, remained motionless, for at such times, says Stephen, you might have cut off her feet sooner than have moved her. But when the crowd had withdrawn, and she resumed the use of her senses, she felt a sharp pain in her foot, and found herself unable to walk. Her companions, perceiving this, had their attention drawn to the cause, and found the bleeding wounds that had been thus wantonly inflicted.[2]

[1] "Se voi aveste sentito il puzzo che io sentiva mentr' ella meco parlava, voi avreste vomitato." (Leg , Part 2, ch iv) St. Antoninus says of this person, " Erat cujusdam magni prælati ecclesiæ concubina."

[2] Process, 1374. The cruel experiment of Elys de Turenne, mentioned above, had once before been tried on St. Catherine by a Dominican Friar, named F. Pietro Landi, who did not believe in her ecstasies, and who, to

There were wiser and more respectable judges than Elys of Turenne, however, who expressed their incredulity as to the real character of her whose name was in everybody's mouth. By desire of the Pope, Catherine had spoken several times in presence of many assembled prelates and cardinals, and her eloquence and heavenly doctrine drew from them expressions of wonder and admiration; "Never man spoke like this!" they exclaimed; "it is surely no woman who speaks, but the Holy Spirit dwelling in her." The report of her marvellous gifts, and of the impression they had made on the Pope and the cardinals soon spread abroad, and three prelates of very high rank sought an interview with Gregory for the purpose of speaking to him on the subject. "Holy Father," they said, "what think you? Is this Catherine of Siena as saintly as she is reported to be?" "In truth," replied the Pope, "I believe her to be a Saint" "If it please your Holiness," they continued, "we will go and see her." "Do so," he replied, "and I think you will be greatly edified." So they proceeded to her house about the hour of None, and knocking at the door, it was opened by Stephen Maconi, who relates the story. "Tell Catherine," said one of them, "that we wish to speak with her." The message was delivered, and Catherine at once came down, attended by Father John Tantucci, and certain other religious. They bade her be seated, and at once began to address her in a haughty and insolent manner, endeavouring to irritate her by their wounding speeches. "We have come from his Holiness," they said, "and we desire to know if it be really true that the Florentines sent you here, as is pretended. Have they not got a man among them capable of undertaking such an important affair? And if they did not send you, we marvel how an insignificant little woman like you should presume to converse with the Holy Father on so weighty a business." Catherine showed no signs of disturbance, but replied

test their truth, pierced the Saint's foot with a large needle during the time she was rapt out of her senses. Simon of Cortona tells the story in his Deposition, and adds that this religious died a miserable death, out of his Order. (Process. fol. 212.)

with a humility and firmness that filled them with astonishment. When she had satisfied them on this point, they proceeded to put to her many difficult questions on the spiritual life, and to examine her touching her ecstasies, and her extraordinary manner of life, reminding her that Satan often transforms himself into an angel of light, and inquiring what means she adopted in order to avoid his deceits. "The conference lasted until late in the evening," says Stephen, "and I was present the whole time. Sometimes Father John would endeavour to answer for her, but though he was a learned doctor in theology, they shut him up in very few words, saying, 'You should be ashamed to speak in such a manner in our presence. Leave her alone, for she satisfies us much better than you do.' One of these prelates was a learned professor of the Order of St. Francis,[1] and seemed as though unwilling to accept Catherine's replies. But at last the other two gave over their attack, and took part with her against him." "What more would you have?" they said; "she has certainly explained all these matters better and more fully than we ever found them set forth by holy writers." On this they began to dispute among themselves, but at last departed, well satisfied with the result of their visit, and reported to the Pope that "they had never met a soul at once so humble and so illuminated." Gregory was not a little displeased when he understood in what manner they had tried to move her to anger, and excused himself to the Saint, assuring her that it had been done without his knowledge or consent. He said, moreover, that should these prelates come again to speak with her, she was to shut the doors against them."[2] The next day Master Francis of Siena,[3] the Pope's physician, came to see Stephen. "Do you

---

[1] This was Bertrand de Lagery, Bishop of Glandevez, afterwards an adherent of the Antipope

[2] Fen, p. 14, c 18.

[3] This was Master Francis Casini, to whom one of Catherine's letters is addressed (Let. 227.) She met him again at Rome, where he was physician to Urban VI., who employed him in many affairs. He wrote several letters to the magistrates of Siena "in so barbarous a style," says Burlamacchi, "as would cause compassion," and became chief magistrate of his native city in

know those three prelates who called at your house yesterday?" he said, "I can assure you that if the learning of those three were put in a balance, and the learning of all the rest of the court of Rome in another, the learning of those three doctors would weigh against it all. Wherefore I tell you this, that if they had not found Catherine's wisdom and virtue truly solid, she would have made as bad a venture in coming hither as ever she did in her life."

No doubt during this singular scene Father John III. made his own reflections; for his memory must have recalled that other occasion when, in company with Master Gabriel of Volterra, he had first entered Catherine's presence with the like intention of "*shutting her up*" [1] The humiliation which he that day received at the hands of the three learned doctors was a fair penance for his former offence; and we would venture a shrewd guess that some of the party did not fail to rally him on so remarkable a coincidence.

1390. His nephew was created a Cardinal, and his tomb may still be seen in S Maria Maggiore. Master Francis himself was a friend of Petrarch, who wrote him a letter.

[1] See p. 147.

CHAPTER VIII.

THE DEPARTURE FROM AVIGNON, 1376.

CATHERINE'S mission on behalf of the Florentines had, as we have seen, been frustrated through their bad faith, and in the eyes of many her journey to Avignon had doubtless been pronounced a failure. But the providential end for which she had been brought thither was yet to be accomplished, and a far more extraordinary success was to crown her enterprise in the restoration of the Sovereign Pontiff to his long-forsaken See of Rome. Not that the first suggestion of this step is to be attributed to our Saint; Gregory himself had long contemplated, and even resolved upon it; and in the beginning of the year 1375, he had solemnly announced his intention in letters addressed to the Emperor and the other sovereigns of Europe. He had done more than this. When Charles V., king of France, filled with consternation at the prospect of such a change, despatched his brother the Duke of Anjou to represent to the Pope that his health would suffer if he ventured to quit his native air, that Rome was a sort of desert, and its citizens a set of turbulent savages, Gregory replied with firmness and dignity that "whatever it might cost him to separate himself from a country so dear to him as France, he felt it his duty in the interests of the Church to return to that holy city which was the true See Apostolic; and that with the help of God he should do so in the coming autumn." [1]

But the resolutions which determine human acts pass through two distinct stages. One is the decision of the judgment, com-

[1] Rinaldi, Ann. 1375, n 22.

paratively easy to men of clear mind unprejudiced by passion.
The other is the far more difficult decision of the will.   That the
two are not identical, who does not know, who to his sorrow sees
the right, but lacks the strength and courage to accomplish it ?
In the disproportion between these two kinds of decision lies
written the history of all mental struggles, and the explanation of
those amazing disappointments which make us marvel how men
so wise in thought and word can often be so feeble and faulty in
action.

Gregory had thought out the problem, and satisfactorily convinced himself that its true solution was in a return to Rome.
Nor was it any wonder that he should have come to such a conclusion.   It was a word re-echoed from the lips of all those whom
men most held in veneration   Full sixty years had passed since
Dante had reminded the Cardinals that it was their duty to elect
a Pontiff who should restore to Rome the sun that had suffered
eclipse ;[1] and Petrarch, to whom, if to any one, Avignon was
dear, had nevertheless nothing closer to his heart than the desire
of witnessing the resurrection, as he terms it, of the 'eternal city.
He even ventured to address a poetical epistle to Benedict XII.,
in which, by a bold personification, he makes Rome plead her
own cause, as a spouse forsaken by her bridegroom.   "Behold
me at your feet," she is made to exclaim ; "were I as in the days
of my youth I need not declare my name, but worn out as I am,
and disfigured by poverty and sorrow, I must name myself to be
recognised.   Know, then, that I am ROME, once famous throughout the whole world : can you discern any traits of my ancient
beauty ? Yet, alas ! it is less age which has effaced them, than
the long regret for your absence !"   It was a strange device for
setting the truth before the eyes of the Pontiff, but in a second
epistle the poet continues his allegory in a yet more touching
strain.   "Holy Father," he writes, "I have seen at your palace
door a venerable lady whom I seemed to know, yet could not
name ; she was sad, and her appearance showed signs of poverty
and neglect, yet withal she bore the traces of unforgotten majesty.

[1] Ep. vii. (ed. Wite.) p. 48.

Royalty was in her countenance, and she spoke with the voice of command; even through her rags you could discern her mighty soul. I asked her name, but she hardly dared pronounce it, only through her broken sobs did I catch the name of ROME."[1]

Yet severer and more terrible were the warnings and remonstrances addressed to Gregory XI by St. Bridget of Sweden Her dying words were carried to him in 1373 by Alphonsus Vadaterra, and were calculated to rouse the most sluggish conscience.[2] And meanwhile his Legates never wearied of conjuring him to come, and to come quickly, if he would prevent a frightful scandal and restore peace to Italy. To one and all Gregory replied by saying that it was indeed his purpose to come; but weeks and months passed on and brought fresh pretexts for delay, and fresh obstacles on the part of the Cardinals; nor was it until he had been fortified by the heroic presence of Catherine that he at length gained from her the courage to obey his convictions In the letters she had addressed to him before her coming to Avignon she had urged his speedy return in words which, if they displayed less poetic grace than those of Petrarch, had yet a winning sweetness that was not to be found in the terrific adjurations of St. Bridget. On her arrival at the court she found the question one of daily discussion, and quickly comprehended where the real difficulty lay The upright mind and tender heart of Gregory were overborne by the opposition of his French councillors, who found no difficulty in devising arguments to support their own wishes. In particular they set before him the example of Clement IV., who made it a rule to do nothing without consulting the Sacred College. A greater Pontiff, they argued, had never lived; and would Gregory depart from this wise precedent, and dare to take so momentous a step on his own sole responsibility? Gregory listened and hesitated, and finally appears to have sent a message to Catherine to ask her opinion of the matter Her reply is worthy of being studied, so skilfully does she in her lucid and inartificial language unravel the fallacy, and

[1] Petrarch, lib. i., epist. 2 and 4
[2] Rev S. Brid., lib. iv. chap. cxxxix.

defeat the manœuvres of these false councillors. "Holy Father," she says, "I, your miserable little daughter Catherine, desire to see you immovable as a rock in your holy resolutions, so that you may be able to resist all the cunning artifices by which the enemy would prevent your return, and hinder all the good which he knows it will cause. Your Cardinals allege the example of Clement IV., who would undertake nothing without the advice of the Sacred College. It is true he often renounced what seemed to him to be best, in order to follow their advice. But, alas! those who cite the example of Clement IV. are careful to say nothing at all about that of Urban V., who in things doubtful did, indeed, ask their advice, but in things which to him were as clear and evident as the duty of your return is to you, he followed his own judgment, and did not trouble himself about contrary opinions. It seems to me that the counsel of the good should always tend to the love of God, the salvation of souls, and the reform of Holy Church, not to the love of self: and that such counsel should be listened to rather than that which proceeds from men who love only the honours and pleasures of this life. Oh, I beg of your Holiness, for the love of Jesus crucified, not to delay. Hasten, and fear nothing; if God is with you, nothing will be against you. Hasten, and you will restore the crimson bloom of life to the cheeks of your Spouse, who is lying now in the pallor of death."[1] The famous appeal to the practice of Clement IV. soon fell to the ground, but the Cardinals had a more powerful weapon in reserve. They urged—as they and their predecessors had continued for more than sixty years to urge—the danger of returning to a country so torn with civil disorders as Italy. Nay, they whispered that the Italians were skilful assassins; and they asserted as a well-known fact that the poison was already prepared which would be administered to the Pontiff as soon as he had set foot within the walls of Rome. He would then leave the soil of France which he loved, and which loved him so well, to find a cruel and ignominious death in Italy! Did not every one know that Urban V. had been poisoned, and

[1] Letter 7.

hat precisely at the moment when he was preparing a second
ime to return to Rome? Would he not take warning by such
in example?

It must be owned that in their eagerness to scare the timid
ieart of Gregory, the Cardinals had here committed themselves
o a notable blunder. For if Urban V., who died at Avignon,
iad been, as they asserted, the victim of poison, it is plain that
he poison must have been administered, not at Rome but in their
iwn city; and if, furthermore, he had been thus assassinated at
he moment when he purposed returning to Italy, the crime must
iave been perpetrated by those who sought to hinder his return,
—a line of argument which would bring the matter very close to
heir own doors. Nevertheless, they made as much as they could
if the spectral fears which they had thus conjured up; and having
liscovered how greatly Catherine's influence weighed with the
?ope, who regarded her as a Saint, they contrived that a letter
ihould be delivered to him, purporting to come from another
ierson of reputed sanctity,[1] which warned him not to go to Rome
f he were not prepared to be immediately assassinated.

Catherine was of too fearless a nature herself to allow of much
mportance being attached to these appeals to cowardice. To
ier it seemed impossible that any man could be held back by
ear from doing what he knew was right. And she quickly ex-
iosed the miserably bad logic of her opponents, and the trans-
iarent forgery of which they had been guilty. "This letter," she
iaid, "purports to come from a just and virtuous man; it will not
ie difficult for your Holiness to ascertain if this be so, and for
he honour of God you are bound to examine into it For my
iwn part, as far as I can understand the case, its language is not
hat of a servant of God. It seems to me to be a forgery, and
he hand that forged it is not a very skilful one; he ought to be
ient back to school, for he writes like a child Observe, Holy
?ather, he tries to appeal to the weakest part of human nature,
he fears which those entertain who have an excessive love of their
iwn ease and safety, and who shrink from the least bodily suffer-

[1] Supposed to be B. Peter of Arragon.

ing. This is his main argument, but by the grace of God I trust your Holiness cares more for God's honour and the salvation of your flock than for yourself; like a good pastor who is ready to lay down his life for his sheep. Then this false councillor goes on to tell you that your return to Rome would, indeed, be a most holy and excellent thing, only that he is afraid they are preparing poisons for you. He advises you to send trusty men before you, who will find poison ready on the tables (that is, no doubt, in the shops, where they are preparing it), in order to give it to you *in a few days, or in a month, or in a year.* For my part it seems to me you might quite as easily find poison on the tables in Avignon, or any other city, as on those of Rome, *and that in a month, or a year,* according as might suit the purchaser; nevertheless, the writer of this letter would have you send some one to Rome to search for it, and meanwhile delay your journey; and all the time he himself is administering the worst of all poisons; he is trying to prevent you from doing that which God demands of you. If now you do not set out, you will cause a great scandal, and you will be accused of falsehood—you, who sit in the chair of Truth · for you have announced and fixed your return; and if you do not keep your word you will cause trouble and scandal to many hearts. I admire the words of this writer who begins by advising good and holy actions, and then desires you to give them up out of a fear of your bodily safety. That is not the language of the servants of God, who would never abandon their holy undertakings for any bodily or temporal fear, not even for the risk of life itself. Otherwise they would never attain their end, for it is perseverance alone that is crowned with glory. Be firm then to your purpose, most Holy Father; it is the only means of securing peace with your revolted children and the reformation of the Church. Then you will satisfy the desires of those who desire to see you raise the standard of the Holy Cross; and then you will be able to administer to those poor infidels the Blood of the Lamb, of which you hold the key."[1]

[1] Letter 10. The letters to Gregory quoted in this chapter were all written at Avignon, and seem to have been summaries of conversations already held

These last words show us that Catherine had not forgotten the Crusade, and that the difficulties of the time did not seem to her by any means to have closed that question. In fact, Raymund tells us that it was one of the chief objects of her journey to Avignon, and that it often formed the subject of conversation between her and the Pope. As has been elsewhere said, the project was a favourite one with Gregory, though probably his views and plans regarding it partook of the same shadowy character which attached to his other resolutions. If so, Catherine was ready to give them substance. One day when she was in the company of Gregory he adverted to the subject, saying, "First of all, we must establish peace among Christians, and then we will organise a Crusade." "Pardon me, Holy Father," she replied, "but the proclamation of the holy war will be the best means of re-establishing peace among Christians. All the turbulent soldiers who now keep up division among the faithful will cheerfully go and combat in that sacred cause; very few will refuse to serve God in the profession which pleases them, and it will be a means of expiating their offences the fire will thus be extinguished for want of fuel You will thereby, Holy Father, accomplish several excellent things at once—you will bestow peace on such Christians as require it, and you will save many great sinners. Should they gain important victories, you could act, in consequence, with the Christian princes; if they are overcome, you will at least have procured salvation to their perishing souls; and besides, you might convert a number of Saracens." [1]

This was the policy she constantly recommended; and she regarded it as the most likely means of putting a stop to that fratricidal contest between France and England which had for years been the open wound of Christendom. Wonderful to say, she made a convert to her views in the person of one who had come to Avignon for the express purpose of counteracting her influence.

with him. They are in Latin, not Italian. Gregory being ignorant of the latter language, the conversations between him and Catherine were necessarily restricted, and she seems, on leaving him, to have dictated their substance to her secretaries, who translated her words into Latin before sending them to the Pope

[1] Legend, Part 2, chap. x.

This was Louis, Duke of Anjou, brother to Charles V. of France. He was the second son of King John, whom he had replaced as hostage in England. His ambition was greater than his ability, but it would seem that his acquaintance with Catherine for a moment awakened in him nobler and better aspirations than any of which he had hitherto been conscious. He was not content with ceasing to oppose her, he desired to be regarded by her as a friend, and even a disciple. No doubt her very appearance in the midst of that gay and luxurious capital read a silent lesson to many hearts, who, while they had no courage to free themselves from the shackles of a worldly life, could nevertheless feel and do homage to the power of sanctity. They listened to her, as in old time Felix listened to St. Paul, and like him they trembled when she discoursed "of justice, and chastity, and the judgment to come."[1] They gave to truth the homage of a passing sigh that bespoke regret for wasted years, and a kind of wish that better things were possible for them; and then they put the thought away "till a more convenient season," and plunged afresh into the old track of habit. But in the heart of Louis of Anjou the Saint appears to have awakened a deeper interest, and he begged her to accompany him to his castle at Villeneuve, that he might introduce her to his Duchess, and apart from curious eyes might open to her his secret heart. It was all one to Catherine whither she went, if there were question of helping the soul of one of God's creatures. She proceeded then to the royal castle with as much readiness and simplicity as she would have gone to the lepers' hospital, if summoned on a mission of charity. Villeneuve was at that time a place of some importance; it was the border fortress of France, and occupied the western bank of the Rhone, Avignon standing on the east. From the platform of the *Rocher des Doms* you look across the river towards its towers on the opposite side, to which you now cross by a wooden bridge. But in the days of St. Catherine the stone bridge built in 1188 by St. Benezet[2] was still standing, with its nineteen arches, and by this

---

[1] Acts xxiv. 25.

[2] St. Benezet was a poor shepherd boy, who, afflicted at the number of

)ridge she crossed to what was then the important border town
)f Villeneuve-lez-Avignon. She remained there three days, during
vhich time Louis gave her his entire confidence. He owned to
ier that he was weary of the vanities in the midst of which he
ived, and that he longed for some way of escape. Would the
Crusade open to him such a way? Should he take the Cross and
ieek the glory which he coveted, not on a European throne, but
imid the lances of the infidels? The thought came to him like
i gleam of light piercing through the clouds, and Catherine hesi-
ated not to encourage him with her joyous enthusiasm. "I am
iure," she wrote to him on returning to Avignon,[1] "that if you
ix your eyes on the Lamb sacrificed and consumed with love
1pon the Cross to deliver you from death, it will excite you to
:arry out your holy purpose, and will soon banish out of your
ieart all thought of the vanities and foolish pleasures of the world.
They pass like the wind and leave death behind them in the souls
)f those who possess them. I speak of those whose whole life is
3iven to pleasure and magnificence, to luxury and feasting. It is
)n these things they spend their riches while the poor are dying
)f hunger. They seek out abundance of everything delightful—
)eautiful plate, delicate dishes, and sumptuous clothing—and
1ever give a thought to their poor soul that is perishing of hunger.
My dear and sweet lord, my brother in our sweet Jesus, do not
et yourself be drawn away by the world in these years of your

1ersons drowned in crossing the river, which at this spot is rapid and very
langerous, devised a scheme for building a bridge, and actually carried it
nto effect, directing the work himself. (For the interesting story see his
Life in the Bollandists, April 14th Tom. 11, p 958) After his death he was
)uried in a chapel erected between the second and third arches of the bridge,
which is still standing, and where his body remained for five hundred years.
In 1669 a great part of the bridge fell, through the swift current of the waters.
The coffin was removed and placed in the church of St. Didier, where it still
1es On this occasion, and again in 1674, it was found perfectly incorrupt,
inchanged in colour, and even with the eyes bright and lively St Benezet
s regarded as the patron saint of Avignon. Four arches of his bridge are
still standing No doubt St Catherine, when she crossed over it, entered the
chapel and venerated his relics.

[1] Letter 190.

vigorous and youthful manhood; remember the words of the Blessed Christ, when He told the Jews that they were like sepulchres fair outside, but within full of dead men's bones and of all corruption. Oh, how true are those words! Yes, indeed; those who seem so fair and beautiful in all their costly finery have death in their hearts, which are full of all that is shameful and detestable. But if, in the Divine Goodness, you are steadfastly resolved to change your life, those words will not apply to you. You will raise the holy standard of the Cross, you will efface all your past offences, and God will say to you, "Beloved Son, you have laboured and suffered for Me, come then to the nuptials of eternal life, where is fulness without disgust, hunger without suffering, and pleasure without shame. Far different are the joys of this world; they cost much and have no profit, and the more a man partakes of them the emptier he becomes; he seeks enjoyment, and finds nothing but sadness. It was but yesterday that you experienced the truth of what I say. You had prepared a great entertainment and a magnificent feast, and it all ended in sorrow. God so permitted it that He might show you and those who were with you how vain and empty are all earthly joys "

Catherine is here alluding to an accident which had recently occurred at a great banquet given by the Duke, in the midst of which a great wall suddenly fell and killed several of the guests. Coming at that moment, the event served to foster the serious impressions which Louis had received, and he authorised her to acquaint the Pope with his determination of taking the Cross. She accepted the commission with joy. "Holy Father," she said to Gregory, "I announce to you that you have *two* crusades to undertake. There must be an interior Crusade against bad pastors and all the vices with which the garden of the Church is overgrown; and there must be an exterior Crusade against the infidels. You will tell me that for this last a captain is needed; he is found, and I can offer him to you. The Duke of Anjou, out of devotion to the death of Christ and to the holy Cross, desires to take on him this office. He will see you soon, and

peak of this great affair ; for God's sake give him good words,
nd promise him that his hopes shall be realised." [1]

The deep veneration which the Duke had conceived for
Catherine, and the opinion he had formed by experience of her
great qualities, led him to entertain the project of taking her to
Paris,[2] that she might negotiate a treaty of peace with England.
n her humility she declined this mission, though, doubtless,
had it been laid on her by obedience, she would have accepted
t with as little hesitation as she had shown on other occasions.
But without some evident and unmistakable token of God's will,
Catherine was never forward in undertaking such responsibilities ;
however, she did not refuse to write to Charles, and we shall
quote from her letter in this place, because for the first time it
brings her before us in connection with the affairs of our own
country.

It is a remarkable fact that in the part which the Roman Pon-
iffs took in the quarrel between France and England, they seem
o have shown more consideration towards the latter country
han might have been expected, either from their own national
predilections, or from what would seem to us at first sight to
have been the merits of the case. A close study of the action
of the Holy See during the whole of that disastrous contest fills
is with admiration for the strict impartiality and zeal for the
nterests of right and justice which were invariably displayed.
The right and justice for which the Sovereign Pontiffs con-
ended were something higher than the claims of any particular
prince or nation ; they pleaded the cause of God , they sought
o stop the effusion of Christian blood and the ruin of souls, far
learer to them than the gain of any national advantage , and at
every pause in the hostilities, their Legates were constantly at
hand to offer their mediation, and urge on both parties to accept
erms of peace. When we remember that the Popes of Avignon
were all Frenchmen, and all but exclusively surrounded by French
councillors, their abstention from a party view in this matter, and
the noble manner in which they acted as the common fathers of

[1] Letter 9.   [2] Process, 1337.

Christendom, is truly wonderful; and it makes us understand Catherine's language in her letter to the king of France, which in a merely political view of the matter would otherwise seem a little hard.

She urges him to observe three things in the discharge of his royal office, and as one worthy of being called the Wise.[1] First, not to look on his kingdom as his own property, but as something lent to him, of which he only has the stewardship, secondly, to maintain justice, and to defend the rights of the poor; "and the third thing," she says,—"and this is the point which my soul most earnestly desires,—is that you live in love and charity with your neighbour[2] with whom you have so long been at war. Remember the example of our sweet Lord, how, when the Jews cried, ' Crucify Him !' He replied by the prayer, so full of meekness, ' Father, forgive them !' Follow His example, show that you have a care for the salvation of your neighbour, yes, my lord, do not trouble yourself about the loss of worldly possessions; such a loss will be a real gain to you, for it will enable you to make peace with your brother. For my own part I wonder that you are not ready to give your whole life to procure this end, considering the destruction of souls and bodies caused by this miserable war. Be sure that if you refuse to do what you can in this matter, you will be held as the cause of these evils. Alas, for Christians ! and alas, for the infidels too ! for it is your policy that has prevented and still prevents the holy war; and had it no other result than this, it seems to me we should fear the judgments of God." [3]

Charles might have replied with considerable show of reason that the policy she here complains of was nothing else than the patriotic endeavour to rid his country of foreign invaders; and Catherine would have answered by reminding him at what a cost. The cost of maintaining the contest was in fact the dissolution

---

[1] Charles V. was surnamed the Wise, and Catherine did not forget the circumstance. *Vi prego che come Savio, facciate come buono dispensatore.* (Letter 186.)

[2] *i e*, the King of England   [3] Letter 186.

of Christendom, and its poisoned fruits were to be gathered in the centuries that followed. In the eyes of the saint the glory of a patriot king would have been surpassed by that of a champion of the Faith ; and she urged him therefore, even at some sacrifice of national interests, to give peace to Europe, that so all the children of the Church might unite together to heal her wounds and check the onward march of the infidels. " Follow," she says, " the way and the doctrine of the Crucified Lamb. You will follow the way He trod if you bear injuries with patience, and you will follow His doctrine if you are reconciled with your neighbour. You will prove your love of God by helping forward the holy war. Your brother Messire the Duke of Anjou has resolved for the love of God to devote himself to this enterprise, and it would be a terrible thing if you were to hinder or prevent it."

Meanwhile the question of the Pope's return to Rome did not greatly advance. When Catherine came back from Villeneuve she found things much as she had left them. Gregory continued to declare that his determination had been taken, and that he was indeed about to depart; but there were no signs of actual preparation. He still hesitated, and desired to obtain through the prayers of the Saint some certain and unmistakable sign of the will of God ; and for this purpose he one day sent her a message that she was to pray for him in a particular manner the next morning after Communion. She obeyed ; and her prayer, uttered in ecstasy, was preserved and written down by Thomas Petra, the Pope's Notary, afterwards secretary to Urban VI., and one who formed an intimate friendship with the Saint during her stay at Avignon. It is printed first in the collection of her prayers, and concludes as follows :—" O Ineffable Deity ! I am all sin, and unworthy to address Thee, but Thou canst make me worthy. O Lord, punish my sins, and regard not my miseries. I have one body, and to Thee I give it : behold my blood, behold my flesh ; destroy it, annihilate it, separate it bone from bone for the sake of those for whom I pray. If it be Thy will, cause my bones and my very marrow to be ground to pieces for Thy Vicar on

earth, the bridegroom of Thy Spouse, for whom I pray; that
Thou wilt deign to hear me, and that he, Thy Vicar, may both
know Thy will, and love it, and perform it, to the end that we may
not perish !   Give him a new heart, that he may increase in grace,
and raise the standard of the holy Cross, and make even the
infidels to be sharers in the Passion and Blood of the Immaculate
Lamb, Thy only Son our Lord !   O Ineffable, Eternal Deity [1]—
Peccavi Domine, miserere mei ! ”

Having ended this prayer she remained for some time in a
state of abstraction, after which she again began to speak; the
prayer she uttered being that which immediately follows the one
above quoted.   Her Pisan disciple, Thomas Buonconti, was
present at the time, and carefully noted every circumstance; and
in the original manuscript he has left a marginal note in his own
handwriting to this effect : “ Having finished these words, she
remained as before,—silent, immovable, rigid and abstracted, with
her arms crossed on her breast—for about an hour.   After that
we sprinkled her face with holy water, and frequently invoked the
name of Jesus Christ, and in a little while she began again to
draw breath, and said in a low voice, ‘ Praised be God, now and
for ever ! ’ ” [1]

When Catherine returned to herself, she addressed two letters
to Gregory, in both of which she refers to the command which
he had given her to pray for him.   “ Holy Father,” she says,
“ Brother Raymund brought me your command to pray to God,
in case you should meet with obstacles.   I did so after Communion, and I saw none of the perils and dangers of which your
councillors speak.”   Then she declares to him, as from God, that
the most certain sign he could receive of the Divine will was the
opposition he was sure to encounter in carrying it out.   But aware
of the immense difficulties that beset him on the part of his own

---

[1] Buonconti collected other prayers made at Avignon, in the presence of
twelve persons who heard the Saint in rapture holding converse with God.
One of these prayers was spoken on the vigil of the Assumption, and he
describes her state as “abstracted, unconscious, and rigid, so that it would
have been easier to break her limbs than to bend them.” See Gigli, Tom.
iv.. Pref. xv.. xvi.

family, she advised him, if he had not the resolution to carry matters with a high hand, to have recourse to stratagem, and while seeming to leave his departure indefinitely deferred, to prepare for it in secret without loss of time. In fact, Gregory's naturally affectionate heart was suffering a martyrdom from the appeals made him by his nearest relatives and the necessity he was under of struggling against his own tenderness. One day having asked Catherine what she would really advise him to do in these difficult circumstances, she turned on him that penetrating look which had read the secrets of so many hearts, and replied, "Who knows what ought to be done better than your Holiness, who has long since made a vow to God to return to Rome?" Gregory started. He had indeed made such a vow long back, but had spoken of it to no living soul. He perceived that in very truth Catherine was possessed of powers given her by God; and recognising the sign of the Divine will which he had asked for, he at once gave orders for the necessary preparations for departure.[1]

Catherine would willingly now have taken her leave of the Court; her mission at Avignon was ended, and she was anxious to find herself once more at Siena, where her long absence was exciting many complaints. But Gregory felt the support of her presence far too necessary for him to consent to part with her, and it was agreed that she should leave Avignon on the same day,[2] as himself, though, as it would seem, not by the same route.

No further particulars have been left us of Catherine's residence in the Papal city, which lasted altogether four months, nor have her biographers enabled us to follow the track of her footsteps to any of the sanctuaries of the neighbourhood. Yet there can be no doubt of her having often visited the Dominican church, now crumbling to ruins, but then enjoying a certain renown as having

---

[1] This narrative is given in the deposition of F. Bartholomew Dominic (Process, 1325). The fact of Gregory having really taken such a vow is corroborated by Baluze (Vita Greg. XI, 949), and by Pius II. in the Bull of St. Catherine's canonisation.

[2] Process, 1337.

been recently the scene of the canonisation of St. Thomas.   In
this church, too, Catherine would have found the tomb of a
distinguished fellow-citizen.   Simon Memmi, the Sienese painter,
had been summoned to Avignon by Benedict XII., to decorate
some of the halls of the Papal palace ; he died while still employed
on these works ; and he whose pencil had left in the church of Sta.
Maria Novella those many scenes from the life of St. Dominic,
which Catherine, during her residence at Florence, must daily
have contemplated, found the fitting hospitality of a last resting-
place among the Holy Father's white-robed children at Avignon.
We need no assurance that Catherine prayed at that tomb, and
that the name of the artist of her native city brought back grate-
ful thoughts of home during these weary weeks of exile.   At
last the welcome day of departure arrived.   Gregory, profiting by
the Saint's advice, had caused his galleys to be secretly got ready,[1]
and on the 13th of September 1376 he left the palace, intending
to journey by land to Marseilles, and thence to embark for Rome.
Up to the last moment the courtiers had refused to believe in
the possibility of such a disaster ; and the Pope's aged father had
the desperate courage to try the effect of one last impassioned
appeal.   Throwing himself across the threshold of the palace
gate, he there awaited a final interview with his son ; and on his
approach, raising a cry of bitter anguish, "How !" he exclaimed,
"can my son so coldly forsake not only his country but even his
old father !   Well, then, before he departs, he shall pass over my
body !"   But at that supreme moment Gregory silenced in his
own heart the cry of nature ; and it was not Peter de Beaufort-
Turenne, but the Vicar of Jesus Christ, who, as he passed the
prostrate figure of the old man, spoke these solemn words as his
only reply : *Super aspidem et basiliscum ambulabis · et conculcabis
leonem et draconem* (Ps. xc. 13).

If Catherine heard them she must have given thanks to God
who had put into the heart of His servant a courage the more
sublime as it was wholly supernatural.   We shall not follow the
journey of the Pontiff and his reluctant attendants any further,

[1] Biondo, lib. ii, cap. x.

though it has been thought worthy to be made the subject of a grand historical poem ; the author of which was no less a personage than Pierre Amely d'Alète, Bishop of Sinigaglia, and the Pope's almoner.[1] But turning our backs on the towers of Avignon we will accompany the little group cf Italian pilgrims who set out the same day, taking the road, not to Marseilles but to the port of Toulon.

[1] This very curious production, which is not without its interest both historical and geographical, may be found in Ciaconius (Vitæ Pont. et Card., Tom. ii. p. 578).

END OF VOL. I.

BURNS AND OATES, LIMITED, LONDON

945301

Printed in Great Britain by
Amazon.co.uk, Ltd.,
Marston Gate.